CHALLENGE AND CHANGE
IN
AMERICAN EDUCATION

CHALLENGE and CHANGE

in

AMERICAN EDUCATION

Edited by SEYMOUR E. HARRIS,

KENNETH M. DEITCH AND ALAN LEVENSOHN

Introduction by SEYMOUR E. HARRIS

Commentaries by KENNETH M. DEITCH

McCutchan Publishing Corporation
2526 Grove Street
Berkeley, California 94704

Preface

This volume is drawn from papers and discussions at the Seminar on Challenge and Change in American Education, held at the Harvard University Graduate School of Public Administration in 1961-62. This was the second of such seminars. The first, *Higher Education, Resources and Finance,* 1962, was published by the Harvard University Press. A third volume, based on the 1962-63 seminar, is almost ready for publication.* Eighteen sessions were held in the 1961-62 session; the speakers and discussants included state and federal government officials, presidents, deans, business officers of several Institutions of Higher Learning (IHL), officers of foundations and thirty-nine professors, among others. At sixteen of the sessions, formal papers were read. A few were not released for publication; the rest appear in this volume. In the two other sessions, no formal papers were delivered. In all sessions, a general discussion of the issues concerned was pressed vigorously, by panels of discussants and by the audience of students as well as by the speakers themselves.

The main responsibility for the seminar was mine, but it was shared by Francis Keppel, then dean of the Graduate School of Education, now U.S. Commissioner of Education. We received assistance and close cooperation from Don K. Price, dean of the School of Public Administration, and from Vernon Alden, then associate dean of the Graduate School of Business Administration. The departure of Dean Alden to become president of Ohio University was a great loss to the seminar.

In preparing this volume I was fortunate to have the assistance of two associates. Alan Levensohn, a professional editor, established the structure of the volume and was responsible for the major editing. He did a superb job. Kenneth M. Deitch, a teaching fellow at Harvard University, helped with the editing and wrote the commentaries, which summarize the discussions and offer further observations and interpretations. These commentaries are Mr. Deitch's work; and though they have been shown to the participants in each session, including myself, they remain wholly his responsibility.

---

* *Education and Public Policy,* McCutchan Publishing Corp., Berkeley, Cailf.

My contribution consisted of planning the seminar (with the help of Dean Frank Keppel of the School of Education and Dean Don Price of the School of Public Administration), obtaining funds to finance it, inviting experts to write papers and comment and others interested, presiding at meetings, and raising questions with the authors of papers as well as helping update the papers after the long gestation period. My introduction is largely an attempt to indicate the range of the papers, to update to some extent, and to introduce some additional relevant material.

My greatest debts are to the authors of papers and comments who gave generously of their time and experience and were most helpful in every way. I take this opportunity also to apologise for the long delay in getting the book published. The fault was mine primarily. I also hope that the drastic editing job required when authors are so diverse in interests and training in no way changed the sense of their contributions.

Miss Marion Wilson assumed the responsibility, not only for most of the secretarial work of the seminar, but also for a large part of its management. She contributed greatly to the smooth functioning of the seminar. I am also especially grateful to Mrs. Joan Burstyn; to my secretary at that time, Miss Mary Watson; and to the stenotypist, Lawrence W. Burt.

The Ford Foundation was most generous in providing the necessary funds. My first consultations were with Philip Coombs; and after he left the foundation to join the United States Government, Clarence Faust was very helpful and cooperative. Without the support of the Ford Foundation we could not have carried through this seminar.

Seymour E. Harris

LaJolla, Calif.

CONTRIBUTORS
(In order of their Contributions)

James E. Allen, Commissioner of Education, New York State.

Homer D. Babbidge, Jr., President, University of Connecticut; Former Assistant Commissioner of Education and Director of the Division of Higher Education, U. S. Office of Education.

Elliot Richardson, Former Assistant Secretary for Legislation, U. S. Department of Health, Education and Welfare.

Robert Rosenzweig, U. S. Office of Education.

Francis Keppel, U. S. Commissioner of Education; Former Dean of the Harvard University Graduate School of Education.

Charles V. Kidd, Associate Director for International Activities and Former Associate Director for Training, National Institutes of Health, U. S. Department of Health, Education and Welfare.

Don K. Price, Professor of Government and Dean of the Faculty of Public Administration, Harvard University.

John S. McCauley, Director, Office of Manpower Training Operation, U. S. Employment Service, Bureau of Employment Security, Department of Labor.

Montague Yudelman, Harvard Graduate School of Education.

Adam Curle, Center for Studies in Education and Development, Harvard University.

John B. Carroll, Professor of Education and Director of the Laboratory for Research in Instruction, Harvard University.

John M. Stalnaker, President, National Merit Scholarship Corporation

Dan C. Lortie, Professor of Education, University of Chicago.

Theodore Caplow, Professor of Sociology, Columbia University.

Charles S. Benson, Associate Professor of Education, University of California, Berkeley.

Herbert S. Conrad, Program Planning Officer, Bureau of Educational Research and Development, U. S. Office of Education.

Otto Eckstein, Professor of Economics, Harvard University, and Member of the President's Council of Economic Advisors.

André Daniere, Assistant Professor of Economics, Harvard University.

John J. Corson, Management Consultant, McKinsey & Company, and Professor of Public and International Affairs, Princeton University.

Glen A. Lloyd, Chairman of the Board of Trustees, University of Chicago.

John F. Morse, Director, American Council on Education; Former Staff Member of the U. S. House of Representatives Committee on Education and Labor; Former Vice President, Rensselaer Polytechnic Institute.

Eugene S. Wilson, Dean of Admissions, Amherst College.

Rexford G. Moon, Jr., Director, College Scholarship Service of the College Entrance Examination Board.

James S. Coles, President, Bowdoin College.

John S. Dickey, President, Dartmouth College.

George R. Waggoner, Dean of the College of Liberal Arts and Sciences, The University of Kansas.

Bernard R. Berelson, Director of the Bureau of Applied Social Research, Columbia University.

John Chase, Chief of the Higher Education, Personnel Section, U. S. Office of Education.

Clark Byse, Professor of Law, Harvard University.

Robert W. Merry, Professor of Business Administration, Harvard University.

Vernon R. Alden, President, Ohio University.

Contents

                                                                    Page

Introduction by Seymour E. Harris   1

PART I: GOVERNMENT AND EDUCATION

1. State vs. Federal Power in Education
   James E. Allen   41
   Homer D. Babbidge, Jr.   46
   Commentary   51

2. Educational Lobbies and Federal Legislation
   Elliot Richardson   55
   Robert Rosenzweig   59
   Francis Keppel   63
   Commentary   67

3. The Federal Government and University Research
   Charles V. Kidd   75
   Don K. Price   82
   Commentary   87

4. Education for Manpower Development
   John S. McCauley   91
   Commentary   97

5. The Goals of Education in Underdeveloped Countries
   Montague Yudelman   103
   Adam Curle   108
   Commentary   112

PART II: CHALLENGES IN EDUCATIONAL PLANNING

6. Learning Ability and the Superior Student
   John B. Carroll   119
   John M. Stalnaker   128
   Commentary   137

7. Social Values and Formal Education
        Dan C. Lortie   149
        Theodore Caplow   156
        Commentaries   161

8. The Teacher Shortage: Causes and Solutions
        Charles S. Benson   169
        Herbert S. Conrad   174
        Commentaries   180

9. State and Local Investment in Education
        Otto Eckstein   189
        Charles S. Benson   194
        Commentary   201

10. Planning Education for Economic Productivity
        André Daniere   205
        Commentary   220

PART III: MANAGEMENT OF COLLEGES AND UNIVERSITIES

11. Roles and Responsibilities in Management of IHL
        John J. Corson   231
        Glen A. Lloyd   239
        Commentary   243

12. Academic Quality and Financial Aid
        John F. Morse   247
        Eugene S. Wilson   254
        Rexford G. Moon, Jr.   260
        Commentary   266

13. The Role of the Liberal-Arts College
        James S. Coles   273
        John S. Dickey   280
        George R. Waggoner   283
        Commentary   288

14. Graduate Education in the Arts and Sciences
        Bernard R. Berelson   293
        John Chase   301
        Commentary   309

Page

15. Tenure and Academic Freedom
        Clark Byse   313
        Robert W. Merry   321
        Commentary   328

16. The Challenge of Growth for University Management
        Vernon R. Alden   333
        Commentary   342

Introduction[*]

By Seymour E. Harris

This book is concerned primarily with issues of educational policy and management. Today's policies are reflected in tomorrow's management problems. We have not tried to cover all the issues. Rather we have invited participants who might have something helpful and interesting to say about educational problems. Any reader who looks hard will find gaps, e.g. we have not given the civil rights issue the space it should get if this volume were a complete and systematic review of management and policy in education. We have not concentrated on economic issues of education as we did in earlier volumes, although we have not exactly neglected these issues.[1]

In the seminar upon which this volume is based, we have invited State Commissioners of Education, officials of the Office of Education in Washington and other high ranking Federal personnel, college and university presidents and deans, school superintendents, and college professors—psychologists, sociologists, political scientists, economists, teachers of law, and others. Here we publish 33 papers covering 16 sessions; and the able commentaries by Kenneth Deitch, Teaching Fellow at Harvard.

I [2]

Our first of three parts deals with government in education; and we begin with a discussion between the Commissioner of Eduation in New York State, James E. Allen, probably the most distinguished Commissioner of Education in the country, and a young and rising university president, Homer Babbidge, head of the University of Connecticut. The latter had an opportunity as an assistant to Mr. Marion B. Folsom, then head of Health, Education, and Welfare, and as Assistant Commissioner of Education, to view the relevant problems from Washington as well as from Storrs, Connecticut.

Compared to many countries—e.g. the United Kingdom and Germany, F.R.—the Federal Government in the United States contributes

---

[*] This is a summary but includes some updating and additional comments.

1

little relatively to education: roughly $2+ billion, or about one-tenth of the total bill, though by 1965-66 the cost may exceed $4 billion. In view of the large variations in economic status among states and the rich tax program of the central government, the financial participation of the Federal Government is slight indeed. Moreover, with the increased emphasis on tax cuts as the road to a healthy economy and government deficits, the central government educational outlays are likely to rise less than might have been expected a few years ago.

Yet the Federal Government contributes crucial sums in many fields: loans and fellowships to students, building grants and constuction loans to Institutions of Higher Learning (IHL), operating subsidies to schools in areas where the impact of defense outlays greatly increases educational outlays and (anticipated in 1965) special help to low income places, special grants for improving the teaching of sciences and languages and for increasing the utilization of teaching aids, and for many other purposes.[3]

What especially interests Messrs. Allen and Babbidge is the manner of disbursing and controlling the use of funds under these numerous federal programs. Should the intermediary be the State Government, as under the original Land Grant College program, or the IHL as under the loan program of the National Defense Education Act? A related issue is control by State vs. Federal Government. In these opening essays the reader will get some insight concerning the case for State intervention or (and) assumption of responsibilities in general, and in particular the competence of the State or the IHL (and Federal Government) to assume these responsibilities in general, and in conjunction with different programs.

II

One reason for the slow advance of federal aid to education lies in the failures of the professional educational lobbies. Elliott Richardson, the top government official responsible for formulating and pushing through the important National Defense Education Act (NDEA) under President Eisenhower, throws light on the lobbying activities, helpful and harmful, the failure of lobbying groups to achieve unity of action, the conflicts between educational objectives and other aims of these groups; and he details the steps and processes by which the government was able to achieve passage of the NDEA.

Conflicts of interest between large educational organizations, e.g. the American Council on Education (ACE) and the National Education Association (NEA), between constituent elements of the ACE (e.g. public vs. private universities) and of the NEA, e.g. early conflicts of university administrators and school teachers—these contribute to an understanding of the inadequate achievements of the educational associations. The current Commissioner of Education, Frank Keppel, traces the history of these conflicts within the organizations and among them.

A puzzling aspect of federal educational history is the success with specific programs and the failure to obtain general aid. Robert Rosenzweig, a former official of the Office of Education, explains the small successes and the large failures. He also says some interesting things about the political activities of educational leaders which helps us understand the evolution or non-evolution of federal aid.

III

Federal expenditures on research raise many thorny problems. Dean Don Price of the Harvard University Graduate School of Public Administration and Charles Kidd, Associate Director for International Activities, Public Health Service, H.E.W., suggest the causes of disagreement between government and universities, the extent to which differences are being reconciled, and the extent to which through dealing with specific issues the government has been able to provide aid without getting into troublesome issues of general aid to IHL. A major source of disagreement is that government is interested in getting particular tasks done; the university is primarily interested in its objective of adding to knowledge and helping to pass it on. Messrs. Price and Kidd are eloquent on the sources of misunderstanding as well as the degree of reconciliation. University officials often seem to forget that the research programs are not merely aid programs to IHL.

I cannot resist adding a few supplementary facts and points to the excellent discussion by Messrs. Price, Kidd, and others. First, the amount of money involved is large. Whereas in 1947-48 research income of IHL from the Federal Government amounted to $95 million or 6 per cent of the educational budget, by 1961-62 the sum had increased to $1,274 million or 17 per cent of educational and general income. In fact, government now provides about one quarter of the income of private (?) IHL, and most of this is research grants or contracts. Research expenditures of the Federal Government of about $15 billion yearly are a maximum in relation to GNP,* a ratio matched nowhere in the world with the possible exception of the United Kingdom. A significant part of these funds goes to IHL.

Second, the participants in this session show clearly some of the difficulties of arriving at mutually agreeable terms for coverage of costs of federal research projects. I need add only that university administrators often underestimate the gains to the IHL of research grants. In discussing this problem with many university presidents, I was impressed by the extent to which these federal grants lighten the burden for IHL—e.g. training in the medical schools. Yet one is also impressed by the better terms that business groups obtain from the Federal Government than IHL. A more generous treatment of IHL is supportable by the general view that the Federal Government does not adequately help higher education. Here is an easy way out without getting into the troublesome issues of general aid.

Apparently the Appropriation Committees of Congress are unwilling to provide the full overhead costs. One of the difficulties is, of course, that it is not easy to estimate what these overhead costs are, and they vary greatly from institution to institution. For example, according to a National Science Foundation study for 1958 of 74 medical schools, 8 estimated that their indirect costs, as a percentage of research operating expenditures, were less than 18 per cent, and 6 estimated the figure at from 40 to 49.9 per cent, and 45 at from 20 to 29.9 per cent. Obviously adequate treatment would require special agreements with each institution. The National Science Foundation concludes:

> . . . The Bayne-Jones Report recommends an approximate three-fold increase in research funds by 1970. Should this sum for research materialize, and with no change in the present formula for allowances for indirect costs, by 1970 the medical schools would have to invest approximately $25 million more of their own funds toward defraying indirect costs of research than they did in 1957-58. Within ten years, if the present trends persist, the indirect costs to the medical schools of research will represent a sum more than twice the total amount for separately budgeted research expenditures by all medical schools in 1947-48.

---

* Gross National Product.

Third, the federal research programs, as Clark Kerr in his famous Godkin Lectures so well showed, fundamentally change the nature of the university. Kerr also discusses the effect of these grants in diverting faculty to the universities, and also increasing the responsibilities of other IHL for the teaching function.

In the last few years a number of universities have studied the problem of federal research and its relation to the operations of universities. A Princeton and a Harvard report have stressed the fundamental changes being experienced by the university.

After a survey of 36 IHL, Orlans[4] has this to say:

> Now teaching loads have been reduced so drastically at some institutions that they can hardly get much lower. In 1960-61 scientists at Group I universities (these are the twelve universities receiving the largest sums for research funds from Federal Government) taught an average of 6 hours a week; at three universities, their average load was down to 3.9, 4.5, and 4.9 hours, respectively; the reductions are more widespread; and the Government is reimbursing institutions for the time faculty members devote to federally financed research during the academic year—in short, the Government is paying scientists to teach less. 'We have a leaking bucket,' said one science dean discussing his teaching problems, 'and more and more people are punching holes in it.'

> Institutions have tended to increase the size of undergraduate lecture classes, in order to handle enrollment increases economically while maintaining low teaching hours. The result of these and other developments has been to diminish personal contact, particularly between senior university faculty and lower division students.

> Federal programs have had a powerful but indirect influence on these trends because their emphasis on research has served to reduce teaching hours and to strengthen long-established tendencies to devalue undergraduate teaching at the great universities. It can be shown statistically that in every major field and type of institution, a high degree of involvement in research is accompanied by reduction of time spent teaching undergraduates.

Finally, in 1963-64 Committees of the Congress have been studying the allocation of federal research grants. Under pressure of politicians speaking for Southern States and also for the smaller IHL without research funds and speaking against the 10 or 20 IHL which receive such a large part of the federal funds, a greatly changed distribution of these funds is likely. Politicians have learned that jobs follow the research dollars—consider the effect of the University of California and Cal Tech on California contracts from the federal government, and the large gains accruing to Massachusetts in recent years, largely as a result of the research funds going to M.I.T. and Harvard at a time when electronics and missiles have fundamentally changed defense operations. It is most likely that the allocation of funds now well related to effective use will change for the worse in the years to come. This is not to deny the point that many IHL of quality could use effectively research funds that they are not now receiving.

IV

In general American IHL do not directly prepare their students for jobs. Teacher colleges, undergraduate business and engineering schools are important exceptions. There is much more emphasis on general education in higher education in the United States than there is in Western Europe or the USSR. One explanation of this fact is that the relevant age at IHL in Europe is from 20 to 24, as compared to 17 to 21 here. General education comes largely in the gymnasium or lycée in Europe, and similar institutions. It therefore follows that the curriculum of students in higher education in the United States in the first two years corresponds to what is covered in the last two years in secondary schools in Europe.

But increasingly, both in the United States and in Europe, the emphasis is being put on more general education and less vocational education. This is the result of the fact that our institutions are changing rapidly, as technology and automation are bringing tremendous changes in a relatively short period of time. What a worker learns after he gets out of school or college may be of little use by the time he has finished with his 40-50 years on the labor market.

In the discussion in the seminar, John McCauley, Director of Manpower Training Operations of the Department of Labor, brought out the relevance of various bits of legislation, e.g., the Area Redevelopment Act, the Youth Bill, the Manpower Training Act, and the like. They are really concerned with the retraining and education of workers. It was also pointed out that the Government, on the whole, has not done a very good job in encouraging retraining and education of workers. Some studies have suggested that the large corporation tends to go in for further training and education much more than the small corporation, the explanation being the fact that the large corporation has large resources, and also is not so likely to lose a worker and its investment as is a small corporation. It hardly pays a corporation to invest large sums of money in training a worker if he is going to leave the corporation fairly soon. By providing vested pension funds and the like, a corporation, of course, has considerable hold on the worker. Seniority rights also are another factor discouraging large losses on workers who are retrained.

But all of this does suggest the great need of general education. The point is that the student should be trained to think, to organize materials, to make mature judgements, and to communicate so that, as the economy changes, he can quickly adjust to the new situtation. It is less important than it used to be to cram the student with cases based on current experience or on present techniques.

What is being done to train members of the labor market by industry and by government is well described by McCauley. But in view of the changing structure of the labor market, one may be surprised at the failure of the government to do more. Indeed at one point the government studied the training and educational requirements of 4,000 jobs. Moreover, occupational outlooks are a periodic presentation of the government. On the basis of expected income, spending patterns, productivity trends and the like, the government can make some estimates of the workers required in major occupations and industries.[5]

The modest steps detailed by McCauley are only a beginning. In some European countries, e.g. France, the government looks ahead as much as 20 years and attempts to project economic trends, estimate manpower needs, and adjust educational programs to them. In other countries, e.g. Great Britain, the authorities are skeptical of the usefulness of long range plans. Uncertainties about future productivity, of relations of workers trained and available, the structure of industry and other relevant matters—these suggest to the British that the number to be educated at different levels should be determined by the capacity to profit from these educational steps and the demand for secondary and higher education. Increased supply will induce increased demand, and as requirements change, members of the labor market broadly trained will respond to the new market conditions.[6]

V

Having devoted the first four sessions to the relation of government to education in the United States, we moved on in the last session devoted to government and education to an examination of the problems of the underdeveloped countries. In the advanced countries of the world, there is a clear-cut relation of expenditure on education and economic conditions. Countries that spend much on education tend to have high per capita incomes. A cross section examination country by country at any one time, a historical relation of outlays on education and per capita income, or even the relation of the rise of input of resources into education and the gains of national output—all of these reveal generally that education pays as an investment. This is aside from the consumption, e.g. cultural contributions, of education. It is not surprising then that the underdeveloped countries tend to become excessively interested in pouring their limited resources into education.

Dr. Montague Yudelman, a student of economic development and an expert for the International Bank's Uganda Mission has had much experience in theory and practice in considering the allocation of resources in underdeveloped countries. In his essay, he raises some penetrating questions of the educational policies of underdeveloped countries. How much does education contribute to growth? Is there a conflict between growth and educational objectives? How much can underdeveloped countries afford to spend on education? Are past programs realistic? Yudelman not only raises these questions but, based on practical experience, he also gives some thoughtful answers.

Underdeveloped countries are confronted not only with the problem of how much to spend on education in dollars and in resources but also the manner of allocating these funds. Should the money be spent for primary, for secondary, for vocational or higher education? That underdeveloped countries have small total resources is relevant. Although their average income is of the order of $100 per capita per year in comparison with about $1,000 in Western Europe and $2,500 in the United States—with substantial variation from $25 to several hundred—their outlays on education in relation to income are a smaller percentage of their income than similar expenditures in advanced countries. They also suffer from another disability. Their operations are small and hence tend to be costly per student per year. In fact, they are unnecessarily expensive because of mistakes in curriculum and other wasteful practices, e.g. heavy reliance on board ing schools, and because of the kind of personnel in charge of education. Adam Curle, in charge of a large program for education in the underdeveloped countries at the Harvard Graduate School of Education, explains well the pressures to spend on education and the mistakes in allocating resources to education.

VI

We now turn to Part II, *Challenges in Educational Planning.*

At our seminar three authorities in particular dealt with the problem of superior talent: John Stalnaker, Head of the National Merit Scholarship Corporation, Professor John B. Carroll of the Harvard Graduate School of Education, and Richard Titmuss, the well-known British sociologist.

No one would take exception to the general conclusion that we do not invest adequately in the education of those with superior talent. We are just beginning to provide special facilities and special curricula for the highly talented students that come to American IHL. For some wise remarks on the failures and recent advances in the education of superior talent, the reader will find Carroll's essay especially helpful. Only in the last few years, for example, did Harvard provide special freshman seminars largely taken by able freshmen, who had been so well trained that they generally lost interest in their studies in the first and second year at Harvard. After an experimental period of several years the faculty almost unanimously approved of the special seminar program in 1963 and urged its continuation. What the seminar program offers to the freshman is close contact with senior members of the faculty, opportunities to work on his own, write papers, defend them, and, in general, pursue independent work. Advance standing, discussed by our guests, is, of course, another approach to improving the training of the talented youngster, making it possible for a student to advance in a manner consistent with his development.

Carroll examines differences in the selective process in the USSR, the United States, and the United Kingdom. Here we find similar results for the USSR and the United States even though in theory the Soviet is unwilling to acknowledge innate differences. For an understanding of the British approach to the discovery of talent, Carroll examines the underlying psychological theories and in particular the typological theory which supports an allocation of British youngsters among three different types of schools and the more acceptable multidimensional theory of individual differences upon which American education is based. But the British system moves in the direction of more democratic approaches, and especially since Carroll wrote his paper.

In the important British Crowther Report *(15 to 18, Report of the Central Advisory Council for Education,* 1959) the following was said:

> Why the Schooling Age should be Raised:—The National Interest
>
> A. The country is a long way from tapping all the available supply of talent by present methods—half the national service recruits to the Army who were rated in the two highest ability groups had left school at 15.
>
> B. It is most unlikely that this waste of talent can be remedied within a reasonable period without compulsion, because leaving at 15 is so deeply imbedded in certain parts of the social structure. Among national service recruits in the Army, coming from families of manual workers, two thirds of those rated in the two highest ability groups had left school at 15.

The British *Robbins Report on Higher Education* issued late in 1963 devoted much space and time to the British educational system and its failure to make the best use of talent:

"Throughout our Report we have assumed as an axiom that courses of higher education should be available for all those who are qualified by ability and attainment to pursue them and who wish to do so. . . .

". . . we do not believe that modern societies can achieve their aims of economic growth and higher cultural standards without making the most of the talents of their citizens. . . ."

The Robbins Committee is eloquent on the greater percentage of early school-leavers from the working classes. Thus the percentage of leavers of all ages who leave at age 18 and over is 55 for children from parents in the professional and managerial occupations, and 23 per cent for those with parents in the semi- and unskilled occupations.[8]

Another study shows a gain of almost 50 per cent in the proportion of children from the working class entering Independent Efficient or Grammar Schools from the 1930's to 1946-51.

Jean Floud commented as follows on recent trends:

> It should be made clear that these trends cannot be accounted for over social bias in the selection process. There is conclusive evidence to show that awards of places in grammar schools and universities are made today (they were not before 1945) to children of all classes on equal intellectual terms; that is to say that the social distribution of available places closely reflects the social distribution of latent ability.[9]

In trying to assess who are the most able students and to make sure that they get higher education, dependence to a considerable extent has been on the aptitude tests. Indeed the knowledgeable college administrators have depended heavily upon school grades, letters, and the like. The tendency in recent years has been to minimize the importance of the I.Q. test and, in fact in many countries it is frowned upon, and particularly in Western Europe.

It is well to be reminded of some wise remarks made by John Gardner.[10]

> An acquaintance of mine who recently visited a provincial school in France reported, 'The teacher seems to find it impossible to separate his judgement of the pupil's intelligence from the judgement of the pupil's cleanliness, good manners, neatness of dress, and precision of speech. Needless to say, his students in the upper and upper-middle social classes excel in these qualities.' Before the rise of objective tests American teachers were susceptible—at least to some degree—to the same social distortion of judgement. Against this background, modern methods of mental measurement hit the educational system like a fresh breeze. The tests couldn't see whether the youngster was in rags or in tweeds, they couldn't hear the accents of the slum. The tests revealed intellectual gifts at every level of the population.

Indeed the tests do not tell us everything we have to know about the student. All kinds of other qualities make for success in life, and those qualities measured for entrance to college are not equally important in determining the later success. The tests were never intended to provide that kind of a guide for later success. It is well known now that training, enviroment and experience with tests have a considerable effect upon the scores that are made. But I should not anticipate the helpful comments in Carroll's paper on these issues.

In his able paper on the National Merit Scholarship Corporation (NMSC), Stalnaker has made clear the great dependence on intelligence tests in picking top talent for the NMSC. No one reading Stalnaker's paper can deny the great contibution of the NMSC in identifying talent. But it is clear the NMSC is not entirely satisfied with these tests and is trying to supplement them with some selections not based exclusively on these tests.

A similar reservation on usual admission criteria has influenced President John Sawyer of Williams College, who is now experimenting with the help of the Ford Foundation with the admission of students who ordinarily would not be accepted on the basis of the usual aptitude tests, letters, and similar criteria. There are, indeed, many students of outstanding ability in mathematics who could not succeed in history, and vice versa. A first-class man who is excellent in one area may spoil his record by being rather poor in another. Yet many men and women of this type achieve greatness. This is the type of youngster, I understand, that Williams College is going to experiment with over a period of years. They will study what happens to these youngsters as they move along.

In actual practice it is not easy to select the students who should profit from special financial help. This problem has been a serious one for the NMSC. The tendency is, of course, to assume that abilities are evenly divided among states and, therefore, the candidates would be selected on the basis of the relative number of, say, high school graduates. But this may very well mean a large number of high school graduates in New York State with aptitude beyond 700 would have to be sacrificed in order to allow a few students from Mississippi with an aptitude test of 600 to make the grade. I leave to Stalnaker the task of telling the reader how choices are made, the selection of IHL by the National Merit winners, the issue of whether the NMSC should assume responsibility for this choice. On one point raised by Stalnaker I cannot refrain from noting my assent. The large achievements of the students of the prestigious IHL may too readily be interpreted as their contributions; but it is well to consider also the input, that is the quality of the student when he enters.

VII

Two sessions on Social Values and Formal Education exploited the talents especially of Dr. Dan Lortie; Professor Theodore Caplow, the author of the famous *Academic Market Place;* Professor Richard

Titmuss of the London School of Economics and advisor to the La-
bour Party; Professor Everett Hughes, current president of the American Sociology Association; and Professor David Reisman.

As an economist determined to economise on scarce resources,
for years I have been urging greater use of educational television,
recourse to programed instruction, team teaching and aptitude testing.
I need not here go over the arguments for each of these innovations.
But briefly the case for television is possible economies and more
effective use of teaching talent and of improved materials; for programed instruction, adapting the rate of progress to the student's
capacity to learn; for team teaching, saving the teacher from chores
and adapting responsibilities to capacities at the different levels of the
hierarchy; for testing, the conservation of manpower involved in choice
through testing as against the greater emphasis on social background
in the pre-testing era.

Hence to the economist, Lortie's approach to the use of these
modern tools is both provocative and disturbing. He has some interesting things to say about each of these programs, and in particular
their contribution to uniformity against pluralism.

Caplow is concerned over the problem of exporting educational
systems of this country to Latin America. The peculiar history and
traditions of higher education in Latin America, e.g. the tie-in of
the university and students to political operations—these among other
things impede the impact of the American product. Obstacles to im-
portations, and notably cultural differences, are under examination
in Caplow's paper as well as suggested therapy. Again, the economist
is impressed by differences in economic resources which in itself ex-
cludes the imitation of the American product.[11]

Since Caplow wrote his essay, the John Gardner report on the
universities in relation to our AID program has appeared.[12] What
concerns this committee especially is the failure of universities to put
adequate resources into these programs and, unlike some other federal
agencies, the failure of AID to deal effectively with universities. This
is a serious problem with 72 universities involved in 129 separate
agency contracts worth $158 million. The Gardner Report is addition-
al evidence of the failure of higher education in this country to
contribute much to Latin American education.

Is the British system of selecting students to study further and
gain entry to IHL a democratic one? Is the Grant System under
which the government pays most of the higher education bill to be

preserved, or is it in fact a program for government controlling IHL? Titmuss has some interesting things to say about these problems. His views should be compared with those expressed by the Robbins Report of 1963 *(Higher Education)* and also with the Report of the Grants Committee,[13] both of which appeared after the Titmuss presentation. They are much less critical of the British system.

VIII

In two sessions of the seminar we discussed the problem of recruitment of personnel. It is well to remember two points—the first made by Professor Oscar Handlin—that there have been crises before, and second that despite the fact that this is a period of substantial unemployment there still are great shortages of manpower in the professions. In other words, though there is an excess of labor or labor surpluses in many occupations, this does not reduce greatly the shortage in the teaching profession. The transfer of skills from those areas where there is surplus labor to teaching is not easy. In the long run, as education becomes more general, this unevenness of supply and demand in special categories of employment will be reduced.

In the schools the supply of teachers is not adequate, and especially at the desired quality. In the public schools there are still eight states with less than 60 per cent of the teachers with four years or more of college, and there are two states—Nebraska and South Dakota—where more than 17 per cent of the teachers have less than two years of college. Shortages are of course much greater in some fields than others.

In the schools a large part of the problem is the heavy attrition of teachers, estimated at about 11 per cent per year. This does involve a certain amount of waste, though as Professor John Meyer of Harvard pointed out, the consumption gains of education are not to be dismissed even though the potential teachers leave relatively early.

In the colleges there are also shortages. On the average it is expected that there should be a net rise of 100 per cent in the number of college teachers in fifteen years, an increase much beyond what is expected in competitive occupations. The increase should be about four times that in all employment, and two and a half times that of white collar workers, and almost twice that for all professional persons. Obviously some improvement in conditions, especially pay, would be a necessary cost of this increase.

In order to get such large increases, the colleges depend not only on the graduate schools that provide, perhaps, half of the numbers required, but they depend to a considerable extent on manpower drawn from educational services, business occupations, government service, and the like.

This is not merely a problem for the United States. Almost every country in Western Europe, for example, is concerned over the inadequate supply of teachers. The shortage prevails especially in the sciences; but it is also quite general. In response to shortages, the authorities tend to increase the student-teacher ratio. But there are many other correctives, such as later retirement, reduced chores for teachers and hiring part-time teachers. [14]

Why, it may be asked, is the supply of teachers so inadequate? Undoubtedly as has been argued before, pay is a very important factor, but there are other issues. I refer the reader to Charles Benson's able discussion of reasons for the shortage, and short-run and long-run correctives.

One approach is, of course, to increase the size of the class. But most of the experts seem to think that an increase in the size of classes in the public schools would be a great mistake and reduce the effectiveness of teaching.

In higher education, I am not so sure about this matter of size of class. An ideal arrangement is large lectures and small classes or seminars. Undoubtedly much manpower could be saved by eliminating unnecessary courses, alternating small classes, and eliminating many of the small classes that in educational product are not justified in view of the costs. Of course, especially in the last two years of college, there is great need for small classes in order to facilitate concentration. Lectures given by able people, and not merely a compilation of what is already available in the textbook, can often be an inspiration to students, and can provide at relatively low cost an excellent type of education. It is the intermediate size classes, from 25 to 75, where wasteful exchanges between the teacher and a few students prevail, and if one is to have a class of 25 one might as well have one of 50 or 75. There is no evidence to show that the larger class really doesn't do as good a job as the smaller class. In fact, most studies seem to indicate the reverse.[15]

Are there any other approaches towards solving the problem of the shortage of teachers? (Benson has a few.) The Ford Foundation, of course, has put its finger on one important matter, namely the fact that teachers spend a great part of their time doing menial tasks that could be done by younger technicians, and even by janitors. It is uneconomic to pay a teacher $6,000 a year and have him (her) do the kind of work that could be done by others at half the price. Besides it is degrading for the teacher. Anything that can be done to increase the status of the teacher in the community would also be helpful; for example, providing him (her) with fellowships to travel abroad, summer refresher courses, prizes for achievements, and the like.

Dr. Conrad develops an interesting idea. I leave to him the privilege of presenting his incentive program that would increase total supply, takes into account excesses and shortages in different markets, and yet would not be too costly nor excessively tied to pecuniary motivation.

Under the pressure of inadequate supply of teachers, colleges have used all kinds of approaches to economising on teachers and increasing supplies. For example, the following have been used: employment of retired professors and other retired persons; employment of some faculty members beyond mandatory retirement age; employment of part-time persons; sharing instructors and instructional facilities with other institutions; employment of new faculty less qualified; employment of new faculty at salaries higher than formerly; employment of new faculty at ranks higher than formerly; accelerated promotion; increase of the established mandatory age limit; new fringe benefits; salary increases; larger lecture sessions; reduction of duplication and overlapping course offerings; a significantly larger responsibility placed on a student for his own learning; use of non-professional assistants to help relieve faculty of non-teaching duties; reduction of the number of small classes; courses given completely, or primarily, by television; and courses given completely, or primarily, by films.[16]

Perhaps more than anything else, the emphasis has been on raising pay. I would support an increase of pay in stable dollars of at least 50 per cent in the 1960's for school teachers and even more for college teachers, since the latter's real incomes have fallen greatly in relation to income of the working population since pre-war. But the National Education Association proposes rises for school teachers way beyond this. The guide should be an increase large enough to assure the supply and quality needed.

IX

In the past there has been much emphasis on the need for the Federal Government to subsidize public education. The major reasons for this are the large variations of resources among states and the interest of Federal Government in correcting low standards. That poor education in Mississippi is costly to the rest of the nation, is an argument widely used. In one respect the argument is not as strong as it used to be, because there has been a tendency toward equality of income among the states, though the dollar difference continues to rise:[17]

Year	Per Capita Personal Income (Ratio Delaware to Mississippi)	Dollar Difference
1940	4.6:1	$ 786
1950	2.9:1	1,413
1960	2.6:1	1,840
1970 (Projected)	2.5:1	2,210

But it is extremely doubtful that any large Federal legislation for subsidizing schools is likely to be had in the next five or ten years. (Written before Johnson's 1965 proposals.) The reason for this is partly the great burden on the Federal Government of Defense and related programs. Moreover, the introduction of a tax cut program in 1964 suggests that the United States Government is going to try to stimulate the economy, increasingly not through spending but through reduction in taxes. Insofar as tax cuts bring large deficits the possibility or practicability of raising deficits through increased federal spending in welfare areas is, to that extent, reduced. In his paper, Professor Otto Eckstein presents the case against general federal aid to state and local governments for education at this time.

It is not easy to estimate how much money will be required in the next ten years. I have, myself, estimated that the increased need of public funds would be about $11 billion for public schools, and perhaps $4 or $5 billion additional for higher education. (Actually recent increases suggest larger growth). These are the burdens that may be put on state and local governments as a result of the rising costs of education. In making these estimates I assume a large rise of enrollment, as well as improved standards of education commensurate with the rise of general standards for the population in the next ten years. But I should also point out that the National Education Association suggests an increase in current expenditures for public schools from $12.3 billions in 1959-60 to $33.6 billions in 1969-70, or a rise of $21 billions for current expenditures alone, and obviously there will be several billion dollars additional for capital. An increase of these dimensions would clearly be most difficult to achieve. The estimate is based on the theory that the current expenditure per pupil enrolled would rise from $341 in 1959-60 to $720 in 1969-70. An increase of these proportions would mean a rise of expenditures on schools and higher education in excess of $25 billion over a period of ten years. Even on the optimistic assumption of a 100 per cent rise of state and local revenues in the 1960's as suggested by Eckstein, this would be an excessive burden.[18]

To those who are puzzled by the possibility of a rise of state and local expenditures by $50 billion or 100 per cent in the 1960's, I recommend Eckstein's essay. He assumes a 50 per cent rise of Gross National Product (GNP), no substantial improvement in standards of education, and no significant inflation. In this connection, a rise of $14 billion in the 3 years 1961-63 is strikingly close to the projection of $50 billion for additional state and local expenditures for 10 years. (The inflation was slight.) Yet a rise of 100 per cent for state and local outlays in the light of a gain of only 50 per cent in GNP may be troublesome. (The rise of GNP from 1960 to 1963 was $12\frac{1}{2}$ per cent in stable dollars or 50 per cent for a 10 year period if the 1961-63 unusual recovery can be maintained.)

In his essay, Professor Charles Benson shows how additional numbers are gradually imposed on the public schools. In an interesting calculation, he shows that from 1929-30 to 1957-58, the "annual rate of increase in real inputs for elementary and secondary instruction was thus 0.7 per cent." This is a disturbing statistic, for it suggests that the real input in public school instruction rose only about one quarter that of the output (manpower productivity) of the economy.

This relatively large rise of output reflects the increasing productivity. In a study of the period 1869-70 to 1955-56 I found that the average annual salary per member of the instructional staff rose from $189 to $4,156, an increase way beyond that in prices. This rise reflects to some extent the general rise of productivity which in turn is to some extent experienced by the schools.

The gains of productivity in the schools have, however, been less than in the economy generally. As the economy reflects the rising productivity in increased income, the schools are affected adversely; they pay more for services but the additional pay is not offset, as in other parts of the economy, by corresponding rises in productivity.

My own interpretation of rising outlays in the public schools from 1900 to 1956 is as follows:

First is the doubling of enrollment.

Second is the even greater increase of average daily attendance.

Third (related) is an increase in the number of days in the school.

The fourth reason for the increase of expenditures is the rise of prices and the increased productivity of the nation (reflected especially in the large increase of pay of teachers).

Fifth is the increase of capital costs.

Sixth is the increase of proportion of high school students. Per unit high school students cost about 60 per cent more than elementary school students, and their proportion has greatly increased.[19]

X

In the last five or ten years we have had a spate of studies on the relationship between education and income, and some by leading economists. The objective has been to discover to what extent education contributes to income, growth, and productivity. In some instances we have some fairly precise answers. This search has gone so far that the conclusion has even been included in the President's 1963 White House Message on Education—reflecting recent work in this area. I quote:

> This Nation is committed to greater investment in economic growth; and recent research has shown that one of the most beneficial of all such investments is education, accounting for some 40 per cent of the Nation's growth and productivity in recent years. It is an investment which yields a substantial return in higher wages and purchasing power of trained workers, in the new products and techniques which come from skilled minds, and in the constant expansion of this Nation's storehouse of useful knowledge.

Economists have been struck by the fact that when one compares the input of the factors of production, such as labor and capital, and the output, that output seems to rise more rapidly than input. The difference between output and input is what is known as the residual. Obviously the more items (factors) that are included in the input the less will be the difference between output and input. In this respect Edward Denison for the CED in an ingenious study of this problem has added to the items covered under input, and therefore to that extent reduced the excess of output over input. But even Denison has had to make many simplifying assumptions in order to achieve his general goal, that is, to estimate the relationship between education and productivity or growth. In fact, the President's estimate of 40 per cent seems to come largely from Denison's work. Yet in his input Denison does not include such contributions as government or management, and in estimating the contribution of education he assumes that one day at school in the 19th century is equal to a day, say, in 1955. Obviously days at school differ from place to place, from school to school, from time to time, and a day over the years is not a homogeneous product. In Denison's analysis a large part of the residual is related to education. But of course housing and health are also relevant, and there are many other items that might be included in the residual that Denison has not really treated, though he recognized their relevance. He concentrates to a considerable extent on improvement in knowledge as probably the most important factor in the residual. But others have emphasized the point that one must also weigh heavily the contribution of capital. Technology makes the great difference, and technology is tied to education, but technology without capital is not of much use. In discussing the Denison book, Abramovitz writes as follows:

> . . . He calls the ultimate residual the Advance of Knowledge, but of course this category which nominally accounts for just 20 per cent of total growth during 1929-57, is not in any meaningful sense a measure of that alone, and it may not be a measure chiefly of that. For, as a residual it is the grand legatee of all the errors of estimate embodied in the measures of national product, of inputs, conventional and otherwise, and of the economies of scale and other factors classified under productivity growth. . . .[20]

Other approaches are also possible, and we owe a great deal to H. P. Miller of the Census Bureau who has contributed much to an understanding of the relations between education and income. He relates income to years of education. Schultz has developed these matters further, and he has included in the costs of education the income foregone by those who go to school or college. Indeed, for any one worker it may be assumed that in going to school he has lost a corresponding amount of income. But when there are several millions at school and unemployment is high, especially among the young, it is easy to exaggerate the income foregone.

It is also well to note that to a considerable extent the investment in education may be excessive in the sense that employers demand qualifications that are much beyond what is necessary for a particular occupation. When large numbers of college graduates appear on the market, the employer tends to exploit this situation and demands a higher level of education than is required. Moreover, the "guild" in order to keep numbers down may set high educational qualifications. Over-qualification, however, is not necessarily a net loss, because one also has to consider the consumption gains of education for the individual who profits from it. Where there is a shortage of manpower, however, there is a tendency to reverse the movement and to upgrade the worker so that, for example, the technician performs the tasks previously the responsibility of the engineer with four years of college. A considerable amount of progress was made in this direction during World War II when there was a considerable shortage of highly skilled workers. In the same manner wastage can be avoided by reducing the tasks, especially the menial tasks, for the highly qualified, say the teacher, and imposing them on assistants. In the medical profession, in recent years, the tendency has been to save the doctor for the highest type of work and to increase the contribution of the medical team. In this manner it is possible to reduce the degree of over-qualification.

This brings me to the essay of Professor André Daniere. He is very critical of some of this recent work on the relation of education, productivity and income. I, myself, also believe that some of the innovators in this field have tended to give their results a degree of precision that is not justified by the analysis and numbers to be found. Yet if they often have been too audacious, nevertheless we owe a great deal to Messrs. Theodore Schultz, Gary Becker, E. F. Denison, Robert Solow, J. W. Kendrick, and others.

I shall not go over the details of Daniere's complaint. But I should warn the reader that for the non-economist, Daniere's paper may be a little difficult in spots. In a general way, Daniere objects to recent procedures. He prefers to deal with these problems by estimating the need of manpower, total and by categories, and on the basis of this to estimate the required years of training and education. To this extent Daniere shares a view held by many European economists. The French, for example, plan their economy and education in a manner similar to the one proposed by Daniere. A number of British economists have repudiated the whole marginal approach, that is, comparing alternative additional inputs of impersonal and personal capital and the resultant rises of income, and on this basis determining alternative kinds of investment. They prefer to stress the complementary aspects of the problem—e.g. the introduction of the automobile requires impersonal capital, education of the driver and the public generally, and technical advances related to education. That is to say, instead of estimating the return on investment of impersonal capital against that of personal capital they prefer to consider the complementarity aspects.[21]

In Part II the contributors to the seminar dealt with certain aspects of educational planning: treatment of the superior students, educational programs and their effect on diversity, causes and treatment of teacher shortage, the contribution of government at different levels, and the relation of education to productivity and income.

XI

The last part includes discussions of management problems. At the first of these sessions we concentrated on roles and responsibilities. At this session we profited from the presence of a management expert (John Corson), the chairman of the Board of Trustees of one of our great universities, the University of Chicago (Glen A. Lloyd), law school professors who also are experts of the American Association of University Professors in these areas (Clark Byse and John Dawson), and college heads (Margaret Clapp of Wellesley and James Coles of Bowdoin). Hence we were able to sound out interested groups: trustees, administrators, faculty, and management experts.

What these experts really brought out is the difference in operation between IHL and business enterprises, the effect of the absence of the profit motive in IHL on operations and results, the significance of the dual role of faculty as part of management and as employees, and in general to what extent IHL should seek the hierarchical organization of business enterprise and concentration of responsibility at the top.

At the seminar John Corson suggested that the most important objectives were an efficiently operating institution, with the maximum of freedom. But it is not easy to run a highly efficient IHL. As Corson suggests, there is a great diffusion of responsibility among alumni, trustees, administrators, faculty, and sometimes of course the Government is involved. Without the hierarchy and the authority that prevails in business institutions, the college or university is likely to experience much less than a high level of efficiency.

In American higher education the control of the lay board is important. Unlike European universities, the lay board has considerable authority in the running of the university or college. This is the result, in part, of the fact that in the early colleges in the United States the teaching was done by very young tutors and fellows, and obviously the control of the enterprise could not be put in their hands. It was therefore necessary to rely on a mature President and leaders in the community, and notably ministers.[22]

Trustees are indeed responsible for the financial operations of the IHL and, to a considerable extent, for the allocation of resources among different uses, They are also responsible for obtaining adequate financial resources, and also for the appropriate investment of endowment funds. But as Dean Carman has so well said, the trustees have tended to delegate authority over the curriculum to the President and the faculty. Indeed Beardsley Ruml wanted the trustees to retrieve control over the curriculum, not a likely outcome. How far the trustees as against the faculty should assume responsibility for curriculum and educational policy is a matter discussed especially by Messrs. Lloyd, Corson, and Byse. The division of responsibility of the President against faculty and trustees is also under examination.

By determining the curriculum and educational policies, the faculty also, to some extent, controls the financial arrangements. The trustees are confronted with a new program, say in tutorial work or in general education, or a house plan, and these involve large expenditures. Indeed, if the resources are not available, the trustees may then veto a large new program. But within the limits set by available funds, or those likely to be had, the faculty, to a considerable extent in cooperation with the Administration, can more or less determine educational programs and relevant expenditures.[23]

One of the troublesome problems is the relation between faculty and trustees. In general there seems to be a widespread view that the faculty should not deal with the trustees directly, and that only the President should have access to the trustees. The American Association of University Professors, however, urges greater participation of the faculty in trustee deliberations. At Harvard there is no disposition on the part of the faculty to discuss policies with members of the Harvard Corporation that assumes substantial responsibility for policy.[24]

As an observer of the economics of higher education over more than 40 years, I have been very much impressed with the inefficiencies of universities and colleges generally. The explanation, I believe, is in part that the college is run, to a considerable extent, by the faculty. Each member of the faculty considers himself a member of the managing board, rather than as an employee. Where there are so many who determine policy, obviously the result is not likely to be as good as in private enterprise. These wastes are, for example, to be seen in the excess number of courses and of small courses, duplication of curricula, the failure to make effective use of plant, the unscientific and uneconomic selection of sites for colleges, and so on.[25] To some extent, of course, the responsibility here lies with the trustees as well as with the Administration and faculty.

These wastes are undoubtedly a price that is paid for the control of the curriculum and educational policy by the faculty. But it is also possible under the pressure of limited funds and the great demand for entry to eliminate some of the inefficiencies, for example, the inadequate use of plant, and even, for example, to try to cut down the number of unnecessary courses. But these objectives are not easily reached.[26] Beardsley Ruml would return authority over curriculum to the trustees. I doubt that this is a practical solution.

> Bad as the quality of the liberal college curriculum is, its efficiency is even worse. The damage done to the liberal college by its economic poverty is beyond all estimation. . . .
> . . . The Trustees, therefore, must take back from the faculty *as a body* its present authority over design and administration of the curriculum. Trustees must take back this authority, but not because the trustees, *as a board,* are able to exercise it better than the faculty as a body. . . .[27]

XII

In recent years, there have been many complaints of the trends in the relative position of public vs. private IHL, of prestigious private IHL and of other private IHL, and also of the declining weight of aid to students as college costs continue to soar.

An eloquent commentator on some of these issues is John Morse. Morse sees the public IHL gaining at the expense of the private, and the prestigious, e.g. the Ivy group, improving its relative position. As the privileged few attract increasing numbers, some of their gains spill over to a limited number of others. But I leave to Morse the elaboration of this position, and also his proposals on how to treat this problem. In this connection, recall also President Clark Kerr's remarks in the Godkin Lectures on the increasing tendency of the great universities to hoard faculty for research, and thus keep teachers out of the other IHL.

Undoubtedly despite the large rise of entrants a limited number of IHL gain especially, and others experience losses. This raises the question of why the favored few. Dean Wilson's paper is largely concerned with the problem of how one measures the output of Yale (say) against Texas. The general thrust of his essay is that it is most difficult to appraise the net contribution of the institution, for the favored few have entirely different materials to mold. This is the ancient error of equalising output with contribution. The higher income of Harvard, Yale, and Princeton men in later life reflects not only the educational gains while attending these institutions, but also environmental factors and considerable differences in native ability.[28]

A final issue in this chapter is that raised by Moon, namely the declining relative numbers of students aided in recent years and the rising dependence on loans as against grants. Indeed costs in the last few years inclusive of tuition may have been rising faster than per capita income, and hence in that sense higher education is increasingly expensive. But one should also point out that from pre-war until the late 1950's, per capita disposable income or family incomes were rising substantially more than tuition or even college costs. By making this point, I am not, however, denying the need of additional assistance.

It is well also to be clear on a number of additional points.

First, aid to students can come in various ways. The public IHL offers an education that costs undergraduates about $1,500 for about $175. For the average non-public IHL average costs are somewhat higher but the charge is around $800.[29] Here is a direct subsidy available to all irrespective of need. One can argue that there are elements of waste here. Why not charge more and use the proceeds to subsidize a larger number of students with increased stipends? This seems to me an impregnable theoretical principle, although some problems arise in practice.

Second, why not introduce a system like the British? In Great Britain 80-90 per cent of students in higher education receive maintenance grants averaging about $1,300.[30] A maintenance grant of about £460 sterling is the equivalent of about $1,300 at the £1 = $2.80 exchange rate and probably a few hundred dollars more if allowance is made for the difference in purchasing power. At any rate, a maintenance grant or a scholarship of $1,300 in Great Britain is equivalent to one of at least $2,500 in the United States.

Why, it may be asked, should a country with a per capita income about one half of ours pay such large and almost universal scholarships, when in the United States scholarships of a few hundred dollars on the average are available only to about 20 per cent of the students. I think the answer in part is a hostility to large and numerous scholarships in the South and West and hence opposition to governmental intervention, arising in part from a fear of loss of talent to prestigious IHL in the East, and in part from a fear that increased scholarships will bring about higher tuition and thus impair the competitive position of the public IHL. Hence if the United States ever embarks on a comprehensive scholarship program, it is likely to be one with small maximum stipends. Grants at these levels will keep regional mobility of students to a minimum.

Whereas in the United Kingdom, the problem is to obtain entry in higher education—entry assures economic security—in the United States entry to some IHL for any high school graduate is virtually assured; but economic capacity to pay is denied to a substantial proportion who otherwise would find places and graduate.

XIII

At a seminar on the Liberal Arts College (LAC) Presidents John Dickey of Dartmouth, James Coles of Bowdoin, and Dean George Waggoner of the University of Kansas raised some fundamental problems confronting the LAC. In addition we profited from helpful comments from Presidents Mary Bunting of Radcliffe, Margaret Clapp of Wellesley, John Sawyer of Williams and Professor Earl McGrath of Columbia University.

All participants wanted to see the LAC survive as a vital force in American education and life. Among the problems confronting them are the divisive effects of the explosion of knowledge and the growth of research financed by outside interests; the increasing loyalty of faculty generally to the profession against the institution; the tendency to telescope curriculum of the LAC to 2-3 years instead of 4 years as students enter earlier and gain entrance to professional schools at the end of the Junior year; the demands made upon the LAC by professional schools, with the result that they increasingly become service branches for them; the increased attractiveness of the university for students and faculty because of the availability of research programs and advanced courses there, and the pressure to become increasingly vocational in a world where change is accelerated and hence where training in fundamentals is more necessary than ever. These are the issues that our guests identified and attempted to treat.

The gradual encroachment of the professional school especially troubles the supporters of the LAC. The vocational curricula have become much more important as has the university, which of course generally has an LAC connected with it.

Criticism of the LAC goes back a long way. A hundred years ago widespread criticism broke out, partly because of the method of teaching, with students required to memorize and recite, partly because of the small contribution of LAC faculty to research and the advance of knowledge, and partly because of the absence of any vocationalism in the colleges. One result has been the growth of the technological institute, and also the emergence of the university.[31]

In a recent book, Dean William De Vane of Yale wrote that the Liberal Arts College

> . . . comes nearest to Oxford and Cambridge in their great goal of providing a *Studium Generale*—and providing an advanced stage of general studies as a broad, humane, and integrated preparation for life, the object being to make the student *transform himself* into a more real, more substantial, more three dimensional person. They rarely carry their students as far as Oxford and Cambridge, and increasingly the modern undergraduate feels it necessary to supplement his bachelors degree with further work in a professional graduate school.
>
> The curriculum "must be clear and strong against the many pressures that threaten its integrity—the desire of the students for the immediately practical, the pressure of the society for the specialist at too early a stage in his career, the encroachment of demands of professional schools and associations. . . ."[32]

Undoubtedly one of the disadvantages under which the LAC operates is its size. The vast majority of the unattached LACs are church related, and have inadequate resources, an inadequacy partly related to size. In the late 1950's, the median size of a LAC was 723, the maximum 16,214, and the smallest 20. Median enrollment in the upper quartile was 1,401, and in the lower quartile, 396. In enrollment the average LAC is only one-tenth or one-twelfth as large as the average university, a disparity giving the university a large advantage in attracting students and also in cutting unit costs. This does not mean that the unit costs are less in a university than in a college, but it does mean that for the high level of instruction in graduate work and the like, the unit costs are much lower than they otherwise would be. The university has a great advantage, as most of the members of the seminar realized, in being able to attract the best students because of the special attractions for students in the large universities. The first-class junior or senior, for example, can exploit the graduate courses and the seminars that are available in a great university.

Most LAC are private. In one year in the late 1950's there were 653 private and 79 public LAC. The average educational income of the private LAC was $700,000 and the public, $2,250,000. An average educational budget of $700,000 for from 600 to 700 students is not likely to yield a high-quality product. Possibly, as a result of increasing demand for college space, the LAC will be able to expand in the sixties until the average, or median figure is 1,500, a much more likely figure for achieving the greatest economies and strongest competitive position.[33]

It is especially in its command of research resources that the LAC competes unevenly with the university. Whereas in a recent year federal research funds provided about 17 per cent of the educational income of IHL, the contribution of federal research to private LACs was less than 1 per cent of its educational income.[34]

One indication of the economic disabilities of the LAC is given by a study of the median salary for faculty members in the university and four year colleges for the year 1960-61. With an enrollment of less than 500 the average salary was $5,250 for private IHL, for private universities and four-year undergraduates colleges. The figure gradually rises to $6,980 with enrollments from 2,500 to 4,999, and $7,970 for enrollments of 10,000 and over. Since most LAC come in the first two classes, that is, enrollments of less than 1,000 with mean salaries of $5,250 for less than 500, and $5,930 for enrollments from 500 to 999, and since the universities are primarily in the two top classes in enrollment, with salaries of $7,160 and $7,970, it can be seen that the university has a substantial advantage in attracting faculty. To some extent this may be offset by the fact that the small liberal arts college is likely to be in a less populated area where the cost of living is somewhat lower. But these are not large offsets.[35]

In conclusion let me say that the unattached LAC, pressed by professional schools, by the desire for vocational education, by the spread of advanced standing by the university college, and even by the junior colleges, has certainly lost ground. Whereas before the

Civil War the LAC had a virtual monopoly, it now accounts for only about one-third of the baccalaureate degrees. The university college has large advantages with greater research and higher pay rates, and this is related in part to the operations at a higher level of output per institution. An increasing tendency of students to go to graduate professional schools increases the attraction of the university college. At some places, for example at Harvard, where 85 per cent of the students go on to graduate work, the advantage of being in a university college seems great to many students. The university, in turn, profits to a considerable extent from this relationship. For example, I recently, in estimating the proportion of the 30 most distinguished economists that the Harvard Graduate School of Arts and Sciences turned out in a period of about 40 years, found that about 18 of the 30, or 60 per cent, had been Harvard *College* graduates. In other words the undergraduate college provides the graduate schools with some of their best material.

But the unattached LAC also has some advantages. They often do a much better teaching job for the undergraduate. The professor is frequently not interested in research and scholarship, and he is hired primarily as a teacher. It should be said, however, that the best teachers, or at least the teachers for the best students, should be at the frontier of knowledge.

The reader of Chapter 13 will, I believe, agree that the LAC is losing ground. He will find out why, and discover the means of stopping the decline and even recouping past losses.

In short, though the unattached LAC has lost ground, it is far from dead. With the increased demand for space it may well be that the LAC will be able to increase their enrollment to a point where they can do a more economically effective job, and thus be able to compete with universities in salaries, and in related fields. The LAC will continue to guard the integrity of the curriculum, stress broad learning and the ability of the student to think, organize materials, and to form mature judgements. The emphasis on general education and broad training is not entirely separate from vocational objectives.

XIV

Bernard Berelson, both in his book on *Graduate Education in the United States* and in a paper to the seminar, spent much time discussing the problems of the graduate school, problems which have troubled educators for many years: the time to be given by graduate schools to training teachers as against research workers; the time to complete the PhD; the wisdom of saving the MA; the loss of the PhD to non-teaching fields; the shortage of PhD's; the quality of the PhD; the spreading of PhD curricula to inferior IHL. In almost every instance Berelson concludes that the situation is far from hopeless. In fact he generally comes out on the optimistic side. For example, in this kind of a world he sees no reason for debasing research in favor of training teachers. John Chase is not equally optimistic. The latter is concerned also with the responsibilities of the deans of education and the effectiveness of the divisional against departmental organization as well as the relation of departments and deans in their quest for power.

Perhaps Berelson is a little overly optimistic on the production of PhD's. The proportion of PhD's to the total faculty is on the decline. Here the increased attractiveness of non-teaching opportunities is a relevant consideration. Indeed, there is enough talent around so that the number of PhD's could greatly increase. Wolfle has pointed out that 7 per cent of the population can score 130 (the minimum PhD level) or higher in the AGCT (Army General Classification Test), but actually PhD's account for only about 2 per cent of the relevant age group. It is of some interest that of those who attain a score of 130 or higher, 97 per cent finished high school, 53 per cent entered college, 46 per cent graduated from college, and 1.7 per cent received their PhD in a recent year.[36]

One of the intriguing questions is the net effect of the growth of the graduate school on undergraduate education. A view widely held is that increasingly the graduate school develops at the expense of the undergraduate.

As the number of students in graduate schools increases, the cost of higher education will rise greatly. Despite the shortage of graduate students, it is well to note that from 1890 to 1959, undergraduates increased by more than 22 times, and graduate students by 127 times. Even from 1938 to 1958 the graduate increase was about three times as large as the undergraduate increase. The financial burden of increased graduate instruction can be suggested by the following: the relative costs of one semester for (1) freshmen and sophomores, (2) juniors and seniors, and (3) graduate and professional studies varies for one institution in California from 1 to 1.6 to 6. Similar figures are found in other IHL. Actually the genuine costs may be a higher ratio for graduate instruction than is even given here. When one allows for the fact that the high priced professors generally tend to concentrate on graduate work, also that they tend to teach in small courses and seminars for graduate students, which are costly, and also the fact that they tend to give a much larger amount of time to each graduate student than they do to undergraduates, the ratio of costs for graduate instruction may be even larger than is here suggested in relation to undergraduate instruction. That is to say, it is not clear that the above ratios fully take account of the relative costs.

Undoubtedly the cost per graduate student is much greater than that for undergraduates. Yet the graduate student pays no more and frequently less, and, moreover, he is supported much more relatively by financial aid. It may well be that undergraduate education improves, as is widely held. But if it does, then it is despite the diversions of funds to the graduate students. If the average undergraduate student is subsidized by about $1,000 per year (paying, say, $500 for a $1,500 education), the subsidy may well be $3-4,000 for the graduate student in arts and science. (He pays, say, $800 for a $4,300 education. He pays more in part because graduate instruction, at least in private IHL, is in the higher cost IHL.) But this does not necessarily mean that the undergraduate loses correspondingly. His subsidies are somewhat smaller. Since graduate enrollment is only about one tenth of undergraduate (and part of the tenth is outside of arts and science), the total subsidies to all graduate students in arts and science are about one third of those to all undergraduates. If allowance is made for student aid, then the figure may well be closer to one half than one third.

Moreover, it is well to remember that in some IHL the enrollment in the graduate school of arts and science is of the order of one half of the undergraduate enrollments. In such IHL, e.g. Berkeley, Harvard, the "deprivation" of undergraduates becomes much larger.

XV

At the seminar Professor Clark Byse of the Harvard Law School expressed well the general view that tenure is the price that has to be paid to assure academic freedom, that is, freedom to express ideas without interference, whether the issues are baptism, the erection of lightning rods, evolution, oleo margarine versus butter, greenbackism, the theory of Marxism, or Keynesianism. The parallel of the lifetime judge immediately comes to mind.

But there is no doubt that the system of tenure is in many ways costly to the IHL. At the present time a commitment for tenure may involve 30 or 40 years of teaching under tenure, and for those who obtain tenure, say in 1963, this may involve a commitment by better universities to pay as much as a million dollars or more before the professor retires. This problem clearly concerned Byse and he discussed various criticisms of the system and suggestions for its improvement, e.g. the tendency for many professors to become deadwood and not carry through well their assigned functions, the proposal that the situation be reviewed every few years, to see whether retention of the tenure member is justified. But Byse would not compromise with tenure. He would even go so far as to seek enforcement of tenure in the court, though there are certain difficulties involved here. His case for tenure and academic freedom should be studied by every reader.

It is very important that greatest care be exercised in selecting tenure members. A mistake may be very costly. Moreover, the earlier the appointment is made the more likely mistakes are to be made. In a market where the shortage of teachers is very great, the tendency is to make these appointments at earlier and earlier ages. For example, when the Harvard Committee, appointed by the President to *Report on Some Problems of Personnel in the Faculty of Arts and Sciences,* reported its findings in the latter part of the 1930's in the midst of the Depression, the assumption was that the tenure members would be appointed in their later thirties. Actually, in recent years with the change of the economic situation and the rising excess of demand over supply for teachers, tenure appointments tend to be made in the early thirties. In the physical sciences this may not involve large risks. But in the social sciences the risks are much greater.

IHL can protect themselves in various ways. For example, the salary range for tenure members may be, say, from $12,000 to $25,000; the president of a IHL may retire a professor at age 60 to 70 at his discretion; and there are other weapons available. But it should be noted that any exercise of discretion of these proportions may also involve an impairment of academic freedom. A professor who may be retired at 60 rather than 70 may well become most timid once he is in his fifties. For retirement often means a cut in income of $2/3$ or $3/4$. Hence defenders of academic freedom and tenure often demand a narrow range of salaries of tenure members and a fixed retirement age.

Indeed there are some difficulties involved in making the best appointments to tenure positions. Inbreeding is a charge that is often made against the major universities. For example, in the Harvard *Report on Some Problems of Personnel in the Faculty of Arts and Sciences,* the following appeared in the late 1930's:

> . . . During the last 34 years, including the last part of President Elliot's, the whole of President Lowell's, and the first part of President Conant's administration, for every 2.2 men the University appointed from within it took 1 from outside. The Committee sees no reason to doubt that approximately this ratio will maintain itself at an average over a long term of years.[37]

This might suggest that too many Harvard products receive tenure from Harvard, even admitting that, especially in earlier years, Harvard was getting high quality graduate students, and perhaps as high as any university. It is of some interest that over a period of 2 years in the middle 1950's the University of California appointed faculty members with doctorates from the following: University of California = 22%, Harvard next = 11%, then Yale = 4%, University of Michigan = 4%.

It is, indeed, difficult to assume that with Harvard turning out less than 5 per cent of the total PhD's, that the best possible selection of tenure members would be in the proportion of 2.2 Harvard PhD's against 1 from the outside—or a ratio of about 44 to 1 in favor of tenure appointments of Harvard PhD's, as compared to its proportion of total PhD's.[38]

On the history of academic freedom, Professor Robert Merry, who is in charge of the Harvard Business School Management Schools for College Presidents and Deans, has something to say. He also raises a crucial point: faculty associations protect the academic freedom of their members, but with much less enthusiasm and effort do they protect the public and the IHL against abuses of tenure and academic freedom—e.g. against irresponsible statements by faculty members in fields where they cannot speak with authority.

XVI

In the academic there is less disposition to investigate costs than in the business world. Faculties frequently are much more concerned with educational values and think that costs are irrelevant. But so long as there is a shortage or limitation of resources, one has to take into account the cost of doing a particular task. One has to compare alternative uses of limited resources.

In the academic, as in the business world, it is sometimes difficult to estimate the cost of doing a particular task. This is especially true because of the relevance of joint costs—that is, the university or college performs more than one function, and it is not always easy to estimate the costs of each of the functions performed by the college. An extreme case of this kind is, of course, the medical school, where the school not only trains undergraduates, but also graduate students, internes, residents, PhD students, provides services for hospitals and others, and carries on research. How much of the total cost of the medical school, therefore, should be allocated to the four-year undergraduate medical student? Failure to allocate costs properly to the other services of the medical school sometimes results in the absurdly high costs being allocated to the four-year undergraduates. Actually, in most medical schools, and especially in the top medical schools, the costs of the four-year medical school curriculum are only a small part of the total cost of medical services. Proper allocation of costs is not a precise science and depends on intuition and judgment.

In our seminar discussions President Alden particularly brought out the importance of proper budgetary control. He emphasized especially the point that what is required is to find out the cost of doing a particular task, not merely to indicate how much is being spent for salaries, construction, taxes, and the like. What one really wants to know is how much, for example, does the advanced management program cost the business school, and how much does the ordinary two-year curriculum cost? How about the special management program for Radcliffe?

Should one examine the usual Treasurer's report in most colleges and universities, he would not find the breakdown generally very helpful. For example, the departmental summary of expenses for Harvard University is broken down by different branches of the University—for example, Arts and Sciences, Business Administration, Education, Law, etc. Then there is another category, other academic departments—for example, the Arboretum. In addition, there are departments like Dining Halls, University Health Service, Harvard University Printing Office, Special Research and Development. What the Treasurer's report gives, for example, for the Faculty of Arts and Sciences are the salaries paid, wages paid, equipment and supplies, retirement and allowances, scholarships, and other student awards, and then in addition, charges by other departments and miscellaneous expenses. Similarly, with the Graduate School of Business Administration. This amount of information does not tell us very much about the costs and receipts from each program. Nor does it tell us much about how much it costs to educate a law school student, or a graduate student in law, or a medical student. This is the sort of cost accounting that President Alden would like to see established in most universities and for most programs.

With experience as a business school dean, President Alden is in a unique position to deal with problems that stem from the limitation of resources. One would expect him to become interested in such problems as branch operations that are especially cost-saving for students, cooperation among IHL which results in additional services and economies of operation, the use of new teaching techniques that save manpower and economize on scarce resources. Alden's paper reveals him as an unusual innovator in higher education and one not enslaved by generally accepted procedures.

REFERENCES

1. See *Higher Education: The Economic Issues,* S. E. Harris, ed., Harvard University Press (1962) ; S. E. H., *More Resources for Education,* Harpers (1960) ; S. E. H., *Higher Education: Resources and Finance,* McGraw-Hill (1962) .
2. Numbers refer to chapters.
3. The best available study of federal programs is that by John Morse for the House Labor and Education Committee, *The Federal Government and Education,* 1963.
4. *The Effects of Federal Programs on Higher Education,* 1962, pp. 57 and 67.
5. Cf. U.S. Department of Labor, *Manpower Report of the President,* 1964, pp. 34-37.
6. OECD, *Economic Aspects of Higher Education,* S. E. Harris, ed. and Rapporteur, 1964, especially pp. 201-248; and UK, *Higher Education Report,* 1963, pp. 71-75.
7. UK, *Report of the Central Advisory Council for Education,* 1959, p. 453.
8. *Higher Education Report,* 1963, pp. 8, 53. Also see *Ibid.,* Appendix Volume One.
9. *Ability and Educational Opportunity,* A. H. Halsey, OECD, Paper by Jean Floud, 1961, pp. 97-99.
10. J. W. Gardner, *Excellence. Can We Be Equal in Excellence Too?,* 1961, pp. 48-49.

11. Compare Chapter 5.
12. "Aid and the Universities," *New York Times,* May 17, 1964.
13. UK, *University Development,* 1957-1962.
14. See especially UK, *Higher Education Report,* pp. 26, 202; *Ibid.,* Appendix Volume 3, 1963; and University Grants Committee, *University Development, 1957-1962,* pp. 35, 145-6; *Educational Policy and Planning in Sweden,* Appendix 12, 1964; OECD, *Greek Education and Economic Development,* 1964, Chapter 2, pp. 62-64.
15. I have dealt with this problem more fully in Chapter 44 of my *Higher Education: Resources and Finance.*
16. C. D. Lindquist, "Recent Practices Relating to Faculty in Institutions of Higher Learning, Preliminary Report," *Higher Education,* November, 1958, p. 44.
17. The National Education Association, *Financing of Public Schools, 1960-1970,* 1962, p. 14.
18. See National Education Association, *op. cit.,* p. 16; and also United States Census, *Governmental Finances in 1960,* p. 18; and *Economic Report of the President,* 1964.
19. S. E. Harris, *More Resources for Education,* John Dewey Lecture, 1961, pp. 13-14.
20. M. Abramovitz, "Economic Growth in the United States," *American Economic Review,* September 1962, p. 775.
21. See, for example, OECD, *Economics of Education,* 1964, S. E. Harris, editor and Rapporteur, essays by Vimont and Moberg; and forthcoming OECD volume on *Education and Growth,* edited by J. Vaizey.
22. See especially Hofstadter and Hardy, *The Development and Scope of Higher Education in the United States,* 1952, pp. 123-129.
23. See *Administrators in Higher Education, Their Functions and Coordination,* edited by G. H. Burns, Chapter 5, *Board of Trustees and Regents* by H. J. Carman, Dean Emeritus, Columbia College, 1962.
24. L. W. Eley, "The University of California at Berkeley: Faculty Participation in the Government of the University," *Bulletin of the American Association of University Professors,* March, 1964.
25. I have discussed these fully in Part 7, Chs. 42-52 in my *Higher Education: Resources and Finance,* 1962.
26. On some of these matters see M. A. Rauh, *College and University Trusteeship,* 1959.

27. B. Ruml and D. H. Morrison, *Memo to a College Trustee*, 1959, pp. 8 and 13.

28. Cf. Chapter 6.

29. HEW, *Higher Education,* "Basic Student Charges, 1962-63," pp. 9, 11. The average costs are estimated on the basis of HEW statistics on educational expenditures and enrollment.

30. See UK, *Higher Education Report,* 1963, especially pp. 26, 402.

31. On these issues see E. A. Krug, *Charles W. Eliot and Popular Education,* 1961, Chapter 1; Richard Hofstadter and C. DeWitt Hardy, *The Development and Scope of Higher Education in the United States,* 1952, pp. 137-142; G. P. Schmidt, *The Liberal Arts College,* 1957, especially Chapters 7 and 11.

32. W. C. De Vane, *The American University in the Twentieth Century,* 1957, pp. 20-21, 29-31.

33. S. E. Harris, *Higher Education: Resources and Finance,* p. 581.

34. HEW, *Statistics of Higher Education,* 1957-58, Receipts, etc., and Faculty, etc.

35. HEW, *Planning and Management Data,* 1960-61, pp. 30-40.

36. D. Wolfle, *America's Resources of Specialized Talent,* 1954, pp. 182-83.

37. *Report on Some Problems of Personnel,* p. 25.

38. See B. Berelson, *Graduate Education in the United States,* 1960, p. 93.

Part I:
Government and Education

1. State vs. Federal Power in Education

PAPER BY . . . *James E. Allen*
Commissioner of Education, New York State

Let me say at the outset that I cannot claim objectivity in any discussion of relations among the Federal, state and local levels of government in the field of education. I firmly believe that America's greatest hope for meeting the challenges of education lies within the individual states. Among the more obvious of these challenges are: to provide more teachers and classrooms, to improve the training of potential teachers, to modernize curricula and to raise adequate funds to accomplish all these tasks. I shall say nothing more directly about these challenges, for they have been amply dealt with in numerous places (including this volume). Rather, I shall set forth some personal observations on the relationship between government and American education.

It seems important to keep the central purpose of education clearly in mind. In my view, this purpose is to develop each individual's rational powers; this is now a crucial need, for we live in the era of rational man. In addition to this central purpose, education performs another vital service for society: it acts as a stabilizing influence which makes change constructive rather than chaotic. Of course, in order to be stabilizing, education must itself be stable; and although it needs flexibility, it must also possess a certain steadfastness of purpose. Unfortunately, there are factors at work today which threaten this stability of purpose. One is simply the tremendous size of the educational enterprise; another is the necessary growth of Federal support. A third is the fact that society's needs dictate that the individual be molded to fit the educational system, rather than conversely, as it should ideally be.

Turning now more explicitly to the matter of Federal, state and local relations, it seems to me that we must face two major issues. *First,* we must develop a new pattern of economic support for the educational system. Some drastic changes in this area are inevitable if educational needs are to be met. *Second,* there is a pressing demand for improvement in the quality of education—a demand which underlies the need for increased and broad-based public support. These two issues suggest two questions: what influence will increasing Federal support have upon Federal control, and how effective can local control be in providing educational excellence?

It seems to me that America is now approaching a complete re-evaluation and readjustment of Federal, state and local relationships in education. The fact that "state" is listed in the middle of this triad is not merely an accident of the logical arrangement based on size; its position has a deeper significance and is indicative of the role which, in my view, the states must play. Emphasizing the states' role in education is, of course, hardly revolutionary, for their educational responsibilities are firmly embedded in American tradition and law. They are based upon the Constitution's exclusion of education from those direct concerns which it delegates to the Federal Government.

Perhaps the outstanding characteristic of the system whereby states govern American education is its diversity. America has fifty major educational systems, one per state, and no two are likely to have much in common. Each state's system is composed of many local constituencies. These local school districts may coincide with towns, with townships or with counties, or they may conform to some other, intermediate pattern. There is also broad diversity in the structure through which state educational systems, are controlled. In a few instances, state boards of education have jurisdiction over all the educational enterprises within the state, higher as well as lower, and may even deal with certain matters that are not strictly education. In other states the boards have very narrow functions.

Members of the boards of education are chosen in a variety of ways. Usually they are either appointed or popularly elected, but in some states they achieve office through other means. In New York State, for example, the Legislature elects the board of regents. Some states, of course, have no state board of education or its equivalent. Similarly, the various states select their chief educational officers in diverse ways; they may be elected, or appointed by the governor, or appointed by the board of education.

Traditionally, the states have attempted to let local authorities retain a wide discretion over educational matters. The premise underlying this policy is that, by and large, local problems require local solutions. It is accepted almost on faith that safeguarding local control of education is a way of strengthening the states, and ultimately, the nation. While upholding the principle of local autonomy, however, each state has attempted to improve the quality of education within its boundaries and to provide standards and leadership for the enterprise.

The crucial question we must ask is: how effective can the present system be for solving tomorrow's problems? I believe that state departments of education have, in the past, been a constructive force, but it would be naive not to recognize that they all need to improve—some, of course, more than others. Even today, most of them are not able to offer the type of leadership which they should be providing, for in recent years (if my impression is correct) state machinery has grown in size but not in effectiveness. The major focus in our thinking, therefore, should be to make state departments of education increasingly effective, both on their own account and as clearing houses for coordinating Federal and local roles in education. Generally speaking, the primary need at the state level is not physical growth but conceptual, philosophical growth implemented by action.

Realistically, what do these proposals entail? *First,* I think the states must be forthright in accepting the task of identifying, analyzing and solving educational problems. This is especially important because many states have abdicated their authority and wasted opportunities for guiding educational development, even though numerous legal documents assign precisely to the states much of the responsibility for managing the educational enterprise. I strongly urge that the states become increasingly vigilant in carrying out this responsibility.

Second, the existing legal structure, though it is clear enough, is in many ways far from adequate. I propose, therefore, that the legal structure governing the relationship between the states and education be strengthened. I am firmly convinced that each state should have the power and means to enforce high educational standards within its own borders. If necessary, it should be able to reorganize the local school districts—and to enlarge them so that they can operate efficiently. Larger districts would also increase the likelihood of having able people as members of the school board, since there would be more to choose from. The wisdom of such a course hardly seems challengeable.

In New York State, the commissioner of education has a great deal of power at his disposal. At one meeting of the Northeastern State Board of Education, I happened to mention that, as commissioner, I have the authority to remove from office a local school board member or other local school official "whenever it should be proved to [the commissioner's] satisfaction that [such official] has been guilty of any willful violation or neglect of duty. . . ." Many of my colleagues found this fact shocking; they themselves have no such power over local boards, even if the boards are inept or corrupt. Yet, when we give state officials so weak a mandate, how can we expect them to promote excellence in education? By both informal tradition and law, this is precisely what we expect of them, but no state can honor such a commitment unless it has broad power to use corrective measures where and when they are needed.

Let me emphasize that strengthening a state's machinery does not automatically imply increasing its control vis-a-vis that of local authorities. It only means insisting upon adequate management of local affairs, with the proviso that if a local board is not performing adequately, the state will take corrective action. Defining adequate performance is, to be sure, a sticky issue, but I feel confident that it can ultimately be handled in a way which satisfies the majority of those concerned.

Third, much of our current educational dilemma is attributable to the fragmented purviews of the state boards of education. Often they concern themselves with only a very narrow segment of the entire spectrum, such as primary, or elementary, or vocational education. This approach seems unwise, for the lines of demarcation are thin at best, and it is far from clear that drawing them is useful. Even museums and libraries, though many are not formally affiliated with institutions of learning, are nevertheless central to the educational process and might well be administered as part of it. I suggest, therefore, that a state board of education should coordinate the total educational effort within the state, rather than simply focus its attention on one aspect of that effort, as now happens in too many cases.

And *fourth,* the relationship among able men, politics and education cannot be ignored. The over-all caliber of any committee is directly related to the caliber of each member, and so it is with a state board of education. A capable board requires members who are not only capable but also dedicated, for ability without dedication is hardly helpful. Too often boards consist of educators from private schools who have no real commitment to public education. Above all, the members of the board and of the department of education must be free from partisan politics. Maintaining such freedom will not be easy in these days of rising costs, for the more education costs, the more the politicians are to control it. Some elements of political control are, of course, legitimate; but politicians must not be allowed to interfere in matters which are purely educational in nature, matters which are the rightful province of professional educators. One of these matters, incidentally, is choosing the state's chief educational officer. In my view, the state board of education should appoint that official.

There is much debate these days about the role of the Federal Government in supporting education, so a word on this subject is in order. Federal participation is growing—it will and should continue to grow—but the major task which the Federal Government must set for itself is to help the states become masters of their own schoolhouses. It is quite true that many states' systems are inadequate, but this is all the more reason why our national effort to improve education must be directed to the structure at the state level. The aim should be to make states an effective arm of the Federal Government, capable of administering Federal programs wisely. Indeed, it seems to me that the surest guarantee against Federal control is to apportion Federal money directly to the states for use at their discretion to solve their individual problems, which are, of course, different from state to state. The current trend—epitomized by the National Defense Education Act, which apportions Federal aid for very specific purposes —runs contrary to this wise idea. It leaves little flexibility for state authorities to spend Federal money as they see fit, and it harbors the undesirable potentiality of Federal control.

If Federal control is to be avoided, the states' educational apparatus must be improved. Yet, ironically, those who advocate most vehemently that we avoid Federal control are the very people who block legislation designed to effect the requisite improvements at the state level. It is amazing to listen to some of our governors and legislators talk about their concern over Federal encroachment and, at the same time, to observe their failure to provide the type of leadership within their states which can make Federal encroachment unnecessary. A major part of our urgent task, as I understand it, is to make political leaders recognize the importance of strengthening the educational machinery in their own states.

I am advocating, in short, a vigorous renaissance in state educational leadership and a commitment to those revisions and reforms necessary to make that leadership strong and fully effective. The state, being in a sense the middle link in the three-way partnership which guides American education, is in a strategic position; it is big enough to have broad perspective yet sufficiently small to deal with the concerns of individuals. I have said that education's fundamental task is to develop the rational powers of every individual. A strong system of educational administration and guidance at the level of state government will be instrumental in achieving that end, as this nation moves in many directions concurrently to meet the exciting challenges of our times.

PAPER BY . . . *Homer D. Babbidge, Jr.*
President, University of Connecticut; Former Assistant Commissioner of Education and Director of the Division of Higher Education, U.S. Office of Education

I want to discuss a question which I think is particularly crucial, not only for education but for the whole field of intergovernmental relations: To what extent should the Federal Government deal with higher education through the state governments? But it may be helpful, before getting to that question, to point briefly to some of the principal characteristics of the Federal Government's involvement in American higher education.

First, it is important to note that Federal involvement is not new. The Ohio land grants of the late eighteenth century were the first evidence of Federal provision for higher education. Economic historians are inclined, I think, to look upon these as primarily an effort on the part of the Continental Congress to encourage development of the Western lands, but they are nonetheless the earliest concrete evidence of interest expressed by our national Government in the field of higher education.

The establishment of West Point in 1802 was the first evidence of the Federal Government's direct concern for trained manpower. Much of what the Government has done subsequently can be traced to this concern, expressed initially in an area which is clearly the sole concern of the Federal Government—the defense of the nation. A still more striking evidence of Federal involvement was the Land Grant College Act of 1862, a remarkably radical piece of legislation in its day. I doubt that such an act could be passed today, providing, as that Act did, direct assistance to institutions for general purposes.

Second, Federal involvement has become extensive. Former Secretary of Health, Education and Welfare Abraham A. Ribicoff testified a few years ago that twenty per cent of all higher educational income is now derived from Federal sources. Estimates of current Federal expenditures in institutions of higher education range from $2- to $2.5-billion a year. Federal funds now support some seventy per cent of all organized research in universities; in 1959-60, for example, doctoral candidates in American universities received 3425 fellowships from one Federal program or another.

Third, the impact of Federal involvement is academically uneven. Federal programs place great emphasis on the physical and health sciences; they provide relatively little assistance for the social sciences and humanities. Some fields, such as the classics and fine arts, are consciously denied assistance under existing Federal programs.

Fourth, the present pattern of Federal involvement is institutionally uneven. Because of the scientific and research orientation of many Federal programs, the bulk of this Federal money goes to research-minded institutions. More than half of all Federal research dollars go to a group of perhaps twenty universities. Ten universities, in fact, derive more than 50 per cent of their current educational and general income from Federal sources; it is not surprising that this group is headed by research-oriented institutions such as the California and Massachusetts Institutes of Technology.

Fifth, the administration of Federal involvement is fragmented. Some forty-six identifiable agencies of the executive branch administer programs which have significance for higher education. Probably twenty committees of the Congress have some degree of jurisdiction over these programs. As a consequence, complex relationships have developed between particular agencies of government and specialized constituencies in the academic world. Medical research is probably the best example of this.

Finally—and I think this is very important—these Federal programs are influential in the educational world. They affect both the organization and the operation of institutions of higher education to a significant degree. This is apparent in the remarkable proliferation of organizations in the field of higher education which maintain headquarters and paid, full-time representation in Washington. These national organizations used to be limited to a handful whose members were institutions of higher education; the newer ones are increasingly representative of individual researchers and specialists in particular fields.

The influence of these Federal programs reaches into individual institutions. Indeed, it frequently weakens the authority of what might be called the central management of the institutions. As the Federal Government deals increasingly and directly with deans of medical schools, for example, one may sometimes wonder whether the president of a university has any real say about its medical school. On the other hand, while weakening the central authority, Federal influence has tended to strengthen the power of other officials within the institutional structure. The deans of medical schools are a clear example. The deans of graduate schools have also been considerably elevated in their standing in the institutional hierarchy because they now play a major role in the various Federal fellowship programs.

The major concerns which are raised by these developments are (1) the extent to which these Federal programs are creating imbalances among the disciplines and (2) whether these programs may not have the effect of making rich institutions richer and poor institutions poorer. These concerns have been the focus of a number of recent and continuing studies, including those of Harvard University, Princeton University, the Carnegie Foundation for the Advancement of Teaching and the U.S. Office of Education.

Given these characteristics of Federal involvement in higher education, and given the widespread and growing feeling that the time has come to think through more clearly the rationale for this involvement, it seems important to ask what role the states should play in the relationship between the Federal Government and higher education.

At present, the states are not significantly involved in this relationship. It has been the habit and pattern of the Federal Government historically to deal directly with individual institutions of higher education. This pattern may simply reflect the fact that Federal programs have been highly specialized and particularized. In the case of research, for example, the states would be hardly more than middlemen in the effort to link individual researchers with the Federal funds available for research in a given area. Indeed, as I have suggested, the institutions of higher education themselves are hardly involved in that relationship.

But what happens when the Federal Government begins to express concern for institutions of higher education as a whole? At this point, it seems to me, the states sit up and take notice. They recognize an identifiable interest and concern. The Land Grant College Act is a good example, for even though the states have now effectively bowed out of that program, they played a key role in its inauguration. Moreover, the Act gave not to the Federal Government but to the several states the authority to deploy the Land Grant funds; each state could decide whether to put them into an existing institution or to create a new institution for the purpose.

Having once made that basic decision, the states have effectively withdrawn from the relationship. Yet the authority, though it goes unexercised, still rests with the states. There may at any time be—and there have been—some modifications of those decisions. This situation has not been without its complications, as the practice of maintaining separate institutions in southern states suggests. The decision having been left to the states, the customs of the individual states have prevailed.

Recent Congressional legislation providing Federal funds for construction of housing and academic facilities has contemplated a role for the states in establishing priorities where the demand within a state exceeds the Federal funds available. The operating and financial relationship, however, is directly between the Federal Government and each institution of higher learning.

The various recent proposals for a Federal scholarship program have taken two major approaches toward administration. One approach calls for administration by the states, either through existing authorities or through newly created scholarship commissions; the other would have the institutions of higher education receive funds directly from the Federal Government and administer them on behalf of the Federal Government, as is now done under the National Defense Student Loan Program. This ought to be a classic issue in probing intergovernmental relations and their impact on sound educational policy; but the debate on this issue has in fact centered, not on the principles of intergovernmental relations, but on the question of who can do the best job of identifying submerged talent. If the states can do it best, the argument runs, let us turn the program over to the states to administer. If the colleges can do it best, let us turn it over to them.

The states are becoming more and more concerned about their role with regard to higher education. The pressures are mounting, and the question must soon be resolved. Commissioner Allen, who is in many respects the ablest spokesman for the states, has presented effectively the argument for state involvement. I would like simply to raise a few of the questions about state involvement, questions which trouble those who find the historical arrangements—that is, direct Federal-institutional relations—convenient.

First—and this is perhaps the biggest question—should state governments have authority over private institutions of higher education? Twenty-two states now have some kind of statewide organization in higher education, ranging from coordinating bodies and advisory commissions to boards of control with very real authority. But as far as I know, only one state body—the New York State Board of Regents —has anything like authority over private institutions of higher education within the state. Others are limited in scope to state-supported colleges and universities. With state administration of Federal funds in the realm of higher education, would not private institutions be drawn into the orbit of state governments? And would this not constitute the use of Federal funds to vest states with authority they do not now possess?

Second, would statewide coordination or statewide control have good effects? A principal claim for state involvement is that it would help to insure that funds are deployed most efficaciously. But is it not true that the states' tendencies toward equalization sometimes mean strengthening the weak at the expense of the strong?

Third, are state governments capable of sufficiently strong organization? There is no point in ignoring the widespread skepticism about the quality of state governments. State departments of education bear their full share of these doubts.

Fourth, is the logic (or illogic) of state arrangements alien to the values of higher education? Do not state boundaries impose unfortunate limitations on the scope and quality of higher education, when they get translated, for example, into limitations on the number of out-of-state students to be admitted and when they tie down institutions to the happenstance of the economic base of a given state? Can the concepts of civil service and of the unfettered re-examination of traditional ideas be reconciled? Is the perspective of states broad enough to serve the national and international objectives associated with higher learning?

And *finally*, would state involvement mean anything more than a highly bureaucratized obstacle interposed between the Federal Government and higher education? The U.S. Office of Education has encountered the problem of state concern in the realm of data-gathering. The Federal Government, in seeking information on college enrollments, faculty salaries and the like, has always gone directly to individual institutions of higher education. Certain states are now asking that requests of this sort be channeled through the states and that the responses be funneled back through state organizations. The net result from the Federal Government's point of view (apart from whatever beneficial or deleterious effects there may be at other levels) is further delay in the collection of important information. Is the injection of a middleman into such a relationship anything more than a burdensome administrative complication?

I do not want to leave the impression that I am conscious only of the negative considerations. I am, however, concerned lest their significance be overlooked.

This basic question of state vs. Federal power in higher education is very important. Pending legislation touches upon it, and existing programs are under some pressure to accommodate themselves to the states' growing concern. We would be well-advised to reach some decision as soon as possible.

The tradition at the elementary-secondary level has been different. The states are solidly involved in virtually all programs of the Federal Government at that level, with the notable exception of the school-assistance program in Federally impacted areas. Can one argue that all educational relationships should be the same? Or do historical and other differences between higher education, on the one hand, and elementary-secondary education, on the other, warrant different administrative relationships between the Federal Government and higher education?

COMMENTARY *

Multilevel governmental jurisdiction makes the American educational system somewhat analogous to the proverbial dog whose head was severed from his body, then inadvertently reattached near his tail so that he was ultimately able to bark at both ends and run in two directions concurrently. In less fantastic prose, the existence of

---

* All commentaries are by Kenneth Deitch. They are based on the stenotypist record and have been checked with relevant participants. s.e.h.

government at the Federal, state and local levels, though it has advantages of its own, still makes achieving educational goals, whatever they are, a more complex task than it might be if power were less widely diffused. It was in the ramifications of these remarks, widely interpreted, that the members of the seminar found subject for discussion.

It is no secret that the Federal Government's involvement in education is growing. It is not so well known but nonetheless true that this development is creating pressure to define the states' role more precisely. The states hope to avoid becoming simply middlemen operating between the Federal Government and institutions of higher learning. According to Dr. Allen, states should have large discretion in determining how to spend educational funds, even though it is generally acknowledged that many would be unable to handle such an assignment satisfactorily unless their agencies dealing with education were greatly strengthened. In fact, John F. Morse, director of the American Council on Education and former staff member of the House Committee on Education and Labor, attributed much of educational legislation's failure to a stalemate between those who claim that government's increased role in education should be concentrated primarily at the state level and those who argue that many states' educational bureaucracies are unqualified to assume such responsibilities. Moreover, Morse suggested that this latter problem is particularly serious in those states where the educational system most needs strengthening, and thus he argued that pouring Federal funds into states which need them desperately but are unable to administer them well is not a happy solution.

The appropriate function for a state department of education is not an all-or-nothing proposition. The alternatives are not either that it does everything or else ceases functioning altogether, but rather that it makes certain types of decisions and not others. Indeed, some wish to distinguish between those states in which the apparatus for administering educational matters is first-rate and those in which it is not and to give more financial autonomy to the former than the latter. Even, however, if a state's educational bureaucracy is extremely able, the Federal Government should not operate exclusively through that bureaucracy and never directly with institutions in the state. Instead, the issues themselves should determine the optimal *modus operandi*. For example, according to Dr. Babbidge there is general agreement that the states should have large discretion in allocating funds for constructing academic facilities, whereas their proper role in the awarding of scholarships is not so clear and perhaps should be considerably less than all-influential.

The major rationale for working through a state department of education, even when the task is to allocate Federal funds, is that this department is a going concern and thus has, at least in quantitative terms, the requisite administrative machinery to accomplish the task at hand. If the Federal Government were to act in its own behalf, it would have to duplicate facilities which already exist. Such reasoning prompted Dr. Allen to argue that his department should have primary jurisdiction over the awarding of Federal scholarships in New York. On the other hand, working through the states is not a single-sided coin; it has disadvantages as well. Typically a state's government is more constrained than its Federal counterpart in the matter of whom it may aid. Specifically, operating through the states would limit the Federal Government's ability to subsidize private higher education. Dr. Allen reported, for example, that New York State's constitution prohibits using public funds to aid private institutions. Furthermore, many influential institutions, public as well as private, simply do not want to deal with the Federal Government through their state department of education and would vigorously oppose any increase in their obligation to do so.

The requirements of managing its expanding role in education—particularly of being in touch with numerous, widely scattered institutions of higher learning—have prompted the Federal Government to establish several regional offices of the Department of Health, Education and Welfare. These offices have siphoned off some of the business which previously went to the state departments of education. Massachusetts Commissioner of Education Owen Kiernan noted that many matters which until recently were considered the rightful concern of the commonwealth's department of education are now brought directly to the attention of HEW's regional office in Boston. To avoid such conflict, Allen proposed that HEW consider each state a region and then do its regional work through the states' educational bureaucracies, but someone else suggested that this plan would produce too many regional offices, most of which were smaller than might be ideally desirable. Although this entire argument was made in concrete terms, spelling it out more abstractly might be useful: the Federal Government is increasingly eager to by-pass the states and deal directly with institutions of higher learning, whereas the states wish to avoid having Washington decide matters over which they themselves feel entitled to jurisdiction.

There is a plausible resolution of the conflict between some people's desire to increase—or at least maintain—the state's educational responsibilities ,and their knowledge that many states are not well qualified to handle such an assignment. It involves allocating Federal funds to the states precisely for the purpose of improving their departments of education. This scheme is not unchallengeable, however, for its raises the interesting question as to whether money alone can assure that the job will be done. Messrs. Kiernan and Morse argued on opposite sides of this issue, the former claiming that supplying money was tantamount to a guarantee of desirable results, the latter, that it was by all means necessary but in no sense sufficient. Unfortunately, neither Morse nor Kiernan had time to spell out the reasoning which underlay his conclusion.

Throughout the meeting there was talk about curing America's educational maladies by appointing prominent citizens to high-minded boards having discretionary power to regulate education more or less by fiat. This plan's major asset is that it avoids the usual political frustrations inherent in any attempt to pass legislation concerning education. One participant reminded the members of the seminar, however, that such a scheme is utopian, unrealistic and, in the most literal sense, not American. He views America's political power as being divided into many small, separate fragments. The Tariff Commission and a few similar groups notwithstanding, such power is not generally given to a committee which can rule by decree for long periods and over so broad an area as education. Whatever the merits of operating by decree à la Caesar, this technique is not often used—nor is it soon likely to be—in America. The participant emphasized that to discuss improving education in such terms is a vacuous activity. A more fruitful endeavor is to assume that America's political structure for generating social decisions will remain relatively constant and to design solutions which are feasible within the existing framework, rather than attempt implicitly to remodel it.

2. Educational Lobbies and Federal Legislation

PAPER BY . . . *Elliot Richardson*
Former Assistant Secretary for Legislation, U. S.
Department of Health, Education and Welfare
(now Lieutenant Governor, Massachusetts)

I should like first to submit some general observations about lobbies and then to discuss certain aspects of lobbying for education in particular.

It is important, I believe, to recognize that every organization which is devoted to advancing the interests of a particular field, profession or activity—that is every lobby—quickly becomes a known factor in support of or in opposition to certain types of legislation. The congressman, who is considering whether to vote for a given bill in the field of health insurance, for example, does not need to be told much about the American Medical Association's opinion of the bill. He may want to learn the strength of the AMA's feelings in the particular case at hand, but for most practical purposes its general position is a constant to him, as familiar as the economic and occupational facts about his own constituency (so many farmers, so many blue-collar workers, such-and-such type of production and so on). This sort of pegging is inescapable for any long-term lobby, and the people who run a lobby in Washington are deluding their members if they suggest that the lobby can bring any special weight to bear on any new issue.

So much for lobbies' limitations—what they cannot do. In a more positive vein, what can and should they do? Their first basic function, I think, should be to provide accurate information to legislators. To a considerable extent, their effectiveness depends upon the confidence that congressmen and senators have in such information. If the legislators do not feel that these facts and figures are reliable, then after a while, when the lobbyists come around to distribute their latest brochure, they will not even be welcome at the door. As by-product of maintaining the confidence of legislators, the lobby preserves such weight in the political scales as it may have. The lobbies' second basic function is a corollary: to serve as an effective medium for communicating intelligence to their members about what is going on in Washington.

When a lobby wishes to put over a particular bill, it must, of course, do more than simply supply congressmen and its own members with information. The crucial requirement is to recruit support that is not already a known factor in the relevant legislators' minds. Any group which is genuinely concerned with passing a bill—as distinguished, for example, from the National Education Association, whose primary aim is not to secure legislation but to attain a membership of one million—must devote its best energies to developing a coalition of groups, preferably ones whose support of the bill is not already taken for granted. A good lobbyist will also look to the districts and decide who should be heard from there. He will attempt to have expressed from back home those views which are likely to strike a pivotal congressman or senator as being entitled to weight, since their proponent is one of his consistent supporters, or is a man of generally high standing in the community, or has some other special claim to be heard and heeded.

Given this context, we can understand why a congressman or senator pricks up his ears when he hears that an organization outside the field of education, such as the League of Women Voters, the AFL-CIO or the Congress of Parents and Teachers, favors or opposes a specific bill on education. It would be news indeed if he learned that the U. S. Chamber of Commerce, which maintains an active interest in the field of education, favored a given Federal-aid bill. Such support would certainly make a difference in his thinking.

Let me now say a few words about certain of the tactics which we in the Department of Health, Education and Welfare used in our campaign to win Congressional support for the National Defense Education Act. Along with several of my colleagues at HEW, I was involved in supporting this bill, and certain special factors eased and complicated my efforts. On the one hand, I had the advantage of being, in effect, the bill's lobbyist without having to bear that functionary's usual cross of selling the proposal to the members of his own association. On the other hand, I had to curtail my activities somewhat in order to comply with the antilobbying statutes applicable to Federal officials.

Our first step was to consult those people, in each field of education touched upon by the bill, who we thought could offer us the most useful judgments on the proposals under consideration. This put us in touch with people who carry weight both in their communities and with their congressmen and senators; and although we approached them initially for advice, they were ultimately of value as sources of support.

Our second tactic in developing the legislation which later merged with the Hill-Elliott bill to become the National Defense Education Act was to keep in touch with each of the organizations concerned with the legislation. We talked first with those groups that were directly concerned, such as the language teachers, the counseling and guidance people and the Association of Graduate School Deans, which we consulted about the title providing grants and fellowships for graduate students. We also kept in contact with the major lobbyists for education, as well as with certain peripheral organizations. In fact, during the entire time I was in HEW, I had periodic meetings with these peripheral organizations simply to keep them abreast of our thinking and to seek their support tacitly, as well as to elicit their views while those views might still influence our eventual proposals. (These so-called peripheral organizations were the AFL-CIO, the American Legion, the American Association of University Women, the American Parents' Committee and half a dozen others.)

When we reached the actual phase of legislative battle—we started with the House, believing that our aims would be better served by beginning there, rather than in the Senate—it seemed important to broaden our activities, especially in communicating directly with congressmen. And so there was formed a group called the Emergency Committee for the National Defense Education Act. This committee had a staff man, who worked very closely with my assistant, the Congressional liaison officer for HEW, and who acted as a clearinghouse for all the various groups interested in the bill. He kept a record of who was getting in touch with which people back home, what they were going to do and so forth. His work made it possible for diverse efforts in support of the bill to proceed with a minimum of confusion; his coordination also enabled us to achieve the best possible results from the potential contacts in the home districts.

Our approach to the NDEA was a practical—and successful—application of the fact which I mentioned earlier: if you really want to do a lobbying job in the field of education, you cannot depend upon the regular education lobbies alone. They can never exert, in any special case, more influence than they bring to bear at any other time. They are a voice reaching the ear of Congress with a constant volume at a constant pitch, and such a voice is easily tuned out.

Let me turn now to certain other problems which beset organizations that lobby on behalf of American education. The one obstacle which prevents American higher education from obtaining a really effective voice on Capitol Hill is the issue of church and state. One personal experience of mine may help to illustrate this point. The American Council on Education is regarded as the spokesman for American higher education, and its Federal Relations Committee meets from time to time in Washington to discuss legislation of possible interest. I met with the committee several times, and in the last two or three of these meetings we discussed the Eisenhower administration's program for higher education. That program provided for making grants—very modest ones, but grants nonetheless—available to all institutions of higher learning without regard to denominational affiliation. The committee had prepared a memorandum denouncing the administration's proposal, and I was asked to meet with them. The essence of their argument was that they feared the potential repercussions of such grants. I said to them, "Gentlemen, do I understand that you would prefer sacrificing substantial help from the Federal Government, rather than facing up to the issue of church and state among yourselves?" They nodded around the table. Their answer was "Yes."

I believe this incident conveys a message. While this situation prevails it is impossible for the American Council on Education to determine a uniform and effective policy concerning the appropriate relationship between the Federal Government and the complex of American higher education. But unless such a determination of policy is forthcoming, it will be difficult to achieve legislative progress. Congress will probably not act unless it believes that its action represents, at least in the minds of higher education's leading spokesmen, a genuine step forward.*

Another of the issues which are troublesome for educational lob-

---

* Under Logan Wilson, the American Council on Education is becoming a more effective organization than in the past. s.e.h.

bies may be illustrated by an incident involving the National Education Association. Roughly ninety per cent of NEA's 700,000 to 800,000 members are teachers, and there is inevitably some conflict between the interests of teachers and those of education; the two are not identical.

During the summer of 1957, one of the most important developments in NEA's history took place at Atlantic City. The AFL-CIO met and, at the instigation of its American Federation of Teachers, adopted a resolution condemning NEA as, in effect, a company union. NEA's membership includes representatives of educational management—superintendents and school administrators—as well as teachers, and AFL-CIO's theory was that such an organization cannot effectively represent the teachers' best interests in negotiating wages and working conditions.

One result of the AFL-CIO's slapping NEA in this way was that NEA withdrew the limited support it had previously been willing to give the administration for school-construction legislation. The teachers had always suspected that matching dollars for bricks and mortar might reduce the funds available for their salaries, and now it became vital to NEA to cement the loyalty of its teacher-members. At HEW we worked hard to mollify NEA and to recultivate its support for our program, which, with that support, would certainly have been enacted within two or three years. Unfortunately, our efforts were unsuccessful.

Our failure to sway NEA's leaders was largely attributable to their intensive concern with their dues-paying membership, rather then with the broad needs of education. As a matter of fact, they had recently increased membership dues to finance what they had advertised as a full-scale blitz on the Congress for Federal aid to teacher's salaries. They were so deeply committed to this program that they could not turn back in a direction that might have accomplished specific results for education.

PAPER BY . . . *Robert Rosenzweig*
U. S. Office of Education

In these brief remarks I wish to set forth and discuss two general observations. Let me come directly to the first. Elliot Richardson has pointed out that organizations concerned with higher education have been unable to come to terms with the church-state issue—specifically, with the matter of how the Federal Government should apportion its resources between public and private institutions and, within the latter, between secular and church-affiliated institutions. But the basic question is: why do such matters become problems in the first place? The reason, I think, is that they are most often raised by people who, in view of their interest in achieving particular legislative aims, should not be considering them.

This inappropriate raising of certain issues results from one fairly simple fact: as a group, those educators who are involved in higher education have an incurable urge to act as statesmen. There are now encouraging signs to the contrary, but until very recently higher education's administrators have seemed unable or unwilling to distinguish and to make a rational separation between their role as educational statesmen and their role as political operators lobbying on behalf of their own institution's interests. The closer any one of them gets to the position of college president, the stronger that urge becomes; and when he actually reaches that status, it is clearly an obsession. The historical record supports this observation. Since World War II, the reports of proceedings of such organizations as the Association of American Colleges, the American Council on Education and the Association of State Universities and Land-Grant Colleges have contained some of the most agonizing groping imaginable toward an official position on the issue of the Federal Government's proper relationship to public and private institutions.

The general tendency of these administrators to try to say too much has been detrimental to their cause. In many cases, it seems to me, college presidents (and it is almost always the presidents who are involved in these matters) have leaned over backwards to tackle an issue of public policy which they could and, from a political standpoint, probably should have avoided. The church-state issue, for example, has never been as pressing, either from the public's or the Congress' point of view, with reference to higher education as it has been in elementary and secondary education. Yet representatives of institutions of higher education have felt compelled to stake out a public policy position on this issue, even though there was no special pressure on them to do so, and their voluntary pronouncements immensely complicated their legislative efforts.

The tendency of higher education's administrators to say too much is not, of course, all bad. In some ways it is laudable. These men are among the nation's intellectual leaders, and we look to them for guidance on important questions of public policy. I must stress, however, that there is a genuine conflict between the role which they seek for themselves as educational statesmen and their role as political operators lobbying on behalf of higher education. For these men are not inherently naive or unable to function as good politicians. They only act so when they are operating outside their academic environments, in the public arena. When they turn to the internal affairs of their own institutions, most of these gentlemen readily put aside the postures of the statesman and become shrewd, very effective politicians and administrators. They manage, where necessary, to avoid issues that can only get them into trouble and involve them in needless controversy.

This ability to function effectively as a politician or administrator is not dishonorable in our society. It is done every day, and having to do it is simply one of the prices a man must pay for having power conferred upon him. But higher education's administrators have not resorted to it enough. They should use these tactics, I believe, not only when they handle the daily affairs of their own universities, but also when they enter the public arena and become lobbyists on behalf of higher education. Modifying their approach in this way might diminish the glory that reflects on them personally, but it would certainly give the cause of higher education more than compensating benefits.

I come now to my second major point. It has always been taken for granted that there is a coincidence of interest among all organizations which represent higher education. In fact there is no such widespread coincidence. It is patently clear that there are matters upon which the interests of public and private institutions, for example, diverge. Scholarships are certainly one such matter. Public institutions have never been happy about raising fees and then compensating for the higher prices by more and larger scholarships, and they are not happy about it now. Whenever a real effort has been under way to secure legislation for a national scholarship program, they have generally been dragged along—but never with any great joy about the course upon which they were embarking. Private institutions, on the other hand, have traditionally felt that a national scholarship program was clearly in their interests.

It seems to me that a great effort is made within the educational community to wink at these points on which the interests of the various subgroups diverge. The general—and to me very dubious—reasoning which underlies such action seems to be: "After all, fellows, we're all interested in better education. Getting into squabbles among ourselves doesn't look right to others. There must be some way of avoiding them. Let's simply pretend that these differences don't exist and try to present a united front." United fronts work sometimes but not always, and the unwillingness of higher education's administrators and lobbyists to come squarely to grips with their own conflicts of interest has undeniably handicapped their attempts to get educational legislation.

Let me spell out the implications of this last point. It has been and is still unambiguously true that the narrower and more specific an educational legislative proposal and the more clearly identified the goal to which it is directed, the better are the chances of Congress passing it. Conversely, the broader the program—the more closely it resembles general aid to education—the less likely it is to pass. Why is this true? Why has it been possible since the first Morrill Act, or for roughly the past one hundred years, to get aid from the Federal Government for categorical or specific purposes but not for the general educational programs?

The most important explanatory factor, I think, is that a proposal for general aid brings out all the contradictions within the educational community, whereas a specific proposal does not. A proposal for general aid to education brings to the forefront the public-private split, the church-state issue, the conflict over segregation, which is certainly one of the crucial issues in education today, and so forth. Categorical programs, on the other hand, whatever their educational merits may be, have one great political virtue: they can normally mobilize the support of interested groups without rallying the opposition of other groups. Thus it is often easy to pass specific proposals because they are supported but not opposed; it is difficult to pass general proposals because they call forth not only support but also opposition.

Let me mention two of the more successful specific programs which have developed as a result of Federal legislation. One is the vocational education program, perhaps the classic success story of educational legislation. Since 1917 this program has been supported by national generosity; it has had no trouble getting money and expanding into new areas of vocational training. The program has for its lobbyist the American Vocational Association, which is one of the most effective interest-protecting and interest-promoting groups that exists anywhere. It also has the support of the U. S. Chamber of Commerce, which has, of course, been helpful.*

---

* Since this paper was presented, substantial new advances in vocational education involving Federal outlays have been made. s.e.h.

The second example which I should like to mention is the program for language development provided for in the National Defense Education Act. This program had strong support from the Modern Language Association, and although there were other reasons for its passage as well, MLA's support was crucial. I mention this case with special emphasis because it is a good example of a situation in which one profession was able to generate, both within and outside its own ranks, enough support to get for Americans the kind of a program that we have needed for a long time.

My primary contention, then, is that the best educational programs which have found their way past the potential barrier of Congress have met two important tests. First, they have provided specific rather than general aid. And second, they have mustered sufficient support from particular interest groups without alienating any other groups in the educational community.

PAPER BY . . . *Francis Keppel*
U. S. Commissioner of Education; Former Dean of the Harvard University Graduate School of Education

In the United States today there is an incredibly large number of associations representing schools, colleges and universities. The directory lists more than 500 regional and national educational associations, nearly 150 college professional societies, 50 religious educational associations and 15 international educational associations. In all there are about 1100 private associations that describe themselves as having something to do with education.

Such a conglomeration of associations, as you would expect, exhibits a tremendous variety in size and intent. Nevertheless, they share certain common characteristics; and I believe that two can fairly be said to typify a majority of all these associations' purposes, interests and lobbying aims. These are the National Education Association, which today deals primarily but by no means exclusively with matters in primary and secondary education, and the American Council on Education, which represents a variety of interests primarily in higher education. The activities of NEA and ACE are not totally separate. There is a certain degree of overlap—enough, in fact, to result in some friction between them. However, I shall concentrate here on NEA, since the problems facing the Federal Government in elementary and secondary education are perhaps more difficult then those in higher education.

Before embarking on a discussion of NEA, it is worth noting that most of the Federal legislation that has affected education has been the by-product of other legislative purposes. Most of the Federal Government's policies and programs which have influenced education were undertaken for some reason other than a conscious concern with the network of schools or colleges. The legislation establishing the Northwest Territory may have been an exception: it provided land for churches and for schools, and this was indeed general aid for education. We cannot overlook the possibility, however, that the legislators were not motivated primarily by a love for the schools. Their primary aim may have been to attract settlers to the territory, and providing general aid for education may have seemed a good inducement, an attractive fringe benefit.

A debate which sheds some light on the early activities of NEA and which has a fascinating history of its own concerns an American national university. It was in 1787, the year after the Northwest Territory was established, that Benjamin Rush first proposed that the Congress establish a national university. Many illustrious Americans favored the proposal. Madison tried to provide for such a university explicitly in the Constitution, but his attempt failed. Washington endorsed the project in his first and last messages to the Congress and even bequeathed money for it. As you might expect, Jefferson favored it; and so, perhaps more surprisingly, did John Quincy Adams, who proposed it around 1825. For more than a century the idea of an American national university was enthusiastically discussed at educational meetings. Just after the Civil War, at the time NEA was founded, these debates were especially lively. Then, around 1905, the issue was removed from the NEA agenda. The circumstances surrounding this event are instructive.

Late in the nineteenth century and until about 1905, although NEA claimed to be primarily concerned with elementary and secondary education, it was directed by university presidents. These men, for obvious reasons, were unsympathetic to the idea of a national university, and it was they who removed the idea from NEA's agenda for good. What they did was to appoint a committee to deal with this topic; the chairman was President Harper of the University of Chicago, and the other members were Presidents Angell of Michigan, Butler of Columbia, Canfield of Ohio state, Draper of Illinois and Eliot of Harvard, along with two superintendents of schools. Somehow that committee managed to by-pass the topic, and it never really appeared on the NEA agenda thereafter.

In the first decade of the twentieth century there was a mild revolution within NEA. The school teachers had come to feel that the university presidents did not have their interests centrally in mind, and Nicholas Murray Butler, to his distress, failed one year to win re-election as president of NEA. His successor represented the interests of the primary and secondary schools. Around this time one sees the beginning of a trends towards the separation of the interests of the primary and secondary schools, on the one hand, and the colleges and universities, on the other. I think it is fair to report that the trend towards separation has continued to the present day. Certainly since 1910, as expressed in their resolutions and in such lobbying as they do, NEA's major concerns have been with the primary and secondary schools. The American Council on Education, which was established some years later, has become the largest organization whose resolutions concern primarily higher education.

Let us consider briefly NEA's legislative accomplishments in the Federal Congress. If asked what, on balance, it has accomplished during the past century on behalf of the primary and secondary schools, one would have to reply, "Not much." NEA has tried. It has been both vocal and active. It has presented many resolutions in various forms to the Congress; and in these resolutions and through other channels, it has proposed appropriations by the Federal Government for both general and specific purposes. The question of Federal appropriations has found its way into many topics raised for discussion at NEA meetings throughout its history. There were very active efforts to win legislation in the early 1920,s and in the early days of the New Deal. Yet even between 1933 and 1938—a time when this country should have been ideally receptive to notions of social reform—NEA's efforts bore little fruit.

How can we explain that limited success—and the comparably limited success of the groups representing higher education?

First of all, where one might reasonably have expected to find alliances between educational and other groups seeking reform, particularly in the 1930's, such alliances were not made. This was due in part to the split between organizations representing higher education and those representing primary-secondary education. It was due also to the collapse of the alliance between the progressive movement in general and the forces urging the spread of education. In the nineteenth and and early twentieth centuries, this alliance had been informal rather than tight-knit; by the 1930's it had disintegrated. Schools had by then spread all across the country, and education was simply no longer part of the reform movement.

Another set of reasons explaining NEA's near-failure to affect national policy relates to its internal structure. NEA is constantly aiming for but has not yet achieved a membership of one million, and this effort pre-empts much of its energy. Moreover, the rate at which teachers leave their profession is far higher, I suspect, than for any comparable group seeking to influence Federal policy. Studies from the Department of Health, Education and Welfare indicate that every year nearly eleven per cent of all American school teachers leave teaching altogether, while another eight per cent move from one school to another. Hence, at the start of each school year, roughly one-fifth of the teachers are new in their schools. This turnover must seriously impede NEA's ability to perform its dual task of designing policies and mobilizing public support for those policies.

NEA is also a holding company for numerous specialized interests in education. Among its members are a large number of commissions, committees and the like, as well as many superintendents and principals. These more permanent elements tend to counterbalance the effects of the high rate of turnover of NEA's teacher members, but they may seriously hinder the association's efforts to achieve overall educational objectives. The views of the various blocs of members inevitably diverge as much as they concur.

NEA's policies have been directed primarily to encouraging Federal appropriations of funds, yet it has often taken the position that, in effect, "we need the money, but we oppose Federal direction of how to spend it." By now the American people and the Congress are persuaded that the United States wants no part of Federal control in education. The idea has become so axiomatic that a Congressman would have to be supremely courageous—or extremely ill-advised—to speak out in favor of Federal direction of curriculum. NEA's efforts alone may not have created this situation, but its efforts were surely influential; and its very success in this matter has created a barrier to Federal aid. There is an inherent conflict between desire for freedom from legislative limitations and desire for Federal appropriations. The debate should turn, it seems to me, from the matter of Federal control, which no one wants, to the nature and extent of Federal influence and aid to special fields, which seems to me a very different matter.

Let me say just a few words about the American Council on Education, the largest organization for higher education. Its membership includes institutions of higher learning, represented by their presidents, and groups such as the Association of Land Grant Universities and the Association of Urban Universities, which have subgroups for their members. Like NEA, ACE is troubled with a changing membership, though to a lesser degree. An additional problem for ACE is the range of its constituencies: among its members are the smallest colleges and the largest universities, as well as both public and private institutions.

Some groups supporting higher education have been especially successful achieving legislative aims. The Association of State Universities and Land Grant Colleges is a prime example. Its long-standing relationship with the Department of Agriculture and other agencies of the executive branch, as well as with the Congress, is a noteworthy phenomenon. But we should not forget that, in general, the very large constituency formed by schools, colleges and universities in the United States does not have an influence on the Federal Government commensurate with its size.

COMMENTARY

It is often assumed—not always correctly, incidentally—that the distinction between what is good, for example, for business and for labor is clear-cut; but there is general agreement that the distinction between what is good for education, on the one hand, and for high school history teachers, university presidents, school superintendents, post-doctoral research fellows and so on, on the other, is somewhat obscure and difficult to make clear. This point is suggestive of some of the general issues which the members of the seminar discussed. They also, however, considered a few specific examples of the interrelation between private support for and Congressional action on educational legislation, and it seems worthwhile to begin by mentioning these latter points before presenting the former.

As a first example, Elliot Richardson described a lobbying effort which is not made under the banner of one of the big associations and which does not attempt to proclaim the general glories of education in broad and glowing terms. It supports a narrowly defined program and does so in an unpretentious though highly efficient way, using what one might call pyramid-building tactics. The program involved is the so-called P.L. 815-874 proposals for impacted-area funds. Currently, about 320 Congressional districts receive such funds. The lobbying is directed by a superintendent of schools in Oklahoma. Whenever support for or opposition to a given piece of Federal legislation is needed, all he does is dictate a single telegram to his secretary in Oklahoma City. Within hours that telegram reaches every superintendent whose school system is in a Congressional district which receives impacted-area funds. In turn these superintendents and any additional people they may approach immediately send appropriately worded telegrams to their congressmen in Washington. The crucially effective characteristic of this lobby is that each congressman hears directly from home, rather than from some association that only professes rather mystically to favor "better education."

In a slightly different vein, recent events in Massachusetts indicate clearly, according to Commissioner of Education Owen Kiernan, that the interests of educational personnel, mostly teachers, and those of education are far from identical. Over seventy-five per cent of Massachusetts teachers belong to the Massachusetts Teachers Association and a somewhat smaller percentage to the American Federation of Teachers (AFL-CIO). These associations tend to lobby for teachers rather than for education. Recently they have been bolstering a bill to raise the teacher's minimum salary from $4000 to $5000. The General Court, Massachusetts' Legislature, senses that professional groups like MTA and AFT represent vested interests other than those of education; and now, when helping education per se is the task at hand, the General Court is correspondingly less sensitive to the views of such groups than it used to be. Recently education's strongest lobbying support in Massachusetts has come from organizations whose titles do not intuitively suggest that they would have much direct concern for that cause at all. Some of these noneducational organizations which support educational measures tend to be for motherhood and against sin, so to speak; their support is, in Kiernan's view, somewhat too general to be helpful and cannot be accepted. Among education's staunchest and effective supporters are the League of Women Voters, the Federation of Women's Clubs of Massachusetts and, perhaps surprisingly, the Taxpayers' Federation; and all of these groups are powerful voices on Beacon Hill. Labor, too, has rather consistently supported programs of high quality in education. Thus education's very effective lobbying support in Massachusetts now comes from groups that are not directly connected with the educational establishment, rather than from groups which are, like MTA and AFT.

One incident which occurred when the Eisenhower administration was drafting its contribution to the National Defense Education Act sheds additional light on the political realities of the matters at hand and also indicates something important about the character of the National Education Association. Richardson put the matter this way: the administration wishes to add English teachers to its program for foreign-language and science teachers, but it sensed that NEA would undermine such as amendment and so, before drafting it, decided to sound NEA out. The administration's initial instincts were correct. NEA said that if the provision for English teachers were included, it would lobby to extend that provision, across the board, to all teachers. In this vignette NEA clearly indicated where its true allegiances lie. There is nothing culpable in this sort of loyalty. Steel workers have a union, and teachers are certainly entitled to one too. What is important is for NEA's officers to honor the simple allegorical rule that if an implement has a long handle and a small, flat head and is useful for digging, they will call it a spade. This rule obliges NEA to remind the public that they are at least as dedicated to the interests of primary and secondary school teachers as they are to those of education in general.

The members of the seminar did more than consider isolated incidents in the recent history of these matters. They dealt with this basic issue as well: wherein does the system in its present form, the form which is politically feasible, fail? One basic flaw is that America's approach to these matters has always been fragmentary. There are no influential educational lobbies which take a truly global view. All of the associations pay lip service to the general and lofty goal of improving American education, but in reality many are single-mindedly dedicated to little more than raising the salary of the teacher of Hindi in the junior high school in East Noplace, Wistucky. The Office of Education has always been a good candidate for leader of a successful lobbying movement on behalf of American education in general, but that role has never materialized. Similarly, a number of factors have prevented the American Council on Education from assuming such a role itself. Not the least of these, according to Robert J. Koblitz of the Carnegie Foundation, is its diverse constituency, which includes, among many other groups, the American Red Cross and the AFL-CIO. With such a membership, achieving agreement on the most narrow proposals has historically been a chore; coming together on the general ones has been unthinkable. Now changes are occurring within ACE, and its current able president, Logan Wilson, is trying to guide it towards a broad and coherent policy on higher education.

The second shortcoming is that, historically, Federal aid has been appropriated for specific rather than for general educational purposes. References to aid to education in the Federal budget help to clarify this point. The Federal Government now spends approximately $3-billion annually on what may reasonably be defined as education, and yet in the 1960 Federal budget only about $100-million was actually called aid to education. Most of the money was appropriated in terms of narrowly defined categories with special names, rather than simply as "general aid to education." This result is a corollary of the first flaw, the nature of the lobbies, but is, in a way, not something bad but rather a tribute to their success. One may believe that specific aid is bad and general aid good, but one must also recognize that the lobbies have worked wholeheartedly to get specific aid. Thus, when someone says that there has been too much specific and not enough general aid, what he is really condemning is the very success of the lobbies in achieving what they have sought.

In treating general versus specific aid, it makes some sense to start by considering what these terms really mean. Rosenzweig emphasized that the distinction is one of degree. No one close to these issues has ever yet seriously advocated completely general aid. The system's critics simply feel that, historically, aid has gone too far in the direction of catering to the rigidities of American politics at the expense of the needs of American education. It has been sought and received in terms of categories—packages, if one prefers—whose titles have strong and seductive political appeal: let us help the teacher of Latin; let us support education of the blind. In the view of Edward C. Banfield, professor of government at Harvard University, narrowly defined programs have the political virtue of being able to muster support without also rallying opposition. As an approximate goal for primary-secondary education, the proponents of more general and less specific aid would favor appropriations to school systems in the future which are, if not quite this extreme, at least of this sort: so many dollars per full-time student per academic year. For higher education, particularly when funds are appropriated for research rather than directly for instruction, the formula could not be quite so simple. Without being exhaustive, these remarks perhaps suggest roughly what the distinction between general and specific aid to education means.

To be sure, the present system has its flaws, but still there is no unanimous evaluation of the entire structure in simple "good" or "bad" terms. Two schools of thought emerged at the meeting, one arguing that things now are terrible indeed, the other, that the situation may not be so bad after all. The system's most severe critics argued along several lines. They claimed that specific Federal aid tends to disrupt the academic balance within universities and thus fundamentally works to change their nature. Over ninety-five per cent of the approximately one billion dollars which the Federal Government spends each year on research in institutions of higher learning is allocated to the sciences, and the best estimates are that this percentage will increase before it gets smaller. Many of the large universities are now devoting their unrestricted funds increasingly to the humanities and, to a lesser extent, to the social sciences, in an effort to redress their internal balance. Their resources are not sufficient, however, to allow them to hold the line indefinitely against the effects of specific Federal aid to the sciences, and several of those present predicted that if present trends continue, sooner or later the academic character of these universities will be permanently altered.

Another major complaint set forth is that the piecemeal approach to Federal aid prevents discussion of lofty issues from taking place in important public forums. The argument is that having these issues debated in Congress would contribute to society's general enlightenment. Those who took this view did not do so uncompromisingly. They admitted that the time is not yet right to debate publicly all controversial issues, that in the interests of legislative progress some, notably those which evoke the specter of the First Amendment, such as the church-state issue, should for now be avoided. But they feel that certain others, the matter of public versus private education for one, could now quite profitably be discussed on the floor of the Congress and that the general interests of social enlightenment would be well served by such debate.

The final line along which the system's major critics argued is that using the fragmentary approach is tantamount to rejecting the value of any scheme of over-all social planning or, to use a less controversial phrase, social accounting. André Daniere, Harvard economist, suggested that the educational system now stands at the head of the path down which American agriculture has already walked. The program of agricultural price supports probably would have produced tolerably good results had it been developed in the context of a broad, forward-looking agricultural policy. Instead, we have had a piecemeal, commodity-by-commodity approach, with temporary pressure from one group after another. As a result, the system is now a mess and probably an irreparable one at that. Daniere made the inductive leap from agriculture to education, and his message was clear: failure to introduce a broad approach will cause the system to get out of hand—cause the tail to wag the dog, so to speak—and will cause this generation of Americans to bequeath to its heirs an educational nightmare comparable to the present-day agricultural enterprise.

The system has more than critics. Some members of the seminar, although they admitted it can be improved, were more or less its defenders. They argued that the present system is not as bad as one might think and objected strongly to the strategy of debating the large, abstract issues in Congress on two grounds: First, it hinders legislative progress; it is not feasible. Second, and crucially important, there are many, many things which can be done to aid education without raising these issues. The system's advocates accused its critics of Utopian tilting at windmills, of holding the naive view that things can only be "right" when society has finally solved every one of its problems. No society, they argued, has yet achieved that end, and America is unlikely to be the first to do so. Matters like church-state in education have existed since the founding of the Republic and will probably never be definitively resolved. Dealing with the problem of improving education on the level of legislative action is difficult and complex. One does not raise the status of teachers, for example, simply by proclaiming that they ought to have more prestige. Finally, they emphasized that their argument should not be construed to mean that they would not like things to be different, to be in many ways as their opponents imagine them. They simply stressed the element of political feasibility and claimed that their approach is mandatory **because their objective is to help education,** rather than simply to engage in "what we would do if we could do" type of talk.

There is one point which is vital for an understanding of the controversy over general versus specific aid to education and which therefore warrants being spelled out explicitly and with special emphasis. In discussing this issue, people often lose sight of the fact that every dollar of aid to education, no matter for what purpose and in what language, general or specific, it was initially appropriated, is in the end allocated to a very specific objective. For example, it either goes to raise a teacher's salary, or for the purchase of a new school bus or an additional dormitory, and so on. The real issue, therefore, is more precise than what has by now become the cliché, general or specific aid. The real issue is: at what stage in the process of transferring a dollar from the taxpayer's pocket to the educational system should that dollar be specifically earmarked for a particular use? Should the label be appended as it passes through Congress or when it arrives at the educational institution? More pointedly, the question is really: who is better qualified to do that earmarking, the congressmen or the deans?

The members of the seminar also discussed the direction in which the system could profitably evolve, the nature of the changes which might be worthwhile. There was general agreement that policy makers should work towards broadening the categories in which aid is appropriated. Such broadening, it was suggested, will help to insure the autonomy of the United States educational institutions, and autonomy for those schools and colleges is a cornerstone of the entire American notion of what is right. A satisfactory compromise must be worked out between the desire to furnish those people nearest to the ultimate use of the funds—college deans, school superintendents and so on— with wider allocative power than they now have and the awareness that the lobbies with the strongest vote-getting influence in Washington have rather narrowly defined goals and may look upon general aid with a somewhat jaundiced eye. Stated more simply, a satisfactory compromise must be found because the kind of aid it is possible to obtain is not always the most desirable kind of aid. Some added that the general aim of making aid less restricted has already been and can continue to be well served by making the regulations governing Federal and state matching funds more flexible.

A second major aim generally advocated by the members of the seminar is to improve the administrative coordination of the various Federal programs, especially within the Department of Health, Education and Welfare itself, by merging certain agencies and departments to eliminate the overlaps, duplications and gaps which now exist. Third, in the near future the policy makers should probably place special emphasis on those measures which can help education without bringing to the forefront of legislative battle sticky issues that might block their passage. Although it does not entirely avoid the troublesome issues, aid for constructing schools should probably be supported now. Certainly, increased aid for training teachers, similar to NDEA's provision for modern-language teachers, can gather wide support and is also a program which should be pushed right away. Finally and in general terms, those present agreed that policy makers should continue to frame programs in the best interests of education, but they must be ever mindful of the fact that if progress is really to be forthcoming, the programs they design must strike a sensible balance between the conceptually ideal and the politically feasible.

3. The Federal Government and University Research

PAPER BY . . . *Charles V. Kidd*

Associate Director for International Activities and Former Associate Director for Training, National Institutes of Health, U. S. Department of Health, Education and Welfare

During the past twenty years, we have lived through a period of continuing change in the relationship between university and the Federal Government. Support provided by the Government for research in universities has been the prime source of these changes. The sheer increase in the volume of Federal research funds has exerted powerful forces, but this is not the only significant factor. The purposes for which Federal funds are made available to universities have also been changing in a fundamental way.

Behind all these changes, the role of the Federal Government has been continually expanding. The original center of gravity of Federal support was in programs relevant to the operating missions of Federal agencies. Gradually the Government is becoming, not merely a major patron of science in universities, but a source of funds for all of the functions of universities. In this role it tends to act as the state, responsible for the general national welfare, rather than as a collection of operating agencies.

Stress is inherent in such a situation. Indeed, when one views the forces at work, it is remarkable that universities and the Federal Government remain on speaking terms. I should like to consider first the factors in this relationship that have tended to drive universities and the Government apart and then the forces that are tending to draw them together.

The strain between the Federal Government and the universities, where support for research is concerned, can be traced to a number of sources. Among the more troublesome are:

First, the wartime contract-research system. The major precedents for postwar Federal support were set in the World War II contract-research program. Many characteristics of this system were basically repugnant to universities. Among them were pressures towards applied work, security classification and the use of procurement-contract philosophies and methods.

Second, the dispersion of sources of research support among Federal agencies. After the end of World War II, the practice of supporting research in universities on a substantial scale spread from the Armed Forces to a wide variety of Federal agencies. These Federal activities were largely uncoordinated. As a result, the universities were faced with diverse rules and found themselves unable to resolve many important problems. They also incurred heavy research costs, for which they were only partially reimbursed by the Government.

Indeed, there has really been no such thing as the "Federal Government" in support of research, except in the sense that the independent actions of a number of largely autonomous agencies constitute the action of the Federal Government. The Federal agencies have tended to view universities simply as places where administrators can find brains and other resources useful to the accomplishment of agency missions. They have not viewed universities as institutions whose total health is important to the welfare of the nation. This conflict between the Federal administrators' views of universities and the universities' views of themselves has contributed to the strain.

Third, the concentration on support of science research. Under Federal statutes, hundreds of millions of dollars annually are poured into the research function of universities; virtually all of this money has supported research in the physical and life sciences. A reasonably balanced research effort in a university, however, requires research in the arts, social sciences and humanities as well.

Furthermore, a university is more than a research institute, and the discrepancy between the research authority of Federal agencies and the total role of universities has been a continuing source of tension. The universities have not been reluctant to criticize the agencies, and their criticism has at times been misdirected. Some university commentators have scolded bureaucrats for lack of vision and understanding, when they might more logically have been lobbying for general Federal aid to higher education.

Fourth, the dissimilarities of the bureaucrat and the academician. Federal employees and professors often have different values, different languages and different approaches. But the importance of these differences can be overestimated, and no more need be said about them.

And *fifth,* the direct alliance between the professor and his patron. A salient characteristic of Federal support for research in universities has been the extent to which decisions are negotiated directly between bureaucrats in Federal agencies and professors in universities. Given the fundamental purpose of Federal support for research, this sort of arrangement was inevitable. However, this direct dealing has tended to frustrate any joint attempts by Federal agencies and universities to establish a system under which the Federal Government as a whole could view the research needs of universities as a whole. It has also tended to complicate the universities' need to exert a reasonable degree of control over the total size and content of the research activities of the faculty as a whole.

This list of sources of strain between the Federal Government and universities could easily be extended. One might include the rapid change in the Federal agencies' ends and means, the persistence of a perhaps inappropriate philosophy that universities should pay part of the cost of research, and the inadequate structures of many universities and of the Federal Government for the formulation of research policy. But the list is already so formidable as to raise the obvious question: How has the system survived without exploding?

Fortunately, many forces are at work which tend to reduce the strains—or at least to make the parties ignore their differences. Let us examine five of the most promising:

Mutual dependence: To an unprecedented degree and with extreme rapidity, science and technology have become interwoven with the essential operations and decisions of the Federal Government. Virtually all significant operations and decisions are affected by or affect scientific and technological matters. The Government, therefore, cannot operate effectively without a highly complex and penetrating involvement with science and technology.

Because the resources and the brains of the nation in these fields are found largely in universities, the Government depends on universities to an extraordinary degree. In turn, the scientific and technological enterprise of universities depends in a decisive way upon Federal support. Universities would be impoverished and crippled in science if Federal support were to decline substantially or to cease.

The situation brings to mind a cartoon which showed two mountain climbers dangling above a chasm a mile deep. One was barely holding on to a pick caught precariously on a rock. His companion, in turn, clung to his ankle. The top man was shouting to the bottom man, "Let go of my foot, or I'll hit you with this pick."

Universities and the Federal Government depend upon each other so fundamentally that efforts to establish a smooth relationship must be exerted on both sides. But it is more harmful than helpful to describe the relationship, as is sometimes done, as a partnership. Matters are better arranged if universities have a clear idea of their missions and if they bargain with the agencies at arm's length for the things they consider essential or desirable.

On the other hand, neither the individual Federal agencies nor the Federal Government as a hole has authority to operate as if Congress had enacted a law providing for general Federal aid to higher education. Some criticism of Federal agencies relating to such matters as inadequate attention to the general financial structure of universities and failure to support the humanities is, in effect, a plea for general Federal support of higher education. In the absence of such a law, administrators are not in a partnership with universities. They are responsible for administering laws which can be responsive to the universities' needs only to a limited degree.

One of the most interesting reflections of the lack of identity of purpose between Federal agencies and universities is found in the long and, at times, acrimonious debate over whether the Federal Government has an obligation to pay the full costs of research which it supports. This debate has centered primarily on the issue of indirect costs. For years, the National Science Foundation and the National Institutes of Health have operated on the principle of paying only a part of the indirect costs. These agencies assert, among other reasons, that they are not responsible for the total financial soundness of the universities in which they support research. The universities, on the other hand, insist that if the Federal Government expects them to remain strong intellectual centers, it must be concerned with their long-range financial stability. (This is only a partial sketch of a very complicated issue, but it shows that issues which seem superficially concerned with details of administration actually go to the heart of the university-Government relationship.)

Once universities become engaged with the Federal Government to a significant degree, they become engaged in politics; otherwise, major decisions in which they have a stake will be made without them. Political involvement is, of course, nothing new to state universities and to many private universities; but the extent of their involvement with both the executive and legislative branches of the national Government is a fairly new phenomenon. The situation is epitomized by the adoption and later repeal of the disclaimer provision in the National Defense Education Act.

Almost certainly, as the array of Federal programs affecting universities becomes larger, Congress will consider adopting other legislation repugnant to them. Almost certainly, universities will urge more frequently upon Congress the adoption of substantive laws and appropriations to which other groups and forces are opposed. The further development of the political role of universities on the national scene will be interesting to observe.

The rise of the civilian research grant: One of the most important factors easing the strain between universities and the Government has been the relative decline of the military research contract as the source of Federal funds for university research. In the decade 1952-62, for example, the percentage of Federal research funds in universities which came from military research contracts declined from 70 to 28 per cent. With a few notable exceptions, research grants administered by civilian agencies are fundamentally more congenial to universities than those let by parts of the Department of Defense.

Dispersion as protection: The dispersion of Federal support among many Federal agencies, though it causes annoyance and expense to universities, also gives them a fundamental protection. A tidy concentration of most Federal research support in a single agency might make university bookkeeping departments happy, but the real cost to universities would be high. Their capacity to influence Federal policy would be reduced, and the danger of the dominance of a single philosophy and a single group of advisers would be increased. By dividing their eggs among many baskets, the universities can conquer some of these dangerous potentialities of Federal support. It is widely believed, therefore, that a heavier concentration of research support through any single agency of Government would be a mistake.

On the other hand, the evolution and broadening influence, within the executive branch, of a central structure for developing a policy towards science represents a sensible balance between the complementary needs for diversity in operations and unity in general policy. All thing considered, there is too little unity; a great deal more could be done to establish unified policies without harmfully reducing the diversity which is such a basic protection to universities.

(A prime example of *un*desirable diversity—and one of great significance to universities—is the difference among Federal agencies with respect to the charging of faculty salaries to Federal research grants and contracts.)

Faculty involvement: The tendency of the Federal support system to stress aid to an individual or to parts of the university, rather than support of the whole, is a blessing as well as a curse. It is basically healthy to have a system of national competition for research funds, in which decisons are made by qualified peers rather than by mechanisms confined to universities. The involvement of scientists in making these decisions is an effective way to maintain an open system and to avoid detailed decisions by a bureaucracy which is almost certain to be less competent than the broad scientific community. Furthermore, the many advisory committees which are integral to the current system have become a very effective mechanism for scientific communication.

Despite all their actual and potential defects, then, the scientific advisory groups are an administrative innovation useful not only to Federal agencies but also to scientists and universities. The widespread use of advisers has certainly been a major factor in reducing the strain between Federal agencies and universities.

Shift of mission: The most fundamental force for harmony between universities and the Federal Government has been a *de facto* change in the functions of Federal support. This has been reflected in changes both in the terms and conditions under which funds are provided to universities and in the purposes for which funds are made available.

Federal research support is no longer restricted, for example, to narrowly defined research projects. The agencies have evolved diverse forms of support which include quite stable aid to broadly defined research and research training—for example, the institutional grants of the National Science Foundation and the general research support grants of the National Institutes of Health. Such grants, together with markedly expanded support for students, faculty and construction, have transformed the Federal science-support system over the past few years. As a consequence, the earlier complaints about the narrow-project system (that it threatens to inhibit free-ranging thought, and so forth) are scarcely heard these days.

These changes represent major steps in the evolution of Federal research support. Provision of funds for broadly defined research signifies a more sophisticated understanding on the part of Federal agencies of the conditions prerequisite to effective science—and hence to more efficient fulfillment of the agencies' aims.

Among the most significant changes has been a substantial shift towards support for expansion of resources for research, as contrasted with support of research with existing resources. Support for training and education in the sciences has become much more widespread. Science students are receiving extensive support through various kinds of Federal stipends, and employment on research grants is prevalent among graduate students in science. An increasing proportion of faculty members are securing all or part of their salaries from research grants and contracts. The approaches to education are more diversified, including many improvements in high-school teaching as well as aid for construction of research facilities.

The fundamental reason for this growing concentration on expanding research resources is that Federal agencies are viewing their tasks over a longer perspective of time. The new concentration implies a decision not only to use but to expand the scientific capacity of the nation. Aid to the development of resources which have a long lead time—notably, high-school students—implies a continuing, general commitment on the part of the Federal Government.

All these movements toward a long-range, general commitment tend to make Federal support more congruent with the total mission of universities. They also signify a fundamental change in the role of the Federal Government. The Government, to an increasing degree, reflects the nation's need for a strong science structure in its universities. The Federal Government is progressively less a collection of individual operating agencies and more a channel through which the broader needs of universities are met.

Nevertheless, there remain obvious gaps and imbalances in the Federal programs affecting university research. Let me briefly list a few:

These programs do little to aid universities except in the physical and life sciences. Certain areas of science are relatively poorly supported; most areas in the social sciences and all the arts and humanities are ignored. A change in this situation awaits public recognition of the significance of all areas of higher learning to the national welfare.

Since Federal support has been directed primarily toward the producation of research findings, the funds have been channeled into the universities with the most powerful research faculties. Much more could be done within existing statutory authority, if Federal agencies were to exert a concerted effort under strong leadership, to diversify the geographical base for science research. However, deliberate use of Federal funds to establish a wider network of centers of intellectual excellence—an objective both feasible and desirable—is difficult on a large scale until this objective is ratified by the Congress.

Despite the growth of Federal support for students, that support remains limited in terms of fields of study, numbers of students supported and the amount of support per student. Very few Federal scholarships are provided in mathematics, physics and engineering, though an extensive Federal program of aid to students in these fields has been advocated. No Federal scholarships are available to those earning an MD degree, and there appears to be little prospect of such aid. Only in the life sciences and medical sciences *after* the MD degree is Federal aid to students at a level approaching adequacy.

Finally, there is every prospect that the physical facilities of universities will not expand on an adequate scale during the 1960's without a much wider program of Federal grants.

If some or all of these measures are to be adopted, the general concept of the role of the Federal Government in supporting universities must continue to evolve. In recent years the actual role of the Government has broadened substantially, in concept as well as in scale. It seems likely that this trend will persist into the future and that most if not all of the present gaps in Federal support will be filled. If they are, the Government will soon be concerned even more directly with the total affairs of universities. Universities will find it progressively more important to exercise vigilance and effective political power in order to define and protect their essential areas of freedom.*

PAPER BY . . . *Don K. Price*
          Professor of Government and Dean of the Faculty of
          Public Administration, Harvard University

Charles Kidd has said most of the things which ought to be said about this topic. My remarks will be a bit more informal and are intended to cover a few additional points, both general and specific.

The relationship between the Federal Government and universities is not today what it was twenty-odd years ago. I am not yet

---

* In 1964, the Federal Government increased its support of higher education, particularly in subsidizing construction. s.e.h.

ancient, but I can well remember the characteristic attitude of educators and scientists from private universities and research institutes when I began working for the Government. At that time, the notion that private universities would ever ask for Federal funds or that the National Academy of Sciences would ever find it respectable to discuss the possibility of Government support for basic science would have seemed absolutely unthinkable. Since then, such attitudes have changed fundamentally.

What caused this revolution? The massive support of science during World War II and the subsequent pressure to maintain that support for reasons of national defense go far toward explaining it, but there were also institutional adjustments that made this new system very tolerable. Today it is not only full-time Federal officials who make the basic decisions concerning the relationship between Government and universities. Private institutions, through part-time committees and consultants, help to formulate these decisions, and they clearly have a vested interest in receiving the aid.

This development has not evolved in secrecy. Indeed, it has in part been forced upon the agencies by Congress. Those agencies which were initially reluctant to include private institutions in the decision-making process found their position politically untenable. In the case of the National Institutes of Health, the association was deliberately created so that authority would not be completely contained within the full-time machinery of the Federal Government.

Let me generalize and suggest that we are witnessing a true breaking down, for better or worse, of the distinction between public and private agencies. It seems to me that this disintegration explains the change in the attitude of scientists and educators since the late 1930's. Perhaps an analogy will be of some use in supporting the point. (The analogy is highly speculative, and I confess that I do not know how to validate or reject its relevance though I should certainly like to see someone proceed in a scholarly way to do one or the other.)

Early in this century there were bitter arguments in America about states' rights. We still have such arguments, but they are now rather superficial, for with Federal grants-in-aid to states, the arguments have become mere theorizing, void of any political meaning. Thus an agricultural program that would be considered socialism in any other sector of the economy is considered a defense of the normal American way of life and is favored by the farmers. The program of Federal contracts to research institutions and universities is, I think, cloth from the same bolt. Political antagonism between the Federal Government and universities has lessened because their common material interests have increased.

Obviously this problem lends itself to a materialistic interpretation, but I think there has been a genuine institutional adjustment. The change has been so profound that we do not yet have a terminology which accurately defines certain features of the new system: who is responsible, what are the limits of that responsibility, where does the role of the agency official begin, what is the function of the part-time adviser, to what extent are all these questions handled at the political level, and so on? I am not attempting to suggest definitive answers. However, a number of commentators have pointed out that there is no longer a clear conflict of interest between the Federal Government and universities. I should like to go further and state the proposition affirmatively: it seems to me that there is now a true mixture, a harmony of interests, and that the terms "public" and "private" are of very little use in helping us to understand the issues.

Some people maintain that each university should assume full responsibility for handling the problems which have recently arisen in its dealings with the Government. This worries me; it is too much like substituting a moral exhortation to drive safely for good traffic regulation. Things are moving too quickly and the amounts of money involved are too large to make that sort of solution feasible. I do not doubt that each university has and should accept a tremendous responsibility in these matters, but no one institution can solve all these problems in isolation. The proper path is cooperation among all institutions of higher learning and the Federal Government to work out carefully defined procedures of operation. Some conflict is unavoidable, but in general there will be a large base of common interest upon which to build.

Let me now make a few specific points relating to the matters at hand. In recent discussions about the Government and universities, overhead, or indirect costs, has been the most difficult and tiresome question. I once served for a year on a committee of the National Science Foundation that had been set up to consider the entire range of Government-university relationships. It started with the overhead problem, got bogged down in it, never managed to consider any other matters and never solved that problem either. If nothing else, we at least substantiated that to argue this problem in terms of technicalities is no help.

The problem of overhead has been especially difficult because it embodies a complete spectrum of cases. At one extreme are the small private foundations, whose staffs can visit a scholar at his university and immediately arrange to provide him with a modest sum to bolster his research. At this extreme, compensation for overhead is nonsense; the very idea is almost immoral. But at the other extreme, where vast amounts of money are involved, the argument against overhead seems sterile, and the entire institutional health of a university becomes a matter of Federal concern.

None of the proposed solutions seems to me quite so meaningless as the formula embodied in one Congressional report specifying that the amount of overhead should be determined by which side took the initiative. I see, on the contrary, a genuine merger of interests. When a bank loans money to a corporation, it is concerned about that corporation's total policy. There is no moral issue of initiative: who asked whom when for what? I sense that we have reached the same point in our dealings between universities and the Federal Government.

Another specific and much discussed issue is the balance within the universities among the various academic disciplines. The Government's influence on that balance has, I think, been no different from that of the private foundations. Federal policy today is almost a macrocosmic caricature of the Rockefeller Foundation's policy of the mid-1920's. To put that policy in crude and exaggerated terms, those who now grant money to universities for research apparently believe that our salvation depends entirely upon the natural sciences. Anything the social sciences and humanities are likely to receive in the near future will be more or less decoration. I myself do not believe that this policy is the wisest attainable, but inveighing against it seems fruitless. If balance is to be restored, the impetus must come in part from aggressive seeking of private funds and in part from efforts to induce the Government to give increased general support for total university programs. Here political action by the universities can be extremely important.

One of the major problems in this entire area is that of simple misunderstanding between the Government and the foundations, on the one hand, and the universities, on the other. A basic cause of this misunderstanding is that many personnel of the Government and the foundations are unaware of the real social and administrative structure of universities. Perhaps the major characteristic of a university which all these people fail, in varying degrees, to comprehend is the tenure system. Except for this system, a university could be looked upon as just another research institution. One could give it additional jobs and expect it, when necessary, to recruit additional personnel to handle them. It could be expanded one year, cut back the next and, in general, treated as flexibly as General Motors or a military laboratory.

But a university is different. If there is any central concept in its nature, it is the notion of a self-governing community of scholars. To be sure, one hears a generous amount of nonsense on this point from scholars, who naturally tend to exaggerate its normal qualities; I do not wish to endorse everything I hear in academic meetings about the community of scholars. Still, it is an important factor and deserves proper emphasis. Indeed, it is the controlling element in the internal power structure of any university. Research administrators in foundations and the Government alike have made many mistakes by overlooking this fact, which imposes a clear limitation on a university's ability to expand to perform certain services for them.

One final point seems worth making. Since all the language and all the procedural apparatus in this area are geared to specific projects and special-purpose grants, the Government can continue to insist that it has no over-all policy for higher education. In a sense that is true: it has no formal policy. But, in another sense, Congress has simply been willing to wink at the development of a real system of aid to higher education; in this way it can support the system without raising many difficult issues. The present system is illogical and scattered, but in the eyes of politicians it has the great merit of leaving dormant these issues which people simply are not willing to face. The two most important of these issues are (1) the line to be drawn between secular and religiously affiliated institutions, and (2) the balance to be kept between institutions of higher learning with strong research programs and institutions which concentrate their resources not on graduate research programs but almost exclusively on teaching.

The system has not camouflaged these matters completely. I used to spend a disproportionate part of my time in the Defense Department drafting replies to southern senators, explaining why southern universities received so few grants for research. Still, for practical purposes these issues have been well covered up. The tactics for doing so have been to make the awarding of grants for research turn on professional standards and to distribute the grants in a huge number of small packages, so that an attack on one does not jeopardize the

entire enterprise. I find these tactics lacking in symmetry and superficial logic, but I must admit that they have a great practical advantage. Frankly, I am skeptical whether we are yet ready to incorporate a
higher level of sophistication into our system of awarding research
grants to universities. I wish we were.

COMMENTARY

Unquestionably Federal sponsorship of research is an important phenomenon for American higher education. On the other hand, it is
not of such Gargantuan proportions as followers of the daily press
might be led to believe. Federal funds for research are popularly
thought to be disbursed among a sizeable proportion of all institutions
of higher learning. Fortunately this proposition is testable, and
tested, it turns out to be wrong. In all there are approximately two
thousand American institutions which more or less qualify for the
title "institution of higher learning." Of these, twenty according to
Mr. Kidd, get about sixty per cent of the Federal funds, and fifty
get roughly ninety per cent of them. These figures fail to account
for research centers and agricultural experiment stations. When such
institutions are included, eight universities receive about sixty per
cent of the funds. At the outset then, it is well to note that the
research which the Federal Government sponsors, though voluminous,
is concentrated in a relatively few institutions.

Within those few favored institutions, significant changes are
occurring. Federal funds are altering their very nature, causing variations in the balance among their constituent parts. Teaching is becoming less respected, less glamorous, less remunerative than doing
research. Also an increasing percentage of the faculty has nontenure
rather than tenure appointments, and in some sense these institutions
are hoarding and underutilizing potential teachers. Finally, the
humanities are losing ground relative to other academic disciplines.
In order to counterbalance this tendency, many of the institutions
involved are using their unrestricted funds to bolster the humanities
vis-á-vis the natural and, to a lesser degree, the social sciences; administrators generally view this strategy as crucial for preserving an acceptable distribution of resources.

There is some sentiment to the effect that the Federal Government exploits those universities which it retains to do research. It
underwrites only direct, not total costs, so the argument goes, and
as a result the universities must themselves pay the residual overhead.
Professor Harris is not convinced that such exploitation is widespread,

but there is good evidence that at least sometimes it does exist. For example, Francis Keppel, then dean of the Faculty of Education at Harvard University, now U. S. Commissioner of Education, cited instances when administrators failed to apply for Federal research grants which their institutions might easily have been awarded and which were attractive on all grounds except financial and organizational. The usual case is otherwise, however, for in general, universities have been eager to do Federal research. Therefore, the question of why they undertake such extracurricular projects, when by doing them they may not so much as break even, remains to be asked. In a very general way the answer is simple: competition for prestige. Interesting research attracts good scholars, who in turn attract able students, and so on. Eventually the result should be a stimulating academic environment and, ultimately, prestige. Acquiring top-flight research being at least one way of initiating the cycle, institutions are eager to obtain it, and often this means bidding below cost in order to win a contract. The only way to avoid the losses inherent in such tactics is for universities to act monopolistically, to cartelize, and thus to raise, in unison, the prices at which the Federal Government can purchase their services.

Fully independent from considerations of whether doing research for the Federal Government is financially feasible, there is the important question of the effect of such research on an institution's educational product. Some types of research directly induce improved teaching, while others do not. It is Mr. Kidd's judgment that much of the research performed in American universities today is of the latter variety, classified research being perhaps the prime example. Such research must be performed in a communicatory vacuum, since not divulging its results is deemed vital for national security, and therefore one of the most potentially fruitful outgrowths of research—trading fresh findings in the free and unbounded market place of ideas—must be foregone. Whether universities should undertake classified research is a delicate issue and one on which each institution must formulate its own policy. Many believe that they should in times of national crisis, not otherwise, and the problem then becomes one of defining national crisis. The pros and cons of doing classified research is not currently the central issue, however. Rather what is of importance for now is to observe that much of the research which universities do is purely and simply noneducational public service; it contributes virtually naught to the cause of current education, conventionally defined, except perhaps in the most obscure and far-fetched sense.

In discussing the relationship between research and education. it is somewhat improper to bring all types of education together into a single package. One useful distinction is that between education at the graduate and undergraduate levels. As a general rule, graduate students are much more likely to reap fruits from research than are undergraduates, and it is the latter about whom designers of policy should be most concerned when they study possible conflicts between education and research. One escape from this dilemma is to support two faculties of arts and sciences, one primarily responsible for teaching undergraduates, the other for teaching graduate students; and in fact some universities have already taken steps in this direction. Unfortunately the scheme has several disadvantages. For one thing, it might discourage able undergraduates from enrolling in graduate courses, though this difficulty hardly seems insurmountable. Of more concern is the fact that supporting a dual faculty of arts and sciences would be extremely expensive, primarily because it would make exploiting whatever economies of large-scale operation universities may already have discovered—such as having graduate students teach undergraduates—difficult if not impossible. Nevertheless, whatever the objections to this specific plan, the general notion that, in diverting resources from low-level teaching, research is capable of doing more harm to undergraduate than to graduate education (although Mr. Kidd does not believe that this has yet happened) seems undeniable and worth bearing in mind.

From the point of view of the Federal Government this entire subject of research raises an interesting issue. Should it purchase all its research from those few universities of unquestioned excellence, or should it perhaps offer some contracts to lesser lights in the educational world in an effort to help them attract more able faculty than they now have and thus ultimately to improve the quality of their product? As spender of public funds the Government should attempt to purchase the best services available, but as regulator of social institutions in response to national needs it should try to improve the caliber of some of America's potentially good but as yet unfulfilled institutions of higher learning. One participant doubted that giving contracts for research to some of America's less well-known universities would do anything more than redistribute the fixed stock of exceptionally talented faculty and students among institutions of higher learning. Its net effect on those institutions raided and on those aided would, in his view, be almost precisely zero. Most members of the seminar, however, criticized this view as exceedingly pessimistic and too intensely focused on static phenomena in the very short run. For the most part, they felt that American education as a whole would gain if a top-notch member of, for example, Harvard's faculty were induced by the promise of Federal funds for research to join the faculty of some reasonably good but not yet outstanding university. The large majority of those present thus favored having the Government spend money for research not only as a narrow-minded rational consumer but also as an enlightened advocate of a policy to increase America's supply of centers of educational excellence.

In these times of huge appropriations for and endless publicity about research, there is inevitably some curiosity about the quality of the work being done and the factors which influence that quality. If a respected member of a university's faculty wishes to apply for Federal funds, his dean generally sanctions the application so long as it includes a reasonable request for funds to cover the overhead allocable to the project. Rarely therefore do a university's administrators control the quality of research which its members carry on. To a certain extent the disbursing agency does exercise such control. Rather than simply filling each outstretched hand with cash, it attempts to evaluate the applications it receives and to reject those which seem least worthwhile. But realistically, much of the information, especially about scholars, is on the level of hearsay, and there are thus strict limits to how enlightened its decisions can be. Mr. Keppel suggested that a man's colleagues ultimately control the quality of his work via covert pressure, since scholars who are themselves engaged in outstanding research simply pay scant attention to a fellow member of the faculty whose work is regarded as third-rate. Proposing an alternative view, Professor Harris argued that this Veblenesque keeping-up-with effect exerts less control over the quality of research than Keppel suggested. According to Harris, there is a strong element of senatorial courtesy of the don't-look-over-my-shoulder-and-I won't-look-over-yours variety in these matters, and he is thus not so optimistic as Keppel about the efficacy of automatic incentives for promoting excellent research within universities. Irrespective of whose view is more nearly correct, however, the truly important consideration is the general point: research—its design as well as its performance—can be carried on both badly and well. Since vast sums of money are currently being spent on the activity, it is crucial that policy makers be aware of methods to elicit research of high quality, as well as to discourage work which is slipshod.

4. Education for Manpower Development

PAPER BY . . . *John S. McCauley*
Director, Office of Manpower Training Operations,
U. S. Employment Service, Bureau of Employment
Security, Department of Labor

A great deal of consideration has been given in recent years to the role of America's formal educational system in developing our human resources. Although we in the U. S. Department of Labor are interested in many aspects of this question, I would like to focus attention on what happens to the career development of the younger worker after he has left school. What opportunties does he have for continuing to develop his skill and knowledge?

Continued career development is an important matter for several reasons. First, many workers in the labor force today did not complete high school and need to fill in some of the gaps in their education. Second, technological change is so rapid that even high school graduates who have had excellent preparation for their careers will need additional education during their working lives. Finally, there is evidence that some persons derive more benefit from educational experiences after they have gone to work than from schooling at the beginning of their careers.

Professor Harold F. Clark of Columbia University was very impressed, when he was visiting classes conducted in industry, by the intentness of the worker-students. They were literally sitting on the edge of their seats. When asked why they had this tremendous interest, the instructor explained that they knew they might be required to apply that very afternoon what they had learned during the morn-

91

ing class. This sense of urgency often seems to be lacking in the regular school system.

The need to develop opportunities for workers to continue their education raises many questions. What is industry's responsibility for conducting this type of education? What should state and Federal governments do to encourage training in industry? What role should the public school system play in promoting adult education? What help can community service organizations provide? I should like to explore these questions briefly and touch on some of the programs sponsored by the Federal Government to meet certain aspects of the problem.

Some large companies have already developed comprehensive formal educational programs for their personnel. For example, the Ford Motor Company has established a broad range of programs, beginning with orientation when an employee starts to work for the company and continuing for perhaps several years. Programs are maintained to develop crafsmen, technicians, engineers, supervisors and even managers. Some employees who have taken part in a series of these programs have advanced very high in the company's hierarchy.

How prevalent are training programs in industry? Some information on this matter was provided by Professor Clark and Professor Harold S. Sloan in a study of the educational programs of the nation's five hundred largest corporations.[1] They concluded that these large corporations are making a significant contribution to the development of their employees' careers. For example, the Martin Company in the outskirts of Baltimore has a number of employees who earned bachelor's degrees in engineering several years ago. The company, in cooperation with the Drexel Institute in Philadelphia, designed a very attractive program especially for these employees, whereby they can earn a master's degree in three years in physics, aeronautical engineering, mechanical engineering or electrical engineering. The classes are taught in the late afternoon in a building close to the plant. Because so many employees wish to take advantage of this very convenient opportunity, only those who agree to complete the entire program are permitted to enroll. However, other courses are offered on a selective basis, and an employee who needs time off to complete a thesis or other graduate work may be given one day off a week at full pay for this purpose.

Although most large corporations provide training opportunities for their employees, relatively few of the smaller firms do so. Small companies usually lack the staff required to plan and conduct educational and training activities. Some of them also fear that after an employee has been trained, he will move to another company. The large corporation has a considerable advantage in this regard because an employee usually has opportunities to move to more responsible assignments without leaving the company.

To obtain more information about training in industry, the U.S. Department of Labor's Bureau of Apprenticeship and Training has undertaken a nation-wide study. Questionnaires were sent to a sample group of ten thousand establishments in different sectors of the economy. Information was requested on whether or not they were providing any training for their employees; what staff they had assigned to plan and administer training programs; what use they were making of the facilities of local high schools, colleges and universities; and what incentives the employees were offered to participate. Training was defined as any prearranged system of instruction designed to equip employees to perform their job duties better. It included instruction provided on or off the job by the firm, by an employee organization or by an educational institution.[2]

Although the results of this study are not yet available, a preliminary study found that only 16 per cent of the establishments in New Jersey were conducting training for their employees. As might be expected, there was a strong relationship between the size of the establishment and sponsorship of training. Of the larger employers (those with 500 or more employees), 82 per cent were providing training. Of firms employing from 100 to 499 workers, 50 per cent were conducting training; while among the small companies employing from 4 to 19 workers, only 11 per cent were sponsoring training programs.[3]

The U. S. Department of Labor's Bureau of Apprenticeship and Training encourages and assists industry in developing training programs. The bureau employs about three hundred field representatives who work with employers and labor organizations for this purpose. In some states, state agencies are also promoting the development of industrial training programs.

A useful technique to encourage training in industry is to help organize a program sponsored by a group of employers. For example, an apprenticeship field representative may assist several employers in the same industry—and perhaps also the union with which they bargain—in establishing jointly an apprenticeship and training program. This approach is widely used in the construction industry, where approximately 3,500 joint apprenticeship committees sponsor training programs. An important value of group programs is that they enable small employers to provide training for their employees.[4]

A great deal more might be done on a community basis to assist those segments of industry which are not able to conduct educational and training programs by themselves. Although the apprenticeship field representatives deal for the most part with individual employers, they are working to an increasing extent with community organizations, such as chambers of commerce, Kiwanis Clubs and Rotary Clubs, which are often interested in sponsoring manpower-development projects in their communities.

To provide the information needed in planning community manpower projects, surveys of the educational and skill requirements of industry are conducted by the local offices of the various state employment services, in cooperation with the U. S. Employment Service. These studies also help to promote closer working relationships between industry and the public school system. However, a major obstacle to planning community programs to meet future needs is the fact that many employers are not in the habit of looking very far ahead. Expenditures for vocational and adult education often look worthwhile only if one takes a sufficiently long view, perhaps ten or fifteen years ahead.

A powerful stimulus to community planning, including manpower planning, was the enactment in 1961 of the Area Redevelopment Act,[5] which provides that an area with substantial and persistent unemployment may be designated a redevelopment area. To secure Federal grants and other benefits for the area, an over-all plan for its economic development must be prepared. The plan is based on the area's prospects for attracting new or expanding industries, evaluated in the light of its population, labor force and other industrial resources. The Act also provides for training programs to help prepare unemployed or underemployed workers for the new jobs expected as a result of economic-development activities and for other available jobs. Emphasis is given to training for jobs in the same area; however, training may be undertaken for employment anywhere in the country. Although allowances can be paid to trainees for only sixteen weeks, this does not necessarily limit the length of the training. In a few communities, programs have been approved for twenty weeks of training.

Additional training for unemployed and underemployed workers was provided by the Manpower Development and Training Act of 1962.[6] Under this Act a trainee may receive fifty-two weeks of training allowances. Training opportunities are not limited to workers living in redevelopment areas; they are extended to unemployed and underemployed workers throughout the country. Before training may be conducted, the local office of the state employment service must determine that there is a reasonable expectation that, as a result of the proposed training, the trainees will obtain employment.

The local office also provides school officials with information, not only on the type of skills and knowledge required by prospective employers, but also on the previous education and work experience of unemployed or underemployed workers who are likely candidates for admission to the proposed course. Planning and conducting school programs under MDTA is the responsibility of local educators under the general supervision of the state board of vocational education and the U.S. Office of Education. When on-the-job training needs to be developed, arrangements with employers and labor organizations to conduct such programs are worked out by the Bureau of Apprenticeship and Training in cooperation with state apprenticeship agencies.

Another measure to develop human resources is the proposal for youth employment opportunities introduced in the Senate by Senator Hubert H. Humphrey.[7] The bill provides that young men be given an opportunity to enroll in camps similar to those once operated by the Civilian Conservation Corps. It also provides that public-service projects be established for both boys and girls who would live at home. Public libraries, hospitals and other non-profit organizations would be encouraged to sponsor public-service projects that would provide training as well as employment. Participation in these programs would doubtless help many young people, particularly members of minority groups, to get started on careers. Several months of training and work experience in one of the youth programs should increase their productivity sufficiently to qualify them for regular jobs.

It must be stressed that efforts of the Federal Government to train the unemployed are not intended to replace existing programs sponsored by employers, unions and educational institutions. Indeed, it is important that the new Federal programs be planned and conducted in such a way as to encourage the continuation and development of other training efforts. To help accomplish this objective, the Labor Department has encouraged the establishment of advisory committees in all communities where it is likely that manpower-development projects will be developed. Advisory committees also have been established at the state and national levels. These committees generally consist of representatives of labor, management, education, training and the general public.

The use of advisory committees helps to guard against the approval of a training program which might favor any particular employer over his competitors. Review of proposed training schemes by advisory committees also gives labor leaders and employers an opportunity to discuss any proposals that may be made to train workers for employment at less than the prevailing wage—a step which might adversely affect both the trade unions and the employers. The advisory committees also help to obtain employer and union cooperation in surveys of training needs and to increase in still other ways understanding of and support for manpower-development projects.

All these programs are more likely to bear fruit in a rapidly expanding economy than in one in which few new jobs are emerging. Measures to promote the general growth of the economy are, therefore, complementary to the manpower-development approach. However, even in communities in West Virginia, where there is widespread unemployment, several hundred persons obtained employment after completing training programs.

Furthermore, training tends to raise the level of employment without building up strong inflationary pressures. It helps to prevent bottlenecks from developing as the economy expands. This was demonstrated in Hazleton, Pennsylvania, when a shortage of technically trained machinists increased production costs and threatened plans to expand a plant which had been operating only a few months in that area. The firm was considering moving to a city with a better supply of machinists, but it decided to stay when training programs designed to provide the necessary skills were established on a community-wide basis.

Although considerable progress has recently been made in providing opportunities for occupational training to adults, a great deal remains to be done. Additional training programs need to be established by employers, labor organizations and government agencies at all levels. In determining the social and economic value of additional programs, consideration should be given not only to the benefits received by the trainees but also to the contribution such programs make to economic growth.

REFERENCES

1. Harold F. Clark and Harold S. Stone, *Classrooms in the Factories* (Rutherford, New Jersey: Institute of Research, Fairleigh Dickinson University, 1958).
2. Results of the nation-wide study will be published by the Bureau of Apprenticeship and Training in a forthcoming report, *Training of Workers in American Industry.*
3. U. S. Department of Labor, Bureau of Apprenticeship and Training, *Employee Training in New Jersey Industry,* September 1960, p. 31.
4. For a discussion of group apprenticeship programs and of the methods used to promote them, see John S. McCauley, "BAT and Community Apprenticeship Committees," *Journal of the American Society of Training Directors,* November 1958.
5. U. S. Congress, *An Act to Establish an Effective Program to Alleviate Conditions of Substantial and Persistent Unemployment and Underemployment in Certain Economically Distressed Areas,* Public Law 87-27, 87th Congress, 1st Session, 1961, pp. 47-63.
6. U. S. Congress, *An Act Relating to Manpower Requirements, Resources, Development, and Utilization, and for Other Purposes,* Public Law 87-415, 87th Congress, S. 1991, March 15, 1962. This Act was broadened and its coverage extended by Public Law 88-214 (HR8720), enacted in December 1963.
7. In the 1st Session of the 88th Congress, the Youth Employment Opportunities Act was passed by the Senate. Title I of the Economic Opportunity Act of 1964, introduced in the 2nd Session of the 88th Congress as a result of President Johnson's poverty message, is an expanded version of this proposal.

COMMENTARY

The relation of man and machine requires attention on many frontiers, e.g. (1) working with and designing today's industrial machinery requires skills which many laborers and engineers were not fortunate enough to acquire when they were learning their trades, and (2) increasingly machines are performing jobs which men once did and are, as a result, causing a form of unemployment which one may describe most succinctly as technological.

In order to keep their employees abreast of their jobs' requirements, many companies sponsor educational programs. The programs are not uniformly comprehensive. Some tend to be narrowly defined and to use the specific industry's jargon, while others seek broad horizons. The latter attempt to teach, as one participant put it, general principles of aerodynamics rather than simply how to design wings for certain types of airplanes. It is the bigger companies, not the smaller ones, which tend to provide the more general programs—those which Dr. Henry David, then president of the New School for Social Research, termed education rather than training. There are several partial explanations for this fact. For one thing, it is the larger companies which are invariably blessed with generous Federal defense contracts and which are thus easily able to transfer the costs of educational programs to society at large rather than having to assume them alone. Second, just as beer, so to speak, is very satisfactory until one tastes champagne, so education will often prompt a man to want to change his occupation. If he works for a large and diversified organization, he is likely to find another job more to his liking within the same company, whereas if he is employed by a small firm, he would no doubt have to search for work challenging to his new skills in other industrial pastures. It seems clear, then, that large companies are less likely to lose the services of the people they educate than are smaller firms, and they can thus be correspondingly more willing to invest in broadening their employees' minds in a general way. Perhaps in a realistic sense the best solution is for the community to underwrite formally some of the cost of this instruction. It already does so informally through defense contracts, but the rationale for formalizing these public subsidies is that even though any company can reap negative benefits if a man it trains seeks work elsewhere, American society as a whole cannot so lose, excluding the possibility of expatriation.

Often he who makes moralistic pronouncements is himself hardly a paragon of virtue, and in the matter of providing working people with continuing education, the Federal Government is no exception. It circulates missionaries far and wide to preach the gospel according to John Dewey, Thomas Edison and Willard Wirtz, but its own house is far from in order and the adage about glass houses and stones comes quickly to mind. To be straightforward, one participant emphasized that the Government has been lax in giving its own employees more education than they had already acquired before they entered its service, although it has, in loud and glowing tones, extolled the benefits of doing so to industry. There are some indications that the situation will change. Congress recently authorized the Civil Service Commission to provide more training for Federal employees, and now, at any given time, one per cent of all Federal civil servants can be on leave with pay in order to receive formal education. The State and Defense Departments have been sponsoring similar programs for a long time, but until recently the authorization to make them widespread has been lacking. Thus the members of the seminar were in general agreement that the Federal Government's record in this area is not one of which it can be especially proud, but it also seems likely that the situation is now improving. And no doubt this improvement would have come sooner if the Government had been able to transfer the cost of educating its employees to industry, as industry has, in substantial measure, to the Government.

In addition to keeping employees abreast of developments in their fields, there is another problem, perhaps a more serious one, of retaining and relocating those people who have already become technologically unemployed. It is the dual nature of the task at hand, the fact that people must be taught new skills as well as put into contact with potential employers, which complicates matters considerably. Legislation is developing in such a way that two executive departments of the Federal Government will probably be working to solve this bilateral problem. The Department of Health, Education and Welfare will be primarily concerned with training the workers. The Department of Labor's major preoccupations will be, first, to project the needs for various skills in order to guide HEW in deciding what sort of training to provide and, second, to act more or less as a placement and guidance service, bringing unemployed workers and available jobs together.

It seems clear that one aspect of the cure for technological unemployment is to increase the mobility of American labor, to move towards transforming the currently large number of local markets into one which is truly national. In order to have a displaced coal miner from Pennsylvania return to work, it is not sufficient merely to retrain him for another occupation. In general, he will also have to move to an area where labor is needed. Increasing the mobility of American labor is thus one requisite for reducing technological unemployment, and this raises the issue of compensating those people who, as a result of economic forces which are beyond their control, are forced to leave their homes and re-establish roots elsewhere. André Daniere, assistant professor of economics at Harvard University, argued that society should pay the cost of moving for such people and also guarantee their incomes for one year. Professor Harris, on the other hand, noted that the chances of Congress' passing such a program, especially its second part, are rather slim indeed, though, to be sure, some progress was made in 1962. It was generally accepted that some form of public compensation is probably justifiable in these circumstances, for such compensation would be indistinguishable from unemployment insurance, and that is, after all, a type of transfer payment to which America has long since been committed.

More generally, the problem is whether, over time, the economy is capable of absorbing its increasing supply of labor. This is a complicated issue in economic dynamics, and the seminar did not deal with it exhaustively but rather discussed a few aspects of the matter. One important consideration is the population of young Americans. Between 1960 and 1970 the number aged 14-19 is expected to increase 42 per cent. In 1961, young people already comprised more than a proportionate share of the unemployed, and many who would have had a good position in the labor market several years earlier found themselves without jobs and even somewhat unemployable. A number of techniques for solving this part of the over-all problem were proposed. One is to increase the supply of vocational training available to youngsters. The stumbling block is in providing enough teachers for such programs. Inevitably, if they expand considerably, they will have to be staffed by people who are not college graduates, and although some approve, more than a few responsible policy makers take a rather dim view of such an arrangement. Another proposal is to expand the opportunities for youngsters to combine school and work. However, the important point, as Dr. David noted, is that although combining school and work has been successful in a number of isolated and well-run trials, in general it has been a sorry failure. Attempts to run this sort of program on a large scale have broken down altogether.

We would do well to view these remarks in the light of orthodox economics, textbook style. Static economic theory has numerous well-known shortcomings, not the least of which is its failure to say much that is useful about technological change. We might, therefore, expect that the sort of policy which is derived from static theory would not be very effective as a cure for technological unemployment, and this is in fact the case. Professor Harris remarked that, as any good Keynesian knows, the currently orthodox formula for curing unemployment is to increase effective demand through fiscal policy. In plain language this means government spending, usually deficit spending or tax cuts. Professor Harris reported that he has done some rough empirical work on these matters, and in contrast to the traditional

view, he suggested that technological unemployment can most economically be cured by retraining and relocating people, rather than
through fiscal policy of the usual sort. He estimates that, even under
certain rather pessimistic assumptions, it would cost the Government
only about $1,000 a year to create a job for a technologically unem-
ployed worker if it retrains him, but between $5,000 and $10,000
per worker annually if it operates through the normal channels of
fiscal measures. This is a striking finding because it adds a new dimension to the traditional tools of economic policy. At the same time,
Professor Harris cautioned that there are limits to the number of
unemployed people who can be put to work through the direct
approach. Specifically, the number of unfilled vacancies sets an upper
limit, but it is not one which is guaranteed to create full employment.

For those who are concerned with American education in toto,
one interesting sign of the times is that both the implicit and explicit
requirements for entering many occupations have been expanding
rapidly. This fact caused some members of the seminar to ask whether,
in the light of the soon-to-be-realized heavy pressure of enrollments
on the capacities of American institutions of higher learning, educational standards for certain types of work may not be somewhat
inflated; and in the extreme, several participants were even willing to
say that requiring a four-year liberal-arts education for some—accountants, for example—is wasteful of scarce resources. They wonder
whether this nation can afford the educational luxury which the system presently allows. Thus, while the Department of Labor has estimated America's higher educational needs for the near future, some
view these projections as a gross exaggeration because they are based
on artificially high educational standards for certain occupations.

This line of argument came under heavy attack on several counts.
First, America is a rich country, and in a general cultural sense education is regarded as a good thing per se. Reading *Hamlet* is unlikely
to enhance one's skill as an accountant, but it provides other benefits
which, although they are not easily calculable, are generally thought
to be large. Second, the phrase "college education" has acquired an
entirely different meaning today from that which it once had; its
meaning is currently much more diffuse than it has ever been. If
an appropriate test of the activity's worth is whether today's college
graduates have received roughly the same training as the aristocratic
few who attended college fifty years ago, then what is happening today
is surely wasteful. But the important point is that today's product
is more diversified than yesterday's, and if this modern version is

judged by standards which are appropriate to it, it fares rather well. Even the extremely high rate of dropouts did not disturb many of those present, for, in speaking of a given individual, they emphasized not that he started and did not finish but rather the fact that he did attend college for one, two or three semesters. They seemed to be saying, in the jargon of the adman, that a little goes a long, long way.

In addition to the matter of whether is it wasteful of scarce resources, there is another dimension to the artifical upgrading of hiring standards. Intuitively one might think that it tends to make the normal employee's lot increasingly insecure. In fact, it was argued that its results have not been this one-sided. Having a college education has recently become a requisite for holding many jobs because employers, in their desire to obtain the icing on the labor-market cake, collectively bid up requirements. They use educational attainments as an easy screening device. It is thus at least partially the actions of the employers themselves which make the supply of employees scarce. As a result of the artificial upgrading, many employers must eventually choose between passing up potentially profitable production or, alternatively, hiring people who, although adequate for the task at hand, have limited educational attainments. When faced with this choice, many employers have decided to produce, have lowered their standards for hiring and have found to their delight that their previous standards were inflated. They have thus hired and been satisfied with the performances of noncollege graduates, women, part-time employees and Negroes, many of whom they would have discriminated against if the supply of "acceptable" labor had not been so scarce. But that supply was limited precisely because of the employers' own irrational hiring habits and desires to find easy screening devices. Thus the moral of the story, as the seminar heard it, is clear: the process by which employers initially cause employees to be in short supply comes full circle and, in the end, causes the former to understand the partial fiction they have created and to hire people against whom they might discriminate when labor is abundant.

5. The Goals of Education in Underdeveloped Countries

PAPER BY . . . *Montague Yudelman*
Harvard Graduate School of Education

Nothing pleases me more than seeing people read and write and thus widen their horizons. There is something deeply satisfying in literacy, in expanding ranges of choice and in the ability to enjoy the great literature that has been written over the centuries. In short, I am not against education; I cannot understand how anyone could oppose education per se. But as an economist who has been involved in drawing up several economic development plans for underdeveloped countries, I find that I have had to take a new view.

Education is one item in a development budget, and we economists must make very difficult choices when we allocate expenditures among competing demands for funds. Among these choices is the problem of determinimg how much should be spent on education. Here we have a serious drawback: no one has yet demonstrated conclusively that any given investment in education can or will increase output by a given amount within a given period of time.

There are various schools of thought on the subject. Some economists, including Hans Singer of the United Nations, argue very persuasively that investment in education yields increasing returns. Their view is that if one adds to the stock of educated people and research in a country and continues adding to that stock, the country will derive increasing and expanding returns in productivity from these investments. Consequently, every investment in education will pay off in the long run—or even in the short run.

Other students of the subject have attempted to demonstrate that investment in education yields high returns. Studies by Professor Rob-

103

ert M. Solow in the United States and Professor Aukrust of Norway demonstrate conclusively that there is a residual factor in the economy, something beyond the conventional inputs of physical factors, that has contributed greatly to economic growth in the United States and Norway. Similar studies have been done in the Soviet Union. Professor Theodore W. Schultz of the University of Chicago has also written a great deal about the returns on investment in human resources.

Most of these economists affirm that changing technology is a very important factor in economic development that is closely linked to the existence of an educated population, and that therefore investment in education helps to explain the increase in the growth rate; in other words, the quality of the human inputs is being changed. They also point out that there are great external economies from investment in education. A nation cannot have atomic power plants or an aircraft industry without having a large pool of trained scientists, and it cannot have these scientists without investment in education.

I accept all these views—except, perhaps, the view that education yields ever-increasing material returns. However, if I were a minister of finance in an underdeveloped country, I would find it difficult to justify huge expenditures on education on the theory that they would pay off in the short run, or even in the long run. Unfortunately, no one has demonstrated conclusively that an increase in investment in education will lead to an increase in national output.

It has been estimated that if an African country had 100 per cent of its children in the appropriate age group in primary school, 20 per cent in secondary school and 5 per cent in a university, it would need to spend about 4 per cent of its national income on education. Most of the developed countries have no more than 8 per cent of the national income available for development services; poorer countries, of course, have much less. Can a country afford to allocate more than half of its development funds to education?

When ministers in poor countries consider the kinds of investments they must make, they are faced with very difficult problems of choice—over the long run and over the short run. If they assume that there is a revolution of rising expectations, they must also assume that a demand for higher standards of living, including more and better material comforts, is part of this revolution. It follows that they must allocate their resources in such a way as to achieve the most rapid growth rate possible, taking into account the need to meet as many aspirations as possible. In order to attain this higher growth rate, they must allocate funds strictly for productive purposes. Obviously they cannot have both a generous pattern of educational enrollment and an extensive investment in productive plant and services.

Uganda is a case in point. A small nation with a population of only 6.5-million it is essentially a country of peasant producers who grow cotton and coffee. During and after World War II, the prices of cotton and coffee rose very rapidly, and Uganda suddenly had huge windfall profits. The government took over these profits, and all at once a small, backward country had relatively huge sums of money to invest in development. The nature of its development programs illustrates the problem of choosing among investments in different sectors of the economy.

During a period of ten years, the Ugandans tried three approaches to development. The first was to concentrate heavily on industrialization. Most of the available funds went into programs for developing infrastructure—providing electricity, building roads and a cement factory, and the like. Some progress was made, but very soon the obvious opportunities for investment in industry were exhausted.

The second approach was strongly influenced by the liberal governor, Sir Andrew Cohen, who decided that there should be emphasis on expanding social services. For the next five or six years there was a very high rate of investment in social services, including education.

By 1960, however, the economy was in serious difficulty, and my colleagues and I were sent to Uganda as members of an International Bank mission to frame a new development program. The Ugandans had a very high rate of investment relative to their gross domestic product, yet per-capita incomes were falling; in other words, the population was growing at a faster rate than the national income. At the same time, government expenditures were running ahead of revenues because the educational program required increased capital costs and much higher recurring costs.

As Uganda's experience indicates, a sharp and sizable increase in investment in education will not necessarily yield a parallel increase in economic growth. Indeed, it may not yield any increase in economic growth at all. This may be too harsh a judgment, especially in the short run, but in Uganda there was obviously only a very limited multiplier effect from increased investment in education. Moreover, other investment opportunities that might have had a multiplier effect were neglected because of the large expenditures on education. Our mission recommended holding the line on expenditures on social services but increasing investment in agriculture. We especially urged that agricultural services be improved; these services included a large component of training.

This brings me to a further point: there are different kinds of investment in education. I think it is useful to consider education in the terms used by Professor Arthur Lewis, who drew a distinction between "consumption" education and "productive" education. Educating cooks to fly planes is consumption education; cooks will not necessarily cook better or be more productive because they are also pilots. On the other hand, if an extension agent is taught to improve his work, he will be able to transmit better techniques of production more effectively than before. This productive type of education yields an increase in growth.

Professor Lewis asserts[1] that since most underdeveloped countries have limited resources, these resources must be used as effectively as possible to promote growth. The emphasis, therefore, should be on providing productive education. General education must be viewed as a luxury; this is regrettable, but it *is* a luxury to provide a consumption education for everybody. Until the economy is stronger, the educational system should not attempt to provide everybody with a smattering of general literacy.

What is needed is a very selective process of education. Economists must first examine the nation's needs in order to identify the shortages of skills which are bottlenecks in the economy. Then they must arrange the educational system so that those shortages can be overcome through specialized training. In other words, training and educational programs must be geared to developmental priorities, rather than to some grand design to make the population literate.

Let me illustrate this point by summarizing one proposal for investment in education in Africa. This proposal emanated from a joint UNESCO-Economic Commission for Africa conference held in Ethiopia in 1961. The proposal was that African countries invest something like $4-billion over a period of five years to increase the number of children in primary schools from 40 per cent to about 60 per cent of the age group, to increase the number in secondary schools to about 6 or 7 per cent and to maintain the number in higher education at about 2 per cent. The task of promoting general education in Africa is enormous—more than half the people cannot read or write—but it is absolutely inconceivable that $4-billion could be raised or used by these countries in five years for this purpose.

The total amount that some observers believe should be invested in education is, considering the economies which would have to carry this burden, too huge to be realistic. Moreover, this kind of investment would indicate a misplaced faith in education, for it will not lead to a rapid rate of growth. It will only result in a larger number of people who can read and write. In Tanganyika, Uganda, Kenya and the Rhodesias, the amounts of money invested in education are already far higher than the amounts invested in agricultural development, and these countries depend almost entirely on agricultural development for their economic growth.

Ministers of finance and ministers of economics in underdeveloped countries are confronted by a tremendous demand for all kinds of services. Perhaps the strongest pressure is for increased expenditures on education. This may be related to the undeniable fact that education not only expands horizons but also opens opportunities for individuals to ascend the economic scale, especially as government employees where new governments are coming into being. But, at the same time, there is a great need for investment in services that will produce quick economic growth. In my view, these new governments have to increase their national incomes before they can afford to invest substantially in consumption education.

The essence of the conflict that now confronts members of cabinets is to reconcile the pressure for general education with the need to promote rapid economic growth. These goals are not mutually exclusive, but there must be a system of priorities in expenditures and investments, and there must be a division between long-term and short-term goals.

There is great pressure in underdeveloped countries for education, and ministers of finance will have to be very strong to follow a sound economic policy. This policy, I believe, would be to hold the line on general educational expenditures, while increasing investment in those areas where there will be a fairly quick return, so that these contries can get their economic growth under way.

REFERENCE

1. W. Arthur Lewis, "Education and Economic Development," *Social and Economic Studies*, X (June 1961).

PAPER BY . . . *Adam Curle*
                    Center for Studies in Education and Development,
                    Harvard University

It is easy to criticize the educational policies of some countries—indeed, of whole continents—as being excessively costly and irrelevant to the exigencies of development. Such criticism, however, is often less constructive than it might be because it fails to take into account the pressures behind the policies. Decisions are not always taken on purely rational grounds, and persons concerned with development should understand the political and psychological factors at work, as much as the specifically economic matters.

In what follows, I shall attempt to depict some of the influences at work upon a minister of education and other high officials dealing with education in an underdeveloped country. The picture is both composite and fictional, but it is built out of direct experience in a number of countries and is based largely upon what has been said to me by people involved with education.

In the first place, the minister is usually a relatively junior member of the cabinet. He may be a young man on the way up, or he may be a loyal old party member who has been appointed as a reward for past efforts rather than in expectation of future achievements. It would be interesting to calculate the average duration in office of ministers of education; my own limited experience suggests that it is short. If young and ambitious, they tend to take the first chance of moving on. If they are simply ministerial hacks, they are convenient scapegoats. It is hard, under these circumstances, to establish firmly a rational policy. The problem is heightened by the fact that the public servants in the ministry are frequently of low calibre. The able and ambitious public servant gravitates towards the ministries of finance and foreign affairs.

Even the best administrators, however, often operate under three serious handicaps. *First,* they are attempting with exiguous resources to accomplish gigantic tasks. *Second,* being a small professional group in a society, with virtually no middle class, they are at the mercy of the politicians, who (especially in the recently independent states) constitute the new elite. There is no traditional strength in the public service which could withstand the pressure of an ignorant and impetuous politician with his eye on the next election. This is not a situation compatible with careful planning. And *third,* very few people in a developing society have much understanding of the educational process. In many of these countries, education was until recently —and in some places still is—practised on a minute scale, often mainly by missionary bodies administered from overseas. This provided a quite inadequate basis of experience for the men who are today in charge of rapidly expanding educational systems.

One result of this insufficient acquaintance with education and its problems is an ambivalent attitude towards education; this is a further cause for impractical policies. Education is both undervalued and overvalued. It is undervalued, as I have suggested, in the frequent appointment of men of second-rate ability. It is overvalued in that innumerable people believe it has some magic, some trick, which will help them achieve rapidly an American or European level of development. This belief is heightened by the obvious formative influence of such schools as Achimota, Katsina, William Ponty and one or two others. People do not always understand that there is a categorical difference between these efficient and potent institutions and a one-room bush school run by a semiliterate. To the undiscriminating, it is all education, and all education is good.

The tendency of the underdeveloped areas to overvalue education has been encouraged in some degree by the international agencies. At internationally sponsored conferences in Karachi, Addis Ababa and Santiago, the nations of Asia, Africa and Latin America pledged themselves to ruinously large programs of educational development. These conferences underlined the existence of a new form of rivalry in which the possession of a university or a system of universal primary education are the indices of status.

But perhaps the most powerful pressure towards rapid educational expansion is popular sentiment. Throughout the world, to the ordinary man (though not always to the ordinary woman), education is the symbol of freedom and progress. The clamour for learning is far louder than that for hydroelectric systems, improved agriculture or even hospitals, and it is hard to resist this universal yearning. Expansion of education is therefore a great vote catcher; it tends, of course, to be exploited for political purposes, thus making it still harder for the administrator to devise a sensible policy. Only the most inept (or honest) politician would advocate caution in educational expansion. The majority usually seek to prove their advocacy by arranging for the erection of school buildings as visible evidence of concern.

For all these reasons, more schools—often of an unsuitable type—are built than can be paid for or staffed. There is, moreover, excessive emphasis on primary and university education. Primary schools proliferate because of popular demand and international pressures. Above all, there is emphasis on primary expansion because it is easier and cheaper: a primary teacher (it is often felt) need himself be only a primary graduate, and in order to double a school population, one need only introduce a shift system. Universities are built as an ostentatious expression of national pride, places around which the nation's president may show important visitors.

Secondary education, which is perhaps more important than any other level for purposes of development, has been the most seriously neglected in most poor countries. There are several reasons for this. Secondary schools, while having none of the glamour of a university, cost very much more than primary schools to build and maintain; teachers of adequate calibre are often unobtainable except by importing prohibitively expensive foreigners; and primary education which has been too rapidly expanded often graduates students who are not prepared for a secondary education.

Vocational and technical schools are even more scarce then secondary schools offering general education. This is another cause of adverse comment by the outside expert. He may not realize, however, that it was his colonial predecessors who demonstrated the values of a literary-classical education in attaining the highest positions in the administration and that the example of those men has led the present generation to believe that such posts represent the summit of man's achievement. Young Africans and Asians today feel that if pressure is put on them to enter technical education, they are being fobbed off with second-best. They reject training as agriculturists, for example, because the land represents to them the backwardness they long to escape from. Moreover, if they are stuck in a remote part of the country doing work of low prestige, they miss many glittering prizes—the titles, the appointments, the visits to the United States —which are lavished on the few educated citizens of an underdeveloped country.

The honest official of an underdeveloped country will concede all these points but, having done so, may proceed to another line of argument. He will emphasize that many underdeveloped countries, especially those of Africa, are not yet nations with problems; they are geographical and administrative units facing the problem of *becoming* nations. Many of these countries are agglomerations of tribes having little or nothing in common. Their members have no concept of the nation and attach all their loyalty to the tribe. If tribal integrity is threatened by the state, the tribesmen spring to its defense against what they feel to be an alien intrusion.

The African leaders are keenly aware of these dangers to national solidarity and development, and many believe that education is the best means of opposing them. Education disperses a common language by which the government may communicate with the people—and the people with each other. More important, perhaps, education imparts a sense of universality, or at least a view beyond the next village. This is one of the factors behind plans by which, in the foreign economist's view, education is excessively favored over more productive investment. The African politician may reply, however, that without a greater measure of political unity and stability, any hopes of real economic growth are illusory. He will also emphasize that illustrations taken from countries still under colonial domination are misleading, because the political problems are quite different before and after independence.

He may also put forward a somewhat different point. One aspect of the backwardness of many nations is their rigid social stratification. When power, wealth and education are virtually the exclusive prerogative of a small group, it is inevitable that the nation as a whole will make slow progress. Even a progressive government cannot easily eliminate class barriers and the ingrained habits of mind by which they are supported; it is necessary for the people themselves to shake loose from their bonds, and education will serve as impetus in this direction. In support of some of these arguments, Western economists and social scientists are, from time to time, aptly quoted. Walt Rostow's insistence on the need to break down the pre-Newtonian *Weltanschauung*, McClelland's stress on the importance of stimulating the achievement motive and Talcott Parson's use of the ascription-achievement polarity as a measure of development are used to indicate the social and psychological elements in development. It is not surprising that education is viewed as a lever to pry people away from attitudes inconsistent with the type of activity upon which economic growth depends.

The African politician may also emphasize that the promotion of agriculture, a vital factor in an underdeveloped economy, depends upon the inculcation of a whole new approach to the land and to life in rural areas. Gunner Myrdal's observation that, in an underdeveloped region, the prosperous area draws wealth away from the poorer ones is noted with alarm by thoughtful persons. To their mind, the vicious circle is best broken by taking steps to build up the more backward regions. These steps are largely educational, if the word is taken broadly to include agricultural extension, community development, health education and the like.

Whether or not the western observer is sympathetic to these arguments, he cannot but feel that the policy they represent is imperfectly implemented. Here we may see another aspect of the undervaluation of education. While it is credited with a sort of mysterious potency, the teachers themselves are underpaid (relative to other professions), undertrained and accorded low status. It is indeed ironical that while education is esteemed, the educator has scant prestige! But this may represent a more deep-seated ambivalence: while education is respected as a valuable and creative force, it is also feared as one which will disrupt the traditional way of life. Yet the attitude toward tradition is also ambivalent: the traditional life is lauded over soulless "Coca-Colonization", but those elements of tradition which would weaken the central governments are crushed.

But if the members of an underdeveloped society are confused about their goals, so also is our advice to them. When faced by differing policies propounded by different individuals and agencies, the official of an underdeveloped nation may often feel inclined to keep his own counsel. This is peculiarly so where education is concerned, for no one really wants a stranger to determine the upbringing of his children.

COMMENTARY

As with so many overwrought words, it seems well to pause over "underdeveloped" from time to time in order to polish the blur and restore its true meaning to sharp focus. Basically the word is a packaging device, and often the elements which it unites are quite dissimilar. India and Ghana are both referred to as underdeveloped, but in many ways their similarities seem trivial in comparison with their differences. On the other hand, all so-called underdeveloped countries must naturally have certain rather important characteristics in common, or social scientists would not find the term as appealing as they apparently do. From our present point of view, perhaps the most important of these common characteristics are two. All countries which qualify for the club of underdeveloped nations have miniscule per-capita real incomes and low rates of literacy.

The Western world has an abiding faith in education. In fact, the roots of this faith extend several thousand years into the past, but they are most popularly associated with the eighteenth century's Enlightenment. Today this heritage prompts many Westerners to advise underdeveloped countries to devote expansive resources to education, almost to treat the enterprise as an end in itself. In contrast, the thinking within indigent nations runs along somewhat different lines. Their most influential officials—if not their populations and ministers of education—have a material objective as their primary goal: increasing real per-capita income. In their minds, education is only a means for achieving that goal, not an end in itself. Many Westerners (and local ministers of education) tell the poor nations' ministers of finance that they could increase their rate of economic growth if only they would devote more resources to education. Though sincerely offered, such advice is somewhat misleading because, although there is not sufficient evidence to contradict it, neither is it supported by the facts. The requisite information is simply lacking. As Dr. Yudelman stressed, there is not yet any satisfactory and unambiguous measure of the relationship between investment in education and economic growth. Thus, although the present controversy between those who view education as a catalyst and those who see it as an impediment to economic growth is passionate, it is none the less based primarily upon intuitive preconceptions rather than upon convincing empirical evidence.

Even though the amount of information necessary to reach a definitive conclusion about the relationship between education and economic growth is not yet available, there are still some shreds of information which seem worth mentioning. Several facts suggest that there are areas in which the demands of education and those of economic growth may be in conflict. One major need of underdeveloped economies is to increase the productivity of workers in the agricultural sector. Yudelman suggested that it seems possible to teach a peasant some of the techniques of modern farming—and thus to increase his productivity—without sending him to a formal school for many years. Reading Kant's *Critique of Pure Reason* is not a prerequisite for being able to learn about fertilizer, and Yudelman views in the same light much of the expenditure devoted to giving Nigerians, say, a Western-style liberal education. A second way in which education and economic growth seem to work at cross-purposes concerns the social prestige of a career in agriculture. In general, farming is regarded as an inferior occupation. Thus, even though in terms of social needs educated people could be highly productive in farming, many turn their backs on agriculture and instead enter one of the more prestigious occupations, such as politics and law. Their very educations influence them to avoid the type of work which the society needs most urgently.

There is evidence that some of the educational projects which developing nations have already undertaken are rather wasteful. Many countries have built fancy universities which, although they serve as show pieces and raise the countries' stock in the market of international gamesmanship, are far larger and more lavish than they need be. To be sure, as Professor Curle noted, the excess capacity is not terribly sinful because enrollments are growing and it therefore merely represents building ahead of demand. But the lavishness is another matter, and in many instances it can only be labelled an irresponsible allocation of scarce resources.

From the point of view of stimulating economic growth, one of the best uses of education is as a reward for increasing physical productivity. Education is an especially good prize because members of the population regard it highly, especially now when many are being taught that the colonial rulers deprived them of learning in order to maintain their empires. Yudelman found that in Uganda the cotton growers did not respond to a rise in the crop's price by increasing the amount they supplied. He is certain, however, that if villages were promised that a sizeable increase in output would bring a school and teacher to the community, then productivity would rise considerably. The job is simply one of finding an effective stimulus, and in many cases education seems to be the carrot that whets appetites.

Yudelman contended that many African educational undertakings are being mismanaged, and he accused educational administrators in general of not being imaginative in finding solutions to their problems. For illustration he cited the fact that in many parts of what was once British Africa, the per-student cost is considerably higher for secondary than for primary schools because the former are the result of attempts to duplicate British boarding schools. Yudelman suggested that a system like the one prevalent in America, whereby the students live at home and travel to and from school daily by bus, would be more economical than the present boarding-school arrangement. Of course, such a plan would not be feasible until the network of African roads undergoes dramatic improvement.

Underdeveloped countries' lofty ambitions are one of their major problems. They want rapid progress and seem determined to compress decades into years, to create quickly a way of life which was a long time in coming to the Western world. One necessary ingredient for them to be able to achieve their goals is a generous supply of external aid, but although they have already been remarkably successful in attracting such aid for certain types of projects, they have not found foreign institutions especially enthusiastic about supporting their educational endeavors. The World Bank, for example, is often responsive when the proposed undertaking is what Yudelman called bankable and not otherwise. In this context, bankable probably means capable of exerting much leverage to aid the cause of economic growth in the not-to-far-distant future. Education is not, in general, what the World Bank's managers consider bankable; rather, it seems to them like a bottomless pit. Simply said, they are not sufficiently confident about the returns from education to believe that investment in it is a worthwhile venture. Curle suspects that their reluctance may soon diminish somewhat, but still the message seems clear: unlike steel mills and dams, education in underdeveloped countries in the near future will be obliged to claim internal funds as its major source of support.

In this matter of making economic and educational plans for underdeveloped countries, there is an obvious conflict between their short-run and long-run requirements. Curle mentioned that, in the long run, these countries want and need regular educational systems which begin working with children when they are young and continue the process formally for a number of years. He also noted, however, that during the near future, perhaps the next ten or fifteen years, their educational needs are somewhat different, particularly as a consequence of their desire to initiate rapid economic growth as soon as possible. The majority of people upon whom their economic performance depends in the next few years are already beyond the school age. Thus, if education is to be a tool for rapidly increasing productivity, it must consist of a concrete program of vocational and, perhaps, on-the-job training for adults. Initially, such an educational endeavor can only go forward somewhat at the expense of the more long-run objective of expanding a conventional school system.

People tend to separate the outlets for a developing country's resources into arbitrary categories, which often turn out, upon careful examination, to be rather artificial and, in some cases, misleading distinctions. Health and education are convenient examples of the general thought. Although realistically a country may have the opportunity to build either a hospital or a school, it is also true, as Professor Harris suggested, that there is a strict limit to the rational precautions which people will take to guard their health before they have been educated to a certain minimum level. Because of local taboos, for example, it is virtually impossible to convince pregnant women in parts of West Africa to eat eggs, even though they may provide the most readily available protein and be essential to their own and their unborn babies' health. Other examples could but need not be cited to substantiate this general point: categories like health and education are not as independent as they might at first blush appear, and in order to achieve progress, underdeveloped countries must improve along a number of fronts concurrently. This notion obviously does not mean that all women should be trained as bacteriologists, but it does suggest that elementary hygiene must be taught as a part of the educational program if standards of health are to improve.

It is sometimes assumed that almost none of an underdeveloped country's native citizens possesses a university degree. In many of these countries such is the case, but it is not true for all of them. One of India's major domestic problems, for example, is its superabundance of people who are quite thoroughly educated and yet unemployed. Curle blames this situation on the fact that, in the past, too many Indians, when given the opportunity to obtain a higher education, elected to enter law, which was already overcrowded, rather than some other field in which qualified people were in short supply. Whatever the reason, however, the fact remains that the classic notion of a country in which the shortage of educated people of any sort forms a bottleneck and restrains economic growth is only part of the picture of underdevelopment. Another part relates to the country where it is necessary to increase the rate of growth in order for the economy to be able to absorb the hordes of people who are currently educated but unemployed. This latter situation is at least similar to the problem which many fully industrialized and, in that sense, developed nations also face, though there is little to be gained from carrying the analogy too far.

Finally, Yudelman said that underdeveloped countries' most fundamental current need is a supply of manpower experts who can, when they know a nation's aims, tell its planners the quantity and types of education which they ought to provide. By having this information available, countries could make their plans for economic development and education in a somewhat more rational and therefore less inherently wasteful way than many of them now appear to do, and the desirability of such an outcome hardly seems disputable.

Part II:

Challenges in Educational Planning

6. Learning Ability and the Superior Student

PAPER BY . . . *John B. Carroll*
Professor of Education and Director of the Laboratory for Research in Instruction, Harvard University

It is a matter of common observation that individuals differ in their capacity to be educated. But perhaps these differences are only apparent. Perhaps a sublimely able educator, applying the best fruits of psychological and pedagogical knowledge, could discover a uniform way to educate all children to a common standard of excellence. In the present state of our knowledge, this possibility is so fantastic that we may as well dismiss it from serious consideration, though I shall touch on a watered-down version of it later.

Having disposed of that possibility, we must admit that individual differences in educability are inevitable, and we must take some account of them in our educational policy. In fact, the question of how to handle these individual differences is one of the cardinal questions of educational policy. There is even some question whether we *should* wish to educate all children to a common standard of excellence. If there were no innate differences in individuals' educability, society would probably try to create some. Without wishing to raise difficult questions of value, I must point out that individual differences, in ability and other traits, seem to serve the purpose of a society in which specialization and division of labor are central to the economic structure.

All systems of education are based on certain implicit or explicit theories of individual difference in educability. Even when they proclaim that educational opportunities are made equal for all, there is an implied premise that individuals differ in their ability to take advantage of the opportunities. (They do not say that educational *achievements* are made equal for all.) And where educational opportunities are made deliberately unequal—for example, under South African *apartheid*—the opportunities are likely to be based on real or imagined differences in educability.

Regardless of avowals about equality of educational opportunities, there may be subtle variations in the way individual differences are handled. We may illustrate this point by contrasting the educational theories of the United States and the Soviet Union. Both nations affirm that educational opportunities are to be made equal, that individuals of like capacity should have like opportunity. In practice, of course, educational opportunities in both countries are associated with social status, geographical region and, in some cases, sex, race and nationality.

In the United States, most educational theory assumes that capacities for education vary widely, and it is taken for granted that educational opportunities should be distributed approximately in proportion to capacity. In the Soviet Union, on the other hand, the ideological line asserts that there are no such things as innate capacities. Psychological tests and even objective examinations are strictly eschewed as instruments of a reactionary bourgeois theory of innate individual differences. Yet the school system in the Soviet Union, from all accounts, has approximately the same degree of selectivity that characterizes the American school system. Despite an examination system which we could consider absurdly permissive and unreliable, Soviet educators find a way to recognize and promote talent and, at the same time, to close their doors to students who are not able to profit from advanced education.[1]

A dramatic example of the way in which a theory of individual differences may shape a school system is to be seen by contrasting the British and American systems of secondary education. Let us look first at the situation in Britain. In 1941 the president of the Board of Education of the United Kingdom appointed a committee headed by Sir Cyril Norwood, president of St. John's College, Oxford, and chairman of the Secondary School Examinations Council. The committee submitted its report in 1943, recommending that a tripartite system of secondary schools be established.[2]

The first type of school was to be the so-called grammar schools, embodying mainly the traditional liberal-arts curriculum and leading the student normally to a university. The second type was to be technical schools, devoted to the needs of pupils "whose interests and abilities lie markedly in the field of applied science or applied art." Finally, there were to be what were euphemistically called modern schools, with curricula designed for the pupil who "deals more easily with concrete things than with ideas." The type of pupil for whom modern schools were deemed appropriate was described in a curious sort of double talk: "He may have much ability, but it will be in the realm of facts. He is interested in things as they are. He finds little attraction in the past or in the slow disentanglement of causes or movements. His mind must turn its knowledge or its curiosity to immediate test, and his test is essentially practical . . ." and so forth. In short, modern schools are for pupils who have neither the abilities nor the interests that would suit them for the grammar or technical schools.

Many of the recommendations of the Norwood Report were actually put into practice in the post-war period, and they are still operative in spite of considerable criticism. The system gave rise to the famous "eleven-plus" examinations—that is, examinations given to children finishing the primary schools, at approximately age eleven, to determine the sort of school in which each should next matriculate. The Norwood Report recommended that teachers should be largely responsible for making this decision and that their views should be supplemented, where necessary, by the use of intelligence tests; but evidently the difficulties of administering a system based on teachers' judgments compelled school administrators to base their decisions primarily on the tests, with their greater reliability and objectivity. The Norwood Report also recommended that, for the most part, the three types of schools should be housed separately; I understand that this recommendation has been generally carried into practice.

The Norwood Report was based on a typological theory of individual differences. It appears to have assumed that children can be sorted into three groups. Although the report makes no reference to any scientific evidence for such a typological theory, the members of the committee may have been influenced by certain ideas then current among British psychologists to the effect that there are two major dimensions of intelligence, verbal and practical. The committee apparently jumped to the conclusion that these two dimensions of intelligence represent types and that therefore types of schools should be established to cater to them, one type of school for each type of intelligence. This was not, however, an accurate understanding of the theory about verbal and practical intelligence. As Sir Cyril Burt, a British psychologist, explained in a searching criticism of the Norwood Report, by far the major amount of variation in ability can probably be accounted for by one dimension, often called "g", or general intelligence.[3] Verbal intelligence and practical intelligence are nothing more than specializations of ability—ripples, as it were, on the overall wave of general intelligence. Thinking that children could be usefully sorted into types was a mistake, for many children are specialized in several directions at once—for example, in both verbal and practical intelligence.

It is very likely that, in practice, the assumptions of the Norwood Report are ignored and that the British tripartite system of secondary schooling is actually based largely on three arbitrary levels of general intelligence. The major determinant of what kind of school a child gets into is, in fact, an examination which reflects his general intelligence. That is, it reflects his accumulated skill in understanding language, manipulating ideas and solving problems of various kinds.

In contrast to the British system, secondary education as practiced in the United States is best represented by what James B. Conant has called the comprehensive high school, and it may be said to reflect a multidimensional theory of individual differences. While overall brightness or general intelligence is recognized as a major dimension of educability, educators also recognize that children may have many specialized talents which are largely independent of general intelligence. They also recognize, I believe, that children of high general intelligence are not necessarily strong in all aspects of academic school work; they may, for example, have weakness in mathematics or in foreign languages. Thus, although children may tend to sort themselves into different streams—the college-oriented stream, the stream vearing towards business and practical affairs, the stream directed to the mechanical arts and trades and so on—there is considerable crossing over between streams, and students take courses in a variety of streams. For this reason, there is an obvious advantage in having all the streams housed pretty much under the same roof.

Scientific descriptive studies of human abilities appear to support a multidimensional theory of individual differences, as against a typological theory. That is to say, abilities and capacities vary simultaneously in a number of relatively independent dimensions. Cognitive abilities, however—that is, all the abilities which involve the intellectual operations of the mind—tend to be somewhat correlated, and a favored interpretation of these findings (though not the only possible one) is that one dimension, called general intelligence, accounts for this correlation. We must keep in mind that "ability" is only an abstraction inferred from the fact that people exhibit different levels of performance on psychological tests and other similar tasks. "Educability" is also an abstraction, originating from the fact that children differ in the degree to which they become educated, even when they are exposed to apparently identical school experiences.

Let us assume for the moment that children differ inherently in their capacity to be educated in various sorts of ways. This creates a tremendous problem for education. If children differ in the ages at which they will become ready for various levels of education, the schools must take some account of this complication. One response is to treat children as if they shared a single course of development; American schools have embodied this response to a degree, in their policy of uniform promotion whereby most children simply advance through the grades without either skipping or failing to be promoted. But this policy is not supported by any convincing scientific evidence. The justification which is usually offered is that American children are somehow better off if they are kept with their age-mates throughout their schooling.

Another response to the problem of differential rates of development is to accelerate studies for the abler student and retard them for the slower than average pupil. If this policy were carried to its logical extreme, it might become very difficult to coordinate the varied programs of students working at individual rates of progress. The school might be forced to teach every student in private tutorial sessions. But a moderate degree of acceleration for groups of abler student has been found feasible and desirable. Miriam Goldberg, a writer who has been studying gifted students and their handling for several years, pointed out ·that not a single study has shown any harm at all coming from this kind of moderate acceleration.[4] Yet, until a few years ago, it was extremely difficult to find it anywhere in American schools. One argument against acceleration was that studies of ability grouping showed very little advantage for such grouping procedures. In those studies, however, ability grouping was only rarely accompanied by a sufficient differentiation in curriculum to make any difference in what the pupils learned. Unfortunately, I am not able to cite any very dramatic instances where there was a differentiation of curriculum—but that is another matter.

Another kind of response to the problem of individual differences is to provide varying degrees of enrichment in the curriculum, on the theory that bright children can at least be exposed to a wider range of educational experiences, even if they are not to taste experience at a higher or more advanced level of difficulty. One suspects, however, that enrichment is sometimes another word for padding. Personally, I should prefer to see enrichment used only in conjunction with acceleration. The fears of many observers that serious social and emotional problems will occur under programs of acceleration are evidently almost totally groundless. The problems under acceleration are no more frequent or severe than under the traditional lockstep plan of uniform promotion, for this latter plan imposes its own stresses, both on the bright child who gets impatient or bored and on the dull child who is too soon left behind.

I have been assuming thus far, for the sake of exposition, that individual differences in educability are invariant, that they never change throughout the lives of the individuals concerned. Lately, however, we have become aware that this conception of the nature of individual differences is due for a thorough re-examination. There may indeed be genetic determinants of individual differences, but the role of learning and experience, particularly very early experience, has assumed a larger place in our thinking.

Let me illustrate this point by recounting an imaginary episode in the life of a psychometrician. The psychometrician is presented with two children whom he is to test for reasoning ability. The children are of the same age; let us even assume they are identical twins. Upon testing, one child is found to be far superior to the other. He can solve a certain class of problems with great ease, while the other child stumbles and falters. By using a sufficient variety of problems, the psychometrician assures himself that the better child has not been coached and provided with pat answers. The child really does show more so-called ability in answering these problems. He concludes that the child who performed well is far brighter than the other, and he might even convert the results of the test into an IQ differential, if the test was part of a regular standardized series.

At this point, enter another psychologist, an experimental psychologist who is interested in the science of learning. On hearing the results of the psychometric test, he objects violently. He too had worked with these children, and there had been no difference whatsoever between them in innate ability. He had, however, used one child in a special kind of learning experiment, in which the child was taught to solve problems of the class represented by the psychometrician's test. More precisely, he had allowed this child to learn how to learn, simply by having him practice solving problems of this type. He was planning to get around to the other child later, and he was confident that the second child would learn to perform equally well.

As a matter of fact, this episode could well have happened, for I am recounting the essence of a famous experiment conducted by the psychologist Harry Harlow.[5] Harlow and his associates conducted virtually the same experiment with chimpanzees and with children. In each case, they demonstrated that the subjects learned to learn, simply by being put in a suitable learning situation in which, trial after trial, they were presented with simple problems which required them to identify cues that would produce rewards. In one part of the experiment, for example, the monkey or the child was supposed to figure out that, in order to get a piece of food, he had to select the block with stripes. There were many similar problems, and the cue, or discriminative stimulus, varied with the same problem. In early trials the identification came slowly; but later on, identification was nearly always made with the second setting of the problem.

The lesson to be drawn from this account is that many of the individual differences which have been supposed to be innately determined may actually be acquired. They may be due to accidents of personal history which lead to profitable learning experiences for some children and to little or no learning for others. We may further suppose that small differences which happen to appear very early in life may have long-term effects which become magnified many times over.

If this account is correct, the implication for education is that learning experiences of the widest variety should be encouraged at the earliest practicable ages. I am not suggesting that we try to force children to learn beyond the limits set by normal maturation, but I believe that opportunities for learning at critical times can be made much greater than has been commonly thought. There is evidence, for example, that the kinds of toys we provide our children in their first two or three years of life have an impact on the kinds of abilities they develop. We are now doing a much better job than we previously did of teaching children, among other things, to perceive and manipulate three-dimensional objects.

The role of learning as a factor in shaping individual differences is also seen in the curious fact, which has been studied by a number of psychologists, that current mental age is practically uncorrelated with the next increment of mental age.[6] In plain English, even though you may know a child's mental age today, you cannot accurately predict how much more mental age he will acquire in the next year. He may acquire a great deal, or he may acquire little; the outcome depends upon the kinds of experiences to which he will be exposed. On the average, we expect children to acquire one year of mental age during each calendar year; this is how mental tests are standardized for children in the aggregate. But the system does not enable us to make predictions for each individual child. Thus the mental age of a person at maturity—say, at age twenty-one—is simply the accumulation of a random series of virtually uncorrelated increments.

It begins to appear that the British system of eleven-plus examinations, which assumes that a child's intelligence remains more or less constant, is unfounded. Indeed, Philip Vernon, another Britist psychologist, showed that the degree to which a British boy is able to improve his IQ-test score during his secondary school year is strongly associated with the type of school to which he is sent.[7] If he is sent to a grammar school, he might gain quite a bit; if he is sent to a modern school, anything might happen. IQ scores may not be subject to short-term changes, but they are subject to long-term effects if stimulation towards intellectual activity is applied or withheld over a long time. The same holds true for educability, insofar as it is correlated with IQ.

There are other straws in the wind. The advancing technology of behavioral change (this is Professor B. F. Skinner's term) suggests that learning and performance can be markedly improved by proper techniques of instruction. We are finding that children of apparently diverse talents learn and perform in surprisingly similar ways and at similar rates when they are allowed to learn through carefully programed courses of study. This is a tentative conclusion from recent work; our evidence on this point is not yet completely satisfactory. We have a suspicion, too, that many cases of reading disability, arithmetical disability and so on may be attributable to improper teaching when these skills are first introduced. One is also reminded of the hypothesis, which Jerome Bruner stated in *The Process of Education,* that "any subject can be taught effectively in some intellectually honest form to any child at any stage of development." This is only a hypothesis—unless the ambiguity of statement makes it merely a self-fulfilling prophecy—but the promise of markedly improved learning which it implies is wholly legitimate.

Let me conclude with two thoughts. The first is that, in the light of present knowledge, we must adopt a more flexible view of the nature and extent of individual differences in educability. We must take individual differences where we find them and capitalize on them. As one specific goal, let us try to identify talented children as early as possible and place them in specially favorable learning environments. But this means that we must improve the early learning environments of *all* children so that we can select those children who appear best able to profit from them.

My other thought is that, at the same time, we should not be too ready to regard human talent as immutable. The selection of talented children must be a continuous process throughout all levels of education; a child who does not appear talented in one round of selection may conceivably appear so in a later round, months or years later. Not only should we recognize the role of accidents of personal history in shaping an individual's talents, but we should also have an abiding faith in human perfectibility, at least within the confines to which we devote ourselves in education.

REFERENCES

1. Henry Chauncey, "Some Observations on Soviet Education," *Proceeding, 1958 Invitational Conference on Testing Problems* (Princeton, New Jersey: Educational Testing Service, 1959), pp. 71-85.
2. Board of Education, *Curriculum and Examinations in Secondary Schools; Report of the Committee of the Secondary School Examination Council Appointed by the President of the Board of Education in 1941.* (London: H. M. Stationery Office, 1943).
3. Cyril Burt, "The Education of the Young Adolescent: the Psychological Implications of the Norwood Report," *British Journal of Educational Psychology,* XIII (1943), pp. 126-140.
4. Miriam L. Goldberg, "Recent Research on the Talented," *Teachers College Record,* LX (1958), pp. 150-163.
5. Harry F. Harlow, "The Formation of Learning Sets, *Psychological Review,* LVI (1949), pp. 51-65.
6. See, for example, John E. Anderson, "The Prediction of Terminal Intelligence from Infant and Preschool Tests," *39th Yearbook, National Society for the Study of Education,* Part I (1940), pp. 385-403.
7. Philip Vernon, "Education and the Psychology of Individual Differences," *Harvard Educational Review,* XXVIII (1958), pp. 91-104.

PAPER BY . . . *John M. Stalnaker*
President, National Merit Scholarship Corporation

The identification of highly able students is the chief purpose of the National Merit Scholarship Program. This program came into being about two years before the launching of Sputnik I, which aroused a surge of interest in able students and triggered what amounts to a revolution in the formal educational pattern in this country.

The Merit Program has a certain general social significance resulting from the fact that about 17,000 high schools, enrolling ninety to ninety-five per cent of all the secondary-school students in the country, take part in the program. In March 1964 we tested approximately 800,000 students. Never before, so far as I know, have so many able students been tested at a single grade level. The 9,000 Merit Scholars appointed in the first nine annual programs have enrolled in about 400 colleges and universities.

The Merit Program is concerned with able students throughout the land. It is the champion of able students as such, regardless of their college preferences or curricular interests; in that sense it is unique. We strive to increase interest in these students by the public, the secondary schools and the colleges. If we can judge from the interest which the press displays in the Merit Scholars, public interest in able students generally is widespread at the present time.

The Merit Program does not advocate any particular type of treatment of superior students. In fact, we meticulously keep our hands off such matters. We do not advise or counsel Merit Scholars on educational matters, even when they request us to do so. We refer them to their schools or to their colleges in the belief that these institutions are better able to offer sound advice than we are. Our functions are to identify able students in every state, to make them visible and to help create a climate of public opinion in which they can thrive.

At the same time, we are studying the selection techniques being used by ourselves and by others, the backgrounds from which the able come, their interests, how they select their colleges, how the colleges they select differ and the interaction between the students and the colleges.

I want to tell you something about what we are learning, but you will understand, of course, that these comments are preliminary and subject to change as we learn more. Some of my remarks may be provocative; if they are, I hope they will stimulate further consideration by others. Much of our research, dealing as it does with large and important issues, is more suggestive than conclusive, more exploratory than definitive. We are working in areas where little is really known and where significant work in the past has been sparse. Also, we are dealing with very dynamic situations. We are dealing with growing and changing boys and girls, with an extensive and varied educational system in flux and with a national temper regarding education that is somewhat unsteady at this time.

Let me quickly sketch some background. We are all aware that in the last decade, considerable concern and attention has been given to the discovery of the "talented" student, who is generally taken to be an academically oriented student of superior intellectual ability. Such students are spoken of as our most precious natural resource, and we can probably agree that they are. Many figures are cited to show how large a proportion of the talented are "lost" (that is, did not enter college), and salvage programs of various types have been proposed by the Federal Government and by others.

But until quite recently, very little attention has been paid to what we actually mean by talent or to how it should be developed and utilized. Prestige colleges, for example, have gone to some lengths to attract bright, conforming, grade-getting students, sometimes emulating the techniques of seduction perfected by their departments of athletics. Until the past few years, however, few colleges have shown much concern about what happens to this talent once it has been captured and brought into the institution. Even today, many colleges devote more attention to recruiting able students than to developing their talent after they enroll. Indeed, the evidence suggests that the students often contribute more to strengthening the colleges than the colleges do to developing the students.

In this regard, I was struck by a point made in a report by Wilbur J. Bender, who retired a few years ago as dean of admissions at Harvard. His report, I believe, will be widely quoted in the future because it says so many different things and therefore lends itself to being quoted by people with diverse points of view. The part that lends itself to my argument is Mr. Bender's statement: "I believe that the present student body at Harvard is much the ablest academically in our history. I have more doubts about the ability of Harvard College under present conditions to give these men an education worthy of their quality than I have doubt about them as men or as scholars."

It is interesting to note, too, that most colleges treat their top intellectual talent very differently from the way they treat their top athletic talent. In the realm of intercollegiate athletics, men with superior talent are separated from the rest after appropriate tests and trials. They are given special, intensive and usually very expensive instruction by the best teachers—in some places, they are even called professors—who utilize all known effective teaching aids. The first team, you may be sure, is not taught by graduate students, or teaching fellows, to whom teaching is a means of eking out a living with as little effort as possible while pursuing a graduate degree. The players, for their part, know that they must work hard if they are to stay on the first team. Our institutions of higher education (unlike a few high schools), have no intellectual teams in which at least some representatives of the general public, the press, the donors, the alumni and the state legislators could show anything like the interest they show in athletic teams. As a nation we have not, in general, favored Little Leagues of the mind.

Lest we lose hope, let us also note that on the horizon are signs of favorable developments. These developments are not occurring without cause. Rather, as so often happens, necessity has motivated action. At least three factors are involved. First, the number of second-ary-school graduates is increasing very rapidly. Second, more than half of all high school graduates are seeking a college education, and the proportion is increasing each year. Colleges cannot absorb them all. And third, the pursuit of excellence is earning increased attention.

Institutions of higher education are accordingly undergoing changes. Many state universities which have heretofore admitted any high school graduate from the state are now effectively discouraging applicants whose grade records or test scores appear unpromising. In most colleges—and especially in the prestige institutions the pressures surrounding admissions are growing. In response, the standards for admission are becoming more rigorous, and this change is felt directly by the high schools and their students. The students are forced to take seriously whatever subjects the colleges demand that they take seriously. The pressure undoubtedly is on, and the rapid and wide-spread growth of the advanced-placement program is evidence that high schools—at least, those which are better equipped and staffed —are becoming concerned with able students. Another such sign is the increased offerings of intellectual subjects and foreign languages at the high school level.

At the college level, little attention has been given to the able student in the past, but this situation is also changing to some extent. One can predict with reasonable certainty that the close scrutiny (and the accompanying criticism) which the secondary schools are now receiving will soon focus also on the colleges. I was amused at one meeting, for example, to hear a top official from an organization of secondary schools declare that the colleges are not doing an effective job of guiding the exceptionally able students whom the secondary schools send them. It is quite a change to have representatives from the secondary schools begin to be highly critical of the colleges.

At another conference I attended, a secondary-school counselor had the temerity to point out that, although the colleges do not hesitate to demand a great deal of information from the secondary schools about their students, the colleges in turn give very little information to school counselors about what the colleges have to offer to the ablest students. These are signs that the tide is turning and that the colleges, particularly as their tuitions increase, will come in for some vigorous criticism, both fair and unfair.

Merit Scholars select their own colleges for reasons which they believe sufficient. Once they enter their chosen institutions, we discourage but do not prevent them from transferring. In fact, about ten per cent of the Merit Scholars do change colleges at some time during their undergraduate years. In one case, the lad requesting a transfer explained that he was the top man by a considerable margin in every course he took except physical education. He claimed he was learning nothing, and he therefore wanted to change colleges. This explanation did not sound quite right, and we asked him to request his dean to confirm it before we would endorse his transfer.

Surprisingly, the assistant dean wrote to confirm what the student had said. He explained that the institution was overcrowded and that it had to devote its major efforts to the mass of deficient students who required remedial work. Since this lad was terribly bright and had intellectual interests, said the assistant dean, he really ought to transfer to another institution. Here, then, is a university—and a large one at that—which has no real place for a student with intellectual interests. One college official, at least, saw that such a student did not belong there.

Fortunately, this example is not the whole story. Colleges are becoming aware of the need to devote more time and effort to their able students. One piece of evidence is the astonishingly rapid growth of honors programs, especially in institutions which accept students with a wide range of ability, as most of our large state institutions do. What the state institutions are doing is especially important because they are now educating a large and increasing percentage of all students in higher education. A number of these institutions now identify especially able students before they reach the campus and place them in honors programs where they receive special consideration and privileges. Many Merit Finalists are participating in such programs, and our reports indicate general satisfaction with them. The honors programs at the University of Kansas, Michigan State and the University of Colorado are notable examples, and many other state institutions are making equally successful efforts along the same lines. Such programs can set the pace for their institutions and, in the long run, have a substantial influence on the tone of the institutions generally.

The Merit Program is helping to identify students for such programs by supplying to each of a number of colleges a list of students who have scored within the top 35,000 in the country on its tests and who have designated that college as a first or second choice. In addition, the Merit Program is cooperating with several states by helping each to identify its most able students, so that it may offer them special attention and encouragement to further their education.

In 1964 the Merit Program awarded about 1700 four-year scholarships. Further, each year, by a letter of commendation or by a certificate of merit, the program gives recognition to the top 35,000 students, who constitute roughly two per cent of the high school graduating class. Although these letters and certificates are merely pieces of paper, they are tangible recognition of achievement and are regarded as such by students, schools and the press. The result is that special attention is given to these students, both within the school and in the broader community; and research indicates that such recognition has value. It seems to develop a greater self-confidence in the recipient; it encourages increased intellectual effort; and it results in the setting of higher long-range goals.

Parents are also impressed, as they should be, and tend to exert themselves more to see that their talented children are given a superior education. A few years ago, one parent wrote to us: "I knew my son was bright, but I didn't know he was this bright. Now we shall see that he receives the best that we can give him." Incidentally, in response to a routine question concerning the after-effects of winning recognition in the Merit Program, one lad responded: "Well, for one thing, it gave my teachers and principal the shock of their lives."

As I have said, the Merit Program does not advise students. This policy includes not giving them advice on what college to choose. On the other hand, we do study carefully where the group goes to college, how the colleges differ and what the outcomes of such interactions are. Since the Merit Scholars are selected from every state and from various socio-economic levels, one might expect them to distribute themselves fairly widely among America's roughly 1200 degree-granting institutions of higher learning. This is not the case, however. To date they have limited their selections to about four hundred colleges, and the concentration in a few colleges has been marked. About one third of the Merit Scholars enroll in a dozen institutions. Harvard alone has attracted ten per cent of the recipients; the other colleges popular with this group are (in order) Massachusetts Institute of Technology, Stanford, Radcliffe, Princeton, California Institute of Technology, Yale, Rice, University of Michigan, Oberlin, Swarthmore and Cornell. Michigan is the only state institution in the group (we consider Cornell private), and in many ways it behaves largely like a private university.

This concentration of Merit Scholars is reflected in the college preferences of the top 35,000 students. When we ask them as applicants where they would prefer to attend college if they win a scholarship, we find that one third of the men name ten colleges. The order in this "popularity poll" is Massachusetts Institute of Technology, Harvard, California Institute of Technology, Stanford, Princeton, Cornell, Yale, University of California at Berkeley, Notre Dame and the University of Michigan. A second state institution, California at Berkeley, appears on this list. The girls in this group of 35,000 are somewhat less concentrated in their preferences. The following institutions account for about a fifth of their votes: Radcliffe, Stanford, Cornell, Wellesley, University of Michigan, University of California at Berkeley, Oberlin, Smith, Swarthmore and Northwestern.

Such a popularity vote should not be interpreted to mean more than it really does. It does not show where the "best" education is offered, nor does it show which institution will most effectively meet the needs of any particular student. It simply shows where superior talent thinks it can get the most appropriate treatment at the present time.

What actually occurs is equally interesting. From time to time, individual Merit Scholars inform us through letters of their experiences. "I feel very lucky," one student wrote, "that the University of X [a not widely known but large Midwestern state institution] has turned out as well as it has and that the scholarship has enabled me to study here. Harvard is certainly not as much better than this university as the cost is higher. However, there are influences which taken together empower a man to contribute significantly to society, and it is precisely these that Harvard offers. . . ." He went on to justify a request for transferring to Harvard.

Another student planning to leave a prestige university for one much lower on the popularity list wrote: "I find that the intellectual pursuits around this university consume only a small fraction of my time and—due to the isolated nature of this community, the complete lack of automobiles, and my limited fianancial capability—I find that during the greatest percentage of my time I am, in a word, bored. I have tried participating in various campus activities, but none of them has succeeded in filling the void. . . . Although the academic life here is adequate, the atmosphere of the undergraduate life is not only not conducive to character building but actually destructive to moral and spiritual endeavors. Another reason [for wanting to transfer] is the lack of social life here. Although there is, to be sure, social life available, the expense of bringing in a girl precludes any more than very infrequent participation in this social life. . . ."

The college stated on its part: "Mr. Y is entitled to honorable dismissal. . . . While not brilliant, Y's academic record is good and he has no record of any disciplinary problems." This is the best that any university can say. But in this case there also is an important socio-economic factor to keep in mind. At this university, I would hazard the guess, the median income of the students' parents, including those of scholarship students, is upward of $20,000 a year. It may not be the ideal place for a poor boy from the Southwest to develop most rapidly. We authorized the transfer.

Another interesting case concerns a girl who wanted to transfer from one of the women's colleges high on the preferential list to a large state university in the Southwest. She wrote: "I feel that at the University of X there will be more real experience of life, that I will have to learn to get along in a place that is more like the world around me and not just a slice of the intellectual upper crust. . . . There will be less of an atmosphere of intellectual stimulation at the University of X, I am sure. This fact does not particularly bother me, for I shall be taking an advanced program, and

I feel that my own curiosity has been sufficiently aroused [so] that I can continue without the necessity of extraneous stimuli. . . . I do not mean to belittle the college where I now am. What this college has done for me in two years has been and will be invaluable. It has taught me to think clearly . . . and the value of knowledge as the springboard of creative thought. . . . Nevertheless I prefer to trade the atmosphere of intellectual stimulation for an atmosphere sensitive to and derived from the real communications of real persons."

In all such cases, the reasons given in support of the request to transfer are, in our opinion, not necessarily the basic ones. Students tend not to talk in these terms, but it is possible that being pushed over too many socio-economic barriers, with the help of a scholarship, may not result in the most productive type of education. A dean from a small prestige college on the West Coast reasons along these lines. In writing of a Merit Scholar's leaving his institution, he said: "I have some skepticism about the probability of a boy from a very depressed background vaulting over too many economic and social levels. . . . He was able to do our work academically, although with some effort. We were never able to push or pull him into any vigorous effort to be a part of the social life of the campus. I suspect the cultural jump was too great for him." But the dean then went on to describe the case of another Merit Scholar from an equally depressed background who became a campus leader.

Let me turn from illustrative cases to some of our research studies of colleges and students. We have found a great disparity in the institutional resources of colleges—disparities in the quality of the faculty and facilities, in the quality and nature of the admitted class and in the amount of money which the institution devotes to its educational program. Furthermore, we find some evidence that the rich institutions are getting richer and that the poor are getting poorer. In one study we contrasted a group of thirty high-endowment private colleges— (we used thirty to get some stability in the figures and to avoid getting only extreme cases) with a group of thirty low-endowment private institutions. These sixty institutions were drawn from a sample of 340 institutions. In the high-endowment sample, the average amount spent per student for educational purposes is almost $2000 a year; in the low-endowment sample, it is under $500. We find equally great discrepancies in comparing the high-budget and low-budget public institutions, some of the ratios being as large as 20-to-1.

Our research workers have been impressed also by the importance of the student input to the colleges. They do not believe that the institutions' contributions to students are of no importance, but they find that a careful study of the students admitted—their personality types and abilities, their family backgrounds and economic standings, the ambitions they bring with them and so on—will explain more about the institutions' educational products than can be learned by studying the particular characteristics of the institutions as such.

Let me give a single example. If one wants to determine the productivity of a college in terms of the proportion of its graduating class that will undertake professional education, such as the PHD, MD and LL.B. programs, the best index—and a very good one indeed —is the replies of the entering class, before the institution has had any influence on them, to the question, "Do you expect to study for an advanced degree?" It seems important that the best index we have found of an institution's productivity—if, on the basis of these findings, it can still be called that—is information obtained before the institution has had any direct effect on the students what-soever. In view of these findings, a wag might observe that by a judicious selection of students, where such is possible, an institution can effectively conceal its own weaknesses for years.

Conversely, given certain student bodies, no college—not even the best in instructional efficiency and potency—can hope to exert more than a modest influence in four years normally alotted to its efforts. After all, students attend college for only a very limited period. By the time a student enters college, a great deal of important groundwork has been laid. The college education must take off from the past development which the student brings with him and fit into his plans for the future.

One Merit Scholar, a Negro girl attending a West Coast prestige institution where she was doing B+ work, expressed this point forcefully:—

I have found university life to be intellectually stimu-lating and challenging. At the same time the fact of living in an isolated scholarly community is prone to produce an alienation from the realities of the outside world in which life is much more prosaic and unintellectual. While I enjoy participating in the idyllic existence of the university, I real-ize that success will not always be so easy. My purpose here is not becoming a scholar, but a lawyer. The university is a training ground; it is not life.

In our research efforts, we are making an attempt to characterize institutions and to type students. A tentative conclusion is that when a student goes to a college attracting a preponderance of students of his own type, he will achieve more (in the conventional sense) and change less than he otherwise would. His pattern will be reinforced. As might be expected, changes are greatest when a student enters an institution where his type is in the minority. If he can endure such a situation and even learn to enjoy it, chances are that he will learn and change.

We assume that a fundamental long-range objective of education is to help able, talented individuals become productive—that is, to assist them toward performing tasks with an excellence commensurate with their potential. It is eventual performance that counts, not one's grades in college. We believe that both an early recognition of a great variety of abilities, as well as a tolerance for variation of any kind from the group pattern, is essential for developing talent to a productive level.

Edwin H. Land of Polaroid, speaking in the realm of science, has pointed out that significant developments come from "some individual who has freed himself from a way of thinking that is held by his friends and associates who may be more intelligent, better educated, better disciplined, but who have not mastered the art of the clean look at the old, old knowledge." The average college, I think, has a long way to go before it will be able to encourage a great variety of talented youth to develop, each in his own way, the "fresh clean look at the old, old knowledge." But a survey of the total picture of higher education in America today indicates, I believe, that increasing efforts are being made to find the right path.

COMMENTARY

Russia discovered Sputnik and in response America discovered, within its educational system, defects which the nation is now attempting to correct. One tactic for achieving that goal has been to seek talent for education in the form of bright and enthusiastic students. The fact that the meaning of academic talent is elusive has impeded these efforts. Controversy about an appropriate definition is widespread, and even within the academic community itself students and faculty often disagree on the matter. In spite of such controversy, adopting an operational and useful definition of talent is an important task and, fortunately, not a hopeless one. Many influential groups have defined it rather arbitrarily—but usually in a widely accepted way—and then have simply proceeded to label certain students talented. Of these organizations the National Merit Scholarship Program (NMSP) is perhaps best known and is certainly America's most eminent academic talent scout. Its president, Mr. Stalnaker, has dealt with the program's activities. In the ensuing discussion, additional facts about the program were brought out; it makes some sense to cite that information now before mentioning several of the more general matters which the members of the seminar considered concerning superior students, higher educational institutions and public policy.

Merit Scholars have achieved an impressive academic record; they are doing far better than American students in general. Interestingly enough, they have shown a tendency both to elect initially and also to transfer into the more intellectually prestigious (as opposed to the more vocationally oriented) academic disciplines. For example, they tend to select economics over business administration and physics over electrical engineering. Another important indicator is the fact that the rate of dropouts for the group is extremely low. The national average is between forty and fifty per cent, the precise number depending upon the definition one adopts. For Merit Scholars the figure is seven per cent, and only about half of this group can properly be called academic failures. The other half leave school for reasons which, in Mr. Stalnaker's view, would make it wrong to label them failures, either academic or otherwise. One boy, for example, withdrew from MIT to devote his full time to studying music; and, of course, a number of girls have abandoned their studies for marriage.

The record looks especially impressive because Merit Scholars attend what are generally considered the best schools and thus voluntarily elect to compete with many of America's ablest students, students to whom those institutions themselves have awarded scholarships. Mr. Stalnaker suggested that, in such circumstances, one might expect the members of this latter group to have something of an advantage over the Merit Scholars, for in awarding their own scholarships, institutions are able to consider those characteristics of students which have historically tended to be conducive to success in the environments which they provide. In contrast, each Merit Scholar chooses his own college without receiving any suggestions from the program about where he might be well advised to matriculate. In brief, a student who receives a scholarship from his college knows that some reliable and interested authority judges that he is well suited for that college, whereas Merit Scholars do not enjoy such security, although, to be sure, one must consider this point with caution because in many cases a Merit Scholar might well have won one of his college's own scholarships.

In elaborating on where Merit Scholars go to college, Mr. Stalnaker reported that socio-economic factors seem to exert significant influence upon their selections. There are exceptions, but in general, students from the lower socio-economic levels tend to select the low-cost state institutions, whereas those from the upper strata seem to favor the high-tuition private institutions. Another important point is an amplification of Mr. Stalnaker's findings that the top two per cent of recent male high-school graduates select Massachusetts Institute of Technology, Harvard, California Institute of Technology, Stanford, Princeton, Cornell, Yale, University of California at Berkeley, Notre Dame and the University of Michigan, in that order, as the colleges of their first choice. With the exceptions of Cal Tech, all of these institutions are large. Mr. Stalnaker emphasized that this outcome is directly attributable to the index of popularity which was used: a raw absolute score. Suppose, now, that one were to think that, instead of the absolute score, the relevant index for gauging popularity was some measure of the excess of demand for an institution's services over its capacity. This is certainly an appropriate approach to the problem. Suppose, to be specific, one used (as Merit's researchers in fact did) this index: the total vote an institution receives divided by the size of its freshman class. This index produces a new list of winners in the popularity contest. In order they are: Cal Tech, MIT, Harvard, Rice, Amherst, Swarthmore, Reed, Stanford, Princeton, University of Chicago, Oberlin, Yale, Columbia, Dartmouth, Carleton and Wesleyan. Moreover, it should come as no surprise that, whereas on the first list colleges that may be called small are only one out of ten, on this second list they are seven out of sixteen.

In general, the Merit Program has produced extremely satisfactory results, but, as Stalnaker himself noted, they are not yet ideal. One mildly disturbing matter is the fact that ten per cent of the Merit Scholars transfer from one college to another. The clear tendency for the direction of transfer is away from the prestige private institutions and toward state universities. Taken alone, this fact might be a powerful piece of propaganda. Therefore, before the supporters of public higher education exploit this statistic too much, it is well to point out that, although the fact as stated is true, there is something of the character of a statistical mirage about it. The important point is that Merit Scholars are highly concentrated initially in private institutions. Even if the desire to transfer were randomly distributed among all Merit Scholars, the statistics would still reveal an exodus from the private towards the public institutions. Thus the statistic is somewhat less meaningful than it might appear at first sight.

Apart from the politics of public versus private sector, there is some interest in explaining why, in the aggregate, ten per cent of all Merit Scholars transfer, for that number is larger than the program's officers might both hope for and expect. Certainly, part of the answer lies in the counsel which the Merit Scholars receive. The program itself gives none, and with a very few exceptions, that which the high schools offer is, according to Stalnaker, of poor quality. This set of circumstances led Dr. Anne Roe, lecturer on education at Harvard University, to question the program's wisdom in not guiding its scholars and to wonder what the rationale for this policy may be. Stalnaker replied that it is twofold. First, it is political. He argued that for NMSP to start expressing candid opinions, either publicly or privately, about the quality of various colleges would be tantamount to the program's risking self-destruction. His second point was that since the majority of the scholars live far from Merit's headquarters, any counseling which the program did would have to be carried on by letter, and he and his colleagues object strongly to mail-order guidance.

Dr. Roe acknowledged the soundness of Stalnaker's reasoning but still argued that, in the light of some of the program's plans for the near future, abstaining from guidance may be a luxury it can no longer afford. In addition to their existing awards, the program's officers plan to offer soon some scholarships on the basis of less strictly objective criteria than the ones now operative: exceptionally high grades in high school and outstanding performance on objective tests. These additional awards are designed for students who have been somewhat nonconforming in school and who are thus not fortified with a brilliant record on paper. Already the program offers some scholarships on this basis; the plan is to offer more. Dr. Roe felt that this idea is splendid but also that it has certain dangers for the program and its reputation. She allowed that without much doubt there are important areas in which the potential achievements of individual members of this nonconforming group exceed those of the more conventional, grade-oriented award winners, but she also was certain that their over-all rate of dropouts will be larger than the Merit Scholars' present average of seven per cent. It seems inevitable, she emphasized, that this new group will contain more than its fair share of misdirected genius, and in order to help insure that these people fulfill their high potential, she concluded that it may be either necessary or advisable for the program to withdraw its self-imposed ban on advising its scholars.

Another matter closely related to academic criteria is geographic distribution. In dealing with it, the program's officers have learned an important point of public relations: "quota" is more or less a dirty word, but "representation" is acceptable. Thus they must speak of a state's representation, not of its quota. The basic question about geographic distribution is: should the awards be for the entire nation undivided, or should they be allocated by state, so many for California, so many for Montana, and so on? This problem arises because academic talent, at least as the Merit Program measures it, is not distributed equitably—i.e., in proportion to population—among all states. In some states, even the top few per cent of all high-school seniors are below what the program considers acceptable standards; in other states, the top few per cent do not begin to exhaust the stock of qualified talent. The program's officers must achieve a compromise between the desires of their financial supporters to underwrite the educations of only America's ablest students and their own knowledge that it is probably politically advisable for their organization, which is called "National," to give some recognition even to residents of states with very low standards of education. In general, they try not to make any students suffer because of the educational inadequacies of the states where they live. The actual compromise in current use is to award letters of commendation on a national basis but to distribute certificates of merit and the National Merit Scholarships on a representative basis by state. Thus in New York there may be five thousand letters of commendation, in Mississippi maybe fifty; but there will be roughly the same number of semifinalists and certificate of merit winners in both states, relative to the population of high school seniors.

Having thus discussed the Merit Program, those present then proceeded to consider some more general matters concerning the American educational system's treatment of superior talent. There was a widespread feeling that the system is wasteful because many promising high-school students never enter college. It is important to understand whose education the country is really sacrificing in this way. Some say glibly that half of the students in the nation's top quartile do not go to college. Although this may be true as a statistical fact, it conveys an impression which is not altogether correct. Mr. Stalnaker pointed out that nearly all of America's very best students—those in the top two or three per cent—do go to college. Where the nation is losing valuable talent is from levels below the very top, from perhaps the eighth to the twenty-fifth percentile. In short, the loss involves primarily the very adequate, not the very brilliant students. In one way or another the truly superior students manage to fend for themselves. Indeed, the colleges fight to get them, and their opportunities to receive financial aid are much greater than the chances of those students one notch down. From a policy point of view, America's greatest concern should be with that second group of candidates for a college education; and in the future, organizations which want to locate highly educable students, whose college training it would be worthwhile to subsidize, will find the lower two thirds of the top one quarter of the distribution of high-school students very fertile hunting ground indeed. Of course, NMSP has defined its own task —and, incidentally, a task which those present agreed that it is carrying on with brilliance—somewhat differently. It must therefore leave this latter aspect of the over-all business of financing American education to other worthy and likewise public-spirited organizations.

The discussion's center of gravity shifted from society to the individual. It is rather widely believed that the nation loses when a potentially good student does not go to college and gains when he or she does go. But what about the gains and losses of going versus not going accruing to the student himself? Answering this question is difficult, for it involves defining the educational product of a college. This topic has evoked much talk and no definitive conclusions, but, as Stalnaker began to outline in his paper, the Merit Program's researchers have presented some very interesting tentative answers. Their work, as Stalnaker reported it, suggests that a college's input of students is a better measure of its product than are such conventional indices as the number of books in its library, its salary scale and so on. This is a very dramatic finding, of extreme interest in itself and also pregnant with implications for public policy. Spelling out its precise meaning is therefore vitally important, and a homely analogy may aid in doing so. In an approximate sense, a college is something like a Minute Car Wash garage. If the proverbial man from Mars were to stand before such a garage and observe the shining cars which emerged, he would undoubtedly conclude that they were made inside. In fact, of course, if he were to look at the entrance instead of only at the exit, he would see that functioning cars, albeit dusty ones, enter the garage under their own power. He would thus view the Minute Car Wash in true rather than glorified perspective. There is a limit to how far one can profitably carry this analogy, but the major point seems clear: what Merit's researchers are in effect advising is to look at the college's entrance, as it were, as well as at its exit in the form of the graduation procession. In simple terms, they are saying this: if you want to know what a person will be like after he graduates from college, looking at him before he enters will provide a large part of the answer.

Stalnaker did not intend to suggest that a college gives an individual little. Rather, he argued that the college may give a great deal but that if it admits those who can absorb its offerings readily, the graduates will be "better" than they would be if it admits those who are resistant to its intellectual bill of fare. The input, he stressed, does in large measure determine the output, but the output can still differ significantly from the input. Suppose for the moment, however, that we believed the more extreme claim, that a college gives an individual little that he did not have before he attended, would we then be obliged to admit that America's higher educational system is useless? Not really, argued some members of the seminar. They maintained that irrespective of what benefits the college gives the student directly, it can still perform the valuable social function of labeling him. It can say roughly, "This student has performed all the tasks we have given him satisfactorily, passed all our tests, etc. Therefore we give him to you, society, with the assurance that he has at least a certain competence and energy level." The college, in other words, serves the community by placing its seal of approval, its warranty, on the student.

There is some merit in this scheme, but several of the participants noted that it also has two crippling shortcomings. First, it is too absurdly expensive. Society does not want to pay the cost of a four-year college education only to have the student labeled and nothing more. Second, the entire scheme rests upon the implicit assumption that getting through college is a rigorous chore, that anyone who can manage to do it is necessarily of potentially great value to society. Stalnaker argued that this assumption is not perfectly valid. There are many colleges where simply satisfying the academic requirements is not very difficult for the student once he has gained admission, and therefore one must be cautious in attaching more than nominal significance to the fact that someone is a college graduate.

In fact, Americans often fail to exercise this sort of caution. In spite of the serious flaws in using the higher educational system to label students for their potential employers, this is still one of the primary tasks which society assigns to its institutions of higher learning. Often, all too much of the benefit a student receives from his college is the privilege of using its name, sometimes almost appending it to his own in a manner remarkably reminiscent of the Homeric simile. Odysseus was long-tried, and John Doe is Princeton-educated. The names of certain colleges have the characteristics of potent magic. They confer upon the institutions' graduates a kind of halo effect which is often instrumental in getting them their first jobs. Conversely, the wrong name can make that desirable first job very difficult to obtain indeed.

Having acknowledged that the higher educational product is of considerably lower quality than they should ideally like, the participants then focused their discussion on one of the central causes of the product's shortcomings: it is not sufficiently flexible to serve the diverse needs of the students. Stated another way and with slightly different emphasis, there is not the proper degree of coordination and cooperation between higher education, on the one hand, and primary-secondary education, on the other. Stalnaker reported that some students, who have attended superior high schools, can virtually coast through two years of college on the strength of their previous training. Others, students from high schools of low quality, are frequently so unprepared for the work at high-powered institutions that during their first year of college they can hardly find enough spare time to leave town during vacations or even to see a movie on Saturday evenings.

It is not inevitable that an institution must at one time have many students who are bored and many others who are traumatically overworked. If, however, these extremes are to be avoided, then it is imperative for the colleges to design their curricula to take account of the academic differences that do in fact exist among their incoming freshmen. In addition to smoothing the process of transition from high school to college, such a policy would also meaningfully increase the benefits which many students can gain from their college education. The advanced-placement program has made progress in this area, but much still remains to be done. Another change in the attitude of many colleges that would be enormously helpful would be for them to abandon what has historically been their somewhat haughty attitude towards the high schools, which seems to say, "Just teach them to read, write and add. We'll do the rest." As Mr. Stalnaker pointed out, there have recently been favorable changes along these lines, but again there is ample room for further progress.

In addition to commenting upon the institutional aspects of the matter, those relating primarily to the colleges and their products, the participants also made a few remarks more explicitly concerning students. Along these lines, one of Dr. Roe's findings is encouraging. The best evidence available to her suggests that students are rather resilient creatures. Bad schooling may limit their progress, academic or otherwise, but—and especially if it does not come too early in life—it has practically no chance of preventing them from eventually becoming intellectually creative if they are innately qualified to do so.

A second related point is that, in addition to intellectual aptitude, there is another important dimension to an individual's academic potential, one which Stalnaker brought to the attention of the seminar. It is what the psychologists call the level of mental energy and what may be approximated by the more prosaic phrase, the intensity of interest. Many knowledgable people assert that they would be willing to trade 150 points on the College Board's Scholastic Aptitude Test for a ten per cent increase in their level of mental energy. This claim deserves minor modification. The trade would probably be worthwhile if the points on the SAT were those between 800 and 650. If, on the other hand, they were those between 500 and 350 or below, it is less certain that this particular exchange would bring any special advantage. Perhaps, in this latter case, a twenty-five per cent increase in the level of mental energy might make a fair trade. Quibbling about these trading ratios is not the major issue, however. What is important is that the concept of mental energy adds a new dimension to one's thinking about those factors which make some students superior, others ordinary and still others below average.

It may be recalled that, early in the discussion, Stalnaker identified a group within American society in which there are many able youngsters who are not attending college. The third and final point along the present line is an extension of this previous notion, a similar point but one with even broader social implications. Dr. Roe explained that there are many potentially educable and socially productive Americans who never even remotely approach achieving their potential because they are born into families whose values or economic or social situation is stultifying. One thing that many responsible social thinkers would like to do is to extricate these potentially ca-

pable children from their enervating home environments at an early
age in the interests of both their personal well-being and national
benefit. This is a terribly touchy view, for it comes into direct conflict
with some very strong American notions about the sanctity of the
family. Nevertheless, there is an important problem here, and although
solving it satisfactorily may indeed be difficult, Dr. Roe implied that
it still seems advisable to set forth the facts of the matter.

Finally, the participants said a few words directly concerning
public policy. An interesting question is whether the Federal Government will initiate a program, similar to Merit's and Woodrow Wilson's, whereby it would make scholarships directly available to students and let them use those funds at the institutions of their own
choice. Most experts in this area do not think that such a Federal
program will be forthcoming. The reason is not that it would not
be a worthwhile endeavor but rather that the smaller, less well-known
institutions of higher learning, plus the leaders in regions threatened
with loss of their talented residents, would use their lobbying influence to block its passage. These institutions and leaders would
oppose it purely for reasons of self-interest. In its stead they would
favor a program whereby the Government made scholarship funds
available to all higher educational institutions, allocating them in
proportion to enrollments. Under this plan the worst institution—if
that term has any meaning in this context—would receive proportionately as much of a Federal subsidy as the best.

Those are the facts. Whether the plan which the small, less well-
known institutions would sponsor is good or bad is another matter
and one upon which there is no unanimous accord. Those who favor
it argue along these lines: the rich and superior institutions are already doing extremely well for themselves. What this country really
needs is to reduce the inequality in the distribution of academic
talent, to create more so-called centers of excellence. Thus the Government should give the have-nots of higher education subsidies which
are at least as large as—perhaps even larger than—those which
it gives the institutions which are already thriving. They claim that
unrestricted Government scholarships will not lead to that goal because most of the recipients will elect to attend the prestige institutions. The alternative argument stresses that a student should be perfectly free to choose the institution at which he will receive his higher
education and also that the outstanding institutions can currently
make better use of the proposed type of subsidy than can the others.
Stalnaker argued that the Merit Program now awards $4-million a

year in scholarships, of which perhaps several hundred thousand dollars are spent at MIT. A Government program that cost $100-million and allocated funds to all institutions in proportion to enrollments would, by his estimate, give considerably less than $50,000 to MIT, and this outcome he simply feels is wrong. His emphasis is on putting the money where its current educational value is highest.

Those, then, are the arguments. The matter is not clear-cut, but this is not the place to resolve the dispute, nor in fact to do anything more than present the issue.

7. Social Values and Formal Education

PAPER BY . . . *Dan C. Lortie*
Professor of Education, University of Chicago

Some of the policy questions we sociologists have raised about schools reflect our concerns about social stratification. Schooling plays an important part in determining students' subsequent careers; in sociological terms, it influences life-chances and helps to allocate persons to different social and economic positions. The fundamental question of policy is whether our educational system makes these allocations in ways consistent with our expressed ideals of equality of opportunity and open social mobility.

Schools also transmit significant aspects of our culture to each new generation and thus assist in socializing youngsters into our way of life. Here the questions of policy center on whether students encounter the diversity of values we associate with an intellectually open society. Do schools expose them to a wide range of values from which they may choose, or do they tend to stamp out graduates from a single master stencil?

When we review the work of sociologists who have examined schools, we find two important recurring themes. First, men as otherwise diverse in outlook as Emile Durkheim, William Sumner, Willard Waller, August Hollingshead and David Riesman agree that the schools' effect on students is not limited to intellectual teaching or formal curriculum. In subtle and manifold ways, schools influence the students' concepts of what is true, good and beautiful. These men are not necessarily advocates of broadened school purposes; they have simply observed that academic institutions do in fact convey

149

more than the specifics contained in their curricula. Our schools may not make all Americans into scholars, but they do help to make students into Americans.

The second point of agreement is more surprising. Durkheim, a radical even by late nineteenth-century French standards, referred to "our traditional system of education [which] is no longer in harmony with our ideas and our needs."[1] Sumner of Yale, no radical by any standards, implied constricted schools when he spoke of them as transmitting the orthodoxy of their time.[2] Waller, agitated after years of studying American schools, called them "museums of virtue."[3] Hollingshead documented the preoccupation with narrow middle-class standards he found in the schools of Elmtown.[4] And David Riesman has frequently noted the schools' tendencies to conformity.[5] These commentators, though separated by time, place and political conviction, have all perceived schools as narrow and antiquated in content and tone. Schools, they say, present students with too limited a band in the spectrum of human values.

One approaches schools today, then, expecting homogeneity rather than heterogeneity; one hardly expects to find them citadels of pluralism and diversity. But we cannot argue, I think, that there is less need for such diversity today. On the contrary, we need more. Accelerated social change confronts our nation with numerous new, undefined situations, and we shall cope with them more effectively if our population has the capacity to entertain more rather than fewer alternatives. The responsibility for encouraging diversity falls largely on the schools for two reasons. First, other mass influences in our society will probably not do so: cold-war pressures can and do suppress dissent—and even, at times, reason. Second, our increasingly technical and complicated work processes demand higher skills, give education greater economic value and so place more power in the hands of educators.

Despite increasing college enrollments, most Americans end their formal schooling in public secondary schools. Unlike those who go on the college, they cannot choose between different types of schools but must attend those to which they are assigned. What happens in our schools, then, has great importance for our society-at-large; and if we are to meet societal challenges effectively, innovation and change in our schools are essential.

There *is* change in American education today. We are, some say, in the middle of a revolution in instruction. But this revolution is characterized less by ideological ferment than by technical innovation; we are finding new ways to do old things better. This trend might be called "The New Rationality" in deference to its stress on achieving specific goals through rationally selected means. The key words of this new trend seem to be "efficiency" and "realism"; and the social scientist, rather than the philosopher, symbolizes the mood.

Technical changes, however, involve social values, and it is possible that the New Rationality embodies certain consequences which we would not deliberately choose. I want to discuss four recent innovations which, in my opinion, reflect the new mood of rationality and owe something to psychological and social-scientific thought. These are (1) the acceptance on a broad scale of psychological testing, coupled with homogeneous grouping of students, (2) the use of television for classroom teaching, (3) programed instruction and teaching machines, and (4) team teaching. These four innovations do not, of course, exhaust the current activities in this rapidly developing field, but they do illustrate the general approach which is gaining momentum today.

Each of these innovations is a rational attempt to solve chronic problems efficiently; and taken together, they reflect the thinking of many psychologists, sociologists and economists. Proponents of each innovation can already point to gains that result from its use. I shall call attention, however, not to the undoubted strengths of these innovations but to certain risks which they pose to schools already too narrow in their cultural content. I shall focus on their possible injurious by-products—in sociological terms, their dysfunctional unanticipated consequences.

We shall need intensive research on and thoughtful evaluation of each of these innovations for years to come, and any final assessment should include evidence on how these innovations affect the *range* of student experience. It is still too early to view with alarm or to point with pride, for rational innovation carries a commitment to tentativeness and a willingness to suspend evaluation until the findings are in.

The advantages of psychological testing and homogeneous grouping are well known. Every teacher knows how classes of mixed ability are impeded by differential learning, and most Americans share the respect for achievement norms which underlies the efforts of individual psychologists and large testing agencies. Getzels and Jackson have warned us, however, that our testing procedures may overlook significant human abilities;[6] and if this is so, the risks to variety in our culture are obvious.

But perhaps the most powerful influence towards standardization lies in the application of these procedures in which students are segregated ("grouped") strictly according to test results. Since all these tests are geared to capacities which correlate highly with social class, the net result is that more and more students spend more and more time with others like themselves. The individual student, already limited in his social contacts by increasingly homogeneous neighborhoods, finds his classmates even more similar than students in the school at large. Cliques are not the invention of schoolmen or psychologists, but does homogeneous grouping offer any help in offsetting the tyrannical influence such peer groups wield over adolescents and other children? There are undoubtedly social costs; are the technical gains great enough to offset them?

Television is an obvious instrument for multiplying the audience of a gifted lecturer; it has an obvious value for the economic use of scarce teaching abilities. But it also has profound standardizing effects, since the current format of classroom televison consists mainly of a teacher lecturing to students who are unable to argue back. Furthermore, one television teacher's opinions replace those of several classroom teachers, who would most likely have disagreed among themselves on some points, especially in the humanities and the social sciences.

Since television requires careful scheduling and somewhat formal presentation, it inevitably reduces the spontaneity of the television teacher. Side comments, which can startle a student out of complacency, are less frequent. Students, in turn, cannot interject clarifying or challenging questions because the teacher is out of reach. The range of discussion is narrowed; the initiation of new ideas and active controversy is inhibited. Perhaps television need not be so restrictive a medium; perhaps more experience will yield a more imaginative use of its possibilities. But the enthusiasm of its promoters might well be offset by noting what it does to broaden or narrow the range of ideas and stances to which students are exposed.

Programed instruction and teaching machines, though still limited, are exciting to those who have seen them at work. Students can learn at their own speed, obtain an immediate reaction to their reasoning (or lack of it) and, it is reported, learn more faster. But, ironically, the very strengths of such instruction—high effectiveness and low cost—may pose real obstacles to diversity in the schools. The difficulty arises from the fact that instruction can be programed best in subjects where the logic is most cleanly organized and where the right answer is least controversial.

Imagine the situation a few years hence. Programed instruction has proved its superiority in, let us say, the teaching of mathematics through grade twelve. The school system's entire mathematics instuction is in the hands of a relatively few, highly specialized teacher-engineers, who are capable of programing materials and helping individual students. School boards may then find that, even after paying higher salaries to these specialists, they are spending disproportionately large amounts for teaching in nonprogramed fields, where the teacher-student ratio is much higher. It will take a good deal of countervailing power to offset the financial pressures brought about by these large-scale differential economies.

There are indications that teachers in the fields which resist programing represent cultural values above and beyond the subject matter they teach. They serve as models to students of differing life styles and value commitments. In one school I studied, the social-studies teachers measure their achievement by how much controversy they can evoke in their classrooms; and when asked to nominate an outstanding teacher, they cite a colleague in English who beats them at their own game. Yet these very fields which urge the student to consider alternative values and come to terms with them are those which programers consider "soft" and unenticing. Here, it seems to me, lies the risk: programed instruction appeals to our American passion for technological advance, and it is hard to see how those who oppose it will be able to dramatize their cause. They will appear to be protecting their selfish interests, or they will be accused of resistance to progress.

Team teaching is a long-range strategy, designed to attract persons of high ability to classroom teaching—and to hold them—by offering a phased career in which money, prestige and range of influence increase with time and successful performance. This work arrangement features visibility in the work of participants, and it therefore demands a high level of professional discipline. The risks to variety are subtle and will require very sophisticated observation.

Team teaching features two structural properties rarely found in schools, sharing of work among teachers and a hierarchy-rank within the teaching staff. Team teachers do their core tasks in each other's company, and they frequently carry titles which indicate differences in authority, prestige and income. But close colleagueship and differential rank are a somewhat unstable combination, and it seems likely that teams will emphasize one or the other. In some teams, hierarchy will dominate; in others, equal working relationships will be stressed.

Unless there is a significant change in the teachers' professional status, schools organized with hierarchical teams may pose a real danger to diversity and freedom in the schools. Teachers are now protected from interference in a rather left-handed fashion: their superiors, harassed by detail work, simply cannot give close supervision to the entire faculty. This means that some bad teaching, especially by beginning teachers, is overlooked, but it does afford a certain autonomy to those who teach well.

Team teaching, with team leaders supervising small groups, could mean effective supervision; and an instructional cabinet of team leaders and the principal could dominate the staff. Where community pressures are powerful and line administrators disinclined to resist, integration of curriculum could be a cloak for laying down a safe and banal line. I have more confidence in our public-school personnel than to suggest this will be an automatic outcome, but the danger exists, especially since the distinction between democratic control of school policy and wholesale intervention is not always easy to make or to enforce.

I expect that teams will emphasize equality more than rank, and here the risk is more subtle. Building effective teams will require harmonious relationships among the members of these teams, for many problems will have to be worked out in sharing students, developing common standards and so on. But how will this need for group harmony affect the teachers' expression of opinion in front of students? Will they pride themselves on arguing in class, or will they seek to maintain faculty solidarity by avoiding disagreement? We must keep a close watch on team teaching to see whether it results in heightened dissent and clash or in the muffled tones of clubbiness.

Only time and close observation will tell whether the risks I have mentioned are real or imaginary. But a further and more disturbing question comes to mind: who will watch and report to us objectively what in fact occurs? There are few parties among those concerned, who do not have an interest either for or against specific innovations. Some of the foundations which are openly committed to promoting innovations have announced no plans for objective assessment of their effects. The actions of state and national legislators do not indicate complete detachment, and the Federal Government some-times acts as if education were purely a matter of national defense. Professional educators seem to lack the political power and the resources to initiate and sustain long-range, detached evaluative re-search. School boards, part-time bodies separated from one other and bound to the property tax, find themselves under unremitting pressures to follow the pragmatically "successful" and inexpensive course.

Those who advise caution with regard to innovation will—in many cases rightly—be accused of protecting their narrow interests or of rigid conservatism. There may be noise and argument, but will it be intelligent? As Professor Robert Ulich has commented, Amer-ican education can use even more criticism than it gets, but some of the criticism should at least be informed.

We seem, then, to need a functional equivalent to the routinized reporting and criticism which disciplines certain other fields. Business has men who make their living by analyzing company operations, peeking into corners and giving full and frank reports on the affairs of their clients; certified public accountants, for example, though loyal to the business system in general, live by their reputations for com-plete and truthful analysis. Justices of the United States Supreme Court, I am told, are not unaware of the sharp reviews their decisions receive in law-school publications. Pathologists, perhaps less publicly, keep close tabs on those among their colleagues who may be tempted to operate a little too readily. I do not know what form such close and sophisticated criticism should take in school affairs; but unless we develop some such arrangements, we may find ourselves, twenty years hence, reading sociological analyses which still point to schools as narrow or constricted or unrealistic.

REFERENCES

1. Emile Durkheim, *Education and Sociology*, trans. Sherwood D. Fox (Glencoe, Illinois: The Free Press, 1956), p. 103.
2. Quoted in Everett C. Hughes, "Institutions," *Principles of Sociol-ogy*, ed. A. M. Lee (New York: Barnes and Noble, 1957), p. 231.
3. Willard Waller, *The Sociology of Teaching* (New York: John Wi-ley and Sons, 1932), p. 34.
4. August B. Hollingshead, *Elmstown's Youth* (New York: John Wi-ley and Sons, 1949).
5. See especially David Riesman, *Constraint and Variety in American Education* (Garden City, New York: Doubleday Anchor, 1956).

6. Jacob W. Getzels and Philip W. Jackson, *Creativity and Intelligence: Explorations with Gifted Students* (New York: John Wiley and Sons, 1962).

PAPER BY . . . *Theodore Caplow*
Professor of Sociology, Columbia University

There has been some discussion in recent years of the possibility that America might offer technical assistance to institutions of higher learning in underdeveloped countries, particularly in Latin America. Such programs are in the air. But this discussion inevitably raises the question whether, in view of the differences in social and cultural values between the United States and Latin America, our pattern of higher education is really exportable.

We might even ask whether the same pattern is capable of internal diffusion. New academic institutions are being founded all over the United States, and old ones are being expanded. Most of them hope to develop into research-centered institutions, modeled on the most distinguished universities. The challenge of how to export the pattern of our finest academic institutions is matched by the challenge of how to diffuse it more widely within our own system.

But let us concentrate upon the foreign scene. The American approach to industrialization and economic development is very closely linked with the American system for developing and transmitting technical knowledge. Thus, when we talk about aiding economic development through technical assistance, we imply an intention to transmit to the economically backward parts of the world a characteristic view of science, technology and even the humanities, along with a set of devices for selecting and training the specialists concerned with these matters.

Many of us who have a special interest in empirical social science would like to see a lively, autonomous social-research movement established as part of this development process. A precedent is the Marshall Plan—the only fully successful program of technical assistance so far—and the parallel growth in postwar Europe of social-science disciplines which owe much to American influence but are no longer dependent on this country for new methods or new concepts.

Even the most casual survey of Latin American universities demonstrates that they must be reorganized if they are to play a significant role in economic and social development. With some notable exceptions, they are very weak in research potential. Most of them have been influenced, directly or indirectly, by what is known as the Reform of Cordoba (1918), which established the double principle of student participation in university politics and university participation in national politics—a principle which indirectly reduced the identification of university professors with their academic careers. For this and other reasons, it is almost impossible for most Latin American universities, as now constituted, to sustain large research programs. They lack the physical facilities, the necessary control over students and the full-time, qualified faculties.

The efforts that have been made to overcome these difficulties only highlight the problem. One approach, for example, has been to export an American state university, full blown, to the fringes of Latin America. That is the University of Puerto Rico. In many respects it has been a bold and imaginative effort, but it suffers from a number of peculiar defects—notably, the tendency of bureaucratic procedures to break down when transferred to a more particularistic setting; the distractions of coeducation in a society where relations between the sexes are closely guarded; the conflict between patriotic and merit criteria in the selection of faculty; and the tremendous difficulty of translating the American system of instruction, with its dependence on textbooks, into a society where the appropriate textbooks for many courses do not exist.

There have been several other approaches. A number of new institutions, whose histories are still too brief to evaluate, represent compromises between American and Hispanic forms of academic organization—for example, the University of the Andes in Bogotá, Colombia, and Faculties of Concepcion in Chile.

The principal device for the exportation of the North American system, however, has been the technical-assistance project involving cooperation between a North American and a Latin American university. Adams and Cumberland, working with Widener, evaluated nearly a score of such technical-assistance projects in Latin America; and their report, by and large, was negative. The principal difficulty, as they see it, has been in obtaining effective participation on the part of the receiving institutions. This appears to reflect some essential incompatibility between educational institutions which operate on dissimilar assumptions and follow quite dissimilar modes of organization.

The amount of money spent on these technical-assistance projects has often been disproportionately large, in relation to what is locally available for higher education. The prevalence of large grants, grandiloquent plans and ambiguous results suggests that we do not yet know how to operate with these foreign systems. In the few cases where American universities have tried to establish projects in Latin America without the cooperation of a local institution, the results have been even less satisfactory.

There are some notable exceptions to this general unhappy pattern. Professor Theodore W. Schultz's project in Chile, for example, has had very interesting results. In fact, it is one of the few technical-assistance projects that has an ideological slant: the idea was to introduce a viewpoint in economics (the so-called Chicago viewpoint). This seems to have worked much better than the nonideological projects, such as those concerned with training tractor operators, if only because Latin Americans can understand a missionary effort to transmit an ideology.

Teacher-exchange programs have also been somewhat disappointing in Latin America, and for much the same reasons. If we are to have missionaries, they must be real missionaries, not tourists. So far, there has been virtually no recruitment of American educational missionaries. There are many people who are delighted to spend a semester, or a year, or perhaps even two years, in exotic foreign surroundings, but we have not yet found an academic population willing to serve abroad permanently.

If we search behind these alternative modes of organization, we find strikingly different philosophies of the goals of higher education.

Although there is a superficial resemblance between the Latin American university and the famous student-dominated university at Bologna, Italy, the model for most of the Latin American institutions founded or reformed in the early days of independence was French. Their self-imposed goal was to train an intellectual elite equally qualified for academic pursuits and for the public service.

This decision must be seen against the background of the older tradition, which John Tate Lanning has studied in the case of Guatemala. Colonial higher education in the Spanish Territories had a remarkable intellectual heritage, reflecting first the liberal episcopal viewpoint of the sixteenth century and then the Enlightenment of the seventeenth and eighteenth centuries. Perhaps because of its very merits, it produced a weak system of university organization.

In its primeval form, the problem of technical assistance was raised early in the Conquest, when the Crown set up an elaborate program to develop literacy in Spanish, attaching a school to every parish church throughout the Indian country. It founded an unhappy tradition immediately afterwards by refusing to allocate the necessary funds.

There was also a serious effort to bring the Indian culture into the university. One of the first chairs established in the University of San Carlos (in 1520) was a chair of modern Indian languages. The post was occupied intermittently for more than 175 years without presenting a single doctoral candidate. There were professors of modern Indian languages, but there were no students, because the indigenous students who advanced far enough to pursue graduate studies in the university preferred to separate themselves from the Indian culture and to study Latin and Greek, theology and rhetoric.

Thus, at the very beginning of higher education in Hispanic America, the question of what function higher education ought to serve in an underdeveloped region presented itself insistently.

Professor David Riesman has suggested that college education in the United States serves to separate the upper-middle from the lower-middle class and to change the semiamorphous adolescent into a semi-identifiable adult. Equally succinct generalizations can be worked out for the other major systems of higher education in the western world.

The French system, on which the Latin American institutions are modeled, is explicitly designed to produce an intellectual elite, not only at the top level but also at the intermediate and primary levels. When it worked well, as it did throughout the 19th century and into the 20th, there was at least one individual who represented the dominant intellectual tradition in every village. Although the range and quality of scholarship increased as one moved up the educational scale, everyone trained in the system was heir to the same Cartesian viewpoint.

In contrast the German university tradition, which has recently been subjected to eloquent criticism by von Weber and von Krakow, is dominated by the theme of intellectual efficiency. It is very similar in some respects to the modern industrial corporation's approach to the problem of organization: decentralization, managerial autonomy for the chairholder, multiplication of material resources at the point where research is actually conducted, a harsh and rigidly rational selection procedure, competitive tests at every career level, a deliberate lack of interchangeability with outside careers and a variety of quantitative devices for evaluating output. We can see from the effects of the German system on our own that its clear central purpose is to maintain and multiply the supply of specialized knowledge.

What, then, should be the purpose of higher education in an underdeveloped country? The common assumption is that it should facilitate the transition from a preindustrial to an industrial society by converting students from parochial, local, conservative, agrarian values to universal, egalitarian, scientific, industrial values. If we examine our own system as an exportable pattern, we confront the paradox that it is unsuited in several respects to accomplish this purpose.

First, we have an excessive commitment to the academic prestige order. To solve the problem of pluralistic supports and mulitiple values in higher education, we assign a guiding function to the prestige order, and we assume that the function of increasing knowledge—as distinct from transmitting it—can be adequately performed by the top five or six dozen of our two thousand institutions of higher education. We ourselves regard most of our colleges and universities as unproductive. We are only able to defend the system because, atop a great heap of mediocre institutions, flower a few universities worthy of the name.

Second, our productive academic units are much larger in scale than the units which need to be created in educationally underdeveloped areas. Even our liberal-arts colleges are huge in relation to the human and economic resources that can be made available in new centers of learning.

Finally, an essential feature of our own system is the curious interplay between a professor's local academic rank and his prestige in a national discipline. This relationship is obviously not exportable to an environment where there is no national discipline and where the best hope is to establish one strong local institution at a time.

Yet, however great the difficulties, the problem must be solved. In one form or another, the advancement of the poverty-stricken parts of the world must take place, and that advancement is inconceivable without adequate means of diffusing knowledge. In one form or another, there must be a growth of higher education correlative with industrial growth. We probably do not know enough at this point to propose solutions, either for underdeveloped regions in general or for Latin America in particular, but I think there are some clues to the kind of solutions that will ultimately be found.

First of all, we might weigh the idea of developing a new profession of missionary college teachers, who would not have the characteristic professional attitudes of professors in the United States because their career conditions and their fundamental objectives would be different. A related possibility is to establish a term of missionary service as a normal, early phase of the academic career. There has been a long, vain search in the graduate schools for a nonresearch degree which would nevertheless confer professional self-respect on its holders. Perhaps the answer is to be found here. Potential college teachers might well undergo a fairly extended term as educational missionaries. Five years in Patagonia might be an admirable preamble to a career of teaching in a community college.

A second hopeful point is that national or international competitive examinations, which can be enormously effective in raising educational standards, are rapidly developing in Latin America, though without any deliberate plan. The French system, which in many ways remains the most compatible with Latin American expectations, relies heavily on centralized examinations. Although the Latin American countries differ in many respects, they do not differ so much that a continental examination system is inconceivable.

Finally, possible realignments of primary, secondary and higher-education systems need to be seriously considered. Many exchange programs have encountered a vacuum in secondary education rather than in higher education, and we may not be able to approach seriously the question of higher education in these countries without including a thorough consideration of the supporting secondary structure. If the two are considered together, even our own current experience suggests that the line between the fixed curricular pattern of general education, on the one hand, and the system of specialized studies, on the other, may need to be drawn at different points for different populations and in different settings.

The solution of some of these problems might have unexpected benefits. If we learn how to establish a nucleus of American higher education in Patagonia, we may then know how to diffuse the same pattern at home.

COMMENTARIES

I

One interesting sociological issue is the meaning of a first degree from an American institution of higher learning. Professor Everett C. Hughes of Brandeis University, president of the American Sociological Association, suggested that when one says a person has such a degree, he has done little more than assert that the person has spent sixteen years attending school and college. Interestingly enough, if he has received a degree in less than sixteen years, it is probably rather impressive, indicating a relatively high level of achievement, for in general only the better institutions sponsor accelerated programs. In effect, then, Hughes argued that much of what passes for higher education in this country is in truth a device for occupying the young until they are deemed old enough to work. André Daniere, assistant professor of economics at Harvard University, questioned the wisdom of such an arrangement. He noted that we have many social obligations to perform and wondered whether spending large amounts of resources simply to entertain or, at best, to watch over millions of youngsters in the name of higher education is a worthwhile venture. In responding, Hughes emphasized that he was not advocating such a system but merely pointing to its existence.

When American higher education is criticized for housing more students than it educates, the usual defense is that the system is open-ended and thus democratic. In contrast to European education, it does not deny most youngsters the chance at least to try their intellectual wings when they have achieved a certain degree of maturity. Its doors are, by and large, open to all who would enter; those whose academic performance throughout their early years has not been outstanding are given a second chance. Unlike Daniere, who correlates the inflexibility of education in Europe with the prevalence there of free public higher education and who feels that a free public service is hard to imagine without rigid bureaucracy, many insist that gratuity is the core of what one means by equality of educational opportunity. Moreover, they argue that the restriction inherent in substantial tuitions is too high a price for the potential economy that such modifications might effect.

Another concern of the sociologist is the implications of modern educational technology. It is frequently held that mechanizing teaching with such aids as television will not simply increase productivity but may change the very nature of the educational product as well. Some fear, for example, that television may destroy that aspect of teaching which involves interpersonal relations, questions and answers, the Socratic method and so on. One suggested remedy is to have the teacher, who might be broadcasting to several thousand people he cannot see, not remain alone in the studio but rather teach before a small group of students who may question him and with whom he may converse. Thus an educational television program would become somewhat akin to that eminently successful gimmick of commercial television, the audience-participation show, and presumably in this way teaching could retain its essentially personal and social characteristics.

The potential effects on the educational product of programed instruction, as well as those of television, are also a current concern of many interested citizens. One of programed instruction's major alleged advantages is that by enabling administrators to economize on teachers it will allow them to minimize the number of eccentrics in classrooms and thus to place before a large proportion of students conventional teachers with stable personalities. In fact, however, Professor Riesman claimed that such an outcome may be only an apparent rather than a real advantage. He cited a well-known psychoanalyst who maintained that having, for example, a sadist as a teacher may in itself be an extremely beneficial educational experience for a child—much more valuable, in fact, than being subjected only to teachers from a uniform, button-down mold.

The relation between education and prejudice, in-groups and out-groups, is a further matter of intense interest to the sociologist. Professor Lortie asserted that one of education's results in this country, whether intended or not, is to transform students into Americans. In amplifying the point, however, Professor David Riesman of Harvard suggested that in fact this phenomenon may be a less happy event than one might initially suspect after hearing Lortie's presentation. Riesman said that, according to a recent study, what really happens in college is that the focus of students' prejudice is redirected. Chauvinism replaces the dislike of various minorities. Thus bigotry is not erased; it is merely changed from one form to another. Ethnic foundations for prejudging are replaced by political, nationalistic criteria.

Turning the discussion in a new direction, the sociologists noted that worshiping expansion is a major component of the American ethos in general. This faith has not failed to influence America's institutions of higher learning. Perhaps, either substantively or in terms of their public image, several of the loftier institutions can benefit from their reluctance to expand, but the majority cannot. Riesman suspects that in this decade of rapidly increasing enrollments, the average institution will have to grow, not simply to accommodate its qualified applicants but also to maintain and enhance its reputation. He suggested that if, in any given September, a college opens its doors to considerably fewer students than it did one year previously,

this event will, in the absence of some very unusual explanatory factors, be a reliable indicator that the death of that institution is
imminent.

There was general agreement among those present that in the
near future American higher education might usefully produce a large
stock of educational missionaries to travel abroad and aid in educating
the citizens of those nations which are currently attempting, in one
dimension or another, to enter the Western world's version of the
twentieth century. Some people are skeptical about our ability to implement such a scheme externally, arguing that even though America
has had ample opportunity, it has not even done so within its own
borders. The logic of this assertion is questionable. But the point
itself does focus attention on an interesting fact: although, in addition
to a few centers of excellence, America has many educationally underdeveloped areas, there is no vibrant collective motive to redress
the balance between these two sectors. America's most capable scholars
rarely offer a few years of their time to the mediocre institutions,
partially because the path to what has come to be called academic
Siberia is thought of as a one-way street. Whether the fact that the
missionary formula has not been successfully applied within America
means that it will not work externally is difficult to say. But certainly
we can note that its chances of succeeding will improve illimitably
if we destroy the notion—and to a certain extent the reality—that
having taught for several years early in his career at Patagonia Tech,
a person is unlikely to be able to return to a first-rate American
university. In short, we ideally want to encourage educational missionaries, and at the very least we must avoid penalizing them for their
efforts both at home and abroad.

II

*At another session in the seminar, on the topic of "British
Education," the discussion also turned primarily on the relationship between social values and the structure of formal
education. No speeches were delivered at that session. This
commentary is an elaboration of the major issues raised in
the extended general discussion.*

Individuals rarely view accepting criticism as the most delightful pas-
time imaginable, and in this respect societies are no different from
their constituents. For this reason Americans, who may be discouraged
by the amount of fault-finding to which their educational system has

been subjected, can take comfort in learning that British education seems no nearer perfection than its American counterpart.

British education is elitist; it does not provide all young people with anything remotely approaching an equal opportunity for advanced training. The division between who will and will not receive higher education is made when children are eleven, and, according to Professor Richard Titmuss of the London School of Economics, once removed from the small stream of university-bound youngsters, a person's chances of re-entering it are quite minute.* With extreme good fortune, a few may receive a second opportunity when they are thirteen, but after that the gates are, for all practical purposes, closed. And they are closed with the majority of Britain's youth on the outside, for only six per cent of the college-age population attend universities. An additional three per cent enroll in other institutions of higher learning, such as technical colleges, teachers colleges and nursing schools and so-called further education.* One major current debate concerns whether or not to call these latter institutions universities. In a tradition-oriented nation like Great Britain, such an issue is not so trivial as it might initially appear to an American. Conservatives oppose the change, arguing that the status of university should be reserved for institutions where large amounts of research are carried on. Richard Titmuss, the British sociologist, on the other hand, favors elevating the prestige of these institutions by calling them universities in order to abolish what he considers one unnecessary element of snobbery.

Until recently, the effects of elitism in British education were nowhere more evident than in the medical profession. As in America, doctors in Britain have tended to be men, and men from relatively wealthy families. During World War II, however, the scarcity of males prompted the British Government to pressure the medical schools into reserving ten per cent of their openings for women. This arrangement has not changed since 1946, so that today women still comprise ten per cent or so of the stock of prospective doctors. Incidentally, their academic record is, on the average, above that of their male colleagues.

Members of the Establishment have so far sheltered their own kin from the type of struggle to remain in school which enshrouds

---

* But see Chapter 6 for recent democratizing trends in Great Britain. s.e.h.

* According to the *Robbins Report on Higher Education* (1963, p. 15), of 216,000 full-time students in higher education in 1962-63, 118,000 were in universities, 55,000 in teacher training and 43,000 in further education. s.e.h.

much of American public higher education. The rate of dismissal from Oxford and Cambridge for academic deficiency is minimal. However, the elite are not fully consistent, for they display ambivalent feelings about the appropriate relation between Darwinian competition and education in general. They condone objective tests to separate the university-bound from the others at age eleven, but they oppose using such criteria at age seventeen to determine which students attend what university. How successfully they can continue to dominate the better universities is unclear, for the pressure of numbers may foist change upon the system.*

Recently, the rate of failure in the first part of the London School of Economics' degree course in economics was forty per cent; it was ninety per cent among overseas students taking the degree externally. Titmuss views this latter situation as a public scandal, as well as an effective way to turn the sympathies of foreign students to communism. But perhaps its main significance, from our present point of view, is as an indication that British higher education is now beginning to face problems of sheer numbers similar to those which American universities can also expect in the near future and which have already been highly publicized in this country.

Predictably, conservatives and socialists view Britain's educational ills in rather contrary ways. The former are reluctant, according to Titmuss, to undertake the sorts of projects which are vitally necessary. Among other things, they are unwilling to deal with education's private sector. The socialists, on the other hand, are filled with ideas for innovations which they claim to be worthwhile. For one thing, they favor abolishing the seven-year covenants and other legal devices which, as they see matters, only perpetuate Britain's present inequality of educational opportunity. More generally, Titmuss contended that piecemeal changes are not sufficient, that wide-ranging reform is needed. He argued that the educational system cannot be renovated for use in the twentieth century in a vacuum, independently from the numerous other aspects of British society which are also essentially elitist. In the educational sphere, he favors giving more people larger amounts of liberal education. Placing emphasis somewhat differently,

---

* The *Robbins Report* reveals that only 39 per cent of all undergraduates at Oxford and 25 per cent at Cambridge come from schools maintained by the government. But the authors nevertheless conclude that "the candidate from a maintained school who actually presents himself for entrance receives due consideration of his claims. . . ." *Ibid.*, pp. 80-81. s.e.h.

Professor Daniere suggested that Britain might profitably think in terms of minimum acceptable general-educational attainments for seventeen-year-olds, plan to satisfy these and, beyond that, devote its educational resources primarily to materialistically oriented manpower-training programs in an effort to accelerate its currently unsatisfactory pace of economic growth.

One of Britain's most serious educational concerns—and in this respect Britain and America are similar—is that the system is not fully efficient in its use of manpower. Ideally, one should like to spend resources to train those people who seem most educable, and this consideration is of particular importance when, as with Britain, the society is giving higher education to only a small proportion of its youth. British education violates this seemingly wise dictum for, as Titmuss reported, fifty per cent of all youngsters whose IQ's are above the 120-125 range abandon their formal educations at age fifteen.*

The government of British universities is complex. One aspect of it concerns the University Grants Committee, which is a device for letting the Government hold the universities at arm's length and give them public subsidies without impinging upon their academic freedom and control of curriculum. Perhaps the major proposal which Titmuss advocated is to do away with the committee. He holds that academic freedom need not depend upon its continued operation. Authority over the truly important issues, such as appointment, tenure and promotion, should, in his view, be vested in those members of a university's governing board who are also on its faculty, not in others.** This does not mean that the faculty should be subject to no control. But it does mean that through their representatives they should have ultimate jurisdiction over those matters which pertain to academic freedom, curriculum and staffing. In the debate over abolishing the University Grants Committee, the major issue is to what agency its powers and functions should be transferred. The leading candidates are the Ministry of Science and the Ministry of Education. Titmuss favors the latter because he thinks a bilateral system of control over British education would eventually produce two streams, one for those in universities, one for the others; and this, in his

---

* Cf. Chapter 6. S.E.H.

** The Grants Committee maintains that the universities in fact retain authority in these matters. Cf., for example, University Grants Committee, *University Development, 1957-1962*, 1964, p. 196. S.E.H.

opinion, is an unwise arrangement. Thus he argued that it would serve the best interests of British education if the Ministry of Education were to inherit the committee's activities and, in this way, come to terms with the universities as well as with lower education.

8. The Teacher Shortage: Causes and Solutions

PAPER BY . . . *Charles S. Benson*
            Associate Professor of Education,
            University of California, Berkeley

We might, if we wished, take a comfortable view of the situation in elementary- and secondary-school teaching. At least three significant facts would warrant this. First, although enrollments have been increasing appreciably, class sizes have not. Second, teachers' qualifications have risen, as measured by the average amount of formal training they have completed. And third, their mean salaries advanced steadily over the last decade [the 1950's] at a higher rate than that for all workers: about 5.5 per cent annually, measured in current dollars. This advance augurs well for recruitment in the decade ahead.

This evidence notwithstanding, I would like to suggest that we have serious grounds for concern. These stem from six primary characteristics of the profession: (1) The quantitative demand for public-school teachers seems to depend rather rigidly on the number of students enrolled. It is difficult to substitute capital for labor in the classroom, and there are certain fixed ideas about what the maximum pupil-teacher ratio should be. As a result, the demand for teachers has become so strong that the teaching profession has been growing relatively faster than the population of college graduates. (2) Techniques for measuring the individual teacher's productivity exist only in the most primitive state. (3) Though teaching requires a college degree, the profession relies heavily on the services of women. The large majority of elementary teachers are women; this seems to be inevitable. Some states do have a predominance of male secondary-school teachers; but certain institutional features, such as the almost universal single-salary schedule, tend to blur the distinction between secondary- and elementary-school personnel. (4) The majority of elementary- and secondary-school teachers are public employees. (5) In many states, management of the elementary and secondary schools is a local affair. And (6) the formal hours of work in teaching are set by schedules appropriate to groups of children.

In addition to these primary characteristics, there are three secondary characteristics. The first of these is that the teaching profession is marked by a relative ease of entry. Indeed, it apparently requires less effort to find work as a teacher than as a general machinist. Since the demand for teachers is increasing while the standards of performance on the job elude measurement, it is inevitable that the requirements for entering the profession will be low enough to make the marginal recruit—the one necessary to fill the annual quota—acceptable. This, incidentally, explains the continued existence of small teachers colleges dispersed across the nation, each geographically close to some group of prospective female recruits.

Let us now make the reasonable assumption that, on the average, women's commitment to nonhousehold work is less than men's. Since the profession is composed mainly of women, it follows that the demands made on teachers will have to remain rather low, lest they alienate women whose inclination toward teaching is uncertain. The standards for entering teaching, therefore, though perhaps rising in an absolute sense, will continue to be low relative to the standards for jobs that are dominantly held by male college graduates.

The second secondary characteristic is that teachers, as public employees, are very likely to be paid according to a formal, inflexible schedule. Because charges of political favoritism make good newspaper copy, school boards dare not rely upon subjective criteria in determining salaries, and objective judgments are not to be had. Furthermore, the salary schedule must be simple; otherwise, the board members, who for the most part are not professional educators, would find it awkward to explain their salary decisions objectively. For this reason, seniority is the major criterion used to discriminate among personnel.

Unfortunately, it is difficult to defend high maximum salaries under such a scheme. Hence, education is burdened with top salaries which were adequate in Depression days but which do not impress male college graduates in today's high-employment economy. Education has thus come to be viewed as a low-paying profession. In the light of this fact, there seem to be only two basic ways of satisfying education's manpower requirements. One way is to raise salaries. The other is to lower further the standards for teachers.

The third secondary characteristic is the relatively small number of hours that teachers must spend in actual classroom teaching each week. Teachers apparently do not have to work very hard (in the conventional sense), and this view is supported by the fact that so many of them hold two jobs.

These three conditions—ease of entry, low maximum salary and low quantity of output apparently required—contribute, I believe, to the present situation in which education is ranked as a second-rate occupation by talented, ambitious, energetic young people. These young people recognize, of course, that education is important to America, that it is vital to our national security, our national productivity and so on. But I suspect that this sort of patriotic appeal is more impressive to women, who choose their careers casually, than to men, who weight their choice of career more heavily.

Let me emphasize that by casually I do not mean thoughtlessly. The important point is that a woman's career is likely to be temporary and that her choice of career is less apt than a man's to be troubled by a conflict between obligations to family and obligations to society. Thus many of the top female graduates of the highest ranking colleges and universities enter public-school teaching, while the top male graduates of the better teachers colleges—men who are probably the peers in talent of some students in the prestige universities—turn their backs on the elementary-secondary classrooms. At the moment of choice, lower education often loses the very men who have made a preliminary commitment to it.

Let us turn now to the problem of imbalance in staffing among subject-matter fields. At present there is an excess of social-studies teachers and a shortage of good mathematics, science and English teachers. In 1961, for example, nearly twice as many college students completed teaching-certificate requirements in social studies as in science—and more than twice as many as in mathematics. Moreover, the science group included an unknown number in the general-science category. Of the 85,000 students who received a certificate for secondary-school teaching, only 1500, or 1.7 per cent, are known to have received one in chemistry or physics. A few years earlier it appeared that the situation was improving, but the most recent data are not so encouraging.

These imbalances are, I think, related to the characteristics of the various fields. Mathematics and the sciences are generally thought to be more difficult majors than history, and they are usually considered fields for men. By and large, the bright entrants into teaching—those for whom the study of mathematics and science should hold no terror—are women, and for the most part they do not have a sufficiently strong commitment to the profession to make the unusual choice. The men who enter primary-secondary teaching tend to have less intellectual competence and so are often reluctant to teach mathematics and science, even though they could then expect more attractive offers, (offers, that is, from higher-paying school districts). Furthermore, many potential teachers find the prospect of not having to exert much effort in their jobs a major attraction of the profession; they therefore shun fields, such as science and English, which involve a large work load. Last but not least, the truly ambitious male in education is likely to point himself toward administration, and a math or science background if not a prerequisite for obtaining such a post.

This situation troubles me. School systems enter the market to hire teachers on quite unequal terms. The rich suburban systems have a number of attractions to offer: relatively high salaries, bright pupils, prospects for rapid advancement into administrative positions, opportunities to participate in experimental teaching schemes and so on. Even these systems, however, have to accept rather poor mathematics, science and English teachers. The less well-favored school districts must feel the imbalance with particular severity.

The poor districts contain many young people of average and better than average ability who are unlikely to attend college, either for financial reasons or because not-going is the accepted social pattern in their neighborhoods. This is unfortunate for them individually because there is likely to be a gradual upgrading of jobs in industry, and many which are now held by high-school graduates may someday be reserved for college graduates. There will remain some opportunity for people who, although they did not go to college, have both reasonable ability and a solid high-school background in mathematics, science and English. These people may qualify for a new group of top-level blue-collar jobs, such as programing tape-controlled machine tools or maintaining a battery of automated tools, for which a knowledge of several systems of control is required. But the poor school districts will find it very difficult to prepare students for such vocations because they cannot get good teachers in the essential fields. This equity problem is far more severe than some others which have already attracted the attention of economists, such as the treatment of businessmen's expense accounts.

Let me summarize the three key factors which intensify this equity problem. *First,* although there is an increasing amount of experimentation in primary-secondary education, it is not distributed proportionately among the school systems. This factor alone tends to strengthen the relative capacity of the good systems to attract teaching talent. *Second,* as more students graduate from college, the qualifications for holding certain jobs rise, and the not-so-well-educated man finds himself progressively less marketable. *Finally,* the educational requirements for the top-level blue-collar jobs are also rising. Formerly a man could receive on-the-job training as a tool-and-dye maker. In order to hold the same position today, he needs rather thorough instruction in mathematics and science; and unless he receives it in secondary school, he is unlikely to get it at all.

What should be done to alleviate this equity problem? Basically, we must attract more bright young people into the teaching profession, but this is a long-range challenge. Two not-too-radical changes, however, can be made in the short run. The first is to use the time of those teachers who are in short supply more fully than we now do. It is reported that 23.5 per cent of all men in public-school teaching hold two jobs during the school year, and the second job is often in fields such as sales and service, rather than in education. It seems to me that we might try to induce these teachers to hold their second jobs in other school systems where their services are needed.

For such a scheme to work effectively, school hours would have to be more flexible than they are now. The state would have to participate to make the plan tenable; it would have to set standards for those who hold two teaching jobs, and it would have to determine a proper distribution of their services and time. These teachers would have to be part-time employees of the state and take assignments on the state's request.

The second change is to work towards achieving higher faculty salaries and improved working conditions in the teachers colleges. I know that this proposal is unacceptable to those who believe that teachers colleges should be replaced by regular liberal-arts institutions. It is a fact, however, that the poor school districts hire their teachers almost exclusively from the local teachers colleges, and if we are to raise the calibre of these districts' recruits, we might well begin in the teachers colleges themselves.

In the long run, there may be a solution through the use of television or through other forms of mechanization, which would require a more precise programing of instructional materials than we now have. Such a development might induce the sort of specialization in education which I believe is necessary to raise the prestige of the teaching profession and thus to encourage large numbers of capable people to enter it.

PAPER BY . . . *Herbert S. Conrad*
       Program Planning Officer, Bureau of Educational Research and Development, U. S. Office of Education

[This paper was prepared in the author's private capacity, and no official support or endorsement by the Bureau of Educational Research and Development, or by the U. S. Office of Education, or by the Department of Health, Education and Welfare, is intended or should be inferred.]

According to Seymour Harris, "an estimate of 1961 puts the *full-time* teachers in 1958-59 at 250,000, the new full-time teachers required in 1959-1970 at 346,800. . . . An average projection is a net rise of 100 per cent in numbers of college teachers in fifteen years. This greatly exceeds the expected rise in all employment, or that in competitive occupations. The increase of college teachers, according to projections, should be 4 times that in all employments, $2\frac{1}{2}$ times that in white-collar markets, and almost twice that for professional persons."[1] Mr. Harris observes further that new college teachers in some fields are being drawn to an increasing extent from high schools, which themselves suffer from serious shortages in the same fields.

The prospective need for college teachers is, in fact, even greater than Mr. Harris has indicated. Calculations by the U. S. Office of Education, based on more recent data, project the "degree-credit enrollment" of students in colleges and universities in the fall of 1970 as 6.9-million, or 15 per cent *greater* than the 6.0-million previously estimated.[2] (This later projection agrees with one made also by the Bureau of the Census.)[3] The addition of 900,000 students obviously means a considerable rise in the estimate of additional professional staff needed in colleges and universities.

In testimony before the U. S. House of Representatives Committee on Education and Labor on February 5, 1963, the then Commissioner-Designate of Education, Francis Keppel, stated that "the tidal wave of students moving toward college classrooms will require *at least* 406,000 new teachers during the next ten years. This space-age generation of college students has a right to the same quality of instructional competence as their predecessors, and even higher if possible. That means the number of professors in preparation must be greatly accelerated." (Emphasis supplied.)

I have emphasized the words "at least" in the interest of accuracy. Figures on the professional-staff shortage in colleges and universities are generally expressed in terms of "full-time-equivalent"; but a significant portion of this staff are employed only part-time, especially those engaged in evening or extension instruction, or in fields such as medicine, dentistry, law and accounting. Hence, more than 406,000 persons must be recruited to yield 406,000 "full-time-equivalent" staff members.

A further factor relates to an assumption uniformly made in gross, over-all estimates of the needed supply of college and university teachers. It is assumed that supply is nicely adjusted to demand, that there is no discrepancy between the fields in which persons are trained and those in which these teachers are needed. Actually, of course, a perfect balance between supply and demand never exists. There is some waste, since more students may prepare for a career in teaching, say, history than are needed, while too few may prepare for a career in teaching mathematics. Thus we must be doubly careful not to interpret the figure of 406,000 *teachers* needed as meaning that 406,000 *persons* can fill all the specific prospective needs.

If these needs are to be met, the new teachers must be not only available but also genuinely qualified. On this point Commissioner-Designate Keppel testified: "If the present rate of completion of graduate study continues, probably only 141,000 doctorates will be earned this decade, and of these only 46 per cent will enter or remain in college teaching. Our estimates show, therefore, that by 1970 our colleges and universities will not meet the minimum acceptable standards of a faculty consisting of 30 per cent doctorate holders but, rather, will fall short some 90,000 college teachers possessing the doctorate."

Given this situation, what is the proper role of public policy? And what are the obstacles to intelligent public action?

Three emotional obstacles to intelligent public action seem apparent. The first is the general yearning for a policy of laissez faire: the traditional faith or hope that things will "straighten themselves out," especially "in the long run." In the long run, as Lord Keynes reminded us, we are all dead. Indeed, without an active, aggressive nurture of our human resources on a scale comparable to that in the Soviet Union, most of us may well be dead (or dreadfully disabled) in quite a short run.

The second obstacle springs from the simplistic view that "we cannot overestimate the importance of free choice on the part of the individual." Stated thus baldly and without qualification, the viewpoint is rather obvious balderdash. Conscription in war, the rules of the road (land, sea and air), laws of all kinds and social pressures in a thousand directions—all testify that the gains of civilization extract as their price considerable amenability to social demands. Granted that the implementation of manpower-strategy in peacetime should rely on the voluntary response of all concerned, the system must include effective inducements to channel manpower into areas of shortage. Financial inducements, for example, have always been an essential part of the American way of life and are generally accepted as compatible with the idea of individual freedom.

Finally, there remains the primitive, atavistic notion that all government is bad and that centralized government is especially bad. Political scientists may regard government as one of the greatest inventions of mankind, but many people seem less appreciative. According to opinion polls, the idea that Federal support of education must mean Federal control—and that Federal control is worse than death —prevails more largely in legislative halls than among the people. To date, experience with Federal aid does not support the view that Federal aid to education equals Federal control. But if it did, the people are free to elect officials who could restore the *status quo ante*—unless, of course, the people found the actual degree of Federal control advantageous and to their taste. This is not outside the bounds of possibility; it has happened before.

The preceding paragraphs have, of course, been a defense-in-advance for a proposal which I shall now present. This proposal should be regarded as supplementing other remedies which are already being applied or advocated, such as increases in compensation (in terms of salary, payment for summer work, decreased teaching load, faculty housing, improved retirement provisions and so on) ; increased fellowships for graduate students; increased availability of loan funds for all students; and the development of a national system of scholarships. The problem is so severe, however, and individual remedies are in practice so mild that we shall need all the corrective influences we can marshall.

The proposal is that the Federal Government provide financial assistance to students for college and university education *differentially,* with a view to prospective requirements for college- and university-trained personnel at the time when the students will graduate. One of the prime purposes of such a program would be to mitigate the shortage of college and·university staff in specific fields of study and research, but it would also serve the needs of industry and government.

More specifically, the program should aim (1) to call students' (and prospective students') attention to the opportunities for careers in *all* major professional fields, including college teaching, not just in such traditionally recognized fields as engineering, medicine, dentistry and law; (2) to induce appropriate numbers of capable students to enter colleges and universities; (3) to make sure that students are given the information and inducements needed to attract them to curricula related to shortage areas; and (4) to provide the information and inducements that will encourage them to complete their training.

Let me stress that no compulsion is contemplated at any point in this agenda. Furthermore, the method is not limited to developing professional staff for institutions of higher learning; it is applicable in equal measure to other significant areas of national need for highly trained manpower.

Theoretically, financial assistance affecting students can take many forms. Assistance may be given directly to students; or it may be given indirectly (through subsidies or preferential taxation of parents of college students) to institutions of higher learning, college faculties, educational suppliers and so on. I shall here consider only direct assistance to students, if only because such assistance seems to escape the hamstringing issues of race, religion, economic level and public vs. private institutional control, which arise when other types of Federal aid for education are proposed.

Financial assistance to students can take the form of preferment in employment (as teaching assistants, laboratory assistants, research aides and so on); of loans on favorable terms (such as low interest, deferred repayment and forgiveness of interest or principal, in whole or in part); of scholarships (generally to students of superior academic ability in need of financial help) ; of fellowships and trainee-ships; or of outright grants (with or without conditions attached).

Our purpose is to manipulate student aid so as to achieve appropriately *differential* input into various types of college and university training. The ultimate goal is to assure that the national need for manpower in specific areas will be fulfilled. For this purpose, at least four steps seem necessary:

First, we must determine the trained-manpower shortage areas far enough in advance for students to make educational choices in anticipation of the shortage. Such advance determinations cannot, of course, be made with complete reliability, but they must be made with a useful degree of accuracy and specificity. A classification into such broad categories as "white collar" and "blue collar"—or into "professional and technical," "managerial," "skilled" and so on—would have very limited value.

Second, we must determine the differential inducements which will be adequate to effect the flow of highly trained manpower into desired channels. Here again, it is impossible to know in advance exactly how great the differentials should be, but study and trial should eventually lead to determinations of practical value. The situation is more complex than it may first appear, since a student in a well-managed program of financial aid is now generally offered a package—say, ten hours a week of university employment, a moderately large National Defense Education Act loan and (if necessary and if the student has a good academic record) a moderate scholarship. Calculating the net effect of such a combination of aids may prove elusive.

Care must also be exercised to make the differential in favor of, say, engineering over business administration large enough to produce a significant effect but small enough to minimize the total cost of the program of financial assistance, and it must not be so large that it displaces the students true, spontaneous interest and motivation. The complexity of these problems makes clear the importance of the third step.

Third, we must maintain a careful and more or less continuous check over the first two steps, with appropriate modifications of each as needed, according to the findings.

And *fourth,* we must create an appropriate administrative structure to implement the program. The structure should, I think, be either wholly or basically Federal, in the interest of efficiency and of prompt adaptation to new information. The alternative of fifty separate agencies, operated by the fifty states, seems inefficient and impractical.

Within the Federal Government, an Educational Awards Commission might be set up, similar in political independence to the Federal Reserve Board and equally influential. To the extent desired, the commission could (and doubtless would) make use of information and facilities available in the Office of Education, the Bureau of Labor Statistics, the Department of Agriculture, the National Institutes of Health, the National Science Foundation, the Bureau of the Census, the Federal Council for Science and Technology, the National Academy of Sciences, the National Research Council, the Department of Defense, the Atomic Energy Commission, the National Aeronautics and Space Administration, the Council of Economic Advisers and others. It would also, no doubt, undertake studies under its own authority, either through its own staff or by contract with universities, private research institutes and so on.

The principal functions of the Educational Awards Commission would include research on the adjustment of the supply of highly trained manpower to national needs; determination and coordination of policy concerning highly trained manpower (but the established Federal agencies should retain authority for innovation and experimentation on a limited scale) ; dissemination of information on career opportunities for college and university graduates in relation to national needs; and determination, within limits set by Congress, of the level, types and differentials of financial assistance required to achieve the purpose of the program.

The concern of the Educational Awards Commission would embrace both the science and nonscience fields. In making its decisions, the commission would face the problem of giving proper weight to long-run vs. short-run considerations; of evaluating the significance and urgency of current and prospective needs in the sciences, social sciences and humanities; and so on.

Helping to meet the manpower needs of the colleges and universities would, as I have said, be only one element in the total task of the Educational Awards Commission. The manpower needs of colleges and universities cannot be viewed in isolation from the manpower needs of other sectors of the economy. Except where supply fits demand perfectly, the national interest requires some intelligent accommodation between the different sources of demand. Nor should it be forgotten that the nation suffers from surpluses in the labor force (evidenced by unemployment, underemployment and low compensation), as well as from shortages (evidenced by vacant positions, overworked staffs and high compensation). Ultimately, it may well be found desirable to establish a full-scale National Manpower Commission covering *all* occupations.

Our emphasis on the need for college- and university-trained personnel in general—and on the manpower needs of colleges and universities in particular—is justified only by the clear, paramount importance of these institutions of higher education. Scratch a university, and a public school system (perhaps, indeed, an entire state's school system) bleeds. Create a few research professorships, and an industry may bloom. Lower the quality of college teaching, and the nation's crop of graduates withers. Lower the supply and quality of researchers, and we quickly lose the race for national security and social progress.

Yet there still remains the larger task of determining the *total* manpower needs of the nation and developing a more responsive and responsible system for meeting these needs. This larger task needs urgently to be undertaken. Perhaps the work of an Educational Awards Commission for college- and university-trained manpower can help to point the way.

REFERENCES

1. Seymour E. Harris, *Higher Education: Resources and Finance* (New York: McGraw-Hill, 1962), p. 690.
2. Louis H. Conger, Jr., "College Trained Personnel: Supply and Demand," *Economics of Higher Education,* ed. Selma J. Mushkin (Washington: U. S. Government Printing Office, 1962), Chapter 1.
3. U. S. Bureau of the Census, *Illustrative Projections to 1980 of School and College Enrollment in the United States,* Series P-25, Number 232 (Washington: Bureau of the Census, June 1961).

COMMENTARIES

I

In the eyes of the casual observer, a society's wealth can overshadow its poverty, even obscure its existence altogether. But the presence of one does not preclude the other, for to consider the total is not to heed its distribution. The two are not rigidly related in any pattern that has yet been discerned. It should, therefore, not be surprising to learn that although America is indeed an affluent society, her

supply of talented primary-secondary teachers is far from abundant,
The members of the seminar discussed this problem.

One particularly disturbing aspect of the matter is the high percentage of young teachers who leave the profession each year. The
figure is about eleven per cent, and there is some sentiment to the
effect that this attrition represents a large waste because these teachers,
who are just beginning their careers, fail to pursue the activity for
which society has paid to train them. Calculating the exact cost of
this waste is difficult because a number of elusive concepts, such as
the cost of a teacher's education, income foregone, the number of
years in a full career and so on, must be considered. Nevertheless,
Dr. Conrad estimated that when all of these factors are evaluated,
the waste is about $180-million annually. The crucial point is that
these teachers have not paid the full cost of their education. Society
subsidizes them by charging each only a fraction of what his education
costs the nation to provide. The argument is that because it made
a sacrifice out of current consumption to educate the teacher, society
can reasonably expect that he will remain in the profession long
enough to repay it the cost of its investment plus a fair return for
waiting.

This line of reasoning had critics at the seminar as well as supporters. The critics argued that, for a number of reasons, the desertion
of teaching is not as serious a problem as some might think. For
one thing, those who quit have received higher education, which
for obvious social and cultural reasons is a desideratum in itself.
Many teachers are women who were enrolled during their undergraduate days in a regular liberal-arts program and who simply accumulated a few education credits almost as an afterthought in their junior
and senior years in order to give them some prospect of pleasant
employment between graduation and marriage. André Daniere emphasized that this situation is substantially different from the hypothet-
tical one in which a surgeon might train for twelve years and then
abandon the medical profession shortly after beginning his practice.
In that case the waste would be tremendous, but a teacher's training
is neither as long nor as divorced from the path of general liberal
education as is a surgeon's, and the waste that occurs when a young
teacher leaves his or her profession is correspondingly less serious.

As a second point, Mr. Martin Mayer, author and journalist, proposed that the people who are leaving the profession may be precisely
the ones society should want to leave: the less talented teachers. Before
complaining about losing them, the nation should be convinced they

are worth keeping. It is often far better, Mayer suggested, to have a truly good teacher working with forty students than to have a good one working with twenty and a poor one with the other twenty. Third, saying that eleven per cent of all primary-secondary teachers quit annually does not account for the fact that many of the people who leave the profession, especially women who leave during their initial years of marriage, also re-enter it some years later. Finally, even if one were convinced that the apparently high rate of loss were a very serious problem, he would have to use extreme caution in handling this conclusion, for, as Mayer remarked, it is the most fundamental characteristic of a free society that when a person no longer wishes to hold a job, he leaves it, and nothing that America could gain by reducing the exodus of young teachers would be sufficient compensation for sacrificing one iota of this freedom and mobility.

Two general considerations for public policy emerged from this discussion. *First,* education's policy makers should clarify their thinking on this question: how serious is the waste caused by the eleven per cent annual loss of teachers? If they conclude that it is too large to tolerate, they should attempt to reduce it, not by preventing incumbents from leaving, which would impede individual freedom, but rather by discouraging those unlikely to remain active in the profession for a reasonable number of years from seeking training as teachers. *Second,* they should focus their efforts to recruit teachers on what might be called America's womanpower. In a general sense, they should attempt to enhance the prestige which is accorded to women who do part-time work. Unfortunately women are very often thought to be doing something menial—whatever the endeavor—so long as they are working part- rather than full-time, and in the opinion of some participants, this nexus keeps far too many married women vocationally idle. For a variety of reasons, not the least of them being the hours involved, American women are ideally suited to teach part-time. Many now do so, and to the extent that policy makers could induce more to enter the profession, they could alleviate the chronic problem of a shortage of primary-secondary teachers.

In the long run, the nation can only raise the status of teaching and thus attract able young people into the profession by increasing its economic reward, and for the most part this means raising salaries. According to Professor Harris, primary-secondary teachers have recently been more successful in gaining larger salaries than their counterparts in higher education, but the situation is still not totally satisfactory in either sphere. From a policy point of view, Mayer argued that the crucial concern should perhaps be to raise the maximum salary attainable in teaching rather than the average. The existence of a few teaching jobs which paid between $20,000 and $25,000 annually would substantially increase the profession's recruiting power, irrespective of the fact that the average salary remained low. People in general and Americans in particular tend to be more impressed with the size of the carrot than with the army of other proverbial rabbits who are also trying to grab it. As one participant pointed out, there is, for example, a superabundance of relatively unsuccessful businessmen and lawyers in this country, but the public image is of the few who receive over $50,000 a year, not of the many who earn under $10,000. It must be understood, however, that there cannot very well be two men with the same seniority rating, doing the same job, but with one earning twice as much as the other. As Mr. Mayer pointed out, the crucial task is to develop a scheme for differentiating among jobs which will rationally permit differential salaries that are not based on seniority. Developing such a scheme will no doubt be challenging. Nevertheless, it seems like the best hope for solving the teaching-personnel problem, and there was general agreement that the sooner it is effected, the better.

II

At another session in the seminar, on the topic of "Recruit-ment and Preparation of Teachers for Schools and Colleges," matters related to the teacher shortage dominated the discus-sion. No papers were delivered at that session. This commen-tary is an elaboration of the major issues raised in the ex-tended general discussion.

Social scientists tend to think of themselves as problem-solvers and consequently to identify their professional concerns as problems. In keeping with this tendency, the participants in this session of the seminar considered the "problem" of recruiting teachers. This matter is a problem partially because of two recent demographic develop-ments: a falling off in the birth rate during the 1920's and 1930's and then an increase after World War II, providing America with a legacy for now and the near future of a superfluity of students and insufficient qualified teachers. Oscar Handlin, professor of history at Harvard University, noted that the recent population explosion is not without historical precedent. Indeed, America faced similar crises throughout the nineteenth century, and the nation was as badly prepared for them then as it is now. The current shortage is more intense than its nineteenth-century counterparts, however, because in the past one hundred years the notion of what constitutes a teacher has become increasingly rigid. Today teachers cannot be so easily recruited from those members of the population who are simply not doing anything else. It is no longer regarded feasible to transform an otherwise unprepared adult into a teacher merely by placing a piece of chalk in his hand.

If our mythical social scientist takes his first task to be identifying problems, he takes his second to be solving them. He might therefore be expected to ask: can the problem of insufficient teachers be solved in the near future? Not, according to Professor Handlin, in any absolute sense, for it is not only teachers but rather talented people of all sorts who are in short supply. And since other professions currently pay quite well, they are not readily susceptible to raiding by education. Furthermore, Professor Harris suggested, teachers may soon organize more thoroughly than they now do and, as a result, divert funds which might otherwise be devoted to new teachers' salaries into raising the pay of existing members of the profession. If this prophecy is accurate—and unless the funds available for teachers' salaries become considerably more plentiful than is likely—it foretells another factor inimical to the goal of equating the supply of and demand for teachers in the relatively near future.

All is not despair, however, for even though the problem cannot now be solved, it can be dealt with and ameliorated. David Riesman, Henry Ford II professor of social scienses at Harvard University, proposed doing so by having prospective graduate students in many areas —not simply those in arts and sciences—teach for several years after receiving the BA and before commencing graduate study. Though conceivable and having certain merit, this plan also has several obvious disadvantages. First, it implicitly requires administrators either to relax professional standards or else to be ingenious enough to devise ways of having pregraduate students handle the trivial assignments so that full-fledged teachers can become increasingly productive. Second, it means lengthening the time it takes to get a PhD which, according to many critics, is already much too time-consuming a process.

Another potentially fruitful technique—also advocated by Professor Riesman—for relieving the present shortage is to increase the appeal of secondary-school teaching to those people with scholarly interests who, under current conditions, seek careers in institutions of higher learning or as independent researchers rather than in so-called lower education. Specifically, the proposal was to decrease the hours the teacher must spend in classrooms and thus to give those who wish and deserve it more time to pursue their scholarly leanings. The reasonable premise underlying this proposal is that it is not impossible for someone who enjoys teaching ten-year-olds to want to become, for example, an authority on nineteenth-century Britain as well. And yet the complex of American education today has little room for such an individual. Its schools allow him to satisfy the former desire, its colleges and universities the latter, but virtually nowhere can he do both concurrently. This missing opportunity may be causing a bad allocation of our scarce teaching resources and may therefore be wasteful. It is well to point out, however, that lightening the teaching load in no sense guarantees a solution—or even helpful correction—for the problem. Indeed, such action would initially in-crease the shortage of teachers. It will only ultimately be salutory if the reduction in teacher-hours caused by lightening loads will, in the end, be more than compensated for by an increase in the number of teachers, so that, on balance and other things equal, the total teacher-hours available to America's schools will increase.

It would be shortsighted to discuss the supply of teachers without mentioning America's schools of education, for enrolling in such a school is one path to higher learning and, indeed, the path which those who wish to teach in public secondary schools must usually follow. It seems reasonable to suppose that the ability of schools of education to attract students—and thus, in the long run, the avail-able supply of teachers—is highly sensitive to the quality of education which these schools provide. In fact, that quality has been widely criticized. Some of this abuse is undeserved and merely the result of an insufficient grasp on the part of the critics of what schools of education must accomplish. They are professional institutions and must teach their clientele how to perform a specific job, even at the risk of attracting the epithets "trade school" and "unintellectual." On the other hand, this apology is only part of the story. The unfor-tunate fact is that many regard schools of education—and sometimes with justification—as places to avoid and their staffs and students as people with limited ambition and mediocre talent; as a rule, the best students seek higher learning elsewhere.

These latter remarks bear a message: improve schools of educa-tion. But precisely how best to effect this improvement is far from obvious. Judson Shaplin, director of the Graduate Institute of Education at Washington University, formerly associate dean of the Faculty of Education at Harvard University, reported that Harvard's Graduate School of Education attempts to bolster its faculty by reserving certain appointments for people who would also qualify for the Faculty of Arts and Sciences. Professor Riesman criticized this approach and suggested that schools of education should be daring, should risk being called educationalist for perhaps ten years while they build, with young and as yet unestablished people, an enterprise that will, in the end, put faculties of arts and sciences to shame by luring away many of their undergraduates, if not *in toto,* at least for a course or two. Shaplin replied that Riesman's view was unrealistic because the people required to carry out his plan are simply not available to schools of education. Nevertheless, although there was little concord on the specifics of how to get the job done, there was general agreement on the important point that increasing the supply of teachers is intimately dependent upon the appeal which schools of education hold for prospective students and thus, more basically, upon the quality of the education which they provide.

A final factor relevant to the current discussion is the balance in secondary-school teaching between men and women. Briefly said, the women overwhelmingly out-number the men. One explanation is that many of the available teaching positions are part-time and, for obvious reasons, women are more likely than men to hold such jobs. Parenthetically, Mrs. Mary I. Bunting, president of Radcliffe College, added that teaching part-time is more and more becoming a device which women who have left the profession use to re-enter it. She added that in fact many part-time teachers now remain part-time for only a short while, soon return to full-time status. Whatever the reason and associated parenthetical remarks, however, the important point is that, even excluding considerations of salary, men by and large shun a career in secondary schools because the majority of people who teach there are women and the work is consequently labeled women's work.

The implications of this last point are only fully comprehensible in the light of two additional remarks: as a rule, secondary education's administrators are selected from its pool of male teachers, even when those men are of low quality and exceptionally able women are also available. Furthermore, the enterprise's best hope for the near future is to create a structure sufficiently broad-based and flexible to be able to incorporate novel ideas as they are proposed; creating such a structure is a task for skillful administrators. Assuming then, as seems realistic, that the aversion to having women in high administrative office will not soon change, the task for architects of public policy is clear: they must undermine the stigma which discourages men from entering secondary education, so that in the future the enterprise can enjoy the services of a larger stock of talented men than has been available in the past.

9. State and Local Investment in Education

PAPER BY . . . *Otto Eckstein*
Professor of Economics, Harvard University, and
Member of the President's Council of
Economic Advisors

Perhaps the most useful contribution I can offer on this subject is a view of the over-all financial position of state and local governments in recent history, along with some projections of likely happenings in the near future.

There is a controversy about whether there is now—or is soon likely to be—a crisis in state and local finance. Without arriving at a definitive answer, I should like to present some of the considerations which go into that controversy. For general background, I present two tables which contain some basic data on state and local expenditures and revenues in 1950 and 1960.

The expenditures side of Table I reveals that during those ten years, the total of all expenditures rose from $23-billion to $52-billion—that is, by 127 per cent, or an impressive average of over 10 per cent each year. In the same period, state and local expenditures on education rose from $7-billion to $19-billion, an increase of 161 per cent. The fact that education's increase exceeds the average increase for all items is noteworthy, but it should not be unduly emphasized, for expenditure in many other specific areas also increased rather spectacularly. Highways, for example, is another rapidly rising item and a large part of the total. Interestingly, the one item which has risen very little—if 50 per cent is little—is public-welfare expenditures. Perhaps this is an encouraging indicator of our march to affluence.

STATE AND LOCAL FINANCES: SOME QUANTITIES

Table I: Total revenues and expenditures

(in millions of dollars)

	Revenues				Expenditures		
	1950	1960	% increase		1950	1960	% increase
Total	20,911	50,505	142%	Total	22,787	51,876	127%
Property taxes	7,349	16,405	124%	Education	7,177	18,719	161%
Sales and gross receipt taxes	5,154	11,849	130%	Highways	3,803	9,428	148%
Individual income taxes	788	2,463	213%	Public Welfare	2,940	4,404	50%
Corporation net income taxes	593	1,180	99%	All other	8,867	19,325	118%
Revenue from Federal government	2,486	6,974	180%				
All other revenue	4,541	11,634	156%				

Difference between Tables I and II exist primarily because Table I is on a cash basis and Table II is on an accrual basis. Grants-in-aid for highways are particularly affected.

Revenues, as Table I shows, have also increased considerably. In fact, in this particular decade they grew even faster than expenditures, though this result would not be true for all pairs of years. Had

Table II: Federal grants-in-aid to state and local governments
(in millions of dollars)

	1952	1960
Total	2,635	6,128
Public assistance	1,277	2,132
Education	198	428
Other Health, Education and Welfare	362	631
Highways	460	2,467

Source: *National Income Accounts,* Department of Commerce

you asked one hundred randomly selected experts in 1950 whether state and local governments could raise $50-billion in 1960—an increase of 142 per cent—they would no doubt have questioned your sanity, for the increase in the revenue-raising ability of state and local governments has vastly exceeded everyone's expectations. Between 1950 and 1960 property taxes, which have traditionally not responded to inflation, rose 124 per cent; sales taxes rose 130 per cent. For individual income taxes the increase was over 200 per cent—a rise which reflects the introduction of income taxes in a number of states, as well as rising income. Oddly enough, corporation net income taxes rose only 99 per cent; this low figure presumably resulted from interstate competition for the location of business. Finally, receipts from the Federal Government increased considerably, but in absolute terms they were of only minor significance.

Table II permits us to trace the activities of the Federal Government. Between 1952 and 1960, Federal grants-in-aid increased from $2.6-billion to $6.1-billion. Fundamentally, two things happened. The Federal Government increased its participation in the highway program by $2-billion. It also paid more in 1960 than in 1952 for public assistance. And Federal grants-in-aid for education rose from under $200-million to over $400-million, still a very minor element in the total educational budget.

Projecting all these figures—and there have been a number of such projections—one finds that the total rate of increase in revenues and expenditures will continue to be extremely high. Crudely speaking, one can expect state and local expenditures to double again by 1970. Unless there is a new wave of inflation, there is no reason to think they will rise by as much as 130 per cent; but the increase can hardly be less than 100 per cent, given any reasonable set of expectations. Thus, by 1970, state and local expenditures should be around $100-billion.

One element (this is simply my own private hunch) which is likely to dampen the rate of increase of state and local expenditures is a slowing down in the rate of increase of the salaries of state and local employees, including teachers. In the last five years of the decade, these salaries rose at rates of six and seven per cent a year, considerably faster than wages in the economy as a whole, which rose three or four per cent annually. Assuming no new round of inflation in the 1960's, one can expect these salaries to rise no faster than other salaries and wages—in other words to rise at a slower rate than in 1955-1960.

Still, state and local expenditures promise to be around $100-billion in 1970. And now we get to the controversy: can the state and local governments hope to raise this extra $50-billion in the present decade, or is this fantastically unrealistic—as fantastically unrealistic an increasing expenditures by $29-billion in ten years must have seemed in 1950?

Of all the studies pertinent to this controversy, the most detailed is that by Richard Netzer, who made several projections of expenditures and revenue. Let me, in order to suggest the flavor of his results, present one of those projections. Assume, first, an annual rate of growth of Gross National Product of 4.2 per cent, which is, incidentally, a rather high rate to sustain for ten years. Next, assume some moderate and not carefully defined improvement in the standards of service which local governments provide. In this case, Netzer concludes that the revenues resulting from constant real tax rates would be almost sufficient to equal the increase in expenditures.

If either of these assumptions is modified—if the rate of growth of GNP is assumed to be less than 4.2 per cent, or if the improvement in local service standards is assumed to be quite substantial—the conclusion changes. In the former case, there would be a deficit but not a very large one. In the latter case, however, there would be rather large deficits, around $12- or $15-billion annually; this would mean a state and local debt in 1970 nearly 60 per cent above its 1960 level. Thus a substantial improvement in standards of service could not be financed without an increase in tax rates, but a moderate improvement could be. In short, Netzer reached the surprising conclusion that state and local governments would be able to raise the requisite additional revenue in 1960-1970 without any large new programs of Federal grants-in-aid.

How reasonable is Netzer's thesis? The answer depends upon how one expects the tax system to respond to economic growth. Students have tended to assume that the property tax does not respond to general economic growth, and it certainly does not respond very rapidly when there is inflation. But the figures show a rise from $7.3-billion in 1950 to $16.4-billion in 1960—a rise that is rather out of harmony with such pessimistic expectations.

Something is happening to make these revenues from the property tax increase, and it has apparently not been primarily a large increase in real rates. To be sure, newspapers convey the notion that property-tax rates are rising steadily, but there are two offsetting points to keep in mind as we interpret these straws in the wind. *First,* localities raise rates because it is difficult for them to adjust the valuation of old property to inflation. But these new rates, to the extent that they are levied on old property, are only rising nominally; the value of the property is rising about as quickly as the tax rates. *Second,* an element which was very important in the 1950's and continues to be so in the 1960's is the tremendous increase in the number of homeowners and thus in the total amount of taxable real estate.

Netzer assumes that yields from the property tax will rise about proportionately with GNP. I would make a different assumption: that there is a very substantial time trend in property-tax revenues, chiefly due to the gradual, steady increase of the total amount of taxable property. There is also some response to general economic activity, but I do not believe that movements in GNP determine the trend of future property-tax collections.

If one assumes that the property tax will continue to produce ever-increasing amounts of revenue, and if expenditure projections remain reasonable, then state and local finances are not heading for a crisis. In some of my own recent projections, I found that the excess of expenditures over revenue would increase, but at an exceedingly slow rate, well within the margins of statistical error. Of course, one may take other views on this property-tax question, and one may then become more of an alarmist about state and local finances.

If, for a moment, we accept Netzer's argument that state and local finances will not deteriorate greatly, how does this affect the case for some sort of Federal aid, either for education or more generally? My own view is that the case for Federal aid stems not from fear of an over-all financial crisis but from a desire to support specific programs. If there are some national purposes which the Federal Government wishes to accomplish, the issue can be judged on its merits. Presumably, localities do not have the same concern with national issues as the Federal Government. If any individual shares the Government's concern, he will favor the Federal program to promote that particular purpose.

But this is a different matter from the over-all fiscal concern. The fiscal argument is that there should be unconditional grants-in-aid, that the Federal Government should simply consign money to the states and localities for them to spend as they see fit. I do not think there is now a very strong case for such unconditional grants because there is no convincing evidence that state and local finances are likely to reach a crisis.

I believe we must judge each case on its own merits. I am convinced there are areas, particularly in education, where there is a national purpose beyond the local concern and where, therefore, Federal grants would be appropriate. But that is an issue for another session.

PAPER BY . . . *Charles S. Benson*
                  Associate Professor of Education, University of
                  California, Berkeley

The administration and financing of public elementary and secondary schools is, for the most part, a local affair. This is not to deny that schools are affected by changes in the national economy, by the cold war, by social policy (such as the Supreme Court decision on integration) and by the efforts of the large foundations to alter or preserve aspects of school structure and curriculum. But Congress does not formulate anything that can be described as a national policy on education. Indeed, it does not even establish targets for expenditure —these could be expressed as percentages of the Gross National Product—and its actual appropriations for elementary and secondary schools are, relatively, very small. Nor is there any administrative body at the national level that is able to develop a consensus on educational policy, however limited in scope such a consensus might initially have to be.

At the state level, governments differ in the degree to which they are willing to prescribe standards for the schools and contribute to their support. In the large majority of states, however, the greatest power over the allocation of resources within the educational enterprise, along with the greatest share of responsibility for providing funds, rests in the hands of local authorities, many of whom preside over quite small districts.

During this century the mobility of the population, the media of communication and the interregional volume of trade have all increased vastly. Such changes enlarge the geographic area over which are spread the social benefits of any local educational program, such as its contribution to economic growth. It has come to pass, I believe, that the amount of social benefits enjoyed by the taxpayers of a given school district—except, perhaps, the very large city systems—are as strongly a function of the expenditures of the neighboring districts as of their own expenditures.

For the local taxpayer, then, education is becoming less of a "social want" (to use Richard A. Musgrave's term) and more of a "private want."[1] This does not mean that responsibility for elementary and secondary schooling has been shifted to the private sector; there has not yet been any significant change in that direction. It means that because educational benefits are semi-national in character, the custom of supporting schools out of local finance has become conceptually inappropriate. (Even if support were centralized, parents would presumably receive a larger volume of benefits from school expenditure than nonparents, but education is not unique with regard to this kind of preferential treatment.)

To add a complexity, school expenditures, now as formerly, are regarded as satisfying a "merit want": public policy demands that a minimum amount of schooling be provided for those who otherwise would be unable or unwilling to obtain it. The notion of what constitutes a minimum varies markedly from one school district to another, as can be seen by comparing the education that a low-income Negro child receives in, say, Boston with what he gets in a small town in Mississippi. Without going into details, this diversity of educational standards probably means that support cannot be centralized unless school administration is centralized—a step as unwise, I feel, as it is politically unacceptable.

Someday a general-purpose school-aid bill may be passed by Congress, but it is unlikely that the Federal Government will carry the major financial load of the schools in the next few decades. The state governments can do more (I shall return to this later), but the local districts will probably continue to carry the largest share of the school tax burden and will remain the dynamic element in raising the standards of support and performance. It is important, therefore, to learn what we can about the pressures that play upon local school-spending decisions.

Before we examine some of these pressures, let us look briefly at what has been happening to expenditure. The size of the instructional budget in local public schools, measured in current dollars, rose from $1,318-million in 1929-30 to $6,901-million in 1957-58. The instructional budget, in other words, increased by a factor of 4.2. This rise reflects not only inflation but also the growth in population of students to be served, the changes in standards of attendance and, presumably, some gain in the quality of inputs.

What about real expenditure per pupil? We must first note that salaries of instructional personnel represent over 90 per cent of all instructional expenditures and that the ratio of students to instructional staff has been approximately constant. Hence, deflating the salary portion of the instructional budget by the average of teachers' salaries will show an almost constant flow of real inputs per pupil into the educational enterprise. I am willing to assume that the gains in teachers' pay are not wholly a matter of inflation—in other words, that they have had some effect in raising the calibre of staff. I have therefore used the average of all earned income in the United States as the deflator for the salary portion of the budget. The remainder, less than ten per cent of the total, consists mainly of books and supplies. For this I have used the wholesale price index of the U. S. Department of Labor.

On this basis I estimate that instructional expenditures in constant (1949-50) dollars increased from $.748 per pupil per day in 1929-30 to $.915 in 1957-58.[2] The average annual rate of increase in real inputs for elementary and secondary instruction was thus 0.7 per cent.

The rise appears to have been quite gradual, and I strongly suspect that we shall continue to see a creeping advance in school expenditure. To support this point, let us now consider some of the pressures that tend to force local school budgets up. The discussion will focus heavily on the institutional side, and I do not pretend that it is complete. It does reflect, however, several years of observation of actual practices in the local administration and finance of school systems.

Parents and the demand for special programs: As a society becomes more affluent, the educational aspirations which parents hold for their children naturally rise. In the richer suburbs, where the parents are likely to be articulate, they may form a kind of education lobby, offering support to most proposals for school spending, including higher salaries for teachers.

One of the most interesting phenomena is a process by which the parents broaden the school program. The introduction of French language instruction in elementary schools is a recent example. In many communities this instruction was commenced under private auspices; a PTA group, for instance, engaged a French teacher, with the classes being held in public-school buildings after hours. Before many years had passed, the local taxpayer was providing not just the facilities but the salary costs of instruction as well.

Why should such a service be moved from the private sector into the public? There are, I think, several reasons. The superintendent is anxious that it be done because he sees the existence of any private, formal instruction as a threat to his political and financial base of support. The parents are agreeable because there is no tradition in most communities of private tutorial instruction (except for handicapped children), because they feel the children will take the instruction more seriously if it is done in the regular school context, and because they hope that the language instruction will be more carefully articulated with the French courses given in the junior high schools.

When it is introduced into the public sector, the new program is unlikely to require any large advance in school spending; indeed, it may at first be placed only in "pilot schools" or "pilot classes." If each of these new programs were very costly, the necessary increase in local tax rates might arouse the opposition of nonparents and other economy-minded citizens. But, in fact, it is much easier to add programs than to drop them.

After a few years the incremental expenditure is incorporated into very broad functional classifications in the school budget. The salaries of the specialist teachers, for example, are lumped into the total elementary teachers' salaries (object classification) under the functional category of elementary instruction. This absence of program budgeting makes it very difficult for a member of the school board—and these school boards are voluntary, part-time bodies—to put his finger on an old special program that may be no longer be useful. One simply adds and adds, and the effect on school expenditures over the years is probably not inconsiderable.

Merit wants in the great cities: It is part of the American social philosophy that children should be given a chance to develop their individual abilities, irrespective of their race or income. The doctrine of equal educational opportunity is paid little more than lip service on the national level; this is evident from the differences in standards among the states and among the districts within most states. However, within school districts the situation is somewhat different. In distributing resources among the schools for which they are responsible, the local superintendents are, I have found, strongly egalitarian. (This does not mean that per-pupil expenditures are the same in all schools of a given district, for expenditures must be related to the varying needs of the student population.) This combination of disparities among districts and genuine efforts to achieve equality within them is itself a force tending to raise local school budgets.

Let us take a striking example. As is well known, there has been a large migration of Negro households from the South to the great central cities of the non-South. Many of these households are characterized by low educational attainments and low aspirations. Some of the Negro children fall far below the school performance of white children of the same age. Rather than simply accepting this situation, school authorities in the central cities have instituted special remedial programs for the culturally deprived children, as they are now called. The Great Cities School Improvement Studies Group has estimated that in twelve of our largest cities, expenditures on programs for maladjusted and culturally deprived children will rise from $57.1-million in 1960 to $125.5-million in 1965.

It might, of course, be cheaper to handle this problem by raising educational standards in the South. But to do so will require Federal aid, and the relatively indigent families in the poorer regions of the country have not been inclined to wait for a favorable vote. Migration leads to more equality of opportunity, but in the process it places substantial costs on a few school systems.

A bottleneck in the supply of educational resources: We have noted some demands that create pressures for increased school expenditures in the suburbs and the central cities. On the supply side, there is a bottleneck that also serves to raise local tax rates: the shortage of mathematics and science teachers. Professors Kenneth Arrow and William Capron call such a shortage of human resources "dynamic,"[3] and it certainly appears so to school administrators. From California, Maryland, New Jersey and Kansas come reports that very many science classes are taught by teachers who have had only a few hours of formal instruction in the scientific disciplines. Incidentally, a severe shortage in these fields is also reported in state-supported schools in England.[4]

Since most school systems pay teachers under a single salary schedule, a shortage in a particular field exerts an upward pressure on the salaries of all teachers. For example, if a district finds that it needs to offer an additional $1,000 to attract a suitable teacher of mathematics, all teachers in the district can expect to get a raise of approximately $1,000—provided, of course, that the man is hired.

This practice, so firmly defended by teachers' organizations, may be wasteful of public expenditure, and it may not give the districts sufficient flexibility to hire personnel in scarce fields. The suggestion is occasionally made, therefore, that prospective teachers in scarce fields should be offered an extra stipend—that is, that market forces should be reintroduced in salary negotiations. A disadvantage of such a scheme, it seems to me, is that the richer districts, which also provide an unusual measure of nonmonetary benefits to their staffs, would be much freer to pirate scarce resources from the poorer ones; and high-quality instruction in mathematics and science is needed urgently in the poorer communities, when so few of the high-school students go on to college.

Moreover, if high-grade mathematical competence is absolutely scarce in our society, it is perhaps not good social policy to lure such men into public-school teaching. With the development of newer forms of mathematical and scientific instruction, it may become possible to judge more precisely the level of teaching skills actually needed in the schools. This may turn out to be something less than the highest, in which case it may be feasible to train larger numbers of people (including larger numbers of women) to fill the school posts.

A new view of state aid: It is not a great secret that property-tax rates and property-tax levies per capita have risen sharply in the postwar period. One may well wonder whether voter resistance to the rising levies will not halt the steady expansion of spending on the schools. Also, certain other types of local expenditure are closely competitive with education. To promote greater equality of opportunity in the central cities, for example, it may make sense to spend relatively more on public housing and relatively less on schools. If schools, no matter how fine, cannot really rescue slum children, the higher priority should perhaps go to removing the slums.

However, the expansion in educational expenditures will be made easier by a change that is taking place in the way the state governments distribute school-aid funds to the localities. Historically, the states have paid out general-purpose school aid under a fixed-unit, equalizing formula, according to which each district receives a fixed number of dollars per pupil, less a reasonable local contribution. Under this form of aid, incremental expenditures above the state-support level—and these are often mandatory—fall strictly on the local tax base. Several states, however, have recently changed to a percentage grant, so that the local educational authorities have, in effect, rather direct access to a wide range of state tax sources. With the percentage grant, only a share of the incremental expenditures on education falls on the local tax base, and the share is larger in rich districts than in poor ones.

Under the fixed-unit grant, the formula cannot take account of the varying degrees of access which districts have to the market for teachers' services, yet the quality of teachers hired is the primary factor in determining the quality of education in each district. With the percentage grant, differentials in the real costs of education are borne partly by the locality and partly by the state, so that the impact on the local tax rate of being in a geographic position unattractive to teachers (a condition faced by many of the older industrial towns and cities) is reduced. Hence, the percentage grant seems clearly more equitable than the fixed-unit type. The percentage grant also allows the state to share automatically in the costs of special programs for disadvantaged children in the great cities. Finally, it allows the state to share automatically in the cost of producing the social benefits which flow from the high-quality suburban systems.

But it cannot be said that percentage grants offer as great an incentive to economy in local administration as do the fixed-unit grants. The change in the fiscal structure of public education, therefore, implies a gradual, steady advance in school expenditure.

REFERENCES

1. Richard A. Musgrave, *The Theory of Public Finance* (New York: McGraw-Hill, 1959).
2. Charles S. Benson, "Teaching Methods and Their Costs: Productivity of Present Educational Systems," *International Social Science Journal*, XIV (1962), p. 677.

3. Kenneth J. Arrow and William M. Capron, "Dynamic Shortages and Price Rises: The Engineer-Scientist Case," *The Quarterly Journal of Economics,* LXXIII.
4. John Vaizey, *Teaching in a Modern Economy* (London: The Joseph Payne Memorial Lectures of the College of Preceptors, 1962) .

COMMENTARY

Just as an outdated movie on television can not command a large audience when a modern superstar is appearing on another network, so too the activities of state and local governments are often overshadowed these days by news about the huge apparatus of the Federal Government. In fact, however, the subject of government below the Federal level is of fundamental importance to any study of education and public policy, for although there is much current talk about Federal aid to education, public education is now, and has been for a long time, primarily under the jurisdiction of the localities and secondarily under the states and, at the higher levels, primarily under the states.

This news may not bring pure joy to the heart of the average American breadwinner, but, according to Arthur Smithies, Nathaniel Ropes professor of political economy at Harvard University, many states have not even remotely approached the upper limit of their abilities to raise revenue. Only a minority of states now levy both a sales and an income tax, and Professor Smithies suggested that many might be capable of substantially increasing their receipts from taxes if doing so were judged necessary. This is reassuring news for the cause of elementary and secondary public education, which have traditionally been supported by the localities. The point is that the amount of local revenue that can be collected in the future is limited practically, if not theoretically, by the political infeasibility of raising the rate of the property tax. Since the states have potentially large untapped revenue and since Federal support of lower education raises knotty problems, the states are strong candidates to subsidize schools when local funds become scarce. In fact, many states have already accepted a substantial responsibility for supplying the difference between the total cost of primary and secondary education and that portion of it which the localities can afford to pay themselves.

In spite of the facts first, that Federal aid to local schools raises difficult problems such as the specter of Federal control and second, that many states can afford to subsidize their schools, still, in Professor

Eckstein's opinion, increased Federal aid both needs to be and will be forthcoming. The major explanation of this seeming *nonsequitur* is that opinions differ concerning the total amount of money which it is appropriate to spend on lower education in the near future. Federal officials feel that their counterparts on the state and local level are treating the matter too conservatively, that they are not willing to spend sufficient funds to achieve desirable objectives. To substantiate this point, Professor Eckstein noted that much of the legislation for general aid to schools which the Kennedy Administration sponsored contained a distribution formula only mildly related to the financial need of the states. Primarily, it provided for increased spending everywhere.

Even though the emphasis has not so far been on redistributing funds among states, Eckstein felt that in the near future such redistribution will be imperative. In absolute terms, the range of resources which the various states are devoting to education is extremely wide. According to Herold Hunt, Charles William Eliot professor of education at Harvard University, the most handsomely remunerated teacher in Mississippi earns less than the lowest paid one in California; and although we must interpret such comparisons with extreme caution, this general point is correct and worth noting: in simple economic terms, the cause of education fares much worse in some states than in others. The situation is most desperate in the poorer states, and in this context "poorer states" include especially those in the Deep South and a few others. If the problem were simply that these poorer states are not devoting a sufficiently large percentage of their total product to education, we might be able to convince them to spend more, but that is not the situation. In fact, the percentage of their income which those states do spend on education is above the national average. Unfortunately, what they do spend, in absolute terms, is still not enough by reasonable standards, and "enough" is so large a percentage of their total income that they need help in financing the venture. In short, funds must be channeled from the wealthier to the poorer states, and this means Federal financing.

It seems advisable to sound one cautionary note on this matter of giving the poorer states funds with which to improve their educational systems. The gaudy stories and ridiculing literature about the *nouveaux riches* remind us that people do not always adjust to large and rapid variations in their style of living with taste and grace, and there is no reason to expect that states would be more skillful in making such a change. Thus, although it is difficult to imagine what might be the analogue for a state to the concept of *noveau riche* which we apply to an individual, the basic point seems well taken: we should give funds to these poor states slowly so that they can absorb them productively. We should avoid flooding them with money so rapidly that much of it can only spill off in waste.

As in previous meetings, the seminar made a number of points about teaching personnel. Professor Eckstein suggested that the rate of increase for teachers' salaries may not be as fast in the near future as it has been in the recent past because it has already exceeded the national average for all salaries for some time. Professor Hunt took exception to this view and argued that teachers are still in extremely short supply and are likely to remain so until 1965. Under these circumstances he believes that they will maintain their currently strong bargaining position for several years and therefore need not anticipate an immediate slowing down in the rate at which their salaries are growing. Professor Benson informed the seminar that the National Education Association is exerting special pressure on behalf of better salaries for elementary as opposed to secondary teachers. He also pointed out, as did so many participants in these seminars, that teachers' salary scales do not reflect sufficient ingenuity in differentiating among individuals. For example, all new teachers of a given discipline generally receive the same pay irrespective of their educational backgrounds. Two beginning teachers of mathematics are likely to receive the identical starting pay even though one may actually have studied mathematics intensively while the other only dabbled in it as an appendage to his major studies, say, of history.

10. Planning Education for Economic Productivity

PAPER BY . . . *André Daniere**
Assistant Professor of Economics,
Harvard University

One cannot discuss the productivity of education without narrowing somewhat the meaning of the term, for education is productive in a number of ways. It produces pains and enjoyments while being acquired. It raises the level of one's intellectual and emotional experience in the years after graduation, and it enhances one's capacity to enjoy the rewards of life in a modern society. It adds to the stock of technical skills available to the economy and thereby increases production in many sectors of activity. It procures diffused benefits which improve the tone and comfort of collective, life. And it contributes a myriad of by-products, ranging from child care in relief of families to scientific research and intellectual creation.

I shall here consider productivity only in the technological sense, first evaluating the contribution of education to the economy's measured national product—that is, to the volume of goods and services consumed or accumulated over a year—and then proposing criteria for an optimum allocation of national resources to education from the viewpoint of technological productivity. With respect to the evaluative effort, my concern will be more with criticism of work already done than with constructive contributions: since the task of measuring education's productivity is not urgent, this attitude is, I believe, morally defensible.

---

* Daniere's excellent essay may be a little difficult for non-economists.

I. *The contribution of education to the measured national product*

One is struck, when reading the works of our productometricians, by their feeling that they have revolutionized America's thinking by calling attention to the productive investment which education represents for the community at large. I believe that they are unfair to public thinking and to public opinion. The shock which they perceive in their audiences is evoked, not by the mere application of the concept of economic productivity to education, but by the attempt to measure this productivity solely through the income differential of educated individuals. The public is further shocked by the suggestion, which is sometimes implied, that economic productivity so measured should be the sole criterion for educational expenditures.

To the extent that these analysts of the economics of education address themselves to so-called underdeveloped countries, their emphasis and their admonitions are no doubt right; but they are not right for America. With a few exceptions (including Seymour Harris) they have tended to rely too exclusively on measurable income and to underestimate the consumption benefits enjoyed selectively by educated individuals. The majority of these analysts view education primarily as a process by which opportunities are equalized, economic growth enhanced and social progress accelerated—a perspective which appears to legitimize the bearing of all costs by the general public. This, however, is another story, and I shall not dwell upon it now.

As an illustration of recent attempts at evaluating the contribution of education to measured national product, let us take the work which Professor Theodore W. Schultz has been pursuing at the University of Chicago. His computation runs as follows:[1]

First, he determines the total investment embodied in an individual over successive cycles of education. Thus, over four years of high school (1954-58), an average of $5930 per student was sunk in the form of costs incurred by the institution, direct costs incurred by the student and virtual costs—that is, earnings foregone in studying rather than holding a job.

The next step is to compute the additional lifetime earnings expected after the individual has completed the cycle. In 1958, a high-school graduate could count on earning, over his lifetime, $70,000 more than a person with only eight years of schooling. This sum is taken to represent the addition to national product which an individual contributes through completing four years of high school. Thus, from an investment of $5930 over four years, our society reaps a total of $70,000 in eventual goods and services over some fifty years of the educated individual's active life. The annual yield, or interest, on the investment is approximately 12 per cent, which is good by most standards. Similar calculations give a return of 40 per cent on the investment made during the fifth to eighth grades and 11 per cent on the investment made for four or more years of college-university education.

From another set of computations, Schultz finds that the national stock of education—that is, the accumulated educational investment in the labor force—went up by $286-billion between 1929 and 1957. A weighted average of the yields calculated for various cycles of education in that period is 19.6 per cent. Thus the rise in the investment must have added 19.6 per cent of $286-billion, or $56-billion, to the national product over that period. Since the observed increase in national product was $152-billion, 37 per cent of it is thus accounted for by the educational investment.

This is a dazzling figure, but no less dazzling than the methodology which produced it. To say that education contributed 37 per cent of the increase in measured income (or national product) is to say that, had the stock of education remained at a constant dollar level between 1929 and 1957, the annual product of the economy would have increased 37 per cent less than it actually did. The analysis further implies that a yield of the same order of magnitude can be expected from future educational investments, in the United States and elsewhere. My impression is that both the conclusion and its implication are unwarranted, for each step of the computation opens the way to important errors. (A good deal of the criticism I shall offer has already been set forth by Schultz himself in his cautioning and qualifying statements. My point is that it adds up to more than a qualification.)

Even under the favorable assumption that all men receiving a given education will command the same future income, the observed income differential would only indicate what *marginal* education contributes to the national product. Employers will call for educated employees only so long as the salary differential is no greater than the value added to their product. Furthermore, as more educated people enter the labor force, each one contributes significantly less to productivity. Thus, in a relatively stabilized employment situation, there is near equality between the differential salary paid and the national product to be gained by educating another worker (or to be lost by educating one less).

If, starting with this stable situation, 10 per cent fewer workers were educated, the loss of national productivity per worker would be more than the productivity of marginal personnel and, therefore, more than the differential salary; if a further 10 per cent were deprived of education, the loss in productivity would be even larger; and so on. The loss in national product if only half as many people were educated would be far more than, as Schultz asserts, the observed salary differential times the number of missing educations.

An error of the same nature occurs in Schultz's computation of the virtual costs of education. He computes the cost in income foregone as the sum of salaries which the students could have earned, at prevailing rates, during the additional school years involved. However, the prevailing wage in the school-age group reflects what the economy gains from additional workers in that group when the number actually employed is small. If a large number of those in school had actually been shifted to employment, their average marginal productivity would have been far less than it was.

A second problem is that the differential earnings between differently educated individuals arise from the greater ability of those who are better educated and from the superior opportunities accorded them, as well as from the education itself. Attempts have been made to separate the effects of education per se from these associated factors by comparing the future earnings of differently educated individuals in otherwise homogeneous strata. The figures on returns used by Schultz are adjusted downwards on the basis of computations of this nature carried out by Gary S. Becker. This still omits, however, the fact of interaction between education and the opportunity-ability complex. A high-school education adds, on the average, $70,000 to one's earnings over a lifetime; but the differential is certainly higher in certain strata and lower in others. The specific contribution of education to national produce in any give case depends greatly on the education's carrier.

When speaking of the potential effect of a cut in (or addition to) the stock of a particular education, we must assume that it is effected efficiently—that is, in such a way that minimum losses (or a maximum gain) are inflicted on the economy. This would mean cutting the education of those students for whom the extra education would have meant the least rise in income. For reasonably small cuts, the loss of national product per education foregone would then be far less than the average differential of all similarly educated students. Yet it is the latter which Schultz uses in his computation.

Note that the error on this account acts in an opposite direction from the one mentioned earlier. We found then that earnings *under-estimate* the loss to the extent that a marginal-productivity measure is used to compute the effect of large shifts in the stock of education. There is a chance, therefore, that the two errors will offset one another, but I can think of no good reason why they should.

Next, of course, is the problem of finding how much of the total costs of education, as we know them, are necessary to develop productive skills. Schultz finds it "plausible that approximately one-half of the total costs of high school education and three-fifths of the total costs of higher education represent investments in future earnings." We may interpret this as meaning that the same growth in future earnings and productivity could be obtained with selective educational expenditures equal to one half and three fifths, respectively, of what they are. The remainder is apparently used to increase the consumption content of education beyond what is generated as a by-product of the productive core. (Even the most technical education opens the way to future intellectual pleasures and certainly to a more pleasant and prestigious form of employment.)

Schultz does point out one implication of this dichotomy—that the return of the specific "investments in future earnings" is 24 per cent for a high-school education (rather than 12 per cent, as previously expressed) and 18 per cent for a college education (rather than 11 per cent). He fails, however, to draw explicitly the further conclusion that a failure to increase the dollar stock of education from its 1929 level ($180-billion) might either have wrecked the economy or affected its growth only slightly, depending on what sort of educational expenditures were undertaken.

Assuming that one half of the stock of education represents an unproductive investment for direct consumption, the 1929 *productive* stock could have been doubled, over time, without changing the total stock's value, simply by shifting unproductive expenditures to the area of productive education. This would have meant a growth of $35.3-billion [180/2 x (.196x2)] in a national product, which is only $21-billion less than the increase otherwise calculated. Alternatively, the whole stock could theoretically have been shifted to consumption education, and the national product would have been reduced by at least $35-billion (calculated on the basis of marginal yields) and probably much more. Similar comparisons can be made regarding the effect of the actual increase in the stock of education from 1929 to 1958 under alternative investment policies. There is thus no validity to the notion that 37 per cent of the growth in national product would have been missed without the increase in the stock of education, or that the actual increase in that stock could not have resulted in much less or much more growth.

A more fundamental question is raised by the assumption that there is an effective relationship between earning differentials and marginal productivities. For one thing, earnings measure productivity only from the standpoint of individual employers of the skill. The existence of a large pool of skilled individuals does, however, tend to create a diffused economy, characterized by cross-fertilization, improved communications and conditions for further technical progress —an effect which is not reflected in the salary differentials. In addition, education opens up young minds, and much of it generates a significant by-product in research; both these factors add to the growth potential of the economy yet show no impact on differential earnings.

Another area of discrepancy between earning differentials and productivity is those professions, such as teaching and the ministry, in which incomes are traditionally below their assumed marginal contribution to social welfare. Conversely, incomes overvalue the social product of education whenever jobs are upgraded to require a non-essential high-school diploma or college degree. To illustrate the point, let us imagine that our economy, twenty years from now, has the same population, the same national product and the same jobs, but that, because of extended higher education, the jobs now held by high-school graduates are available only to college graduates. The additional college education would then have no value as a productive investment, for the salary differential does not reflect *acquired* differences in potential productivity.

In this hypothetical society, because of the rigidities of employment and procedures for promotion, the college degree is taken as a fair indicator of inherent ability and acceptability—or, at any rate, of qualities acquired before college. A college-educated salesman may be better, and will in general be no worse, than a man who never met the challenge of higher education. The more graduates there are available, the more tempting it is for management to apply this trouble-free test; and as more young people become aware of this trend, the more necessary it becomes for them to obtain the golden passkey. Millions of employees in clerical, sales and supervisory positions undertake years of education which contribute little to their effectiveness but which enable them to be selected for their jobs.

Clearly, monetary returns in this case bear no direct relation to the productivity of social resources invested in education. The productivity of the educational increment would, instead, depend on how accurately the college degrees identify individuals endowed with certain desirable qualities. The extra investment in education would be justified, not in relation to differential earnings, but by showing that the selection cannot be made at lower cost by other methods (such as general tests administered by personnel officers) and that the economic advantage of the more precise allocation of persons to jobs is at least equal to the cost of the operation.

It is not inconceivable, therefore, that the yield computed by Schultz could, on this account, be cut by fifty per cent or more.

As long as the measures of productivity under review are only meant to illustrate broadly the importance of education for economic growth, their fallacies can do little harm. It is natural, however, that economic planners should refer to these figures—or, at least, to their order of magnitude—in formulating objectives for increased investment in education. To the extent that these planners rely on either the computed yields or the calculated contribution of education to the national product, their chances of getting anything near the expected increase in productivity are remote; and if they are to determine on this basis the effective yield of education relative to that of alternative investments, God in His infinite wisdom must help them.

More useful information would be generated by relating returns to *specific* stocks of education—that is, to the accumulated cost of submitting students to specific programs of training. Even this technique, however, would be ineffective as long as social returns are assumed to be related directly to differential earnings. One may, in fact, doubt the wisdom, practicality and usefulness of computing the dollar value of any stock of education. Investment processes can best be described as optimal investment choices made in terms of resource *flows* applied in successive periods and output *flows* appearing in a related pattern over time. Stocks are indeed created in the process, but it is not always useful, and it is almost never simple, to measure that stock in a single unit.

The general practice of measuring and valuing stocks arises from the fact of individual ownership and exchange of assets, from the advantage it offers in describing or comparing economic systems and from the numerous situations in which investment problems can be analyzed more simply by reference to homogeneous stocks. Awkward valuations of a stock can be by-passed, however, when the investment process does not give birth to exchangeable assets—for example, investment programs carried out through human beings.

Please note that I am bringing forth practical, not moral considerations. For any conceivable practical purpose, all we need to know is what increase in national product over some chosen horizon would result from alternative series of yearly expenditures on alternative programs of education and in alternative channels of investment. Incidentally, the sooner economists abandon attempts at measuring past contributions of "capital," "labor" and the "residual factor" to economic growth and concentrate instead on the choices open to countries at various stages of development, the better off we shall all be.

Before turning to specific problems of planning, let me point out that the danger of resource misallocation remains even if, as some analysts suggest, the task of adjusting educational investments is entrusted wholly to the purchasers of education (students) through the usual market mechanisms. The basic recommendation is that tuitions should be raised so that the students will bear their "proper" share of the cost of education. Purchasers would still come forward as long as the yield, in the form of differential earnings and consumption benefits, represents a favorable investment opportunity. The educational investment would presumably stabilize at an optimum level, since its contribution to national product (inclusive of consumption benefits) would equal, at the margin, that of investment resources in other channels.

The trouble with this argument is that it reactivates the gross error of equating differential earnings with the marginal productivity of education. It mocks reality further by assuming that all potential students can invest—and invest wisely—in education as long as the expected yield is as good as in, say, utility bonds. It also suggests, rather too lightly, that the total costs of education can be imputed separately to the various services it contributes or, alternatively, that there is an expressed demand for each service at different prices. While marketing does indeed have a role to play, that role should be carefully circumscribed, and some external guidance must be provided.

This is not the place, however, to analyze these points in detail. My central concern has been to deflate the advocated dependence on cost-earnings relationships to generate adequate investments in productive education. Such dependence is an almost congenital defect of market schemes, not just an aberration of would-be planners.

II. *Planning for productive education in developed economies*

What, then, is one to do? I suggest that, for planning purposes, marginal productivity and differential earnings can be useful in solving what economists call partial-optimization problems—in the present case, the determination of optimal patterns of education for specific jobs. Beyond this, I think it best to rely on so-called input-output assumptions—to admit, as an approximation, that a given level of production in any sector requires a certain number of jobs of each class and, therefore, a certain number of graduates from each scheduled program of education. Let me first outline the major steps of the computation and then attempt to justify and qualify the procedure.

1——Taking technological trends into account, list, for each sector of the economy, all job categories and attending qualifications in terms of both general education and special skills and knowledge.

2——Assume that a person's general educational requirements are best satisfied before he enters the labor force and best provided by full-time institutions within the framework of traditional *complete* cycles (in the U.S. system: elementary school, junior high school, senior high school, junior college, college, graduate school) .

3——For each job-sector category, list the alternative minimum programs of education for providing the specialized skills and knowledge needed for qualification (the alternative mixes of initial formal education, direct on-the-job training and so on) . Compare the discounted net returns under each alternative by relating costs (inclusive of sacrificed earnings) to earnings over life and to the average yield on long-term investments.[2] Select the educational mix showing the highest discounted net return.

4——For each job-sector category, list the formal courses needed on a yearly average, after qualification, for expected retraining or updating.

5——Given the planned growth of each economic sector and expected workloads, compute the number of jobs in each category in each sector to be filled during each year of the planning horizon. In view of the results of steps 1, 2 and 3, this gives for each year the total need for personnel who have (a) completed specific cycles of general education in full-time institutions before entering the labor force; (b) completed specific programs of specialized education in full-time institutions before entering the labor force; (c) taken specific specialization courses while working over a specific number of years in specific job categories; and (d) worked without concurrent formal training over a specific number of years in specific job categories. In view of the results of step 4, we are also provided with a measure of the annual expenditure on formal retraining and updating expected over each year of the horizon.

Before continuing, let us be clear as to what we are seeking. The plan is to supply at minimum cost, over a certain portion of the future, the trained personnel required by the planned growth of each economic sector. The investment in education which this program implies is not meant to represent an optimum educational investment from the standpoint of national welfare. The investment —at least in the more affluent economies—must expand both in response to individuals' demand for consumption education and in response to the social demand for the many diffused benefits of education.

The schedule of productive education needs should, therefore, be viewed as a minimum objective of planning. Whether the remaining objectives are served through market mechanisms (sale of education at substantial tuitions) or through collective decisions (selective free education), the actual number of students enrolled in the scheduled programs or in broader programs having higher consumption content will far exceed, on the aggregate, the number called for in the name of productivity. The major role of the proposed computation is to provide a guard-rail, a standard against which to measure and correct serious failures of the system in sensitive areas. Only in the least developed economies—where national income does not justify the luxury of intellectual consumption, except as a strict by-product—may the schedule of productive educational requirements be taken as an absolute planning objective.

Note that the objective has so far been expressed in terms of a minimum dated stock over each year of the horizon, a minimum number of people who have been subjected to specific forms of training and are currently available for work in corresponding occupations. It is also possible to compute the educational enrollments required in each scheduled program over the years to satisfy the stock needs at each point of time. One ought to distinguish in this respect between (a) *objective enrollment needs,* assuming that all jobs are filled by persons who, from their first school day, have followed precisely the program of education outlined as optimum for the job, and (b) *effective* enrollment needs, assuming that all enrollments are, at least in part, for the purpose of job training but that individuals will fail at each stage to distribute themselves among further training programs in the correct pattern and that noncompensating losses of individuals will occur at each stage of the training process.

The computation requires information on the age distribution of the population and on the projected pattern of entry into and retirement from the labor force. Note also that, unless the economy is already on the optimum path (or tends to overfulfill its needs for trained personnel as a result of a high demand for the consumption by-product), it will need time to establish a pattern of enrollments that will meet the needs of planned growth year after year. How much time it will need will be determined mostly by the present distribution of education among those individuals who are either in the labor force or intended for it.

It follows that, in the period immediately ahead, growth may have to be adjusted downward because of a limited availability of manpower; the alternative is to proceed with personnel whose training does not meet long-run standards of efficiency. The second solution will prevail in developed economies which have a large base of general education and industrial skill. The first solution is more likely in the case of underdeveloped economies, if they must build their educated labor force from scratch and are engaged in a serious effort to develop. Under this sort of pressure, a computation of optimum patterns of training on the basis of empirical costs and earnings would be meaningless, if at all feasible, and the notion of a leisurely long-run adjustment to optimal manpower structures makes little sense.

An additional complication is that the total expenditure of education required for maximum growth may represent a significant portion of available investment resources in an underdeveloped economy, so that it is not possible, even as a first approximation, to calculate growth independently and then to compute educational requirements. The planning of education may require reference to integrated dynamic models of the economy, with alternative schemes of education compared not on the basis of earnings and costs in each trade but in terms of their aggregate feasibility and their aggregate effect on economic growth in the immediate future.

We may now turn to justifications and qualifications. I have assumed that, given a normal course of advance in technological knowledge, the cost of educating people for the new qualifications required under alternative technologies has no substantial bearing on the choice of technology, including the specification and distribution of jobs associated with it. We therefore operate with independent technological requirements for personnel under each job category, expressed as a function of the volume of production in each economic sector. On the other hand, we take explicit account of substitution possibilities among alternative schemes of specialized education leading to job qualification. For this purpose, even though earnings must be rejected as an absolute measure of marginal productivity, it is probably safe to use them as a measure of relative productivities in a given class of jobs within a single economic sector.

This leaves unanswered a number of questions, and I shall conclude by attempting to answer two which appear most urgent:

First, is it possible to plan or to estimate the growth of all economic sectors without regard to the implied investment in productive education, then to estimate the necessary magnitude of the latter as a function of calculated growth? The answer is: No, it is not, unless growth (as planned or estimated) leaves unemployed a substantial amount of resources, so that the educational investment is sure to be accommodated. Even then, expenditures in the education sector will require increased production in the supplying sectors (construction, publishing, instruments and so on) and, through them, in practically all sectors of the economy. The anticipated educational requirements for trained personnel must therefore be adjusted to the new figures on growth; these in turn must be adjusted to the revised educational requirements—and so on, in an endless cycle. In addition, care must be taken to compute the requirements of trained personnel for the education sector itself, and doing so induces another set of gyrations.

The number of steps necessary to generate sufficiently good approximations need not be large, however. It can easily be reduced to one or two if growth in all sectors is calculated, from the start, on the assumption that there will be annual expenditures on productive education, the amount of such expenditures growing in the same relation to national income as in the recent past.

Calculations of growth must, of course, always reflect an additional expenditure on education to satisfy both individual consumption objectives and the social demand for diffused benefits. Since productive education provides benefits of this type as a by-product and makes it possible to provide consumption education at lower cost, the estimated (or planned) expenditure on this account must be continually adjusted to the calculated volume of productive education. (The combination of consumption courses with programs otherwise designed for productivity, a combination which is traditional in a good deal of our education, allows production at low cost by absorbing the slack in facilities needed for the program's operation; that is, it makes possible a spread of overhead.)

When the whole economy is planned for maximum growth with full utilization of its resources, or when full employment is expected in an unmanaged economy, it becomes necessary to take into account the drain on investment resources represented by the production of education. This computation would, in principle, require the full integration of educational processes in a detailed dynamic model of the economy. The procedure may be simplified, however, by deriving rough but simple relationships between the growth of each sector and the necessary investment in productive education over the preceding years. The optimum growth path of the economy (in societies with over-all planning) or its expected growth (in unmanaged economies) can thus be calculated without inconsistencies, giving good approximations to the production profile in each sector. The detailed computation of educational needs can then proceed on the basis of these production figures, without further reference to their interdependence.

The second question is: Given the fact that productive education and education for other purposes are joint, what is the proper cost to apply in our computation of discounted net returns of alternative productive educations? I speak of jointness because, in practice, education cannot be given for one purpose without serving—and, to a degree, requiring—the other as well. At the same time, given the need for decentralization of the educational plant, production of education for one purpose reduces the costs of producing education for other purposes.

The problem which jointness presents can be illustrated by an extreme example. Let us imagine that demand for formal education in the applied sciences as a consumption good exceeds what can be used productively in the economy. When we consider replacing nongraduates by graduates in occupations where qualification would thereby be accelerated, we find that there are (or will be) available a more than sufficient number of graduates who acquired their education because they—or the community on their behalf—liked it. A decision to employ them in preference to nongraduates will not add to social costs, and it would be senseless to develop an alternative program of on-the-job training on the pretext that formal education is a more costly process.

Before attempting to answer the question, let me eliminate from consideration a by-product of education which we may call research or, more generally, intellectual creation. Because much of the research carried out in association with education displaces outside research, the social cost of education in the research-education package is simply the excess cost of the package over what the equivalent research would cost if produced independently.

If we assume that those who purchase research (governments, foundations and firms) distribute their funds among the producers (government projects, independent research organizations, industrial research units and educational institutions) in such a way that their dollars bring everywhere the same return (some expected value of yield on research), the marginal cost of the research carried out in universities is equal to the sum they receive on this account. The proper cost of education is obtained, therefore, by subtracting revenues earned in research from aggregate costs. (This holds strictly only if there is an excess demand for academic intellectual creation in all fields, not only in engineering and the sciences. It would require, in particular, that the community adequately finance creative work in the arts and humanities through public or philanthropic grants.)

Once the costs of alternative educations have been calculated in this manner, our problem is to adjust our calculations for the diffused and consumption benefits. The true social cost of education absorbed in productive skills should, of course, be computed net of the value of the other benefits created. I postulate, however, that the magnitude of these benefits is independent of the choice among alternative programs. Net costs are thus in the same ratio as absolute costs, and our choice can proceed on the basis of the latter.

As to individual consumption benefits, I shall offer what I consider a reasonable compromise, fully realizing that it lacks both empirical and analytical substance. I assume, first, that it is possible to distinguish between general and specialized educational requirements for any job qualification. What subject matter falls within the definition of a general education is determined by public consensus, but I am ready to accept this consensus. I also ignore the possibility that general

education may, in a sense, be a substitute for specialized training
or that it can be oriented in such a way that the cost of specialized
training will be reduced. Considering the existing educational technologies and taking account of the high consumption by-product of
general education, I finally suggest that one always acquires general
education best in formal programs within full-time institutions before
he enters the labor force. Note that all these assumptions were either
stated or implicitly contained in my earlier procedural sketch. Their
net effect is to limit the problem of choice between alternative educational processes to specialized education.

The next gross simplification which I propose is that the consumption content of specialized education is the same irrespective
of how it is acquired. This would permit a comparison of alternative
educational schemes on the basis of actual cost, without reference
to their consumption component. On the other hand, it is reasonable
to calculate the cost of initial specialized training which is given
jointly with programs oriented toward consumption. At least for the
wealthier economies, we should assume that initial specialized training
will be given in institutions which provide a complementary program
of general education, the latter at a level above the requirements
for the job. The mix may be established on the basis of time or
according to some traditional pattern. We may assume that there
is an effective consumption demand for the general education
component.

The proper cost of the specialized training, therefore, is the cost
of the mixed education *net* of the cost of an equivalent general education independently produced. This will normally be less than the
cost of specialized training produced in isolation, since, as I have
already pointed out, many facilities can be used jointly with a spread
of overhead and it is probable that either type of training is absorbed more effectively when offered simultaneously with the other.

As a last word, I wish to apologize for offering a recipe for
empirical computations without illustrating it with figures or even
suggesting sources for the needed data. This is bad manners, indeed,
and I hope someday to be put in a position to make amends. Mean-
while, I believe that the methodology I have outlined is more promising than its alternatives, even if the cost of obtaining data forces
us to operate at a high level of aggregation or to substitute observed
trends for the calculation of optimal patterns of education.

REFERENCES

1. See, in particular, two papers by Professor Schultz: "Investment in Human Capital," *American Economic Review,* LI (March 1961), pp. 1-17; and "Education and Economic Growth," *Social Forces Influencing American Education,* edited by Nelson B. Henry (Chicago: The National Society for the Study of Education, 1961).
2. For a theoretical treatment of this category of problems, see Gary S. Becker, "Investment in Human Capital" (preliminary draft submitted to the Exploratory Conference on Capital Investment in Human Beings, December 1-12, 1961, National Bureau of Economic Research).

COMMENTARY

American higher education must now come to grips with a multidimensional problem. It must expand, but because the social benefits created by education are not easily calculable, there are no clearly marked guidelines to indicate a uniquely appropriate direction and magnitude for the expansion. Various writers have dealt with the problem and have set forth a universe of suggested remedies. Much of the literature has been controversial, but two important points have gained nearly unanimous endorsement. *First,* a full-fledged market solution—charging full cost and abolishing all institutional subsidies to students—is not a satisfactory policy. John Vaizey of Oxford reminded those present that even such staunch conservatives as the classical and neoclassical economists, from Adam Smith to Marshall, concurred on this point; almost without exception they all flew the flag of universal free education. *Second,* even though the social returns from investment in education are large, they are not infinite; and similarly, even though America is an affluent society, its wealth is not, practically speaking, unlimited. Thus allocation is still a problem. Because resources are limited and alternative outlets also promise high social returns, certain worthwhile educational endeavors cannot be undertaken; investment in education cannot currently be expanded to the point where the expected social rate of return is zero.

For one who thinks of education as an industry, inspection of the recent literature will readily uncover a seeming paradox. In most conventional economic undertakings, sales and profits are positively correlated; more sales generally mean larger profits. A forecast of an expanding market is sweet music to the ears of an industrialist.

For educational administrators, however, the situation is somewhat different. They can confidently expect that undergraduate enrollment in American institutions of higher learning will more than double between 1960 and 1970. And yet their reaction to this fact is more likely, "How can we possibly finance this expansion?" rather than "How fortunate to be in a booming industry"; their reaction is more nearly one of panic than of joy. Resolving this seeming paradox involves making a point which, although perhaps obvious, is nonetheless crucially important and thus merits special emphasis: selling education is not an economically profitable undertaking. The price tag on a unit of education is less than the average cost of providing it. Thus, whereas for industry more sales mean an increase in the excess of revenue over cost, for education permanently increased enrollments may very often mean larger total losses. It is knowledge of this fact which propels educational administrators upon a course of sober thought, rather than upon one of unmitigated joy, when they contemplate the impending expansion.

In addition to the one just mentioned, there is a second factor, a long-run trend factor, which accentuates education's economic woes and which concerns productivity. Admittedly one must exercise the most extreme caution in making definitive statements about productivity, for in addition to the difficulty of deriving reliable empirical results, there is the bothersome complication that the educational product itself has been changing. Early in this century that product was little more than a relatively simple teacher-student relationship. Since then frills have been added, and today medical service, vocational guidance, hot lunches, housing football teams and the like have become an integral part of the product. These considerations are important, but fortunately they are not sufficient to invalidate one general conclusion: during this century education has not received an equitable share of the tremendous gains in productivity with which many sectors of the economy have been blessed. This outcome was not inevitable; rather, it is a direct result of the form in which those sectors which did experience major gains in productivity chose to accept them. They elected rising incomes rather than falling prices. By so doing they managed to hoard the fruits of their progress. Had they opted for falling prices instead, they could have shared those benefits with all sectors of the economy. But they have acted otherwise, and one clear result of that action is that education now finds itself in a relatively weak financial position vis-á-vis those sectors of the economy which have experienced large gains in output per unit of input. Education must pay ever rising prices for those goods and services which it buys, without at the same time falling heir to compensating increase in productivity.

In addition to dealing with aggregate concepts, the members of the seminar also found it useful to distinguish between the public and the private sectors of American higher education. The pressure to expand affects these two sectors rather differently. For private institutions, mandatory pressure to expand is nonexistent; they may enroll as few students as they wish. Public institutions lack such complete freedom. In the past the law required them to admit virtually all applicants who lived in the state and possessed a high-school diploma. Now the trend seems to be away from such rigid requirements, but progress in this direction is even now only limited. Thus it is still generally true that, in order to restrict enrollments, public institutions must limit the number of applicants or, in the economist's traditional language, reduce demand. One readily available technique for achieving this end is raising the price of education.

Having considered these general points, the discussants directed their attention toward some practical measures for solving educational institutions' financial problems. For the public sector there are two alternative proposals which operate within the existing institutional framework. The first, advocated by Professors Harris and Daniere, is for that sector to rely more than it currently does on fees from students. Specifically, the proposal is to raise those fees and to implement, concurrently with the new schedule of fees, some apparatus for providing students with subsidized loans on flexible terms. One plan is to relate repayments to future income and to forgive outstanding indebtedness after a period of years. Such a scheme would have three fairly obvious results. As Professor Daniere noted, it would make the individual's initial decision to seek or not to seek a higher education more of an investment decision in the strict economic sense than it presently is. It would tend to shift the burden of financing higher education away from the general taxpayer and toward the student and his family or sponsor. Finally, it would tend to diminish existing differences between the financial structures of public and private institutions of higher learning.

Public institutions frequently have low standards for admission, a high rate of dropouts and a large proportion of their operating expenditures coming from general tax funds rather than from students' fees. The second major proposal supported by Professor John Meyer, of Harvard University, is not to tamper with this present system in selling the first two years of a college education but to adopt more ingenious pricing policies for the last two years of college and for graduate education. One useful guide for the administrator to consider when he renovates portions of his pricing structure is the student's expected earned income. Although it is surely true that all income differentials cannot be attributed to differences in education, some can; and the case, for example, for charging law and business school students full cost and at the same time subsidizing education and divinity school students is strong. For medical and certain other students the case is less clear-cut. One possibility is to charge them a nominal initial fee and then a small percentage of their actual annual income, if that income exceeds a certain minimum, until they have paid the full cost of their training. Such a scheme is mildly reminiscent of the "guaranteed to work or double your money back" approach to selling. In this case, "work" can be translated as "bring you an annual income of X dollars." Another set of criteria that might be useful in establishing fees is academic performance. Tuition might be only $300 for a student with an A average, $1500 for one with a C average. Obviously this example is only suggestive. To be workable the system would have to allow for the facts that a C is as great an achievement for some students as an A is for others and that there can be much educational value in nonacademic extracurricular activities. A trading ratio could be established between grades and what the administration considers worthwhile extracurricular activities. For example, a B average and no extracurricular activities might be equivalent to a C+ average and participating on a varsity team. Such a plan would admittedly be arbitrary, but it could probably be designed so that it won the majority's support.

The rationale underlying each proposal can be briefly stated. Those favoring the first, making the decision to purchase a higher education more of an investment decision at the outset by raising the price and offering loans, argue along several lines. Daniere's argument is that, given the size of resources involved, it is not possible to give *all* individuals between the ages of seventeen and twenty-four an opportunity to follow *any* program of higher education they may be tempted to investigate. If not restrained by a rational comparison of advantages obtained and financial obligations undertaken, they will have to be so restrained through necessarily rigid and impersonal requirements for admission or continuation. So long as the necessary financing is made effectively available to all candidates and is flexible enough not to create excessive burdens in later life, substantial tuitions accompanied by liberalized admission and transfer procedures represent, according to Daniere, a surer path to freedom and opportunity than to any feasible alternatives. In partial contrast, Professor Harris argued in favor of increasing tuition along the lines of financial expediency and equity. On the one hand, he thinks it doubtful that legislatures will provide sufficient funds to finance the contemplated expansion. On the other hand, by tending to shift the financial burden from the general taxpayer to the user, raising tuition will, Harris claimed, diminish such undesirable results as, for instance, having farmers in northern Michigan subsidize the children of General Motors' executives at the University of Michigan. More broadly, it avoids having the poor subsidize the rich.

Those favoring the second proposal, maintaining the present system for the first two years of college, make several points. They argue that their opponents' notions about equity are badly taken on two counts: as a matter of fact, children of rich parents by and large attend private rather than public institutions of higher learning. Also, they point out that their opponents make only an isolated attack on a single transfer, when in fact many similar transfers continually occur in this economy. For example, Meyer argued that because of the schedule of railroad rates, marginal freight shippers subsidize rich advertising executives living in Westchester County. Correcting single transfers of this sort is not, therefore, the primary concern. The real issue is how the costs of this transfer compare with the costs of abandoning the system. The proposed system of loans would require a complicated and expensive bureaucracy. The open and flexible system of easy admission and a high rate of attrition is simple to administer and relatively cheap to operate. Thus in the end those favoring the second proposal contradict their opponents' initial point and claim that the first proposal is not nearly as economical as its proponents suggest. Finally, they criticize the Harris-Daniere system because it requires a student to make an investment decision at the age of seventeen, even though one of the necessary conditions to guarante that the decision will be sound is not likely to be fulfilled then. That condition is that the student knows for certain what career he wishes to pursue. It is unrealistic to expect a seventeen-year-old to have such knowledge; however, it is not such an unrealistic expectation for a nineteen-or twenty-year-old who has completed several years of college. By then a student is likely to know what he wants to do; the necessary condition for an intelligent investment decision is thus fulfilled; and subject to the exceptions already noted, charging the student the full cost of his education from that time on seems justifiable.

Private institutions of higher learning are another matter. The statement made earlier that these institutions are under no mandatory pressure to expand may have conveyed the impression that they have no serious economic problems. Such an impression is absolutely wrong. Their financial troubles are severe, and not a few thoughtful commentators predict that some of the least hearty among them may soon expire.

A survey of the economic problems of the private sector reveals an apparent anomaly. On the one hand, although the objective differences between the educational product of the private and that of the public sector are rapidly diminishing and are soon likely to vanish virtually altogether, the price of the former is approximately four times as large as that of the latter. This uncompetitive pricing structure seriously endangers the private sector's ability to maintain its share of the market; it is one of the horns of the dilemma which threatens that sector. On the other hand, however, many private institutions now enjoy and, as Professor Meyer mentioned, are likely to continue enjoying an unprecedented excess demand for their product. For a segment of the private sector, the ratio of rejected to admitted applicants is about three or four to one; and in spite of the low prices prevailing in the public sector, a number of private institutions, perhaps 150, could double their prices and still fill their classrooms.

This latter fact helps to explain the anomaly and is especially important because it underlines a crucial point: the private institutions' economic woes are not solely attributable to the pricing policies of the public institutions. To a large extent those woes are self-imposed. Something perhaps best characterized as a sense of social responsibility makes the so-called prestige private institutions unwilling to practice the sort of pricing policies that would restore their liquidity. This restraint is a rather new development. Professor Meyer argued that earlier in this century private institutions had a considerably smaller excess of demand over supply at the prevailing price than they now do, perhaps none at all; supply and demand were then more nearly equal than they now appear to be. Today these institutions are unwilling to accept the sort of student body—certainly rich and probably of questionable academic competence—which such a pricing policy would thrust upon them. There is thus a very real sense, Meyer concluded, in which today's private institutions are acting like public institutions. Phrased in the simplest possible terms, today's private institutions have shown an unwillingness to exploit the economic potential of their monopoly positions but have rather chosen, even at the cost of financial sacrifice, to tailor their behavior to the dictates of broad social needs.

Even though the large price differential between the public and the private sector is not the *sine qua non* of the latter's problems, it is still quite influential in creating them. This fact sheds new light in the controversy between the alternative methods for solving the public institutions' financial problems. The suggestion that the public institutions increase their liquidity by raising their fees has caused some people to wonder out loud exactly whose salvation this proposal is really intended to insure. The public institutions could, after all, solve their problems in many ways, but only the increased-fee solution, by reducing the price differential between the two sectors, would, as a corollary to its avowed purpose, help the private sector to bolster its competitive position. Anyone who advocates increased fees in the public sector as a method for helping the private sector is implicitly suggesting that the former's strong competitive position emanates unfairly from the state's plentiful resources, which are at its disposal and which permit it to sell education at a much smaller fraction of total cost than the private sector, with its more limited fund of resources, can afford. Viewed in this light, the proposal to increase fees in the public sector is an ingenious technique for reducing the element of unfair competition which is inherent in the system as it now stands. Alternatively, however, that proposal can also be viewed in another way: as a reactionary scheme for perpetuating an untenable network of private institutions.

Everything said so far involves dealing with the problem of expansion within a given institutional framework. Implicit in this approach is the notion that the product mix will remain constant—that for example, the four-year liberal-arts divisions of state universities will enroll the same proportion of all undergraduates in 1970 that they did in 1960. It need not be this way, however. Professor Meyer urged that designers of policy should not overlook the possibility of handling the expansion primarily by changing the proportions in which the various types of higher education are provided. Rather than leaving the product constant and working only through the pricing mechanism, which is what those proposals already mentioned basically amout to, administrators could also attack the problem of expansion by diversifying the product itself. Specifically, this approach might mean channeling a large proportion of the incremental enrollment into two-year community or junior colleges. Professor Meyer suggested that such a program would probably better meet the needs of many students in 1970 than would a four-year, Bachelor of Arts program in a large state university. It should be emphasized that the possibility of solving the problem of expansion at least in part by diversifying the product does not devalue the earlier discussion about fees, loans, rationing, more ingenious pricing policies and the like. It simply adds a new dimension to this complex of concepts and one which educational administrators may find appealing.

Part III:
Management of Colleges and Universities

11. Roles and Responsibilities in Management of IHL

PAPER BY . . . *John J. Corson*
Management Consultant, McKinsey & Company, and
Professor of Public and International Affairs,
Princeton University

I should like to direct your attention to a series of fundamental questions concerning the governance of colleges and universities. The core of these questions is well stated in an interesting pamphlet by A. P. Rowe, formerly vice chancellor of the University of Adelaide, Australia. He titled his pamphlet *Efficiency and Freedom,* and in it he demonstrated the dilemma which universities face in seeking to reconcile these two concepts. This is, in brief, the central problem of all governance, whether in a business enterprise, a government or a university: how can the enterprise be efficient and, at the same time, the individual be free to exercise his talents to the fullest?

The ideal which these two terms imply, it seems to me, is not a "tight ship" (on which neither efficiency nor freedom necessarily exist) but an institution that has clear-cut goals and is able to marshal the energies of those who make up the enterprise toward those goals.

There are five important qualities which characterize colleges and universities and which are obstacles to achieving effective governance of them. The first is that most colleges and universities have no explicit statements of purpose. I once questioned Wallace Sterling, the able president of Stanford, on this point. I pressed him to say what was "different" about Stanford, what was distinctive about its objectives, practices and performance? "In short," I asked, "what is Stanford trying to do that Berkeley is not trying to do?" After pa-

231

tiently listening to my persistent questions, he replied, "A university can't have *a* purpose; it has a multiplicity of purposes."

Yet students of administration have long contended that a clear guiding purpose is essential to the effective administration of any human enterprise. To harness the energies of a group of people, a clear statement of purpose is essential. And it has been proved that a guiding purpose can be precisely defined even for an enterprise concerned with the universality of knowledge; witness Princeton, Wesleyan and California Institute of Technology. There are all too few others, but there are some. I am reassured in this viewpoint by Harold Dodds' statement in his book *The Academic President: Educator or Caretaker?*: "Without forcing all components into a single pattern, the preparation of a master plan is an opportunity to consider interrelation of knowledge at its highest level, which a university—in contrast to a multi-versity—should stand for."

The second obstacle to effective governance of a university is the diverging interests and loyalties of the faculty members. The university's decision-making process is complicated by the intense attachment of the individual faculty member to his discipline, rather than to the institution. He makes his reputation and his career in chemistry, say, or in economics, rather than in the institution. He may start out as an assistant professor of economics at Franklin and Marshall, then accept an associate professorship at the University of Pennsylvania and then be invited to Harvard—because of his growing reputation as an economist. His loyalties are to the profession. This attachment of the individual faculty member to his discipline makes it difficult to harness the energies of the faculty as a whole into a single enterprise.

The third obstacle to efficient governance is that the university is seldom an interrelated whole. It is a congeries of schools, colleges, divisions, libraries, institutes and still other relatively autonomous units. It is not a whole. Edward H. Litchfield, Chancellor of the University of Pittsburgh, in his 1961 convocation address, argued brilliantly for an "organic institution," for the logic of relating the disciplines and the professions in a unified attack on research problems, as well as in a unified approach to teaching. But this ideal is rarely met.

The fourth obstacle is the diffusion of responsibility for decision-making. This is probably the central factor which distinguishes the governance of a college or university. In a business enterprise, decision-making is concentrated in very considerable part on the chief executive. He may delegate, but power is concentrated on and in him. In government, the same is true. Indeed, in too many instances, the statutes require that the chief executive be responsible for decisions personally—a provision which tends to concentrate in the chief executive entirely too much responsibility.

In a university, substantially less responsibility and authority are focused in the chief executive and/or the governing board. The unique aspect of the governance of the college or university is, in fact, the extent to which responsibility for decision-making is distributed among trustees, administrators, faculty and staff. Leadership, as a substitute for the exercise of authority, is therefore a highly essential ingredient of governance.

The fifth obstacle, which characterizes primarily state colleges and universities, is the strict limitation of the institution's autonomy. At the State University of New York, for example, decisions as to capital expenditures, the purchase of equipment for the library and the laboratories, the appointment of nonacademic personnel and, to a degree, faculty selection are governed largely by agencies of the state government, beyond the control of the university's trustees, president or staff.

Consider this illustration: At the School of Pharmacy at the University of Buffalo (a unit within the State University), the chancellor and dean had an opportunity, early in 1962, to employ two men whom they regarded as especially able professors of pharmacy. One, an Englishman, wanted to come to this country, but to induce him to come to Buffalo, the university had to offer him a salary $1800 higher than that authorized by the established salary structure. Neither the chancellor nor the trustees of the University of Buffalo, however, had authority to decide whether they should make this relatively minor exception. Nor could the central trustees of the State University make the decision. In effect, it was made by a third-echelon official in the State Division of the Budget. And this instance typifies a whole range of decisions that are not now within the authority of the officials of the State University.

In New Hampshire the president of the state university resigned in mid-1962. He did not state publicly any reason for his resignation, but those who observed the function of the university in 1959, 1960 and 1961 will likely agree that the extent to which this president was denied the freedom to manage the affairs of the institution, by the editorial policies of the *Manchester Union Leader* and by the related actions of the governor, were reason enough to cause a good president to resign.

This sort of external control markedly affects the governance of state universities, except when state constitutional provisions establish the institutions' freedom from control by state agencies. Since an increasing proportion of the growing number of students in higher education in this country are attending publicly supported institutions, this obstacle to effective governance is significant.

In saying that these five obstacles characterize the environment of colleges and universities, we are saying, in effect, that all other enterprises have certain common characteristics and that colleges and universities differ from this common pattern. John D. Millett, president of Miami University, in his book *The Academic Community*, goes further. He contends that "ideas drawn from business and public administration have only a very limited applicability to colleges and universities."

My own reasoning is founded on the premise that the organizational structure found in colleges and universities, like the organizational structure found in business and government, is (in Millett's words) "built around Max Weber's concepts of authority and hierarchy." Millett contends that "these [concepts] are utterly inapplicable to the college and university." He asserts that two assumptions grow out of these concepts: (1) "the board of trustees has final and ultimate authority," and (2) the faculty authority for academic policy is a delegated authority. Millett denies both these assumptions. I accept both.

In this light, let us identify the decisive questions concerning the role of the various participants in the governance of colleges and universities.

The trustees: Laird Bell, a richly experienced (and invaluable) trustee at several institutions of higher education, was quoted in 1959 as saying that trustees are in "an anomalous situation—technically responsible for control and management of the institution but subject by custom to practical limits on their authority. . . . While faculty insistence on autonomy is justified on general grounds, it remains true that trustees, too, have some obligations in the field and should have appropriate powers."[1] Those statements pose the question well. For surely there are many people who question whether trustees do "have some obligations" and "should have appropriate powers," at least as far as the central function of a college or university—education—is concerned.

At one small liberal-arts college, for example, the board of trustees meets twice a year for two days at a time. A meeting which I attended was devoted to three issues: (1) the rate of return on the invested endowment; (2) a question whether a small building, no longer needed for a bookstore, should be used for a faculty lounge or for an alumni meeting place; and (3) the need for additional piping and refrigeration in the dairy barn of the college farm and the yield of the dairy cows. If a man from Mars had attended this meeting, he might have wondered whether the board was responsible for the operation of a bank (for banks do have farms to manage), a hospital or even a chapter of the Salvation Army.

There was little or no mention of students—not even of the proportion of income that should be devoted to scholarships—and none of matters more directly related to education. When the trustees were asked whether they might have considered questions about the admissions policy or the ratio of faculty to students, the tenor of their answers was that they should not concern themselves with educational issues. They indicated that these are specialized matters, which constitute the province of the faculty and the deans, and that they as trustees had no obligation and perhaps no authority to do anything about educational programing.

Harold W. Dodds, president emeritus of Princeton, has written that the president, as the educational leader of an institution, should preside over meetings of the board of trustees and should be the public spokesman for the institution—in other words, that he should serve as chairman.[2] His proposal diverges, of course, from prevailing practice; he argues for this contention on the grounds that the president is the educational leader of the institution, thus implying that the board will consider educational issues. And this is the central question. Few persons challenge the assumption that trustees should be concerned with matters affecting finance, public relations and athletics. The question as to the role of the trustees focuses on their concern for educational issues.

The president: For more than two decades I have been observing executives in business, government, the military, religious bodies and universities. My experience suggests the university president has a more complex, more difficult and more trying job than his analogue in any other field.

This complexity and difficulty grow out of the fact that, to a greater degree than other executives, he *shares* the opportunity and authority for decision-making. He shares with the faculty the opportunity to make decisions as to educational program—if they allow him to participate. He also shares with the faculty the making of decisions regarding the selection and promotion of the faculty members, as well as student admissions and discipline. The fixity of the large expenditure for faculty salaries means pragmatically that the president cannot use the budget to influence the course of educational programs materially; he can influence only the additions. And when new buildings or matters of public relations are being considered, the trustees feel more at home, and he shares with them the right to decide such questions.

The president shares with the alumni, in many institutions, the control of athletics. In many state universities, the president shares with the governor and a variety of lesser state officials or boards the authority to decide matters concerning finance—even to details of the purchasing of equipment—and the design and equipment of buildings. All presidents, especially those of public institutions, share with powerful constituencies (the organized farmers, the organized liberals, the organized conservatives, the organized doctors, the organized church people and many others) the right to formulate policies and even budgets for the institutions for which they are responsible.

The president's task is complicated by still another factor. Warren Weaver, executive of the Alfred P. Sloan Foundation and the Sloan-Kettering Institute, has pointed out that "universities still preserve many of the features of organization that were discernible in the University of Paris in the 12th Century. There are easily recognizable remnants of the regulations set down by Gregory IX in 1231 for three 'superior' faculties of theology, law and medicine and one 'inferior' faculty of arts. There has, of course, been much evolution; but the organization of American universities is not today very different from the one that was common a century—or even two centuries—ago. We still have rigidly organized departments in all the classic and orthodox subjects, each with a stoutly defended and tightly controlled budget—often each with a specified number of formally approved tenure positions."[3]

Finally, in face of the rapid growth of enrollments in colleges and universities, along with the rapid advance in sophistication in and interrelationships among the various technologies, it seems incredible that any one man could give leadership (as Dodds has suggested) to an educational program. Yet some presidents can and do; among them Dodds himself at Princeton, Victor L. Butterfield at Wesleyan, Katharine E. McBride at Bryn Mawr and Clark Kerr at his mammoth institution at Berkeley.

Some observers hold that presidents in the future will not be able to function as educational leaders, that institutions have grown beyond the scope that will permit a president to influence or give leadership to the educational program. Dodds contends that while faculties are growing larger and including more specialties, their independence persistently grows greater. Hence the president, some (not Dodds) argue, will not be able to function as an educator at all; indeed, it is futile for him to try. That question is the central one regarding the role of the president in the governance of colleges and universities.

The faculty: The central question as to the role of the faculty in governance is posed by two contrasting points of view. The first might be expressed this way: "Since faculty members see themselves as self-employed professionals, rather than as employees, enthusiasm in a common enterprise is proportionate to the sense of ownership they have in it by virtue of sharing in the decisions that govern its course." The contrasting point of view might be expressed this way: "The effectiveness of the faculty in the power structure of the major American university is weakened by the professors' lack of real interest in the university as a total institution."

The first statement argues for a comprehensive role in governance by the faculty. The second statement argues that such a role is not feasible because only a minority in most faculties have thought deeply and analytically about educational programs, as distinct from the substance of their particular disciplines.

A third point of view runs like this: "Administrators, no matter what their backgrounds, are not educators. They may have been members of the faculty in the past, but once they have become purely administrators, they are not qualified to make decisions as to curricula or faculty." But if such decisions are denied to administrators, not much of significance is left.

The academic staff: A fourth group within the organization of a college or university has been substantially neglected. These are the academic staff assistants, who deal with an increasingly important segment of governance—the dean of students, the director of admissions, the director of student health, the director of athletics, the chaplain and so on. These academic staff members tend to be overlooked, in many institutions, so far as governance is concerned.

One reason for this oversight is that the tasks which these staff members perform are not yet recognized as professional pursuits. Many faculties do not yet accept the idea that a dean of students has a discipline all his own; they are inclined to think that "any ex-YMCA secretary" can perform this role adequately. Yet an increasing number of deans of students demonstrate, by their day-to-day performance, that a variety of skills are required for the student-personnel profession and contribute significantly to educational achievement.

A second reason for this nonrecognition of academic staff members as professionals is that they perform functions which the teaching members of the faculty regard as their own. Student counseling is a prime example: the overlap of counseling done by the dean of students and counseling done by the faculty is a point of irritation in many institutions. These emerging professional specializations pose serious questions of governance, which warrant more careful investigation than they have yet received.

Governance involves synthesis, as well as definition of the roles of participants. This synthesis is achieved in most business and governmental enterprises by fixing authority in those at the top and creating a hierarchical structure through which they may delegate (and recall) authority.

John Millett argues that these means of synthesis are inapplicable in the college or university. An academic institution, he says, must be considered not as a hierarchy but as a community. "The concept of community presupposes an organization in which functions are differentiated as among faculty, alumni, administration and in which specializations must be brought together in a harmonious whole. But this process of bringing together, . . . coordination, if you will, is achieved not through a structure of superordination and subordination of persons and groups, but through a dynamic of consensus."[4]

In this statement, Millett effectively points up a critical question of governance for colleges and universities: if the roles of the trustees, the president and the academic staff are to be limited and the role of a fragmental faculty extended, how will this synthesis—this "dynamic of consensus"—be achieved?

REFERENCES

1. Beardsley Ruml and Donald H. Morrison, *Memo to a College Trustee* (New York: McGraw-Hill, 1959), pp. 13-14.
2. Harold W. Dodds, *The Academic President: Educator or Caretaker?* (New York: McGraw-Hill, 1962), p. 230.
3. In a speech delivered at the inauguration of George Beadle as chancellor of the University of Chicago, June 1961.
4. John D. Millett, *The Academic Community*.

PAPER BY . . . *Glen A. Lloyd*
                        Chairman of the Board of Trustees,
                        University of Chicago

The head of a large university must provide superb academic leadership; he must direct a staff responsible for spending tens of millions of dollars every year; he must see to it that extensive buildings and grounds are maintained; he is a huge innkeeper, responsible for dormitories, married-student housing, cafeterias and dining halls; he is a merchant, printer, and publisher; he must be adept at relationships with his community and with the Federal Government; and he must be a money raiser *par excellence*. In the face of all this, no one will challenge the need for good management. But what is good management for a university? By what standards can its quality be judged?

John Corson, in his book *The Governance of Colleges and Universities,* has pointed out the vast number of different arrangements and schemes which private universities have used in trying to solve their management problems. The paradox is that almost any of these arrangements seem to work well under some circumstances and fail under others. What are the mysterious circumstances that cause the same management structure to work rather than fail? I should like to try to identify some of them and to emphasize that they have relatively little to do with the form and structure of any particular management arrangement. They stem more from attitudes and points of view. For convenience, we might call these circumstances the essential ingredients of good university management.

The first of these essential ingredients is a clear understanding of the differences between running a business and running a university. The many similarities can largely be taken for granted. There must, of course, be an organization that people can understand; there may even be an organization chart. Jobs must be adequately defined, and every reasonable effort must be made to achieve economy and efficiency. But by what standard are economy and efficiency to be judged?

The central purpose of a business is to make profits, and profit performance is a powerful gauge of how well the enterprise is doing. Profits are dependent upon certainty and stability: changes in products and production methods must be carefully timed and controlled. In a university, on the other hand, the more competent professors become, the more freedom they expect and should have. For the best results, they should not be expected to engage in specific lines of inquiry if they do not want to do so. Similarly, university research has no easy measure of performance. One of its prime objectives is to make existing knowledge obsolete by new discoveries and to develop new knowledge. There is no easy or reliable standard to know when this has been achieved. It is often difficult to distinguish between success and failure; what look like uncertainty and instability may be the normal, temporary characteristics of successful research.

This point of view, essential in a university, would produce much disorganization and inefficiency in a business. The subtler aspects of freedom become obscured by the businessman's insistence on the kind of efficiency essential to success as judged by the profit criterion. There is no easy way clear to delineate these differences between businesses and universities and to decide which are valid. Nevertheless, real differences do exist, and good management in a university depends on the recognition of this fact.

A second essential ingredient of university management is flexibility—flexibility in the educational purpose, in the pattern and methods of the institution, in its budgetary procedures and even in its organizational structure. Most institutions become too easily satisfied with things as they are; changes are disturbing and sometimes dangerous. But if a university is not dedicated to a flexible point of view, it will have difficulty keeping pace with social change. Its evolving obligations to society and to the government, particularly in times such as these, will not be clear. Educational innovations will be next to impossible.

Every institution of higher learning must reappraise itself periodically. It must decide whether some of its educational programs should be discontinued because it lacks sufficient funds, or because someone else can do them better, or perhaps because they do not belong in a university at all. It must decide whether it should add programs for which it is particularly suited or for which someone has offered financial support. And it must decide how its limited budget should be distributed among its existing programs. The way this distribution is made will largely define the areas in which the university wants to become pre-eminent and thus the kind of university it wants to be.

It is too much to expect that these hard decisions will be made regularly merely because they should be. They are likely to be made only when opportune times come along. Such times may follow unusual discoveries or developments within the institution, or they may follow the loss or addition of outstanding department heads. If the budget—and especially the attitude toward it—are so rigid that decisions cannot be made at these opportune times, they may not be made at all.

Flexibility is also useful in some areas of the organizational structure. The chairman of the governing board of one private university has contrasted the use of many standing committees to the use of only a few, supplemented by special and ad hoc committees. Some of the large number of standing committees of his board, he said, had become inactive and ineffective. One reason, he felt, was that the chairmanships of these well-known standing committees carried such prestige in the community that changes were difficult to make and sometimes produced resentments. For these reasons, he advocated a more frequent use of special and ad hoc committees because this put him, as chairman of the board, in a position to exert more pressure for achievement.

These flexibilities permit response to new ideas, experiments and innovations and to social change. But flexibility also is dangerous: it increases exposure to bad ideas as well as to good ones. Care must be taken that it is not interpreted merely as a lack of definite policies and procedures. To say the least, this misunderstanding is not always easy to avoid.

A third essential ingredient of University management is the development of a close and confidential relationship between the head of the institution and the chairman of its governing board. Each is likely to have a substantial following who will quickly communicate to their respective colleagues any differences which arise. This will bring together the best thought of competent, experienced people with different backgrounds but with a common devotion to the institution. Many misunderstandings will be avoided, and the cause of good university management will be advanced.

The fourth essential ingredient is an organic relationship between the governing board and the rest of the university. Neither organizationally nor functionally should the governing board be a self-contained group paralleling other groups within the university, each with its own jurisdictional duties and rights. Nor should the other groups —the students, the faculties and the central administration—operate in this manner. On the contrary, they must recognize the university as an organic whole, dependent on interchange of ideas and close collaboration.

Organizationally and functionally, all these groups should operate up and down the vertical structure of the university at all levels, rather than in a parallel or horizontal structure. The members of each group should be guided by a selfless kind of restraint which welcomes a colleague, places all talents where they are best suited and avoids meaningless and harmful conflicts. The interactions should give the central administration ready access to collaborators and advisers without jeopardizing its proper authority. It should also, though this requires extremely good luck, leave the members of the governing board with a more sympathetic understanding of the important problems of the institution, as well as more knowledgeable for the judgments they have to make.

Let me illustrate. At the University of Chicago, the board of trustees elects the president, adopts bylaws and enacts—in full, voluntary collaboration with the central administration and the Council of the University Senate—statutes for the organization and management of the university's educational affairs. In the provisions of these statutes, the vertical, rather than the horizontal or exclusive jurisdictional theory for the academic management of the university can be most clearly seen.

The statutes, in effect, assign the trustees many specific, integrated duties, but always of a limited nature. For example, in case of an irreconcilable difference between the president and the Council of the Senate, the board of trustees acts, so to speak, as the supreme court, and its decision is final. The trustees do not have to be professional educators to function effectively in this manner, nor are they trying to be professional educators in so acting, any more than members of the United States Supreme Court have to be professionally experienced in admiralty, patent, antitrust or other technical fields of the law in order to render wise and just decisions.

The vertical structure of organization and relationships tends to prevent conflicts about how much authority each group should have. Uncertainties and conflicts seem to flourish under horizontal or exclusive jurisdictional structures. More important, the vertical structure tends to produce extensive and constant teamwork on all kinds of problems, including educational ones, with resulting strength to the institution.

The fifth essential ingredient for good management—irrespective of what the charter, bylaws and statutes may say—is a positive philosophy and practice in decision making. Decisions should be made at the lowest level normal and proper for the subject to be decided. A decision made at a higher level will not only place unnecessary burdens at the top but will also tend to distort the significance of the issue. The locale of a decision has much to do with keeping the issue in perspective. This is particularly true of sensitive subjects related to the academic freedoms, civil liberties and censorship. A decision made in the wrong place or by the wrong people, even though it is the right decision, may not have its appropriate importance and significance.

Among the most difficult but important decisions to be made in any institution of higher learning are those concerning promotions to tenure. The principal purpose of good management is to maintain high academic standards, but this is difficult to achieve if the faculty alone determines who is to be promoted. Under faculty control, it is almost impossible to prevent promotions based on considerations inimical to high scholarship; these range from rewards for long and faithful service to personal friendships. Few of the wrong decisions made in this process result from bad motives. They come from lack of objectivity. For that reason, Harvard and some other institutions in quest of objectivity may obtain considerable outside help in determining who should receive tenure.

The explosions of population, of knowlege and of social and international tensions account for most of the growing demands upon American universities. From all indications, these demands will continue to grow. If they do, universities will have to learn to handle themselves better as the pressure mounts. Improvement in the form and structure of university management is necessary for this purpose, but it is not enough. There must be further development of the factors which lie behind the charters, bylaws, statutes, organization charts and job descriptions—in short, of the essential ingredients of university management.

COMMENTARY

The structure of authority for private universities is amorphous, not clearly defined as it often is for large bureaucratic organizations such as corporations and government agencies. This situation is at least partially attributable to the fact that, in these institutions, administration and faculty do not precisely correspond to employer and employee, respectively. The usual distinction is that employer may discharge employee, but in private universities the permanent faculty hold tenure appointments; they can not be fired except under most unusual circumstances. They are highly regarded, and the administration often seeks and heeds their views on matters of policy. In short, faculty members have a foot in both the management and the employee camps, and this is a major reason why the government of private universities is a subject of almost infinite complexity.

Trustees are another dimension of the management complex for private higher education, and John Dawson, professor of law at Harvard University, suggested that simply defining their role is one of the major issues. Historically, Mr. Corson noted, trustees have performed a visiting function; they have been expected to observe what the faculty was doing. His own tentative view was that trustees should interpret to the institution those changes in society which ought to be reflected in educational programing. Margaret Clapp, president of Wellesley College, on the other hand, cautioned against asking the trustees, who are generally not paid for their services, to do too much lest they resign. She felt that the trustees' major role is to interpret educational policy to the lay public, and this, of course, means that they must first understand it themselves. Another participant, James S. Coles, president of Bowdoin College, saw the functions of the trustees as three: first, to question the faculty and make them justify their positions on educational matters; second, to assess the faculty's recommendations; and finally, once a decision has been made, to stand by the faculty, protect them and see that they retain their academic freedom.

The role of the faculty in policy making is a rather sensitive issue. For one thing, many faculty members disavow having any interest in such matters whatsoever. Similarly, there are many instructors who, although they want a say on crucial matters, judge a majority of the issues which are labeled educational policy as too trivial for them to consider. There is no uniform rule specifying the amount of personal contact between faculty and trustees which is appropriate. At Harvard not even the various deans meet with the Corporation, whereas, as Messrs. Lloyd and Coles reported, at the University of Chicago and Bowdoin such rigid separation is not maintained, and it is not unusual for faculty and trustees to meet and confer.

In the interests of their own professional dignity, faculty members tend to support with firm conviction those projects which they feel will maintain and enhance their institutions' reputations and to oppose those undertakings whose effects will, in their opinion, be otherwise. Recently Bowdoin had an opportunity to rent its theater to a summer-stock company whose repertoire, designed for vacationers in Maine, included primarily musical comedies of the *Guys and Dolls* variety. The faculty adamantly opposed the project, arguing that such shows were not sufficiently intellectual, that they were not consistent with the character of the institution and thus with their own dignity. President Coles reported that a rather bitter debate between faculty and administration took place over this issue, the faculty voicing concern for its reputation, the administration for the fiscal implications of not renting to this group when the alternative was for the theater to remain unused all summer.

Clark Byse, professor of law at Harvard University, felt that Bowdoin's administration and trustees would be perfectly justified in renting the theater. His criterion for determining on what issues the faculty's voice should be highly influential is this: is educational policy directly affected? If it is, the faculty's opinion is very important and vice versa. The matter of renting the theater, he said, contains virtually no educational implications. However, another timely topic at Bowdoin does. The institution is discussing whether or not to re-establish its medical school. Doing so would change Bowdoin's character in a very fundamental way and would affect the arts faculty directly. Thus, on this issue and ones like it, Professor Byse suggested that the views of the faculty should be taken seriously and weighted heavily in arriving at the final decision. Clearly the general conclusion is that rigid rules are difficult to formulate, and the diverse interests involved will be best served if each case is judged individually and on its merits.

Professor Harris argues that the faculty often obstructs attempts to govern an institution economically. While supporting the tenure system, he still maintained that in many institutions there exists a senatorial system whereby each senior faculty member is allowed to build his own academic empire. Each refrains from questioning the usefulness of the courses which his colleagues teach, and the system progresses harmoniously. Every new academic subdivision is given its niche in the university's curriculum, but courses which have become obsolete are seldom abandoned, at least not until their originator dies. Thus the number of courses which most universities offer is swollen far beyond the point of rapidly diminishing returns, and the many courses which are of only marginal educational value represent a fantastically large waste in terms of the foregone alternative uses of the resources which are devoted to teaching them. The message that follows from Professor Harris' argument seems clear although it is likely to be unpopular in faculty clubs across the nation: give our academic senators less rope with which to strangle their institutions financially. Large potential economies exist, but they can be achieved only if the structure of universities' government, which currently gives professors too much unrestricted license in these matters, is altered in some feasible way.

Near the end of the seminar, Don K. Price, dean of the Faculty of Public Administration at Harvard University, brought to light one previously neglected but crucially important point: recent happenings at private universities are only partially the result of internal decisions—made solely by the trustees, administrators and faculty—for the influence of outside agencies, both government and private, now affect greatly most American universities. For one thing, it is often the sponsorship of such an agency which makes it possible for various academic factions to circumvent the departments and thus, in some important sense, to diminish their inordinate power. Two such examples at Harvard come quickly to mind. The School of Public Health's existence as a separate entity independent of the Medical School is largely attributable to the Rockefeller Foundation. Similarly, but for the Ford Foundation, what is now the independent Joint Center for Urban Studies would no doubt be a substructure within the Government Department.

These latter considerations seem to substantiate a very simple but important conclusion: the structures of support—and thus, to some extent, of power—are far different for today's university than they were for its medieval counterpart. The latter was, in a real sense, separated from and not financially dependent upon the external world. In contrast, today's university is neither cloistered nor financially independent. Its support is drawn from many sources which are truly external to it, and this fact must surely be reflected in an evolving balance of power. In short, the old hierarchies, such as they were, are changing, and we would be shortsighted not to keep this point in the forefront of our thoughts as we analyze the government of modern universities.

12. Academic Quality and Financial Aid

PAPER BY . . . *John F. Morse*
Director, American Council on Education; Former
Staff Member of the U.S. House of Representatives
Committee on Education and Labor; Former Vice
President, Rensselaer Polytechnic Institute

The vast majority of America's institutions of higher learning are
fighting for their lives. Their costs are being forced up as they try
to recruit, hold and pay their faculties. As a result, their search
for students who can pay their bills and who also have the kind
of ability which these private institutions exist to nurture is becoming
increasingly desperate. Nothing that has happened in the last few
years has diminished these pressures, but there are straws in the wind
that at least suggest better weather ahead.

Perhaps a few words of background will place this subject in
proper perspective. When I started doing college admissions work
in 1950, speakers almost daily sought to frighten us with warnings
about the coming "tidal wave" of students, which was due to wash
up on the colleges' shores in the early 1960's. I say "sought to frighten"
because at that time most college presidents, treasurers and admissions
deans, while publicly mopping their brows, were privately rubbing
their hands in happy anticipation. Maybe they could fill those top-
story rooms that had been empty since the GI benefits began to expire.
Maybe they would not have to spend every evening at a different
high school's "college night," squirming uncomfortably under the
dual impact of a chicken dinner prepared by the home-economics
class and their undignified role as conscientious counselors forced

to be pitchmen. They knew that the onslaught of students would cause them headaches, but it promised certain benefits as well.

Now the 1960's are here and with them—as the daily press, news magazines and television programs remind us—the tidal wave. The wave is real, all right; but it is an odd sort of wave, for while it has inundated acres and acres of public land and one hundred lush private islands, it has left countless other islands virtually untouched. Literally hundreds of presidents of private colleges are standing eagerly on their shores looking for the wave and finding instead an ebb tide.

The beginning of this phenomenon was indicated (and indeed, I think, predicted) in the early 1950's by Frank Bowles, who was then president of the College Entrance Examination Board. Mr. Bowles pointed to a "pull apart of the colleges," a disruption of the relatively fixed positions which colleges had generally occupied relative to one another. He noted that a fairly small number of institutions were rapidly gaining in strength—strength of prestige, of resources, of faculty, of student body—while much larger numbers were falling behind, not only relatively but absolutely. If his observation is accurate, I suggest that the trend started when the GI bill began to run out: students could no longer select the colleges best fitted to their aspirations without regard to expense but had to choose among those they could afford. One may argue that the strength of the faculty rather than the strength of the student body determines the real strength of an institution, but in my view the two are inseparable. In the long run one does not exist without the other, and it is idle to debate which comes first.

It was at this point, in the mid-fifties, that colleges began to be labeled like steer beef and to group themselves formally, or more often informally, into tight little clubs with tacit bylaws and unwritten constitutions. The phrase "prestige college" was born. That coinage of the New York sports writers, "the Ivy League," proved a greater promotional phrase than anything ever dreamed up on Madison Avenue, and we began to hear about the "Little Ivy League" and the "Seven Heavenly Sisters." Mysterious groups of admissions deans, like the Northeast's Egads and the New York Expendables, met quietly from time to time, particularly before big national meetings, to seek common ground on controversial questions.

The private prestige institutions which were being drawn together in these ways had and have certain things in common. They are the nation's oldest and wealthiest. Traditionally, they have drawn a sizeable proportion of their student body from the high and upper-middle income levels, where the cost of education has never caused distress and a sharp reduction in the family budget at home. Thanks to this large proportion of paying students who can meet unruffled the almost annual rise in fees, these institutions can devote large sums to financial aid for the kind of youngsters whom they want but who cannot pay the bill. Annual financial-aid budgets at some of the smaller prestige institutions are running about $750,000, and they are approaching $2-million at some of the larger ones. This money is going mainly to well-bred, highly intelligent, clean-cut youngsters who live on the right side of the tracks and whose parents, though poor, are thoroughly respected and even prominent in their communities. It is going in very small amounts to the aggressive, steely-eyed, bright youngsters whose personalities bear the scars left from trying to claw their way out of economic and cultural deprivation in eighteen short years.

This process, which has been self-feeding, is now running on its own momentum and would probably continue even if deliberate efforts were made to stop it. The winners of the large national scholarship competitions—students who come largely from the same gentle background—pour into the prestige institutions, bringing with them from foundations and corporations the aid they need to pay their bills plus a cost-of-education bonus. Almost ten per cent of the entire Class of 1962 at Harvard, for example, entered with National Merit or General Motors scholarships. Similarly, almost ten per cent of all National Merit Scholars ever appointed attended or are attending Harvard College. To a lesser degree, this same concentration and this same self-perpetuating force occur in the other prestige institutions.

It seems clear that as the college-age population grows larger, there is (once again, I believe, I am borrowing a phrase from Frank Bowles) a spill-over effect. In general, the colleges we are discussing have sternly resisted expansion; as a result, many youngsters who would easily have qualified for admission in early 1950's were rejected in the early 1960's. To take a single index, over six hundred freshmen entering Harvard in 1952 had verbal scores on the College Board's Scholastic Aptitude Test below 583. Nine years later, in an entering class of the same size, barely one hundred students scored that low. What happened to the other five hundred? They did not scatter indiscriminately to institutions throughout the United States. Rather, they moved down what they thought of as one notch. The spill-over, then, has not been from a few Harvards to 1325 private colleges scattered about the country. It has been, if I may live dangerously and venture to guess some names, from Harvard to Amherst, Bowdoin and Middlebury; from Stanford to Pomona and Occidental. Each year another college or two breaks into the magic circle and decides it is time to publish a profile of its freshman class, but the total number is still very small.

It might be logical to assume that this spill-over effect would be felt all the way to outer reaches, but in fact it is not. I have suggested that the beginning of the pull-apart phenomenon may be traced in large measure to the decline of financial aid through the GI Bill. Another factor in the economic woes of the private institutions is the competition—not simply in terms of price—which these institutions are getting from the public sector. The great tax-supported universities are giving even our magic circle of colleges a terrific run for their money, for corporation and foundation support, for faculty and for students. In fact, once we get outside the magic circle and its immediate satellites, it is almost no contest. The majority of the 1325 private institutions fall a little further back every year in the race for the kind of students they want and need, and it is not hard to understand why. The spill-over never reaches the less well-known private institutions because the youngster who has not quite made the magic circle suddenly becomes price-conscious: he decides that the education at a low-tuition state or municipal college is a better buy than the education at a much more expensive private institution outside the circle. Mother would take a job if he made Old Ivy; she might even do so if he made Little Gothic. But between $2000 at Stubbs and $1000 at State, he will take State, and understandably.

I want to emphasize that in talking about the Stubbses, I am not talking about the colleges which David Riesman has described as man-traps—the places where faculty members, at the risk of their academic lives, say to promising students, "Get out of here. Go to Chicago. Go somewhere else, so that you will not become like us." I am talking about colleges where Professor Riesman could read the student newspapers and be satisfied that the institutions need not be labeled substandard merchandise. In times past, they drew their share of distinguished students; and many are proud of the proportion of their alumni who are listed in *Who's Who,* or who have doctorates, or who have chalked up the other pat accomplishments which we have come to use as measures of distinction. But times have changed, and many of these institutions are now in serious trouble.

The Stubbses of the country have tackled their problem in one of two ways. Some have kept their fees abysmally low in an effort to compete in price. Consequently, they have watched their plants decline, their young faculty disappear and a glaze form over the eyes of their older faculty as they realize it is too late to get out. Others have raised their fees at a far faster rate than the general cost of living and have allocated between twenty-five and fifty per cent of each successive tuition increase to student financial aid. On the whole, this second approach has worked. Indeed, it has enabled some institutions with unusually imaginative leadership to move nearer to or actually into the magic circle. The basic point, however, is that all these institutions are still in a deadly competition for students—and many of them, no matter how low they drop the bars, are not making it.

Looking at the admissions structures of some of the small, private, liberal-arts colleges in the Midwest may suggest what they are up against. The typical institution has at most two men, called director and assistant director of admissions, attached to the campus office; but it has as many as five or six traveling admissions counselors, who have definite geographic areas to cover and who may get to the campus as rarely as once a year. Some counselors have never spent a full week on the campus. They visit schools in a sorry round of college nights and scheduled calls, grateful when a student or two shows interest. They spend every free evening calling on prospects in their homes, following up every lead from whatever source it may come. These are often dedicated men, interested in young people. But often, too often, their honest desire to counsel and to guide is overwhelmed by the sheer agonizing necessity to produce students and fill beds.

One solid though undistinguished college in the Midwest, for example, has a capacity of seven hundred students and a potential income from tuition of $490,000, almost a third of which goes into financial aid. This college maintains an admissions counselor in Nassau County, New York, at a salary of $7500 (higher than the salary of many of its full professors) plus a travel budget of $5000. Yet its freshman classes are consistently and substantially below capacity. Its $5-million endowment is large in comparison to many of its sister institutions; but even so, how long can this college survive?

I said at the outset that there were some signs of better weather ahead, and I think there are. But the front will have to move faster than it has to date if we are to avert disaster. We simply cannot afford to allow this disintegrating process to continue, and I say this not as a sentimentalist with a tear in his eye but in recognition of a hard-boiled economic truth. We cannot allow colleges to fall apart because we cannot afford to replace them.

One encouraging sign is the fact that state scholarship programs are growing rapidly and are providing a transfusion. Based on need, with elastic stipends which can rise fairly high if the recipients choose high-cost colleges, they tend to narrow the gap in costs between public and private institutions. It was precisely to achieve this end—and in the knowledge that it is cheaper for the taxpayer to utilize empty spaces in private colleges than to build new public ones—that the California state scholarship program was launched. This is also the theory behind the New York State program, which now awards scholarships each year to ten per cent of all high-school graduates in the state. Similar programs have been developed in Illinois, New Jersey and Ohio; and almost every state has a program at least in the blueprint stage.

We might one day have a Federal scholarship program, which could tackle this problem on a national scale. However, the hearings in Congress in 1961 made it clear that a Federal program is likely to be directed toward youngsters who are in such poor economic circumstances that they cannot enter college no matter how intellectually talented they may be. It is almost certain that the large majority of these Federal-aided scholars would attend public institutions, and a Federal program might therefore compound rather than cure the economic problems of the private colleges. It seems clear, then, that in dealing with this matter, the roles of the Federal and state governments will be different. It is in the hands of the *states* that the survival of private institutions will rest.

Some state governments are already well aware of the urgency of these matters. In 1960, Governor Nelson D. Rockefeller appointed a commission under the direction of Henry T. Heald, president of the Ford Foundation, to study and report to him the needs of higher education in the State of New York. The commission was a distinguished one, and its report was brilliant. Implicit throughout the report was the suggestion that many private institutions in the state were far nearer bankruptcy than they realized. The commission proposed meeting this problem head-on by developing ways to make outright grants from tax funds to private institutions. This raised a storm of controversy. For one thing, it revived the church-state issue; this is always a touchy matter, and it was especially so in the spring of 1961, partly because of the change of national administration and partly because of the excited congressional debates on Federal aid to education. If the Heald Commission's recommendation ever had a chance, it certainly did not in 1961. The heat of the debate was so withering that the recommendation probably cannot be revived in the near future.

Although the direct attack proposed by the Heald Commission was lost, an interesting flanking operation developed. I have often been critical of this development because it leaves the major problem which the Heald Commission was attacking unsolved, but it does offer great hope for a solution, nevertheless. In a bill that seemed to be a combination of face-saving and of serious concern for solving this difficult problem, Governor Rockefeller proposed what has come to be called the Scholar Incentive Program. Briefly, it provides for paying tax funds directly to students in order to help them pay their tuition; the payment to each student may not exceed his tuition. For undergraduates the annual payments are $100 if the recipient's parents are in the high-income brackets, $200 if they are in the middle-income brackets and $300 if they are in the low-income brackets. Graduate students may receive as much as $800 a year.

The program became operative in February 1962, and so it is perhaps too early to assess its effects. The most rabid opponents of any program of tax support to private institutions have charged that it is merely a subterfuge, an invitation to colleges to raise their fees. In a sense there may be justice in this charge, but the plain fact is that the institutions were going to have to raise their fees in any case. The state program is merely giving them some assurance that they will not, in the process, drive still more students away from the private sector and create an even larger demand for public facilities than now exists. Certainly the program's chief contribution to the health of the private institutions lies in the fact that they will have to devote less of their unrestricted general income to student aid. This factor can be particularly significant in the case of graduate students.

The Scholar Incentive Program cannot solve all the woes of the private institutions. It still leaves them with run-down, outmoded and inadequate plants, which must be replaced or enlarged. But it does suggest a way in which the private institutions can compete for students and, at the same time, devote a greater percentage of their energies to solving their other problems. If, concomitant with such state programs, there can be Federal legislation which provides matching grants to all institutions for the remodeling and construction of academic facilities,* then we may, with our dual system of education, be close to the Jeffersonian goal of providing opportunity for higher education to all who aspire to and can profit from it.

Those who insist that Federal programs must founder on the same rocks that sank the original Heald proposal may temporarily seem right. But no Federal legislation has ever failed to treat equally all segments of higher education. There is wide precedent in almost a score of present Federal programs for providing direct assistance to *all* institutions. So eventually the legislation I am suggesting must come, if only because there seems to be no other way to "provide for the common defence and general welfare of the United States."

PAPER BY . . . *Eugene S. Wilson*
                Dean of Admissions, Amherst College

I should like to direct your attention toward a number of criteria which are often used to differentiate among institutions of higher learning. There is such a variety of these institutions in the United States that it seems important for educators to clarify the things that can be known and the things that cannot be known about them.

In my judgment, an educational institution of high quality is one which accepts the students it can get and then helps them to develop their talents as fully as possible before it discharges them. Whether the students have an average IQ of 110 or 150 is irrelevant. This definition is, of course, in clear contrast with the usual, perhaps largely intuitive, notion that the best institution is the one whose students have the highest innate intellectual ability, as measured by IQ's, Scholastic Aptitude Test scores or any other commonly used indicator.

The same contrast occurs in attempts to measure the worth of high schools through the nation. Invariably, lists of the best high schools include New Trier, Evanston, Scarsdale, Newton and others in the most culturally privileged areas. The worth of these schools is measured by their students' performance on national tests. Obviously, schools that have the top financial resources can hire better teachers,

---

* In December 1963, the Higher Education Facilities Act (PL88-204) was signed by President Lyndon B. Johnson. J.F.M.

buy better equipment and do more materially for their students; but these schools also start with very well prepared students. They *should* produce students who make high test scores, regardless what education they provide. The true worth of a school, like the true worth of a college, depends on what it does with the resources, human and otherwise, which it has at its disposal. No one has yet discovered a formula for this kind of evaluation.

Four popular methods that have long been used to evaluate colleges are to compare (1) the percentage of their graduates listed in *Who's Who;* (2) the percentage of graduates who have won PhD's or listing in some merit index; (3) the percentage (or actual number) of National Merit, General Motors or Rhodes Scholarship winners, or the number of graduates receiving Woodrow Wilson Fellowships; or (4) the percentage of students who pursue graduate education.

These measures have one fault in common: they indicate more about the institution's student body than about the impact of the institution on all its students. The fact that Harvard has more graduates in *Who's Who* than, say, the University of Nebraska may mean that Harvard is a better institution, but it may also mean that Harvard has in its student body many more potential Who's Whoers than the University of Nebraska. Harvard could be doing a very poor job educationally and still have more graduates in *Who's Who* than an institution doing a top-notch educational job with students who lack the potential for a *Who's Who* listing.

I think it would be fun sometime to conduct an experiment in which the 1200 incoming freshmen at, say, Harvard would change places with 1200 male freshmen at some large state university. A follow-up study of the performance of these two groups in their respective institutions might give us some real clues about the true impact of an institution on a student body. I am afraid that only such an experiment could reveal anything important about the nature of institutional differences and how institutions influence the attitudes and achievements of their students.

Another method which is popularly used to evaluate colleges is the ratio of students to faculty members. This index has several shortcomings. In the first place, the ratio is not easy to calculate accurately, especially if the college is part of a large university. Consider the situation at Harvard. Its over-all student-faculty ratio is three-to-one, but the ratio for undergraduates is elusive because there is no unambiguous way to determine how much of the time of professors who also teach graduates is devoted to undergraduates. When one examines the ratio at Radcliffe, the matter becomes more complex. Radcliffe College has no faculty; its students are taught exclusively by Harvard teachers. Radcliffe's student-faculty ratio is said to be four-to-one, and this computation includes Harvard students. Harvard, in arriving at its student-faculty ratio of three-to-one, apparently does not count the Radcliffe women.

Other institutions also encounter confusions in dealing with this ratio. A faculty committee at a large Midwestern university is reported to have conducted a study and concluded that the student-faculty ratio was 28-to-1. When the president heard this report, his response was: "This is out of line. If we are going to compete in this league, it has to be about 15-to-1." So the faculty committee re-examined the evidence and, by a different method of calculation, produced a ratio of 16-to-1, which was low enough to satisfy the president.

In short, any ratio that one arrives at is virtually meaningless because often another ratio could have been discovered just as easily. Even if the ratio is accurately computed, it is still very misleading, for it tells us nothing about what happens when the students and the teachers, whatever the ratio may be, meet in formal learning situations.

Another popular method of comparing colleges is to compare the number of books in libraries. This indicator is also of dubious value because any college in the country has more books in its library than any student will read in four years.

Along similar lines, a very interesting prospective student once visited my office at Amherst on a Saturday morning. He was comparing the intellectual atmosphere at Harvard, Dartmouth and Amherst by studying the activities in the library of each college around nine in the evening. He was most impressed with Amherst, for never in his investigations had he seen such excitement as existed in our library the night before. I was sorry to have to explain to this young man that part of the excitement was produced by a quarantine for polio which had restricted our students to campus for two days and had left the lbirary as one of the few places where they could gather. I did suggest to him that if he repeated the experiment, he might reverse the order and visit Amherst on a Wednesday night and Harvard on a Friday night.

Another method of evaluating colleges is in terms of their graduates' annual incomes. This was done in the book *They Went to College* by Ernest Havemann and Patricia S. West. The book indicates that

Harvard, Yale and Princeton graduates had the highest earnings among the colleges studied. It should surprise no one, however, that their earnings were higher than those of the graduates of other institutions. Many students at the "Big Three" come from economically and socially privileged communities and are destined to enter higher-paying occupations regardless of their success in college. This book does not tell us much about the influence which Harvard, Yale and Princeton have on students; it gives no information about how the students' attitudes and motivation were influenced by the colleges' faculties and environments. It does, of course, reassure us that many of these students were not handicapped in the economic world by their experiences at Harvard, Yale and Princeton.

There are other ways of evaluating colleges. David Boroff, author of *Campus, U.S.A.*, has developed the "I look at them and tell you what they are" system. He visits a campus, chats with a few students and teachers and then informs the world what the institution is like. This method is somewhat too subjective for my taste, but its results have been widely publicized and quoted. Burton R. Clark, a serious social scientist, wrote *The Open Door College*, a case study of San Jose Junior College, which is an interesting description of an institution and its function, but he did not develop a method or model that can be extended and used for measuring institutional differences in general.

Another effort in this area is Pace and Stern's attempt to identify the cultural pressures in an institution through the reactions of students and faculty to three hundred items on a questionnaire. This method, though interesting, is too subjective for accurate appraisal, and I suspect that more research is needed before it can become an accurate instrument for evaluating institutions. Other studies compare institutions in terms of variety of curriculums and intellectual programs, or on the basis of faculty hiring and promotion procedures, variations of salary scales, attitudes toward academic freedom and so on.

Soon we shall have a new measure of colleges, teachers and students—a measure which promises to create some very interesting situations. This new measure is the program being developed by the American College Testing Program for predicting what grades a given student will receive at different institutions, not only averages but also grades in specific courses. The ACT Program is not designed to measure colleges or teachers, but inevitably this will be its result. For instance, a high-school senior will know that at College A he can expect a 72 average, at College B an 82 average and at College C a 92 average. Which college is he likely to attend? He can also discover that in English and economics he will receive 59 and 63 at College A, at College B 65 and 79, and 84 and 92 at College C. Which course is he likely to take if he has a choice?

What will the English department at College C say when it discovers, through published reports of ACT, that it marks more generously than the English department of any competing institution? I suspect that the reactions to this new program will be somewhat violent in some areas. Just how helpful the program will be to prospective students remains to be seen, but it seems to me clear that a new way of evaluating a certain kind of institutional performance will emerge.

All these techniques, interesting and ingenious as they are, tell us little of significance about the one factor that is most important in evaluating a college: its total impact on its students, especially the impact of the teachers on the students. Comparatively few studies, as far as I know, center on evaluating the college teacher and his methods. Apparently this is forbidden ground for the social scientist, or perhaps the ground is too difficult to survey. Successful teaching is difficult to define, and so varied are the personalities of teachers and students that scientific evaluation seems impossible. Perhaps the successful teacher can be so many different things that there is no way of studying him systematically.

Attempts to evaluate institutions are also seriously hindered because there is no common, unambiguous vocabulary for communicating the most important concepts. Messrs. Bloom, Engelhart and Krathwohl have tried to clarify this confusing situation somewhat by writing their *Taxonomy,* which attempts to define terms, but there has been no systematic effort to put these suggestions into practice. Professor W. H. Cowley of the Stanford University School of Education has done some similar work. He has developed what he calls a taxonomical plan whose purpose is to aid in identifying institutions, educational goals and procedures. I have seen a draft of this book, but, quite frankly, its technical jargon hindered me from understanding his suggestions.

One exciting approach to a genuine evaluation of colleges, it seems to me, would be a descriptive study of the academic programs at various institutions. A student who is choosing his college knows that he can take a course called economics at Harvard, Pennsylvania, Duke, Amherst and so on; but he cannot discover from their literature what he will encounter in each of these courses. He does not know how much reading and writing he will be asked to do, whether memory or reasoning ability is more important for success in the course, and so on. If he knew the answers to some of these questions, he could make a much more informed decision about where to apply.

I suggest that we gather this kind of information from students at, say, fifty to one hundred institutions at the end of their freshman year. Each student would list, not his subjective reactions to teachers and courses, but what he has been asked to do in each course in terms of reading, writing, discussion, kinds of examinations taken and so forth. (William Cornog and his faculty at the New Trier High School have begun to experiment with this kind of study by asking their graduates at about fifty institutions to report back on their experiences. This approach seems to me to hold promise.)

We may learn, for example, that in one college a freshman in psychology has no laboratory work, whereas in another college he spends most of his time in the laboratory. These very different courses are probably both called Introduction to Psychology. In one college a good memory may produce top marks in a subject like physics; in another, the use of knowledge may be more important than the retention of knowledge. Similarly, physics students in one college may be asked to use equipment which has been placed on a bench in a laboratory with instructions for solving a problem, while students in another college may be asked to originate their own experiments to prove concepts or principles they have studied. This sort of information may give us a good clue about how institutions differ in their educational impact on their students.

Whatever method is used to evaluate colleges and universities, we must always make clear to prospective students one simple fact: the education a student gets depends much more on his own aptitudes, interest, resolution and dedication than on the college he happens to attend. Every college and university in the United States has produced great men, and every college and university in the United States has produced failures. We must help students to see that, wherever they go, they will get what their interest, ability and resolution deserve. No college gives any student an education; it gives him only an opportunity to acquire one.

PAPER BY . . . *Rexford G. Moon, Jr.*
                        Director, College Scholarship Service of the College
                        Entrance Examination Board

In the face of a firm national commitment to the idea that a majority of our youth should attend college, one of the real paradoxes of our educational system is the fact that students are expected to pay considerable sums to do so.

Student charges bear more than a casual relationship to the questions of who will attend college and where, and whether our national manpower needs will be properly met. Student aids are of corresponding importance, for they serve to minimize the adverse effects of student charges. If charges grow faster than aids, there will be greater national and personal frustrations than ever. Unfortunately, this seems to be exactly the direction in which we are heading.

The need for more doctors, teachers and engineers becomes increasingly apparent every day. At the same time, we are continually reminded of the fact that many of our ablest youngsters do not go to college. For some reason, we never seem to see that these facts are related: by enabling more superior students to attend college, we may develop more professional men and women. Neither of these concerns is inseparable from the problem of financing an education, for these undermanned professions require the longest and most expensive types of higher training.

The latest figures from the Government-supported study "Project Talent" indicate that at least 120,000 youngsters whose high-school performances showed the ability to achieve success in these needed professional areas did not enter college. The number of students who started college but were unable to meet their expenses and did not continue is not yet known, but the loss over a four-year period will probably exceed 40 per cent of the total. Family finances are surely a factor in this problem.

College aspirations are high among both parents and children. Many of these aspirations become a reality, but a disappointing number do not. A representative sample of parents with children under ten years of age (studied by the Survey Research Center) expect that 73 per cent of their children will attend college. A comparable sample of parents with children of college age, however, reported that only 30 per cent of the children were actually attending college. Another recent study (reported by Project Talent) showed that although only 30 per cent of high-school seniors said they were not going to college, 57 per cent actually did not go. About 36 per cent of the eighteen-year-olds in the country entered college in the fall of 1962.

When considered from the perspective of the family purse, these figures are revealing. Among families with incomes over $10,000 and children under the age of ten, 95 per cent expect their children to attend college, while of those with eighteen- and nineteen-year-olds, 70 per cent of the children are going or plan to go to college. Among families with incomes of $5,000 to $7,500, 80 per cent expect their children to go to college, but only 40 per cent of the children actually do so. Among families with less than $3,000 income, only 40 per cent expect their children to go, and less than 20 per cent of the children do.

Any lingering doubts about the importance of money in determining what children will attend which colleges were laid to rest by the results of Elmo Roper's recent study for the Ford Foundation. Drawing from a cross section of American families with children still some years away from college, it indicated clearly the effect which the presence or absence of money has on family attitudes toward higher education. The results might be summarized in ten statements:

1. Financial reasons are given as the most likely major deterrent to college attendance by those of low economic status, but they are not even mentioned as a possible deterrent by those of high status.

2. Those of high and low economic status show equal interest in state-supported institutions, but there is a marked disparity in the aspirations toward attendance at private institutions.

3. Attending college away from home is a probability for those of high economic status but only a slim possibility for those of low status.

4. Families generally underestimate the current cost of attending college and do not anticipate probable future increases in such costs.

5. High-status families expect to pay more for—and a greater share of—college expenses than low-status families, though the latter group still expects to contribute 70 per cent of costs.

6. Interestingly, families of high economic status expect significantly more scholarship aid than families of low status.

7. Willingness to borrow may be assumed to be equal for families at all income levels.

8. Willingness for children to work is lowest in the high-status group, highest in the low-status group.

9. Saving for education is practiced by a small majority of those

of high status but only by a small minority of those of low status; in neither group is the average amount of savings substantial.

10. The greatest certainty about all aspects of the educational future of their children is expressed by high-status families, the greatest uncertainty by families of low status.

This study indicates an obvious cause-and-effect relationship between a family's income and its plans and attitudes related to higher education. It also suggests that even in those economic groups where college attendance is almost a certainty, the parents are not prepared to cope financially or psychologically with the problems of financing an education. (It further suggests that the lower economic groups take a more realistic view toward educational financing than the highest group.)

Two factors are responsible for this: college expenses are much higher than anticipated, and family preparations to meet them are inadequate. Recent studies show that more than half of the parents of precollege-age children expect their children to enter publicly supported universities. Yet at an institution like the University of Illinois, the average four-year expenses for an undergraduate who is a state resident total $6,400. For an out-of-state student, the four-year expense is $8,500. Graduate-student expenses at the same institution average $2,300 per year. Expenses at private colleges now average close to $10,000 for four years and as high as $12,000 at some. Parents, when asked recently about the financial preparations they have made for their children's education, displayed a certain optimistic unpreparedness. Sixty per cent said they would "take things as they come." The remaining 40 per cent, who said they had savings plans for college, had saved an average of $150 in one year for this purpose.

Every indication is that purses are already pinched and that little relief is in sight. College expenses have not stopped rising, nor are they expected to. Experts say that an annual increase of 5 per cent or more is to be expected, at least until 1970. College tuitions increased by more than 35 per cent between 1955 and 1960. During the period 1960-1975, college tuitions are projected to increase by at least another 75 per cent, while disposable income is expected to increase only about 32 per cent.*

Inadequate financial preparation, therefore, is a reality with which we must deal. Much of the student-aid effort in this country

---

* This is a low estimate. Disposable personal income rose by 15 per cent from 1960 to 1963. The average for per-capita disposable income, the more relevant item, was 16 per cent for four years or about 80 per cent for 15 years. s.e.h.

is directed at compensating for inadequate family preparation, rather than at supporting students in dire need. As the following figures will show, these resources are already seriously strained, and they will be strained even more over the next few years as a result of the probable doubling of enrollments.

The college-administered aid funds for undergraduates in 1955-56 and 1959-60 are summarized by category in the table on page 264. Let me point out some of the changes that occurred during that four-year span. *First,* while scholarships increased in absolute numbers and in total dollars, they declined in a significant way. In 1955-56 the number of scholarships awarded equaled about 14 per cent of the full-time undergraduate enrollment; in 1959-60 it equaled only 11 per cent. *Second,* while college-controlled student jobs increased in both number and dollar value, the demand increased faster than the supply. In 1955-56 the number of jobs awarded equaled 16 per cent of the full-time undergraduate enrollment; in 1959-60 it equaled only 14 per cent. And *third,* in the same way the number of college loans declined sharply—from four to two per cent of the full-time undergraduate enrollment.

In the four-year period, the total expenditure by colleges for student aid rose approximately 47 per cent, but this figure does not give an accurate picture of the actual number of students aided. In fact, there was probably a much greater decline in the percentage of students who received aid than the award figures indicate. This lack of consistency results from the colleges' growing practice of giving aid in some combination of scholarships, jobs and loans—a practice much less common in 1955-56 than in 1959-60. A study of ten Eastern colleges showed that 70 per cent of the aid offers made by these institutions to entering students in 1960 were packaged. Had one assumed that each job, scholarship and loan went to a different student, one would have overestimated the number of individual students aided by 40 per cent.

The decline in the number of college-administered loans made during 1959-60 is undoubtedly accounted for by the appearance of the National Defense Education Act loan program in 1958, plus the impact of ever-rising costs on available funds. (One should note that the average value of college loans went up considerably.) During 1959-60, the second year of the NDEA loan program, the number of NDEA loans equaled only four per cent of the full-time undergrad-

COLLEGE-ADMINISTERED AID FUNDS FOR
UNDERGRADUATES 1955-56 and 1959-60

	1955-56		1959-60	
	Number of Awards	Dollars awarded (in thousands)	Number of awards	Dollars awarded (in thousands)
Scholarships	237,370	$ 65,732	288,521	$ 98,000
Jobs	288,479	$ 65,932	347,678	$ 98,900
College loans	77,107	$ 12,463	56,432	$ 14,800
NDEA loans			106,373*	$ 46,485
Total	602,956	$144,127	799,004	$258,185

Average value of
total aid
per student $230

Average value of
total aid
per student: $322

*Includes graduate
students

Source: Rexford G. Moon, Jr., *Student Financial Aid in the United States: Administration and Resources* (New York: College Entrance Examination Board, 1962).

uate enrollment. Currently, the number of NDEA loans does not exceed five per cent.

The NDEA loan program, then, seems to have brought considerable funds to the colleges at a very crucial time. It did not, however, bring the number of awards under college control up to the 1955-56 level. The total of NDEA and college awards (not students aided) in 1959-60 equaled 31 per cent of the total undergraduate enrollment, as against 34 per cent four years earlier. The decline occurred despite an increase of approximately 79 per cent in the dollar value of financial-aid funds available.

If we were to project these figures to 1962-63 at the same rate, we would see scholarships declining to 9.2 per cent, jobs to 12.8 per cent and NDEA loans rising to 5 per cent. The total number of available awards would equal 27 per cent of enrollment, in contrast to 34 per cent in 1955-56. We must remember, of course, the uncertain relationship between the numbers of awards and the actual number of students aided.

The lesson of these figures is clear. Even with the addition of millions in Federal funds, the strength of college-administered aid programs is waning. Only through more support from outside sources will colleges be able to maintain a level of student-aid opportunities consistent with the past.

Although a number of significant Federal programs have recently emerged, Federal support of students in higher education has been on a steady decline since 1948. In 1960-61 an estimated 380,132 awards were available to full- and part-time college students from Federal funds, representing about 11 per cent of the total degree-credit enrollment for that year. This is in sharp contrast to 1947-48, when 1,235,761 students—about 50 per cent of the degree-credit enrollment—were being helped by Federal funds. Again, the GI Bill provided virtually full support for the student in any higher educational endeavor of his choosing. Present Federal programs average about $900 per student aided, and over 30 per cent of the awards at all levels go to support science education. Thus Federal student support changed, in the course of fifteen years, from generous, general support provided for about half of all students to very modest and somewhat specialized support of a rather low percentage of the total enrollment.

The picture from just the undergraduate point of view is even more striking. Assuming that Veterans Administration funds were distributed between graduate and undergraduate support in proportion to enrollment in 1947-48, half of all undergraduate degree-credit students received support in that period. In 1960-61 about 10 per cent (333,981) of all students were in graduate work; the balance (3,502,107) were undergraduates. If we assume that in all Federal programs which aid both graduate and undergraduate students (NDEA Title II; PL 16, 346, 894, 550; Coast Guard; FAA; Defense Department Employees), 90 per cent of the support was apportioned to undergraduates; and if we add to this number the number for Federal programs which supported only undergraduates (ROTC, Indian Affairs), we reach a total of 245,973 Federal awards, or about 7 per cent of the undergraduate enrollment. Conversely, Federal programs of support (including summer institutes) which require a bachelor's degree or higher provided 134,159 awards, or about 40 per cent of the full- and part-time graduate-student enrollment. In short, support of graduate students continued at nearly the level of 1947-48, while undergraduate support fell drastically.

But even graduate-student support has constricted narrowly in another sense. A total of 134,159 graduate awards for all purposes were given in 1960-61. Of these about 100,000, or 75 per cent, were restricted to science (NSF, NIH, AEC research contracts, Mental Rehabilitation, Bureau of Standards). How many unrestricted awards (VA programs, NDEA loans, etc.) were also used in science study is not known, but the number is probably high, adding to the already heavy concentration of Federal student support in the sciences.

In summary, Federal support of undergraduates declined in fifteen years from about 50 per cent to 7 per cent of the degree-credit enrollment. The type and amount of support also changed, from grant aid for tuition and subsistence to predominantly loans averaging less than $500 per student per year. For graduate students, the level of support has remained relatively high, though it is still short of the earlier level. To get graduate assistance, however, a student must have a science objective rather clearly in mind, or the odds will not be in his favor.

If this trend is allowed to continue—declining Federal support for undergraduates, simultaneous with the declining power of college funds—it will inevitably have adverse effects on the accessibility of higher education for our youth at a time when a very sharp upsurge in enrollment is predicted.

COMMENTARY

Some experts suggest that if present trends continue, the angel of death will soon threaten a large proportion of America's private institutions of higher learning, while their critics relegate this vision to the category of unlikely fantasy. In Morse's view the prophets of doom seem more nearly correct. Like so many other Americans, their critics have been shortsighted; they have focused on only the few sturdy trees in the largely disease-infested forest. The popular notion is that business is booming for private institutions, and for a few—but only a very few—it is. Morse emphasized that for the majority it is not. This fact is not well-known because private higher education has mistakenly become synonymous with the relatively small number of institutions whose names are widely recognized; in fact, it is much more than that. Of the roughly two thousand American institutions which have some legitimate claim to be known as institutions of higher learning, about 1325 are private, and a number of them have names which are less than nationally known, treasuries which are nearly empty and prospects which are far from rosy.

In order to explain why these private institutions are in such a precarious position, it will be helpful to introduce the concept of a market. If covered exhaustively, this is a complex subject, but for present purposes one simple point will suffice. Two sellers, institutions of higher learning in this case, are in the same market if a change in one's price induces a change in the other's sales. It is important to note that this definition does not require that the two products be identical. Instead, they may be what economists call partial substitutes—like Pepsi-Cola and root beer or public and private education—in which case their prices may differ. In general, with partial substitutes, customers will only switch from one to the other when the difference in their prices is greater or less than a critical amount. In the light of this groundwork it is easy to see why many private institutions are in difficulty: first, they are selling their relatively high-priced services in the same market with low-priced public education. Furthermore—and this is the crucial point—ultimately they can only underwrite rising operating costs with higher tuitions, rather than, as the public institutions do, with increased subsidies from the state's funds. When they raise tuitions, however, the difference between the two sectors' fees may pass the critical point, and students may increasingly elect public rather than private education. If present trends continue, then, these private institutions have two not very attractive alternatives: facing financial crises with many students, or facing them with few students.

The reason why the unheralded private college—the type Morse has called Stubbs—is in the same market with the merely adequate, low-tuition, public college is that its product is not sufficiently unique or differentiated to create the isolation from competition which the large educational monopolies enjoy. How different is Stubbs's plight from Harvard's. The latter can charge $1750 and not for an instant fear losing students to many nearby institutions which charge very much less. This liberty which is given to Harvard and denied to Stubbs results mainly from the fringe benefits which the one can offer and the other cannot. "Prestige" is the catchall word often used to describe these benefits. Naturally, not everyone would cherish them, but enough people do to place Harvard and Dartmouth in their strong position vis-a-vis their public counterparts and to leave the mythical Stubbs feeling the pressure of competition from State all too keenly.

The members of the seminar agreed that forces are at work which will both intensify and diminish Stubbs's troubles. On the one hand, certain types of public education are already reasonably expensive and promise to become more so. This is true of what Wilbur J. Bender, director of the Committee of the Permanent Charity Fund, called the Ivy League state universities—for example, Minnesota, Wisconsin and Michigan—especially for their students from afar who must pay for room and board rather than live at home. Thus Bender implied that there is some rationale for predicting that private institutions in states which plan to take most of the incremental enrollment in residential public universities, rather than in community colleges, will be in less of a bind than those which will compete mainly with local colleges designed primarily for commuters. From the point of view of the small private colleges, that is the favorable consideration; however, there are also discouraging signs on the horizon. Moon mentioned that historically, and especially in the so-called Bible Belt, many of America's private colleges have been church-affiliated, and to a large extent this association has helped them to hold their clientele in spite of the fact that perhaps equally good and certainly cheaper public education has for a long time been readily accessible. It seems certain that as the long-range trend towards secularization continues, the cheaper public institutions will make large inroads upon the church-affiliated colleges' markets. And sooner or later this movement promises to be not simply a trickle but possibly of landslide proportions.

What is the outlook for these unheralded private colleges? Speaking in terms of the angel of death and so on is useful to emphasize the basic point, but in a realistic sense it is not terribly informative. What in fact will happen if these colleges' present financial troubles— rising costs and a very limited capacity to increase their fees—continue undiminished for several more years? They will be neither abandoned nor physically destroyed. Rather, as with any business failure, when the till is empty and all lines of credit are exhausted, the enterprise will be declared bankrupt. They will, in Morse's view, simply consign their facilities to the state and become public institutions. To some, such events may seem very strange indeed, and to others perhaps even despicable; but they have already been happening. The University of Buffalo has joined the ranks of public institutions, and so also, as Moon reported, has a small college in Illinois which closed one June with about one hundred students and reopened the following September under the banner of Southern Illinois University with an enrollment of 1500. Other institutions have also already gone public, and it was generally agreed that more will soon join this parade, for to an institution's administrators the prospect of public subsidies can look very attractive in comparison with the alternative of having to beg foundations and alumni for funds.

Given this forecast of rough weather ahead for a large segment of private institutions if no countervailing forces intervene, the members of the seminar thought it well to attempt an evaluation of the trend. Is it good or bad? Should the authorities allow it to continue, or should they perhaps intervene? A number of those present found the trend alarming. They maintained that one of the great strengths of American higher education is its dualism, and they fear that if eighty-five per cent or more of all students were enrolled in public institutions, the system's current healthy balance and interaction would be destroyed. It is important to understand that working to keep all 1325 institutions private is not their concern. On the one extreme, there are perhaps six hundred colleges that might very wisely become public institutions. The change would be profitable for them without at the same time upsetting the system's balance. In short, as private institutions they are expendable. On the other extreme, there are perhaps one hundred institutions—Morse calls them the magic circle—which virtually nothing can dislodge. Between the magic circle and the expendables, however, there are about six hundred other institutions; and these, several of the participants agreed, are the ones America must strive to keep going as private institutions. They claimed that the outlook for balance rests upon America's success in this endeavor; and balance, they urged, is a vital requisite for the system's functioning and continued progress.

Assuming the nation wanted to accept their advice and reinvigorate some of the private institutions which are currently faltering, the pragmatic question of how to go about it arises. There are basically two approaches. One is to convince the public sector to join with private institutions in raising fees, for if the public sector agreed to such a scheme, private colleges could close the gap between their prices and costs without losing students to the local competition in the process. In fact, however, Morse argued that even if such a solution were desirable, there are a number of reasons why it is highly unlikely that the public institutions would cooperate in such a venture. For one thing, they wish to enroll the same high-quality students that the private institutions seek and have no particular interest in sacrificing potential students of their own simply to salvage private education. Moreover, they are generally suspicious of the motives of those who argue that increasing their fees will be beneficial and will go a long way toward solving *their* economic problems. Finally, they believe that their institutions already fail to provide adequately for the needs of students from families in the bottom quartile of the income scale, and they know that raising their fees is not the way to solve that problem.

The second tack for salvaging these unheralded private institutions is for them to travel the fee-raising road alone but fortified with a mightier arsenal of scholarship aid than they have ever had. Although private foundations could be helpful in supplying the necessary funds, the job is too big for them alone and can only properly be done if government—at the state level, for reasons which Dr. Morse developed in his speech—finances most of the operation. In straightforward terms, the plan is to improve these institutions' ability to survive by charging roughly what the traffic will bear and providing aid to those who cannot afford to pay the full charges.

Such a scheme can run into two direct snags both of the public-relations variety. First, it will be, as John U. Monro, dean of Harvard College, mentioned, a difficult but vitally important job for administrators to inform poor students, who see the advertised fee of $3000, that they can afford to attend the institution, that the price for them is not that high. It would be much easier to interest a poor boy in an institution if the administrator could advertise a fee of $50, rather than one of $3000 with the attendant job of explaining to him the bureaucracy of obtaining $2950 in aid. The problem, then, is to show poor people that private higher education is in fact cheaper than they might intuitively think, and this is a job of disseminating information. The second snag is a corrollary of the first. A price-discriminating monopolist is invariably better off if each of his customers is unaware of the prices which the others are paying. In their enthusiasm to explain to poor students that the figure $3000 really does not count for them, that it is only for the rich, these private institutions may manage to step rather heavily on the toes of many of their wealthier clientele. One should be cautious not to weigh this factor too heavily, for the rich have historically treated private higher education with extreme generosity. Nevertheless, he should recognize that they both can and are more likely to become offended if price discrimination is heavily publicized rather than done discreetly. These comments should suggest some of the problems involved in aiding private institutions if this second way—that is, by having them alone raise their fees and their scholarship awards concurrently.

In addition to the two direct problems already mentioned, this second scheme raises a third and a broader issue: the political problem of getting state legislators to vote for measures specifically designed to help private education. In a number of cases such efforts have been successful, but for special reasons. One such effort is the Scholar Incentive Program in New York, which Morse discusses. Morse reported that the reason why it is fairly easy to get aid for private education in New York is simply that the public facilities there, though of high quality, are nowhere near adequate in size or comprehensiveness, and the legislators recognize that the cheapest way to get an educational job done is to allocate it to the private sector. This is a special case, however, interesting but not typical. For the country in general and particularly for the states where most of the private institutions currently under consideration are located, the outlook is somewhat different. Opinion there tends to be more sympathetic to public than to private education, and the cause of the latter is hardly helped by the fact that most legislators, at both the state and Federal level, attended public rather than private institutions of higher learning. Those who presented this material did not intend to suggest that the task at hand is hopeless, but they did mean to underline the fact that the political hurdles to be cleared in order to get increased public support for scholarships to private institutions may be considerable.

13. The Role of the Liberal-Arts College

PAPER BY . . . *James S. Coles*
President, Bowdoin College

The residential liberal-arts college is an institution unique to the United States. It developed here in its particular form to meet a particular need. It was not established as a professional school for clergymen, despite the generally prevailing notion to this effect. (Apparently this misconception sprang from the seventeenth-century equivalent of the fund-raising counsel. I dread to think what the future historians' concept of twentieth-century colleges and universities will be if it is based on the descriptions written by our own fund-raising counsels.) Neither was the liberal-arts college conceived to be solely an institution for the cultural education of the landed gentry.

The charter of Bowdoin College of 1794 provides for instruction in the "useful and liberal arts and sciences." This is a broad mandate and it is even broader today, for the distinction between "useful" and "liberal" arts and sciences has largely vanished. We now understand that a liberal-arts education is in itself useful. The testimony of many practical men—scientists, engineers and businessmen—substantiates this claim.

In speaking of the liberal-arts college, I shall limit my definition to institutions within my own experience. Some 1800-odd colleges in the United States claim the liberal-arts designation, but only about six hundred are accredited and are members of the Association of American Colleges. Even so, when the presidents of these colleges gather for the annual meeting of the association, the names of most of their institutions are unfamiliar to me and would be to many others.

Limiting the group further, one reads in daily newspapers about the hundred or so "prestige" colleges across the country. (New Englanders like to think there are fewer, with the typical New England miniaturization of things which are non-New England.) Dr. Earl J. McGrath's group at the Institute for Higher Education at Columbia selected fifty institutions, in some of its studies, as examples of "the backbone of higher education in this country." The group of liberal-arts colleges considered by the Ford Foundation for participation in its recent College Grants Program numbered about twenty-five.

The good liberal-arts college, of which I shall speak, is thus representative of a small and limited group—say, between fifty and one hundred—which usually enjoy some tradition and stature. They generally have significant (but never ample) endowments; good instructional, laboratory and library facilities; and faculties holding enough PhD's so that the colleges are not self-conscious about appointing faculty members who do not have them. They can exercise considerable selectivity of student body because they attract far more qualified applicants than they can accept. These colleges are not fragments of a larger university complex, and they do not have nationally recognized, satellite professional schools. I am probably talking about places like Reed, Carleton, Grinnell and Wooster. I probably am not talking about places like Monmouth and Juniata, even though some of these institutions have excellent records, as measured by the number and quality of scholars they have produced.

These good liberal-arts colleges have largely avoided vocational and professional courses. Dr. Earl J. McGrath disputes this; his studies hold that the liberal-arts college in this century has introduced many vocational and professional courses, as well as degrees in such fields as business administration, journalism, engineering and forestry. This is certainly true of many colleges in the larger group, but for the smaller group of which I am speaking, it is not true. Nevertheless, says Dr. McGrath, vocationalism and professionalism are still present (1) in the combined 3-2 engineering programs with the Massachusetts Institute of Technology, Columbia and the California Institute of Technology; (2) in the preparation of teachers for secondary schools; and (3) in the programs for intensive major and honors work in specialized disciplines and subdisciplines, geared to students who often intend to continue their studies in professional schools.

So far as combined programs with engineering schools are concerned, the charge is in part correct. However, the three years which the student spends in the liberal-arts college are devoted to liberal-arts studies. The courses which he takes are not designed with pre-engineering preparation or vocational goals in mind; they are offered essentially to satisfy his mind's natural curiosity.

It is also true that many liberal-arts college graduates become secondary-school teachers. However, their liberal-arts curriculum has not been specifically designed to train them as teachers. The minimum necessary courses for teacher certification are offered as electives; and these might even be justified as liberal-arts courses, since they provide knowledge of an important part of our culture. More recently there has been a trend to have these professional courses taken in a fifth year—for example, in a master of arts in teaching program.

Major concentrations and honors programs in history, literature, art and chemistry, in these institutions, are offered basically to give each student some experience in the mastery of a subject in depth. This experience also gives him an appreciation of what knowledge is and how it is obtained. It develops in him a sense of competence, an awareness that he is himself capable of becoming an expert to a small degree. Without question, some professors subvert these programs to proselytizing; but this subversion does not destroy the underlying rationale of the programs, any more than a conniving lawyer destroys the underlying rationale of our legal system.

In short, the assertion that the liberal-arts college is "irrevocably committed to professional training," as made by Willis Rudy, professor of history at the Massachusetts State Teachers College in Worcester, is simply not true. On the other hand, I would not go so far as does President Richard D. Weigle of St. John's College in having the curriculum avoid anything which might possibly be of practical use, such as the development of oral fluency in foreign languages. A liberal-arts education is valuable to all men and women, regardless of their profession. It may also be useful to them in preparing for their profession; but this utility must be an incidental by-product, not the main purpose of the college.

Preprofessional training as such, be it for medicine, engineering or law—or for college teaching—should not be the *raison d'etre* of the curriculum. When it is, the college has indeed lost the liberal-arts concept. My strong feeling in this respect does not arise from any antipragmatism. On the contrary, it is essentially pragmatic. One cannot predict the particular specialized knowledge which a person may require for his profession ten to twenty years after he graduates from college. Therefore, college education must be concerned with fundamental truths, rather than with their specialized applications.

The liberal-arts college shares the general problems of admissions, the education of the superior student and the dynamics of management which concern all institutions of higher learning. It has other problems incident to the recruitment of a football team, which it shares with almost all colleges with male students except Reed, Chicago and some Catholic institutions. And it has problems revolving about coeds, either registered or nonregistered, except in such institutions as Wellesley, Smith and Vassar. There are, however, several special problems facing the good liberal-arts college which will have to be solved if it is to maintain its position of eminence and distinction.

The liberal-arts college of high quality is being squeezed increasingly between the better secondary-school training of its freshmen, on the one hand, and the graduate and professional school, on the other. Harvard, for example, now admits a large proportion of its undergraduates with advanced standing. One Harvard professor has been quoted as predicting that by 1970 all Harvard students would be admitted with at least one year of advanced standing. Will Harvard then become a three-year college, offering a three-year bachelor's degree? Chicago tried to do it in two years and failed; perhaps Harvard can do it in three.

Simultaneously, medical schools and other professional schools are suggesting thay they should admit men without bachelor's degrees, men who have completed but three years of college. If the college is to admit students with one year of advanced training and then transfer these students to professional schools one year prior to the baccalaureate, only two years of work remain to be done in the college, which scarcely seems worthwhile. It would be an elegant junior-college program.

The solution will be found, I believe, in maintaining the four-year college and the four-year BA program, and in upgrading the college program itself from the freshmen year onward. This, in turn, will permit the college graduate to be better prepared for his postcollege work.

The liberal-arts college faces another major problem in adapting to the higher quality of secondary-school education. Because more and more advanced course work is being introduced in the secondary school, the college is enrolling freshmen with widely divergent levels of knowledge within given disciplines. How shall it accommodate to this divergence of training? Much work will be required, both to coordinate new college programs and to provide some uniformity of background in the secondary-school offerings. Our faculties and our curricula must be fluid and flexible, without in any way sacrificing their standards and their integrity. It seems clear that the better preparation of the incoming student will permit the college to enrich its own programs throughout.

This enhancement of secondary-school education is developing a third problem for the liberal-arts college: the increasingly sophisticated approach of the prospective student in his choice of college. More youngsters are determining their profession in high school—and at an earlier age—than ever before. Undoubtedly, better guidance programs as well as better courses contribute to this development. In any case, these youngsters are much less often choosing their college because of a winning football or basketball team, because it was Dad's old school or because they like the school colors. They are asking such questions as "How is your psychology department?" "Whom do you have teaching economics?" "Does your chemistry department have a polarograph?" and "What advanced work do you offer in history?"

We like these questions, and we like this attitude. However, these candidates are obviously somewhat professionally oriented, and we want to avoid professionalism if possible. Here, then, is another squeeze for the independent liberal-arts college, as compared with the university college. The latter can admit qualified undergraduates to graduate courses and can thus offer them much more advanced work than the simple liberal-arts college.

The liberal-arts college also has a difficult problem in recruiting and retaining its faculty. It insists upon good teaching, and it can find men who want to be and can be good teachers. At the same time, these colleges know that their faculties must be capable of and motivated toward research if they are to remain alive and up-to-date in their teaching. The quality of faculty to be recruited is therefore high.

We can match the universities on the basis of entering salaries, and we can match them in terms of laboratory facilities in all respects save the larger, team-research projects—cyclotrons and so on. We have been able to match them in the quality of the student body, although I believe we will face greater and greater difficulty in enrolling exceptionally talented students, who seem to be tending more and more toward the larger universities. We can match them fairly well with respect to secretarial and other clerical assistance. We can compete satisfactorily with respect to library materials, particularly with the aid of modern microfilm, microcard, xerographic and other duplicating facilities. We do have difficulty, however, in matching the vibrant atmosphere provided in the large university by the many colleagues with similar specialized knowledge and competences. This presents problems for the liberal-arts college, but they are not without solution.

These are the special problems of the liberal-arts college as I see them. There are many peripheral problems which they share with other institutions, such as the enlarged number of students and the ever-present problem of financing. These are not the difficult problems, however, nor are they the ones of greatest interest to educators. (Professor Harris is going to solve the financing problem for us, with the help of the Federal Government; and the state universities will be providing for the large mass influx of new college students.)

The role of the liberal-arts college in the future is not to become larger. That would dissipate and dilute its resources, and largeness itself can be achieved by other institutions. Neither is it to become a finishing school for the elite or for the idle rich. The future of the liberal-arts college will be assured as it is able to develop and exploit its special talents for undergraduate instruction—and to extend these in dimensions other than mere growth in numbers.

Liberal-arts training will have to emphasize the pure, as opposed to the specialized, the vocational and the explicitly practical. It will do this because fundamental truths are enduring and can be adapted to the many unpredictable needs of the future.

The liberal-arts college will have to take advantage of the individual qualities of the particular institution. If it is isolated—as Bowdoin is isolated "down East" in Maine—it should take advantage of that isolation, providing a more contemplative and less frenetic existence than is possible in a metropolitan area. A sense of detachment and contemplation is not a bad thing in itself; and for a few years it may be essential to the development of independence of thought and action, as opposed to conformity.

The liberal-arts college can be independent, and it can be individual. It *must* be so; it must *not* be a mere imitator. With a smaller number of students and an opportunity for each student to know a score of mature teachers and scholars, the liberal-arts college can provide for an enriched individual development, geared to the student's personality. Through proper "impedance matching," it can and must help to develop each individual to his maximum potential. This can scarcely be done where most of the student's contact is with other students—a terrifically conforming influence—or where it is primarily with immature and inexperienced teachers, such as one finds where graduate students carry the burden of undergraduate instruction.

The liberal-arts college can take the lead in the development of values among its students. Today we are able to train better and better, to inculcate more and more knowledge, to bring greater and greater understanding to our students; but we find them too often lacking in commitment and dedication. Better training, more knowledge and greater understanding mean nothing unless a man has the motivation and desire to put them to use for the benefit of his fellow men. With the diminishing influence of religion in the home, with the easier and easier material lives we lead, this is one of the most serious problems of the future.

The liberal-arts college of the future will have to forge for itself a new dimension of growth different from simply taking more and more students. Other institutions can do this better than ours, and they can do it without losing their fundamental character. The new dimension of growth which seems to me most appropriate for the liberal-arts college is towards a small but very high-quality graduate program in the arts and sciences. This can be done in small institutions, as has been demonstrated by Bryn Mawr and Cal Tech, to say nothing of the nineteenth-century German universities.

The development of a graduate program would answer several needs of the liberal-arts college. The dynamic quality of growth which is demanded by able faculty, interested alumni and competent trustees can be found in growth in this dimension, as well as in terms of mere numbers. A concomitant benefit would be the greater attractiveness of the institution for recruitment of outstanding faculty. It would be able to offer the prospective faculty member an opportunity to teach advanced as well as elementary courses; it could offer him graduate students in his field; and it could offer him the added opportunity for research which a graduate program provides. He is then more likely to feel that the institution offers attractive possibilities as his intellectual home.

The undergraduate would benefit from this arrangement in at least two ways. He would have better qualified professors; and he would have an enriched range of offerings as he enters his senior year, since the beginning graduate courses would be open to well-qualified undergraduates.

Such small graduate schools might also fill a more general need which I believe is developing. Professors in the large universities are depending more and more upon postdoctoral research fellows as their companions in zealous research. The research productivity of postdoctorates, they say, is very much better than that of mere graduate students. If this means that the large university will be devoting less effort to graduate training, other institutions will have to take up this slack, and this burden may well fall upon graduate programs developed in the better liberal-arts colleges. They already have faculty qualified to give this advanced work.

Obviously, money is involved, but money can be and will be obtained—from private donors, from foundations and, without question, from the Federal Government. Money is among the lesser of the many problems we face. The much greater need is for vision and energy. The liberal-arts college has a future as sound and as sure as those persons concerned for it are willing to undertake.

PAPER BY . . . *John S. Dickey*
                  President, Dartmouth College

All of us who seek to serve and strengthen American higher education need to take a fresh, hard look at the nature and essential properties of that complex reality we call a college. By a "college" I mean the organizational unit, whether located within a university or independently, upon which liberal learning in America has historically been based.

A college is a highly developed, changing, living organism. If it is not, it does not have much of a future. As a living organism, it is a unity of parts organized to function in mutual dependence in relation to the whole. This definition, it seems to me, exposes two of the most fundamental problems which confront our major colleges today: (1) the need for a strong sense of *institutional* purpose and (2) the need to strengthen the identification of the constituent parts with the institution as a whole.

If a young faculty member today is to feel a compelling sense of identity with a college and its over-all educational mission, he must develop a commitment to something there which transcends, as it also involves, his commitment to his particular field of scholarship. No major college today can build and maintain a strong faculty by recruiting solely from its own graduates. The transcending force in the formative years of a new recruit must usually be rooted, therefore, in the *work* of the place, rather than in place loyalty. Hopefully, the latter will grow its own roots in the lives of committed teachers today as it did in the past, but in most cases the college cannot start with it.

The one transcending force which has the greatest chance of drawing teachers and students into a commitment to the college is, it seems to me, an articulated institutional purpose which is recognized as a pivotal factor in the educational experience of the college. Conversely, if most faculty members regard the college as simply a facility of convenience for exposing students to their individual offerings, there will be little institutional purpose on that campus. All members of that faculty will eventually regard themselves as committed solely to their specialties and not to the college at all.

The circumstances of contemporary American life generally—and in higher education particularly—conspire to make this problem worse. For example, the increased mobility of our society, socially, physically and economically, works against the stability of employment relationships. Likewise, loyalty to enterprises and institutions is not as much in fashion today as it was in our earlier, less sophisticated society. I am told by my friends in nonacademic enterprises that these factors are clearly noticeable in commercial and professional life.

In the world of higher education, these general forces are augmented by three specific circumstances, among others. *First,* the rise of modern knowledge has created a demand for ever more highly specialized training and scholarship on the part of all scholars and teachers. I have called this the accelerating obsolescence of knowledge. One of its prime results is to draw scholars into an ever-closer affinity with their professional counterparts, regardless of where they are located.

Second, the financing of a teacher-scholar's professional development is increasingly dependent on outside grants from government, foundations and industry. This money is usually available to him no matter where he is located; he can take it with him if he moves, as he is often invited to do.

And *third,* the stronger institutions are in an increasingly stiff competition for the best teacher-scholars. This tends to put a premium on scholarly achievement at the expense, in some instances, of over-all institutional purposes. The most striking example is that of reduced teaching loads: colleges vie with each other is asking their potential teachers not to teach. This is a problem even on the stronger cam-puses. President Robert F. Goheen of Princeton, in his 1960-61 report, stated that "a researching faculty is the only kind of faculty which is able—out of its own passionate attachment to the search for truth —to infuse intellectual curiosity, excitement, and discipline into its teaching in a vital first-hand way." He added, however, that "the pressures of competition [as to lighter teaching schedules] are telling more severely against us in this respect now than they are in the area of salaries."

All of these centrifugal forces are accentuated on the stronger campuses, where academic activity is more demanding for both teacher and student. On such campuses these forces have been building up for at least sixty years, sometimes in spurts but always cumulatively. And there is a quantitative factor as well. Bigness in any human enter-prise introduces various forms of pluralism. (In big government this means federalism and departmental specialization; in big business it means decentralization in the organization and management of great commercial enterprises.) A college with a student body of 3000 and a faculty of nearly 300 is inevitably a different organism from an institution of 500 students and 25 teachers. The larger institution is almost certain to be more pluralistic in all respects, and pluralism is everywhere the enemy of cohesive purpose. But the converse is equally true: a heightened sense of institutional purpose and identifi-cation can turn size and diversity into strength.

This living organism which we call a college has great need to be adaptable if it is to serve significantly our rapidly changing society. And it is a fact that our society and all its constituent parts are irrevocably dependent on the *quality* of our higher education. This is a revolutionary change. Higher education is playing this role for the first time in human experience within our lifetime.

As a result of the ever-higher demands which our scientific and technologically dominated society is placing on higher education,* liberal-arts colleges are finding themselves in a relentless competition in their efforts to excel—indeed, to survive—as purveyors of compe-tence. This competition focuses on the need of every aspiring college to get its full share of top-notch teacher-scholars and students. There is, of course, an inescapable, reciprocal attraction between these two

---

* For example, about seventy per cent of Dartmouth's graduates now require graduate-school training for the kind of leadership life and job they want. J.S.D.

groups. To keep either a strong faculty or a strong student body, a college must attract and keep both.

But the colleges are not struggling unaided. While our society is making new demands on the liberal-arts college for drastically sharpened intellectual work on the part of both students and faculty, it is backing these new demands, particularly in the sciences and technology, with money. At Dartmouth, for example, much of our teaching and a substantial portion of our new facilities in the sciences are financed for us, directly or indirectly, by the sponsored research grants held by our faculty.

I do not say that this is all good, let alone that it is without dangers and disadvantages; but as matters stand today, we would not even be in the race if it were not for these new resources. The refounded and doubled Dartmouth Medical School exists only because it has an annual research program upward of $1-million, as compared with about $10,000 in 1952. These resources are also providing staff and facilities for the departments of biology and mathematics, and they make possible such new ventures as our doctoral-level programs in molecular biology and mathematics.

The primary obligation of the American college is always to society—a society which it both reflects and helps to fashion. The great reality pervading this obligation is the dynamic, changing character of our society. Today's society demands, especially in the foremost colleges, a much higher level of learning from that which was acceptable even ten years ago. And the demand will surely be higher still ten years from now. If the liberal-arts college is to produce men today who will leave their marks on their time as her sons did in earlier days, she must meet today's challenges and competition on today's terms, gladly and confidently, in the spirit of the Dartmouth family motto, *Gauden Tentamine Virtus*.

PAPER BY . . . *George R. Waggoner*[1]
                         Dean of the College of Liberal Arts and Sciences,
                         The University of Kansas

There is a general (if somewhat one-sided) impression, which parents of college-age students generally recite, that it is very difficult to give or get a good liberal education in a large state university. "Look at the size of these colleges of arts and sciences," they say, "three thousand students, or perhaps six. Nobody sorts these students out before admission; some are mediocre, some are brilliant. Besides, there is a graduate school, and faculty members would certainly rather pursue their research and publish and look after a few graduate students than waste their time on freshmen.

"As for curriculum, the professional schools keep demanding that the colleges of arts and sciences give weak service courses for their special needs—English for engineers, chemistry for home economics, math for business administration, and science diluted enough for people in education. And the departments in the humanities, social sciences and physical sciences are all threatening to fly apart, with economics moving into the school of business administration, math into the engineering school and psychology into the school of education!"

Looking at all these handicaps, of which the small, private liberal-arts college is totally free, one might conclude that the size and diversity of the student body, the disparate aims of the faculty and the ambivalence of the administration in state universities create a nearly hopeless situation. And, indeed, two examples from my own experience come readily to mind.

I once spent a depressing year and a half at an Eastern land-grant university where the college of arts and sciences had been drastically dismembered by the professional schools. The only departments left securely in the college were Latin, Greek, French, English and some mathematics which none of the professional schools wanted. Two or three other departments also remained temporarily in the college, but only until it was determined which of several technical schools would absorb them. The battle over these spoils was still going on.

More recently I visited a large Midwestern state university where the college of arts and sciences had quite disintegrated. An institute of technology exists alongside the college of arts and sciences; significantly, this is the only academic community I have ever visited where nobody mentions "science" without adding "and technology." Chemistry and physics have already moved over with the engineers; botany and geology are petitioning to leave the college and join them.

These two colleges are acute cases, but a similar disintegration threatens the liberal-arts college in more than one large public university. And the teaching mission is further complicated by the problem—or the threat, some believe—of sponsored contract research. At the University of Kansas, the dollar-volume of such research is roughly equivalent to the size of the faculty budget. Something over three fourths of the full-time members of the faculty have found one to six contracts for some type of research. Along with this research, we have accepted large responsibility for programs of national and international service.

If these facts add up to a set of problems for the liberal education of undergraduates, they add up also to a remarkable set of opportunities. Before I discuss these, however, I want to state briefly four convictions or assumptions upon which my own thinking is based.

First, I believe that the function of the college of liberal arts and sciences is to produce intellectually minded graduates with some real competence. This does not mean that they should know everything knowable about some subject. That notion is absurd—and not especially related to competence, anyhow. If students are made to feel that they must know everything about their subjects before they are permitted to think, they will not get very seriously involved. Instead, they will doubtless turn up in the graduate schools respectful and with notebook in hand to write down what they are told. We all know that freshmen are very often more prone to imaginative thinking than are beginning graduate students, who have had imagination trained out of them through four years of being stuffed with data.

The competence I would hope for lies in developing the student's critical faculties, his ability to make sound judgments, which I see as more significant than, say, mastery of the whole history of English literature. Such competence is what frees the student to pursue his own development, in or out of the university.

Second, I believe that we worry too much about providing some integration of knowledge for the student. We try to cook our own subject-matter stew, but by the time we pass it along, it is already a little mushy. Perhaps this is one reason why the standard general-education course is being quietly buried in many colleges around the country. The general-education movement did have a certain insight, which has been sobering, irritating and salubrious to higher education. But it also suffered from naiveté, oversimplification and institutionalization.

My own conviction is that integration of knowledge comes most likely, not from a pablum diet of predigested wisdom, but from serious involvement in scholarly inquiry, even in research activity. A student who becomes engrossed, with a first-rate professor, in some aspect of molecular biology is likely to get excited enough to do his own integrating of mathematics, chemistry, physics and biology. He is much less likely to get that excited about a course titled, say, Introduction to Man in the Biological World.

Third, I believe that a college is successful to the extent that it helps each of its varied students to fulfill his own potential. We cannot do this for everyone; perhaps we never do it fully for any one. But at the very least we must create the right kind of model—a primary concern, not for a minimum standard for the marginal student, but for a maximum stretching and challenging of the best students on the campus.

Fourth and last, I believe that no school, large or small, public or private, poor or wealthy, is worth its charter without a learning as well as a learned faculty. The ideal pattern for a faculty member in arts and sciences is, I think, participation in research in company with graduate students, with undergraduates majoring in his field and with freshmen and sophomores. Here is ground for a fusion of teaching and discovery, not for providing mass entertainment before serried ranks of faces. Performance before a large audience may keep the actor stimulated and the audience entertained, but I doubt that the mass lecture is good for the inquiring mind of either the teacher or the student.

Neither lecturing to hundreds nor tutoring one at a time is the pattern I would choose. The simple bench, with Mark Hopkins on one end and an eager student on the other, is not the best pattern, nor is it as practical now as it was at Williams in 1871. But situations abound in which a similar kind of interaction can take place between *groups* of students and faculty, and research can create these situations.

Upon the basis of these beliefs, let me suggest some opportunities inherent in the problems which are besetting the liberal-arts colleges in large state universities. Let us begin with the size of the student body.

We have been so swept off our feet by our publicists' prose that we really believe we are drowning in a tidal wave of increasing enrollments. What actually exists is a slow and steady increment of students. It is predictable, it is manageable, and it is no more alarming than the growth of the teen-age boy whose shirt sleeves never quite meet his wrist bones. We expected it all along, and we also expected to buy him a new shirt. We may as well acknowledge that a growing student population has long been anticipated and not act as if it were some freak occurrence caused by the Russians, radiation or economic upheaval. We may as well expect, also, that most of this increase will be felt in the public institutions. However, the notion that the quality of education in these colleges must consequently be diluted is a popular fallacy, given credence by our own publicity and lack of imagination in finding new patterns to solve our problems.

The increase in numbers actually allows for greater flexibility. With one hundred sections of freshman English and a freshman class of diverse background and ability, the college can more readily adapt its sections to the students' various needs than it could with a total freshman class of three hundred, where all students would have to fit into similar molds, whether these were suitable or not. Such arrangements take a certain amount of trouble; but, after all, administrative officers exist to perform these functions.

One cannot be happy with a perfectly static faculty. Our growth at Kansas is such that in 1962-1963 we added in the college thirty-nine new faculty members. This annual infusion of new members, at the rate of one for each fourteen and a half new students, at the average salary of present faculty, permits us to distribute resources where they are needed without taking anything away from any department —which, as you know, is hard to do. This constant growth in the size of the faculty also makes possible a continuous strengthening of the faculty, partly by introducing new types of people with special and needed talents. If the size of faculty were fixed, only a real crisis would make such rapid change possible.

The existence of graduate and professional schools on the same campus as the college of arts and sciences is also an opportunity, as well as a threat. For some students, having access to only a limited number of traditional undergraduate courses is like being squeezed into a room with a five-foot ceiling when one is six feet tall. The gifted sophomore or junior student who has taken all the courses in his field available at a four-year institution must either abandon his field or move to another campus. He also misses the opportunity to be stretched a bit by seeing what is going on in the graduate school, which may prove to be the stimulus he needs. Conversely, where graduate and professional schools exist on the same campus, the student has a wider window on the world of both work and scholarship.

A real danger to the college of liberal arts and sciences is pressure by the professional schools for special service courses. One conviction upon which all faculty members in arts and sciences unite is that the teaching of service courses for special vocational groups is a dreary and uninspiring task. Special courses in geology for engineers, economics for business students and chemistry for nurses are rarely exciting.

Under the right circumstances, all these courses can be abolished —and with them the numerous courses that exist for special groups within the college of arts and sciences, such as science courses for nonscience students who have no mathematical background, statistics courses for students who lack knowledge of algebra, and the bloodless courses given such titles as Geology and Man. With the disappearance of this kind of course, the resources of faculty could be used to teach sections, within the regular departmental courses, differentiated by ability and general background.

I have already touched on that beneficent demon, research, and its potential contribution to the learning situation for both faculty and students. Let me emphasize now its flexibility. Faculties and administrators are not limited to sponsored research contracts. They can undertake whatever they choose, and they can devise ways to make it productive for students—provided they believe that students can be taught to think, not merely to behave as passive receptacles.

The advantages to undergraduate students of working in the environment of a large graduate school are also clear. The most capable and mature scholars today, while they demand that their campuses have facilities for research, are generally willing to share their time and ideas with undergraduates. Indeed, one distinguished scientist at a large Midwestern university told me that he and his colleagues are convinced that they *must* devote a fair proportion of their time and energy to undergraduates, for the simple reason that there are no longer adequate faculties or facilities in most liberal-arts colleges to give first-class undergraduate education in their science. This point of view is an extreme one, but it has a large kernel of truth.

It must be evident by now that I do not find the size, diversity and complexity of life in a liberal-arts college in a large university alarming, distasteful or threatening. On the contrary, I believe that the most challenging opportunities to participate in the best kinds of undergraduate education in the arts and sciences exist today in the large universities.

REFERENCE

1. An earlier draft of this paper was edited by Barbara Waggoner from the original stenotyped transcript.

COMMENTARY

Robert Hutchins tells us that the purpose of higher education is to unsettle the minds of young adults. Often, however, it appears more profoundly frustrating to administrators than disturbing to students. One aspect of the over-all subject which now concerns policy makers is the current status and future course of liberal education and the institutions which provide it. To this subject the seminar directed its attention.

The supremacy of the liberal curriculum in higher education is no longer unchallenged. One horn of the dilemma is triple-pronged: first, some form of graduate education is now virtually a *sine qua non* for what President Dickey calls the leadership life. Second, most students can devote only a limited number of years to their higher education. And finally, the kinds of professional education which involve training beyond the first degree are becoming increasingly time-consuming. Medical studies, for example, can easily last eight years; and in order to economize on time, students often enter medical school after their junior year in college. There is also a growing tendency for students to begin college with advanced standing. Thus, for the would-be doctor who enters college as a sophomore and then by-passes the senior year, liberal undergraduate education is reduced from the traditional four years to two. Several participants in the seminar proposed ways of dealing with this situation. Richard M. Millard, dean of the College of Liberal Arts at Boston University, noted that his institution has recently initiated for prospective doctors a combined curriculum, which integrates liberal-arts and medical learning throughout the student's entire higher education. Unfortunately, the program is still too new to be evaluated in detail, but the first signs are encouraging. Margaret Clapp, president of Wellesley College, suggested that many colleges might revise their standards for admission, relax their requirement of twelve previous years of schooling and instead admit some students after their junior and perhaps even after their sophomore years of high school.

The intense emphasis on professional education has put some institutions, whose strictly career-oriented programs are limited, at a competitive disadvantage in the market for attracting students. For the small, private liberal-arts colleges, not the few highly prestigious ones but the many others, the situation is extremely serious, in some cases quite drastic. Part of their problem, as was brought out in Chapter 12, is their inability to match their public competitors' low prices. But another and perhaps an equally damaging aspect of their difficulties is that in a number of fields they cannot provide facilities for professional and preprofessional training which are sufficient to satisfy many of today's customers in the market for higher education.

Another contributing factor to liberal education's woes derives from the intellectual context of the times. Traditional liberal education and its recent descendant, general education, honored the belief that in order for one to think, he must think about something. Many students may have been at war with that proposition, but still it has been a major premise of liberal education. Thus the undergraduate had to learn "things." Now, at least in certain disciplines, times have changed. According to Dean Waggoner, general education is dead, and the rapid obsolescence of modern knowledge requires shifting the emphasis in liberal education from material to approach. Basically, the new movement involves treating under-graduates somewhat like mature scholars, rather than giving them down-payment type education of the memorize-now-understand-later variety. The law schools made this transition long ago and apparently with great success, but for undergraduate education the new technique is still a novelty, and it may be a good many years before teachers and students alike learn to handle it with maturity and finesse.

The problems associated with liberal undergraduate education are different for the small college and the large university. For the small institution, a major dilemma involves attracting teaching personnel. In general, the research-oriented scholars, the most thoroughly knowledgeable people in an academic sense, do not generally look upon a career in such a place as a happy prospect. For one thing, because small colleges can afford only a limited curriculum, they would be teaching basic material rather than working on the frontiers of knowledge. Also, if they desired intellectual rapport with more than a handful of people, they would have to seek companions outside their own fields, and many scholars find such companions less interesting. The important general point, as noted by John Sawyer, president of Williams College, is that liberal education stands for—and should stand for—breadth of understanding; and teaching in such a program may not appeal to anyone whose major interest is confined to studying a narrowly defined subject in depth. The problem of teaching personnel for small colleges is simply an outgrowth of this basic situation. In commenting on these matters. President Coles suggested that these institutions might find it helpful to sponsor limited amounts of graduate education in order to attract a few top scholars. It would be wrong, however, to suggest that in this matter of hiring faculty members, the small college has nothing but disadvantages. The people whom they do attract tend to be talented instructors. Indeed, many of them learned the ropes of good teaching—and emptied their systems of all their bad teaching—while they were doing graduate work at large universities. There is, thus, a real sense in which universities subsidize the cost of training teachers for the small colleges.

In contrast to the situation in small institutions, departments in universities are usually large enough to be intellectually self-sufficient. Although faculty members may appreciate this fact, it seems harmful to a university which is fragmented into ever-expanding departments. In fact, the growth of the departments is at least partially responsible for the demise of general education's independent status. They now include in their own courses material which until recently was presented under the separate title of general education. The departments have also expanded in the direction of greater specialization by increasing the number of courses which they offer. Dean Waggoner contends that a large university not only can afford such proliferation of courses but, moreover, must seek it in order to avoid having huge classes. As a result of the pressure to expand and for other reasons, there is often intense competition among a university's departments for students, prestige and so on; but although the seminar identified this phenomenon, it was silent in evaluating it as good or bad. On one related point, however, the members did agree: a university—and not a small college—is the place for a man in a hurry to climb the academic ladder.

One matter which makes planning curricula difficult for administrators in all types of institutions is the fact that an inordinately large number of students who initially choose to major in science soon abandon the endeavor. Dean Waggoner blamed this situation on dull teaching. Mary I. Bunting, president of Radcliffe College, on the other hand, mentioned that the culprit is the fact that it is easier for students in science than for those in many other fields to evaluate themselves in relation to their classmates. She believes that many become discouraged and leave science when they realize that others have abilities which are clearly superior to their own. Along these lines, Professor Harris told a story about McGeorge Bundy, who entered Yale intending to be a mathematician. During his second year he was enrolled in a graduate course with another sophomore, a man named Andrew Gleason. When mathematics was the issue, try as he might, Bundy was never able to finish anything but a poor second to Gleason, and as a result he soon transferred to political science. Bundy, of course, was ideally suited for his new field, eventually becoming dean of Harvard's Faculty of Arts and Sciences, and then the major adviser on national security to Presidents

Kennedy and Johnson. Predictably, Gleason is now a full professor at Harvard and one of the world's most distinguished mathematicians. Naturally, the point of this story is not that all freshman mathematicians are Gleasons and Bundys. Rather, it serves as an interesting and perhaps dramatic real-world illustration of Mrs. Bunting's point: it seems easier for students in science than for those in other fields to become discouraged with their natural abilities.

Near the end of this session, Professor Earl J. McGrath, executive officer of the Institute for Higher Education at Teachers College, Columbia University, reminded its members that liberal education is not a static concept. In fact, liberal education may no longer be an appropriate title because its current form differs as much from its counterpart of fifty years ago as the Boeing 707 does from the Wright brothers' first aircraft. In the jargon of economics, liberal education is undergoing product differentiation, and McGrath thinks it important for people to be aware that it is now perfectly possible for there to be a good college—good in the sense that it serves the needs of its clientele—which is not even remotely like, for example, Amherst. In expanding upon the theme of product differentiation, President Dickey emphasized that this trend is of vital significance for liberal education and that administrators would do well to keep it in mind when they plan changes in undergraduate curricula. Speaking to Harvard's graduating class in 1885, Oliver Wendell Holmes said, "Gentlemen, your education begins when what is called your education is ended." According to Dickey, those words have never been more relevant than they are today, and he urged that administrators give serious thought to the relationship between the new opportunities for continuing learning and the policies which they advocate concerning liberal undergraduate education.

14. Graduate Education in the Arts and Sciences

PAPER BY . . . *Bernard R. Berelson*
Director of the Bureau of Applied Social Research,
Columbia University

During the past several years there has been a great deal of criticism of graduate education in the arts and sciences in the United States. This criticism can be understood, it seems to me, in two somewhat different ways.

First, it might be seen as an accusation that graduate education is in a terribly bad state. I would have to take the opposite side of this controversy: I side with those who feel that American graduate education is sound and that it needs only some marginal remodeling. I believe that many critics are vastly overstating their case and refusing to recognize the many important contributions which this institution has made to American life, to academic life and to the life of the mind. I must add that this belief places me among the minority, if one counts only those people who are most vocal about the subject.

The criticism might also be seen as a concern that the basic conception of graduate education is wrong—that there is too much emphasis on research, that specialization is carried to an extreme, that not enough attention is paid to the needs of the potential college teacher and so on. These critics call for a radical reform of the present graduate school. Here again I must disagree: I believe that the central objectives and tendencies of graduate education in America today are right, though the efficiency with which the graduate shool is administered can certainly be improved.

In presenting my thoughts about the graduate school, I thought I might best put them in terms of my change of mind. I have lived all my adult life in education, in and around universities. In the fall of 1957, when I began the study which led to my book *Graduate Education in the United States,* I had a number of ideas about graduate education, some of which I changed as a result of looking very closely at the subject. Eight of these ideas—these *changed* ideas— might be worth mentioning now.

First, when I began the study, I thought that the continuing debate over graduate education was in a critically new phase. When I finished, I knew that it was not. The sobering fact is that virtually every current criticism, suggestion, complaint, question, problem and proposal dealing with graduate studies has been put forward during every five-year period since 1900, when the Association of American Universities was established.

I have found it always instructive and often amusing to read through the proceedings of the AAU in its early years. At the very start, in 1900, the proceedings covered the role of fellowships, the meaning of research, the character of the dissertation, the quality of students, the foreign-language requirement, the major-minor problems at the doctoral level, the role of the master's degree, examinations, preparation for college teaching, college-university relations and the need for uniform statistics—all in 1900.

It is amusing, as well as cautionary, to note in these proceedings the regularity with which all the topics we discuss today with such urgency have been explored before. In the early 1950's, the graduate deans spent a long time developing the practice of making fellowship offers on the same day and securing fellowship acceptances on the same day. William Rainey Harper, then president of the University of Chicago, presented a program to this effect in 1901, when only a few institutions were members of the AAU, and the dates involved were almost identical with those presently being used. In 1900, Nicholas Murray Butler, who was soon to become president of Columbia University, complained that because of multiple applications by graduate students, Columbia never knew how many graduate students it was going to have, and proposed a system to correct the situation. Charles W. Eliot, then president of Harvard University, complained in 1901 about the length of the doctoral dissertation, which required "greater sifting." In 1912, Dean Andrew West of Princeton was concerned, as he put it, "about the most sordid and dangerous thing just now in our graduate schools, namely, that they are attracting men not because they must be scholars but because they want a job. Why is the degree made the be-all and end-all? It is beginning to be known like a union card for labor."

In 1903, William James wrote a famous essay called "The Ph.D. Octopus." He argued that the degree was strangling the spirit of learning in the universities. James spoke of the smaller colleges which "hope to compensate for the obscurity of the names of their officers of instruction by the abundance of decorative titles by which these names are followed on the pages of the catalogue where they appear. The dazzled reader of the list, the parent or student, says to himself, 'This must be a terribly distinguished crowd—their titles shine like stars in the firmament, Ph.D.'S, S.D.'s and Litt.D.'s, bespangle the page as if they were sprinkled over it from a pepper caster.' "

"Are young men of undistinguished ability and indifferent personal traits diligently grubbing their way to the doctorate?" That question comes from the AAU proceedings of more than thirty years ago. Is the graduate school paying sufficient attention to preparing college teachers? The question was being argued nearly forty years ago, just as it is today; whenever there is a sharp increase in college enrollments, there is a corresponding increase in debate over that issue. Are too many unqualified institutions offering doctorate studies? Over forty years ago, informal efforts were made to restrict the number. Is the doctoral-degree program too highly specialized? Over fifty years ago, the members of the AAU were arguing that point. Nearly sixty years ago, the graduate dean at Princeton said, in effect, that too much research was being published, that no one could keep up with his field because the flood of publications was swamping people. That was in 1905.

I finally came to believe that graduate education is in a state of crisis today only in the sense that it always has been. These issues have always been argued. Indeed, far from being new, the rhetoric of the discussion has become stuck and needs oiling.

Second, when I began, I thought that the system of higher education was caught in a crisis of numbers. When I finished, I thought the problem had been exaggerated. Without going into detail, let me urge you not to accept uncritically the sources which are usually cited to document a supposed severe shortage of trained people on the faculty of higher education. I think that these sources are overdrawn; we are not nearly as badly off as they make us out to be, and we shall not be as badly off in 1970 as most of them predict. There is a problem, but I think that the system is already rising to the challenge.

Third, when I began, I thought that the graduate school was probably seriously deficient in its training of college teachers, largely because of its great stress on research training. When I finished, I was quite relaxed about that issue.

The issue hinges on what I have come to call the market-research argument, made by those who insist that the graduate school is not training people properly for college teaching. They argue that most PhD's will teach in colleges, but the graduate school is training them to do research. The medical school trains people to be doctors; the law school trains them to be lawyers; and the graduate school should train them to be college teachers. I call this the market-research argument because it is based on the position that the product should be packaged for its subsequent use.

As a matter of fact, only about sixty per cent of all doctorate recipients in recent years have gone into educational employment. It varies by field, of course; it is very high in the humanities and rather low in the physical sciences, with the other fields in between. That percentage has been declining steadily since the early part of the century. I think it is still going down, though not very fast. It does not decrease by many percentage points in a decade, in any case, and the recent improvements in faculty salaries should tend to keep the figure up during the 1960's.

Many people decry the fact that only sixty per cent of all doctorate holders end up in colleges and universities; they would like to have many more, if not all. I would like to suggest that it is very healthy for the American society to have a large proportion of PhD recipients move out into the great world of affairs—into industrial positions, government and even private practice. I think this is an important way to bring the academic world and the world of affairs into closer contact. In my view, it is a great tribute to the graduate school that its trained intelligence is wanted outside academia, and it is good for the society that it is wanted and being used there.

The other part of this argument, however, goes straight to the meaning of "college teaching." Not very long ago, most PhD's entering higher education taught undergraduates in independent liberal-arts colleges. But with the rise of the universities, especially the public institutions, most of this sixty per cent now go into universities and not into independent liberal-arts colleges. Only two or three years after they receive their doctorates, they are teaching graduate courses and carrying thesis loads for which research training is the *sine qua non*. And this trend will doubtless continue, for a disproportionate share of the coming increase in college enrollment is going into the universities, rather than into the independent liberal-arts colleges.

It seems clear, then, that PhD's will be increasingly attracted to the universities and that research training at the doctorate level will be increasingly helpful for the sort of teaching they will be doing. Even in the liberal-arts colleges, the presidents believe that research training at the doctoral level is an important preparation for every faculty member, even if—perhaps especially if—it is the last research he ever does. At least he will learn, in writing a dissertation, how hard it is to come by sound knowledge. Certainly every professor in higher education ought to know that.

And then there are the other forty per cent. If we consider the increasing national importance of research, not only for national security but in a great many other spheres, this seems an inopportune time to cut down research training in the name of the undergraduate teacher. If doctoral candidates are to be trained for their subsequent use, training in research must be provided. Yet the strong emphasis on research training is precisely what the critics seek to replace.

Fourth, when I began, I thought that the standards of doctoral study were being unduly lowered by the spread of degree-granting to unqualified institutions. When I finished, I was quite relaxed about that matter too.

In 1900, when the AAU was founded, the major institutions engaged in doctoral work were seven great private universities: Chicago, Columbia, Cornell, Harvard, Johns Hopkins, Pennsylvania and Yale. They awarded over eighty per cent of the doctorates given that year. By the late 1950's, there were thirty-five major institutions in the field; the seven latest entrants were Indiana, UCLA, Boston, Maryland, Michigan State, Syracuse and Washington. All the national graduate schools were established and in full operation by 1930. Since then have come the regional, state and urban institutions, such as Washington in the Pacific Northwest; Southern California and UCLA in California; North Carolina and Texas for different parts of the South; Purdue, Indiana and Michigan State for the Middle West; and Boston for that urban center.

The newer entrants are growing faster than the older ones, and public universities are growing faster than private ones. A few years ago, for the first time, the public universities gave more doctorates than the private universities. Also, the less prestigious universities are growing faster than the more prestigious. In 1925 the top five universities (determined by faculty vote of what the better departments were) produced over forty per cent of the doctorates; and the top ten produced over sixty per cent. In 1957 the top five (by a similar appraisal) produced twenty per cent and the top ten about a third.

With such decentralization there has inevitably come a concern for standards. Fifty years ago, when doctoral training was limited to a handful of the great universities, they could quite readily maintain an even set of standards. Now the enterprise is too large, too dispersed, too disconnected for that. But—and this is very important—the production of more second-class doctorates, even though it may lower the national average, does not affect the production of first-class doctorates, of which we shall also have more than ever. Large numbers of doctorates are needed for a widely diverse set of institutions. Increased production lower down the line, even if it is of lower average quality, as I think inevitably it will be, is useful in staffing institutions which cannot afford or attract the products of the best institutions and whose faculty would otherwise be much worse.

Here, then, is one consequence of America's decision to have a mass system of higher education: that mass system must be staffed, and it cannot all be staffed by doctorates from the great twenty public and private universities. In a country as large as ours, with a mass system of higher education as diversified as ours, there are places for a variety of institutions—that is, for a variety of people who ought to be trained by a variety of institutions. And there is a rough balancing out by quality, as I tried to trace in my book.

I happen to think that a mass system of higher education is a good thing. Also, for whatever it is worth, my own personal impression is that some of the coming institutions today are better than the great private universities were forty years ago or less, when they were running the show and providing most of the doctoral training.

Fifth, when I began, I thought that some radical revision in the system of degrees might be desirable—for example, the rejuvenation of the master's degree for college teaching or the introduction of a second doctor's degree. When I finished, I had given up on the former for this purpose and opposed the latter.

Briefly, I decided that trying to resuscitate the master's degree in the arts and sciences as a respectable degree for college teachers would be futile. It cannot be done, and I now think that it should not be done. I think we ought to stress the efficient production of doctorates instead of one-year masters. This does not mean that I would dispense with the master's degree altogether. It is needed for a variety of purposes—as an insurance policy, a consolation prize, a qualifying certificate. John Peterson Elder, dean of the Harvard University Graduate School of Arts and Sciences, summarized my feeling about the master's degree a few years ago in an article in *The Journal of Higher Education.* "The Master's degree," he concluded, "is, at present, a bit like a streetwalker—all things to all men, and at different prices."

There are too many obstacles to the resuscitation of the master's as a respected, research-oriented, academic degree for college teachers on a national scale. These obstacles include the historical decline in the degree; its lowered prestige now, as against even the time when my generation took it; the diversity of its meaning; the excess of claimants over the number of faculty available for sponsorship and guidance; its competitive disadvantage relative to the doctorate; the coolness of the better colleges toward granting it; the reluctance of the better students to seek it; the poorer career prospects for those who hold it; and consequently its low return on investment.

Many people are now asserting that the time has come to set up a third graduate degree. Some, citing the weakening of standards for the doctorate degree, call for a degree beyond the doctorate. I think that this is neither desirable nor practical. We now have, of course, a great deal of postdoctoral study, especially in the sciences. I think it is here to stay, and I think it can be better rationalized, but I do not think that we need a degree to symbolize it. Indeed, I think that a degree would do some harm if it were put into the system at that point.

Other people think that we need a new degree for college teachers between the master's and the doctorate—in effect, a new two-year doctor's degree. One problem here is naming such a degree, and lest you think that this is a trivial issue, one that could easily be settled, let me assure you that countless numbers of highly placed man-hours have gone into the debate over what that degree would be called. For prestige purposes, it would have to be called a doctorate. For obvious reasons, it could not be called the PhD. This problem could probably be solved, but it is by no means easy.

Such a degree could probably meet the need of a large number of liberal-arts colleges, as well as the undergraduate colleges in some universities, and there are advantages in saving time on the production end. However, I think it would inevitably be seen as a second-class degree. It would attract second-class students; and on the whole, I think it would not be good for the system of higher education to institutionalize this kind of second-class citizenship, especially when the students who take it would be quite close to getting what would surely be called the honest doctorate. In short, I think this is a poor solution, relative to compressing the present doctoral program and making it available more efficiently.

Sixth, when I began, I thought that the doctorate required too much time because of the program and the dissertation. When I finished, I concluded that the trouble was primarily a matter of money.

Let me point to a crucial distinction. I think that the doctorate takes about the right amount of time in full-time equivalence. In all arts and science fields, it takes the full-time equivalence of about four academic years. However, it takes a wide range of *elapsed* time, shorter in the physical sciences and longer in the humanities, as measured by the time between the granting of the BA and the granting of the PhD. This difference correlates directly with the amount and kind of student support available. The science student can write his dissertation while serving as a research assistant in his own or a closely related field. In the humanities, on the other hand, the support comes more often in the form of teaching assistantships in courses not directly related to the dissertation.

People call for a norm for doctoral study, and everyone agrees that it should be about three or four years. In full-time equivalence, the norm is here. It is in fact three to four years, but it is often spread over a much longer period because of the problem of support. If we solved that problem (and here I take the position, unpopular in some quarters, that the student should bear more of this cost out of pocket, including loans in the terminal year) and if we could compress this program into a full-time affair, so that the doctoral student would be expected to graduate with his class, like a medical or law student, I think we would have solved a number of other problems as well. This is the kind of thing I mean by saying that the doctoral program should be made more efficient.

Seventh, when I began, I thought that the doctoral dissertation in the social sciences and the humanities required improvement in quality. When I finished, I thought that such improvement would best be achieved if the dissertation were shorter—not a median of 250 to 300 pages, as is presently the case, but a median of 100 to 125 pages. I believe that this would make for a better dissertation and not simply a shorter one. I commend to you Abel Evans' ironic couplet and suggest that it might well apply to people who perpetrate too long dissertations on their sponsors, their institutions, their libraries and their fields: "Lie heavy on him, earth! for he/Laid many a heavy load on thee."

Finally, when I began, I thought that graduate education was in a bad way. When I finished, I had come to the opposite conclusion.

I have now come full circle, At the risk of giving up my critical credentials in the academic world—and knowing that one of the worst sins a writer on education can commit is to say anything good for the present system—I think that on the whole, by and large, taking everything into account, with due allowances, on balance and in the main, American graduate education is doing a good job. It is by no means a weak link in our chain of higher education. It is making important contributions to the society and to the educational system; and it deserves the confidence, support and gratitude of the nation.

PAPER BY . . . *John Chase*
      Chief of the Higher Education, Personnel Section,
      U.S. Office of Education

I think that Dr. Berelson has covered about ninety per cent of the important topics concerning graduate education, both in his book and in his admirable paper. I agree with about ninety per cent of his points—all of the specific points, in fact. It is just in the conclusion that I disagree with him. I think that, all things considered, graduate education is in a bad state today, not qualitatively but quantitatively. I shall return to this point later. First I would like to note briefly some of the recent criticisms of graduate education.

Let me begin with a preliminary observation. Although it is true, as Dr. Berelson has said, that many graduate deans have been discussing some problems in graduate education since the start of the century, it seems to me that there is a considerable difference between contemporary discussions and those of even a few years ago. One notable difference is in the number and identity of the people who are doing the discussing. It may be that they are saying largely the same things that have been said before; but in contrast with the early 1900's, they are different people, and there are many more of them. They include not just the graduate deans, who used to do most of the discussing, but also foundation and government officials, scholars in a wide variety of academic disciplines, and writers in professional and even semipopular magazines. In other words, the interested public has vastly increased in size and variety, and this certainly makes a difference.

A second notable difference is the increased amount of reliable information available about what actually goes on in the process of graduate education. I do not know who was responsible for starting the collection of objective facts about graduate students and their problems. Certainly the number of statistical reports has increased rapidly in the last several years. It may be only an accident, but I think much of this has occurred since John Peterson Elder, dean of the Graduate School of Arts and Sciences at Harvard University, published his excellent sociological study on Harvard and Radcliffe PhD's. Dr. Berelson's own study presented a tremendous mine of relevant data. Dr. Charles Kidd and a number of Federal agencies have also added a great deal. I think we are now in a position—potentially, at least—to know much more about the facts than we did even five years ago, and certainly much more than we did in 1950.

Turning to some of the specific criticisms of graduate education that have been ventilated recently, I should like to quote a paragraph from Hayward Kenniston's book about graduate study at the University of Pennsylvania: "The American graduate school is a strangely amorphous institution. It has a 'faculty' but the members of the faculty, with rare exceptions, . . . are drawn from faculties of other schools and are therefore engaged in undergraduate and professional as well as graduate instruction. They rarely meet as a group, except for the election of committees. Graduate schools also have a dean, but he usually has no instructional budget, no voice, except by courtesy, in the recruitment, appointment and promotion of staff. His chief function is that of a record keeper. In reality, the graduate school is a loose federation of autonomous departments."

On the whole, it seems to me that Kenniston's statement is moderate in tone; and it summarizes very well, I think, some of the major criticisms that have been made both by the graduate deans themselves and by a number of serious observers. But his statement is much more applicable to some institutions than to others. Indeed, this is one of the difficult things about American graduate education: it has such tremendous variety.

Kenniston's statement, for example, that the graduate dean has neither budget nor faculty of his own is not true of Johns Hopkins, and it is only partially true of Chicago, Columbia, Stanford and the California Institute of Technology, among others. Again, I know for a fact that at many large universities, both public and private, the graduate dean is almost always consulted in the appointment of any senior professor or departmental chairman. Kenniston's statement was obviously meant to be true—and is true—of the University of Pennsylvania, and doubtless it is also more or less true of some other institutions, but there are many exceptions. It is not uniformly true.

Some graduate deans feel quite strongly that they should be consulted at a much earlier stage with regard to senior faculty appointments, but I wonder how, as a matter of practical fact, this could be. A graduate dean cannot be a specialized expert in more than a handful of the fields normally covered in a graduate school. In the last analysis, he must always rely on the judgment of faculty members whom he can trust.

Another complaint mentioned by Dr. Kenniston—and also, I believe, by Dr. Berelson—is that the average graduate dean (if there is any average) is occupied too much of the time with routine record-keeping and mechanical procedures concerning admissions, residence requirements, language requirements and so on. Dean W. Gordon Whaley of Texas has said that in his opinion, ninety per cent of this routine work could be handled by a top-notch secretary, or even by one who is not top notch. As a matter of fact, he might have added that a large part of it *is* handled by the secretaries.

This complaint has merit, of course, but it is easy to exaggerate its importance. Someone has to pass on admissions; someone has to keep records. It makes little difference, I think, whether this is all done in the graduate dean's office or is handled by individual departments or by some central admissions office. As a matter of fact, there are eminent universities which handle such matters in each of these ways and with various other modifications.

At Johns Hopkins, for example, the graduate dean never sees applications for admission; they are handled completely by departmental chairmen. Much the same is true of Cal Tech. These, of course, are relatively small institutions. At Ohio State, admissions are handled by a single separate office. At UCLA, admissions are routed first to the graduate dean's office; there an associate graduate dean in charge of admissions, with a staff of twenty, screens close to 5,000 separate applications each fall, which are then passed on to the department chairmen for further screening on the basis of their differential standards. Berkeley follows a different procedure: for some departments the graduate dean's office handles all admissions, while other departments insist on seeing all their applications. All these different procedures seem to be effective in the different institutions.

As for the other problems of recordkeeping, two observations seem pertinent and perhaps fairly obvious. First, the stronger the departments are, the less need there is for centralized policing. And second, the revolution in business machines is rapidly making possible new and more efficient procedures for keeping records. I suspect that in most graduate schools (including all the larger ones) in the future, all records will be kept on punch cards or electronic tapes, with duplicates available wherever they are needed on the campus. If so, the solution to this problem is already in sight.

With regard to the general organization of graduate work, there has always been some difference of opinion among well-informed people as to the relative merits of the horizontal pattern—the customary graduate school of arts and sciences—versus the vertical organization along departmental or divisional lines. The horizontal organization is certainly followed by the great majority of institutions, but a distinguished minority is organized along divisional lines. This small band includes Clark, Hopkins, Chicago and Columbia, to mention only four of the better known.

Among the advantages of the vertical or divisional organization, the following are usually cited. First, it is supposed to avoid the invidious distinction between a general faculty and a separate graduate faculty. Second, it is supposed to enable bright undergraduates to participate more easily in seminar and other work of a graduate nature; and this, in turn, is alleged to result in a higher proportion of under-graduates going on to graduate work. Third, it is supposed to help break down the barriers between related departments and thus to be especially effective in promoting interdisciplinary work.

Finally, since each division is normally headed by its own dean, the divisional organization is supposed to give equal representation, at the highest level of university planning, to all the major academic areas—the physical and biological sciences, the humanities and the social sciences.

If all these claims were true, it would be difficult to understand why more universities have not adopted the divisional plan. But the evidence for most of these alleged advantages is not convincing; and where the evidence is convincing, there are also some disadvantages. One of these disadvantages is that someone has to coordinate divisional deans, and this simply pushes the problem up to a higher level. It seems to be generally true that in institutions organized along divisional lines, there is a greater number of officials between the president and the dean. It is not clear to me that the proliferation of these intermediary officials necessarily makes for greater effectiveness and strength in graduate work.

It also seems to be true that, in universities having a divisional organization, there is usually an executive vice president responsible for outside contract research. Separating these two responsibilities— for graduate education and for research—seems to be of doubtful merit in principle, though there are very valid practical considerations. In universities organized on horizontal lines, on the other hand, there seems to be a growing tendency to assign the responsibility for contract research to the graduate dean, sometimes with the additional title of vice president for research, as at Tulane, Michigan, Michigan State, Iowa, Pennsylvania and several others. In still other institutions the title may be secretary or chairman of the University Research Council, as in Illinois, Ohio State, Stanford, Cal Tech and Berkeley. Whatever the title, the dean has the power to see and approve every proposal involving outside research contracts. This is, I think, a major change in the function of the graduate dean's office, and it is a significant one.

Returning to recent criticisms of graduate education, no aspect of the subject has drawn so much adverse comment as the protracted delay between the earning of the baccalaureate and the doctor of philosophy degree. Dr. Oliver C. Carmichael of the Fund for the Advancement of Education, in his recent book *The Changing Role of Higher Education,* has used this situation to make something of a capital case against the graduate schools and the graduate deans. He has argued that a graduate student should have the same assurance as a medical or a law student that he can earn his degree in a specified period of time. This seems to me a dubious analogy; in any case, the argument goes a bit wide of the mark. If the graduate schools are in fact responsible for the delays in the humanities and the social sciences, they should be given credit for the shorter time in the natural sciences. Somehow, they never are.

In fact, the more one considers the bill of particulars that Dr. Carmichael has presented against the graduate schools, the more one comes to the conclusion that these same offenses could more appropriately and more truthfully be lodged against the departments. And the departments, of course, reflect the interests and standards prevailing in the disciplines they represent. Fortunately, there are signs that a number of the disciplines are taking a much more active interest than they did formerly. Let me simply mention what has been done in the social sciences, with which I am most familiar. Since Elbridge Sibley's pioneering study in 1948, *The Recruitment, Selection and Training of Social Scientists,* there have been intensive studies by the professional societies of graduate education in economics, history and sociology. Of the major social sciences, only political science has shown almost no interest and taken no steps in studying its own peculiar problems. Perhaps someday it will.

It seems to me that this path is the most likely route of progress. As the disciplines become more interested, the departments will take some active steps for improvement. When they do, perhaps the graduate deans will be let off the hook and given the credit for what the departments are doing, just as now they are taking the blame for what the departments are failing to do.

It does seem curious that, in so much of the recent criticism of graduate education, hardly any mention at all is made of the one university official who, more than any other, is supposedly responsible for general university policy. I would not expect the graduate-school deans to criticize their own presidents, but their silence on this general point is mystifying when some of the most severe recent criticism comes from a man who has, in his time, been both a graduate dean and a president. (This is a striking illustration of how short a graduate dean's memory is after he becomes president.)

The presidents of some universities have exerted distinguished leadership in enunciating policy with respect to graduate work and also in implementing it. Among these are former Presidents Daniel C. Gilman of John Hopkins, Granville S. Hall of Clark and Andrew

D. White of Cornell, to mention only a few. Graduate education can hardly prosper without such firm and consistent presidential support.

At the same time, it seems to me, the presidents must be willing for the deans to speak to the general public and especially—I know this is a delicate political matter—to state and Federal officials. No one expects the presidents to cede to the deans the right to enunciate general university policy; but they might well consult the deans more than they do now before policy has been firmly established, and they might allow them a reasonable public voice afterwards.

Let me now mention briefly two very large unresolved problems in Federal policy vis-à-vis graduate education. Assuming that there is a need to strengthen and expand graduate education in the United States, the issue, as frequently posed, is whether this can best be done by strengthening the existing institutions or by trying to create new ones. My own view is that we must do both. The existing graduate schools are not being fully utilized; they could accept more doctoral graduates in many fields. But I think we are entering a period of acute national shortage of highly trained manpower in practically all fields, and even the full utilization of the existing graduate schools will not produce anywhere near the number of doctoral graduates we need. Therefore, there is a very strong case for programs designed to broaden the base of graduate education by creating new centers.

Precisely how to do this is a terribly difficult problem. Pouring new money into universities does not necessarily accomplish the task, for the institution with a large new grant frequently uses this money to buy a distinguished faculty member from another institution. This may be fine for the individual and for the institution which has benefited, but shuffling major faculty members around from one university to another does not broaden or strengthen the enterprise as a whole. In the long run, the only answer is to increase both the number of good graduate students and the number of centers in which they can be trained.

The second unresolved problem is related to the first: should the Federal Government shift from its present policy of support for specialized projects to general, noncategorical support? There is at present no general Federal, noncategorical support for education as such, with the possible exception of a few small programs operated by the National Science Foundation and the National Institutes of

Health. But the desirability of such general, noncategorical support has been widely discussed at a very high level in the Government, including the President's Science Advisory Committee. The specific problem is, of course, to find a formula for general support which would be acceptable to Congress, on the one hand, and would be beneficial to education and acceptable to the universities, on the other. To be politically acceptable, any formula for general aid would have to be simple in conception; applicable to all institutions, public and private; and based on some objectively verifiable criteria, such as the number and level of graduate students enrolled or of graduate degrees conferred, or the total tuition costs.

University administrations could perform a very valuable service if they would devote some attention to this problem. We are apparently going to be forced into trying something of this kind, and unless someone has carefully studied and analyzed all the various proposals, the result may be less satisfactory than those involved—among others, the universities themselves—might wish. I should add that there is a law which prevents Government bureaucrats from advocating legislation, so I want to make it very clear that I am only trying to analyze the situation, not advocating increased Federal support.

I would like to conclude with two quotations, which seem to me to sum up the major features of graduate education as it exists today, and to comment briefly on them. The first quotation is: "The wants of the American community have far outgrown the capacity of the University to supply them." When President Charles W. Eliot of Harvard made that statement in his inaugural address in 1869, he probably meant it in a much more restricted sense than we would understand it today. We could certainly agree with it if we understood "the American community" to mean the whole of American society, and if we further qualified it to include the interests of other nations with which we are more or less formally allied.

If Eliot's comment is understood in this larger sense, it is true: the universities, and especially their graduate schools, are being called on today for more and more help in every national endeavor, from improving public-school teaching at home, to raising living standards abroad, to furthering our achievements in outer space. The accumulation of these national demands is, of course, creating many stresses and strains in the universities; and much of the recent criticism of graduate education stems precisely from the uneven impact of these demands on university programs and personnel.

The second quotation is much more specific. It comes from the 1961 report of the Association of Graduate Schools' Committee on Policies in Graduate Education: "The greatest single need of graduate education in the United States and Canada is an orderly, rapid growth in the training of qualified PhD's." I doubt whether anyone who has studied the situation carefully would disagree with this conclusion. But the AGS report simply states a goal; it does not say how the goal is to be reached. If it is to be reached, large additional sources of money will have to be invested in graduate education. Harvard, Princeton and Stanford have drawn heavily on private financial resources for their capital-fund-raising campaigns. But does anyone imagine that the other sixty-odd private PhD-granting institutions can all be equally successful in resorting to private donors, or that the eighty-odd public PhD-granting institutions would be equally successful in winning greater support from state legislatures?

The need for substantial action becomes more apparent every day. If private donors and state legislatures do not respond quickly, then, as on so many other issues, the Federal Government will probably step in—as indeed it has already, though only in a limited way. This, it seems to me, is the largest unresolved issue facing graduate education today.

COMMENTARY

American graduate education in the arts and sciences is many things to many people. To some it is the life's blood of basic scientific research and thus of progressive industrial technology. To others it is the proper breeding for the incipient scholar. And inevitably there are those, participants and critics alike, to whom the institution seems little more than a safe shelter from the real world.

Historically, America's balance of trade in the graduate-student account has been shifting. At the beginning of the twentieth century, this country was a net exporter of graduate students. Dr. Berelson mentioned that one motivating force which drew members of the American Association of Universities together around 1900 was their collective desire to present a united front to the German universities, which were attracting many of America's ablest graduate students. Since then the balance has shifted radically. America is now a large net importer of doctoral candidates, and, both at home and abroad, the stock of American graduate education is clearly on the upswing.

The flowering of graduate education prompts many to wonder whether this development has occurred at the expense of undergraduate education. Decidedly no, was Dr. Berelson's answer. In his view, undergraduates at universities now receive better education than they ever did because graduate programs have brought to the institutions specialists—men who know their fields well—in contrast to the untrained men, often ministers, who were, by and large, charged with undergraduate instruction in the nineteenth century. Arguing somewhat differently, Professor Harris acknowledged that undergraduate education has improved in the past sixty years, but he suggested that this improvement occurred in spite of, rather than because of graduate education. He reasoned that undergraduate education might have improved more than in fact it did, if graduate training had not absorbed so many scarce resources.

The similarities between one graduate school and any other often begin and end with the fact that they both award a degree called a PhD. Thus American graduate education is a diverse enterprise, but whereas this is often interpreted to mean different standards in the various institutions, Dr. Berelson thinks that the students may be a prime source of institutional diversity. The students at some universities, he claimed, are simply better than those at others. This is an interesting way of looking at the issue. However, since the rigor of an institution's requirements and the ability of its students tend to form a which-came-first-the-chicken-or-the-egg? progression over time, the debate about whether diversity comes through students or standards seems at least partially artificial.

Although Dr. Berelson contended that diversity among institutions is desirable, he also argued that in one dimension, administrators should strive to introduce uniformity into all doctoral programs. That dimension is time, the time that elapses between registration in a doctoral program and the awarding of a degree. Specifically, he favors awarding all PhD's at the end of a specified number of years of study, probably four. In addition to increasing support of full-time study, one innovation that would be helpful in making such a plan feasible is shortening the dissertation, and Berelson suggested reducing the average length of thesis by about one half. This suggestion is intimately related to another matter: the amount of advice that one who is writing a thesis receives from his adviser. In general, American educators are ambivalent about how much advice is appropriate. They desire to help the student produce a good book in a responsible amount of time, but they also want to apply sink-or-swim tactics to cultivate his talent for doing effective work independently. Most educators agree that the adviser's virtually holding the student's hand, on the one extreme, or disappearing into Tibet for two years to carry on his own research, on the other, is wrong; but they have not yet agreed on an acceptable mean. Doing so, however, seems a prerequisite to carrying out Dr. Berelson's suggestion about the duration of graduate studies.

We might expect university administrators to be initially unreceptive to the notion of shortening graduate education because often graduate students are for them a form of cheap and, in some sense, exploitable labor—academic coolies, as it were. Such reluctance on the part of administrators to accept Dr. Berelson's scheme would, according to Dean J. P. Elder, be unfounded. He estimated that teaching rarely delays any individual's getting his degree by more than half a year. He thus concluded that even if Dr. Berelson's plan were implemented, the universities' supply of cheap labor for the more mundane teaching jobs would not be seriously reduced—not enough, in any event, to justify administrators' opposing the plan.

Elder reported that the crucial concerns of the graduate dean are admissions and scholarships. In general, standards vary from one department to another, and there is always some conflict between the departments and the dean about whether to admit certain marginal students. On the whole, Elder finds this conflict healthy, for it applies a useful set of checks and balances to the process of admissions. Closely related to admissions is the matter of scholarships, for accepting an impoverished student but offering him no financial aid is often tantamount to refusing him. In awarding scholarships, Elder noted, it is crucial to watch the market and estimate competitors' actions. The dean wants to attract the best students, but he also wants to avoid wasting money. It is thus helpful for him to know how little he can offer someone without losing him, for the competition for talented graduate students is keen. In fact, American graduate schools now seem to look upon budding first-rate scholars the same way that the traditional college football coach views a fleet-footed high-school halfback.

There is good reason for believing that in the near future, the demand for people possessing doctorates will be tremendous in most fields. A recent study revealed that at the University of Pennsylvania, the senior faculty members in the humanities and social sciences are old, on the average. Many will soon retire and will thus have to be replaced, and Dr. Chase thought it likely that in his regard Pennsylvania typifies the majority of America's universities. In the sciences the story is a familiar one. Chase mentioned that as a result of America's decision to land a man on the moon, the National Aeronautics and Space Administration alone could absorb every doctoral graduate in engineering, mathematics and most of the physical sciences during the next decade. And in the life sciences, the National Institutes of Health has put in its claim for a large share of the young doctors, biologists and so on. Clearly, then, the evidence indicates that higher education may soon find itself hard-pressed to hire the number of qualified teachers it ideally needs, especially since enrollments are expected to expand enormously between now and 1975. In any event, one thing is certain: the market for Ph.D.'s is now and will be for some time a seller's market. An otherwise qualified person with a doctorate need not anticipate filing claims for unemployment compensation for many years to come, if ever. (As a rule, he is not eligible, I might add.)

Like all markets, the one for Ph.D.'s is two-sided, and doctorates are now at a premium, not only because the demand for them is especially strong, but also because the rate at which they have recently been supplied is unusually slow. Between 1890 and 1954 that rate had been steady and sufficiently high to double our stock of Ph.D.'s roughly every decade. Between 1954 and 1960 that stock increased by only ten per cent. Many explanations of this falling off have been advanced. Some blame the birth rate in the 1930's; others blame the G.I. Bill; but neither explanation is completely satisfactory.

Whatever the reason, the rate at which our stock of Ph.D.'s is increasing is insufficient to satisfy the demands in the near future. As a result, one of our universities' major current tasks is to increase the rate at which they produce PhD's and to raise that rate to its 1890-1954 average level and perhaps higher. There is, however, a major controversy about how best to achieve this end. Some people, Chase included, emphasize the need for quantity without diminishing quality. Chase argued that even if all American institutions which now award PhD's were working at full capacity, they could not produce degree holders fast enough. He thus advocated establishing new centers for educating doctoral candidates. Berelson, on the other hand, emphasized the quality of the product. He advocated using the facilities of roughly our top seventy-five universities at full capacity, but he opposed spreading the programs elsewhere en masse because, in his opinion, this latter alternative would represent a less efficient investment of the inevitable scarce resources available.

15. Tenure and Academic Freedom

PAPER BY . . . *Clark Byse*[1]
Professor of Law, Harvard University

The most widely accepted statement of academic tenure is that of the Association of American Colleges and the American Association of University Professors. This document, called the *1940 Statement on Academic Freedom and Tenure,* provides that "after the expiration of a probationary period teachers or investigators should have permanent or continuous tenure, and their services should be terminated only for adequate cause, except in the case of retirement for age, or under extraordinary circumstances because of financial exigencies." There are, of course, many variations. But the essential characteristic of tenure is continuity of service; the institution in which the teacher serves has in some manner—as a legal obligation or as a moral commitment—relinquished the freedom or power it otherwise would possess to terminate his services.

The principal justification for academic tenure is that it frees the faculty member from a large number of restraints and pressures which otherwise would inhibit independent thought and action. It gives him, in short, academic freedom. A similar justification accounts for the provision in the Bill of Rights that the government shall not abridge any citizen's general freedom of expression. This general freedom exists largely because of the pragmatic recognition that free trade in ideas is an indispensable condition to enlightened community decision and action.

But there is more to academic freedom. In our society, teachers in colleges and universities have a responsibility to help students

313

develop their critical capacities. Teachers must not only strive to make available the accumulated knowledge of the past and to expand the frontiers of knowledge; they must also appraise existing institutions and seek their correction or replacement in the light of reason and experience. If they are to perform these indispensable tasks, there must be free inquiry and discussion. As Professor Fritz Machlup, Walker professor of economics and international finance at Princeton and recently president of the American Association of University Professors, has noted, this demands more than mere "absence of governmental sanctions, more than a guarantee that . . . [professors] will not be jailed for the expressions of their thoughts. If they are to be encouraged to pursue the truth wherever it may lead, to 'follow out any bold, vigorous, independent train of thought . . .,' they need protection from all more material sanctions, especially from dismissal." Professor Machlup adds:

"With regard to some occupations, it is eminently in the interest of society that men concerned speak their minds without fear of retribution. . . . The occupational work of the vast majority of people is largely independent of their thought and speech. The professor's work *consists* of his thought and speech. If he loses his position for what he writes or says, he will, as a rule, have to leave his profession and may no longer be able effectively to question and challenge accepted doctrines. And if *some* professors lose their positions for what they write or say, the effect on many other professors will be such that their usefulness to their students and to society will be gravely reduced."

This point deserves emphasis. Infringements of academic freedom and tenure bring lasting damage not only to the very small group of teachers directly affected but also to society as a whole. Conversely, the ultimate beneficiaries of academic freedom are not those who exercise it but all the people. Academic freedom and tenure are not grounded in a peculiar solicitude for the human beings who staff our academic institutions. They exist so that society may have the benefit of honest judgment and independent criticism, which otherwise might be withheld for fear of offending a dominant social group or attitude.

A helpful analogy may be found in what may be termed judicial freedom and the tenure of judges. The Constitution provides that "the Judges, both of the supreme and inferior courts, shall hold their Offices during good behavior, and shall, at stated times, receive for their services, a Compensation which shall not be diminished during their continuance in office." Alexander Hamilton declared in *The Federalist* that this "standard of good behavior for . . . continuance in office . . . is the best expedient which can be devised in any government, to secure a steady, upright, and impartial administration of the laws." In the same way, tenure for teachers in colleges and universities "during good behavior" provides the best safeguard from restraints and pressures which otherwise might deter a "steady, upright, and impartial" performance of their indispensable task of critical thought and analysis.

This, in brief and general terms, is the argument for tenure in American higher education. But does it not oversimplify the case? Does it not gloss over difficulties and problems that should be considered?

More than one academician asserts that tenure, rather than advancing scholarship and talent, often perpetuates incompetence and mediocrity. Edgar F. Borgatta, a social psychologist with the Russell Sage Foundation, for example, objects to the principle that retention of a teacher beyond a stated probationary term confers tenure. To confer tenure on this basis, he avers, is "to support the banner of mediocrity rather than the herald of achievement." He argues further that "if the ideal of the university is scholarship and scientific production, emphasis on tenure . . . is hardly coincident with the ideal."

Professor Charles Gordon Post of Vassar is far more extreme. He urges that tenure be abolished, partly because it keeps salaries low. Presidents and trustees, he says, have reasoned (perhaps subconsciously) that "if teachers, many of them inadequate, were going to have this form of security, drawing salaries for years with no chance of dismissal, their salaries had better be kept low." He expresses his concurrence with this reasoning as follows: "If I had to keep a man on for 15, 20 or 25 years—not knowing whether in the long run he would be worth it—but having to pay him month in and month out as long as he was doing a passable job, and couldn't dismiss him, my tendency would be to pay him as little as possible."

But Professor Post's argument goes beyond the economic aspects. Tenure, he says, "provides the conditions under which bad or mediocre teaching may be perpetuated . . . There is no room for the teacher who was a poor teacher to begin with and who after years of service is promoted and given tenure simply because there is nothing else to do with him. . . .

"Tenure is small-time security and reaps small rewards. . . Perhaps the best that can be said for tenure is that it gives the timid a sense of security, the mediocre the right to continue to be mediocre, and all teachers the right not to be fired except for reasons none of which have anything to do with education. . . .

"It seems only fair that a president and board of trustees should have the right periodically to review the work of a given professor throughout his working life and to determine even the question as to whether he should be continued on the staff."

One answer to Professor Post is that while tenure, like many other institutions of a free society, can be and sometimes is misused, this does not mean that it should be abolished. It means only that protective measures should be utilized, principally (1) careful selection of those to whom tenure is awarded and (2) courageous actions by administrators and faculties to weed out those who thereafter become professionally unfit. Unfortunately, this answer is not really satisfactory because these protective devices are not always—perhaps not often—employed.

It takes a great deal of time, ability and often courage to reach wise tenure decisions. If the tenure plan provides that a teacher who is retained after service of a specified number of years automatically secures tenure, there is a danger that those responsible for the decision will shrink from making a negative judgment. They will tend first to postpone and then to avoid concluding that a teacher does not deserve tenure. An additional complicating factor is the present great influx of students and the shortage of even barely qualified teachers. The result, I am afraid, may well be the appointment to tenure positions of many persons who are not thoroughly qualified.

This problem is aggravated when the probationary period is less than the seven years suggested in the *1940 Statement on Academic Freedom and Tenure*. A number of tenure statutes and plans do provide for shorter periods. The question is, of course, very controversial. At a meeting of the American Association of University Professors a few years ago, a delegate proposed that the period specified in the statement be reduced to three years. The discussion which ensued indicated clearly that a number of other delegates did not agree.

Although the questions involved in promotion to tenure are difficult, far more complex problems are inherent, as Ordway Tead has said, in keeping "faculty members at concert pitch throughout a long professional life." He recommends that "whatever procedural provisions we make, we must supplement them with plans for review and appraisal of the teacher's work, and for occasional stimulation, in order to minimize the dangers of faculty deadwood. The procedures of tenure need more solicitous attention from trustees and administrators. So also do the measures which will keep the tired teacher from tiring his students to the point of boredom." He did not, however, outline any specific measures for review, appraisal and stimulation.

A perhaps more intractable stand is taken by the Committee on Academic Freedom and Tenure of the Association of American Law Schools. In its 1961 report, the committee called for a revision of the *1940 Statement on Academic Freedom and Tenure* and for a new set of procedural rules to govern academic-freedom and tenure cases. The committee specified that "such a Statement and set of rules should, for the protection of students, make appropriate provision for the dismissal of teaching personnel who have become incompetent after acquiring tenure." While the committee emphasized "protection of students," it should be noted that a main purpose of tenure in many institutions is to foster creative scholarship. Proposals to cope with the incompetent classroom teacher should, therefore, deal also with the incompetent writer and researcher.

I myself disagree with Professor Post's radical remedy of abolishing tenure; and I doubt that Mr. Tead, the AALS committee or anyone else can develop rules and procedures for review, appraisal, stimulation and termination which will be any more practicable or appropriate than those which now prevail at institutions of higher learning in this country. At the same time, I recognize that the ideal of tenure is not often realized in practice. If there is a remedy, it has, alas! escaped me. All I can say, in full humility and with a measure of sadness, is that I believe the good in tenure outweighs its defects.

I also believe that faculty members who support tenure—and who claim, as I do, that selection, promotion and dismissal of faculty are faculty prerogatives—have inescapable responsibilities which must be discharged with the utmost fidelity. They must exercise extreme care, independence and courage in matters of appointment and promotion to tenure. They must also strive, by precept and otherwise, to maintain a spirit and atmosphere that will promote the persistent pursuit of excellence in the classroom, the library and the laboratory.

Let me turn now to a consideration of the role of law in the enforcement of tenure. Two sharply contrasting views have been expressed. According to Russell Kirk, "The courts, when all is said,

remain the chief defense of academic freedom when a right to tenure
. . . can be proved." But Robert M. Hutchins asserts that the "issue
of legal control is not basic. Academic freedom comes and goes because
of some conviction about the purpose of education on the part of
those who make decisions in society."

I am afraid that Kirk overstates the case. There are so many
limitations on legal enforcement of tenure that a simple assurance
extended by an institution with a long and honorable tradition of
academic freedom and tenure will be more meaningful than an express legal obligation grudgingly assumed by a lesser institution. Some
of the drawbacks to legal enforcement are judicial reluctance to order
specific performance of personal-service contracts (which means that
although a teacher with tenure who has been wrongfully discharged
could secure judgment for damages, he might not be able to secure
a court order requiring reinstatement) ; the expense and delay incident to judicial vindication; the difficulty of proving money damages
to the degree of certainty the law requires; the wide scope of discretion
retained by the institution in most tenure plans; the decisions of
a number of courts that governing boards cannot, by contract or
otherwise, legally limit the power to dismiss teachers bestowed on
them by constitution, statute or corporate charter; the understandable
reluctance of an individual to litigate publicly his fitness as a teacher
or scholar; and the tendency of some—perhaps many—courts to reflect
community prejudices in times of stress.

Despite all these limitations, I believe that tenure which is enforceable in law does have certain advantages over tenure which rests
on the legally uncontrolled discretion of governing boards. The very
fact that judicial review of an order of dismissal is available can
operate as a curb on the occasional arbitrary administrator or
governing board. The fact that the teacher has legally enforceable
rights may strengthen the hand of the conscientious administrator
or trustee when inflamed public pressures unjustifiably seek the
teacher's discharge. Most important, the existence of a disinterested
tribunal to resolve differences, when all efforts to do so amicably
have failed, removes the teacher from a demeaning position of
dependence on a governing board's benevolence. It thus helps to
create a milieu of independence and freedom in which a scholar can
work most effectively.

Essentially the same considerations which have caused the demise
of benevolent despotism as a system of political government argue
against vesting unrestrained power in administrative or trustee groups

in academic government. As James Madison so well said (in *The Federalist*), "If men were angels, no government would be necessary. . . . but experience has taught mankind the necessity of . . . precautions." In academic government, although the wisdom and uprightness of administrators and trustees may provide a primary safeguard, one important precaution is legally enforceable tenure.

This argument that courts should have a more active role in the enforcement of tenure has been questioned by some and opposed by others. Those who doubt the desirability of increased judicial intervention tend to be distrustful of the courts' competence. Robert K. Carr, for example, wrote in 1959 that the "great majority of American judges, state and federal alike, have up to now shared with the public many misconceptions of the meaning and purpose of academic freedom and tenure."[2] In the same year Edward C. Kirkland, after expressing doubt whether "resort to the courts as a palladium of . . . [professors'] liberties would be beneficial," noted that the courts' "record in civil liberties in the last few years is spotty and not untainted with political considerations." He concluded, "I am loath to take any step which would give judges a handhold to weaken private education's comparative impregnability to government interposition."

The most extreme argument against legally enforceable tenure which I have encountered is stated in a 1960 report of a faculty committee of the State University of South Dakota School of Law. The following excerpts are indicative:

"The idea of academic tenure developed, in the first place, as a principle governing the policies of private colleges and universities. To this day, hardly a soul has dared to suggest that the principle be specifically enforced by courts of law against a private university. Like other moral obligations, such as the support of aged relatives, rewarding a rescuer, taking one's hat off in church, or giving one's seat to a lady or one's elder, academic tenure finds its sanction in custom, tradition and good faith. Moreover, the sanction has proved itself real. In many ways a violation of the principle of tenure by a college or university is something even worse than 'illegal'—it is, to use the jargon of our British friends with whom we share the tradition of academic freedom, 'unthinkable.'

"This, at least, is the situation as it exists today at such private universities as Harvard, Yale, Princeton, Stanford, etc. At none of these great institutions is tenure *legally* enforceable, yet one would be out of touch with reality if he denied that it exists or contended that faculty members of such institutions are not protected by its reach."[3]

Messrs. Carr and Kirkland and the South Dakota committee perform useful functions when they warn against undue reliance on judicial protection of tenure. But it is absurd, it seems to me, for the South Dakota committee to suggest that the tenure obligation is like other moral obligations, such as "taking one's hat off in church, or giving one's seat to a lady or one's elder." Furthermore, the committee's report contains no support for its flat assertion that at Harvard, Yale, Princeton and Stanford, tenure is not legally enforceable.

The judiciary has played an important role in protecting the citizen's political freedom. I see no valid reason why it should not, in time, perform an equally important function in protecting the teacher's academic freedom. For despite the arguments adduced against judicial enforcement of tenure, I believe that the reasons in favor of judicial enforcement are more persuasive. I would urge, therefore, that the creative judge should recognize the vital importance of academic freedom in our society and should extend full judicial protection to the teacher with tenure who has been wrongfully discharged. Except possibly in the most unusual cases, full judicial protection would include an order for reinstatement.

Far more important, of course, than the role of the judiciary are the responsibilities of the three groups most directly concerned— governing boards, administrators and faculty members. As Edmund Burke said, "Constitute government how you please, infinitely the greater part of it must depend on the prudence and uprightness of ministers of state." And so in the case of academic government, the primary requisite is prudent and upright trustees, administrators and faculty members, whose wise tenure decisions will obviate any recourse to the judiciary.

REFERENCES

1. These remarks are based largely—at times verbatim—on the report on tenure in American higher education which Louis Joughin and I wrote for the American Academic Freedom Project at Columbia University. See Clark Byse and Louis Joughin, *Tenure in American Higher Education: Plans, Practices and the Law* (Ithaca, New York: Cornell University Press, 1959).

2. Mr. Carr pointed to the following statement by the Supreme Court of South Dakota as an example of the judiciary's failure to under-

stand academic freedom and tenure: "The exact meaning and intent of this so-called tenure policy eludes us. Its vaporous objectives, purposes, and procedures are lost in a fog of nebulous verbiage." The opinion from which this sentence is quoted is criticized in Clark Byse, "Academic Freedom, Tenure, and the Law: A Comment on Worzella v. Board of Regents," *Harvard Law Review,* LXXIII (December 1959), p. 304.

3. The report appears in Kenneth F. Simpson *et al.,* "Academic Tenure at South Dakota's State Supported Colleges and University," *South Dakota Law Review,* V (Spring 1960), pp. 31-35. For a more temperate statement by one member of the committee, see Frederick Davis, "Enforcing Academic Tenure: Reflections and Suggestions," *Wisconsin Law Review,* MCMLXI (March 1961), p. 200.

PAPER BY . . . *Robert W. Merry*
Professor of Business Administration,
Harvard University

Academic freedom is a developing, changing concept. Its source was belief in the freedom of the mind, the freedom of the individual. Faculty sought first freedom to control its own affairs, then freedom from ecclesiastic control, then freedom from political control and finally freedom from internal administrative control. Faculty has made some headway in each of these efforts; it has achieved complete freedom in none.

Faculty's effort to gain personal freedom to control its affairs was evident at the first university, the University of Bologna, in the twelfth century, when the faculty sought and obtained compensation from the town in order to avoid dependence on the students, who had previously employed them. The students had forbidden faculty members to leave town without permission, had prescribed the books to be read and the number of pages to be covered in a class period by the professor, and had even established fines for professorial tardiness![1]

In the thirteenth century, at the University of Paris, where the church was in control, soldiers of the regent killed several students over town-gown brawls. Faculty threats to leave Paris—and the actual departures of many—led to a papal bull giving the university substantial control over its own statutes and discipline.[2]

From the Middle Ages until the nineteenth century, society generally held that either the church or the state has the right of censorship in matters related to theology. In other areas, however, freedom of thought was developing. Thus, in 1673, Spinoza was offered a professorship at the University of Heidelberg on conditions granting freedom of thought, provided that "it would not be abused to disturb the religion publicly established." Although concern over the implications of the priviso led Spinoza to refuse the invitation, the major thrust of the invitation is significant.[3]

In judging the terms of that offer, one might keep in mind the prevailing attitude in the United States as late as 1825. In that year Thomas Jefferson, founding the University of Virginia, which was to be based "on the illimitable freedom of the human mind," and asserting that "here we are not afraid to follow truth wherever it may lead, not to tolerate error so long as reason is left free to combat it," nevertheless sought to lay down through the board of trustees the principles of government to be taught by the faculty, so that students would be indoctrinated with Whig ideas and set in opposition to those of the Federalists.[4]

The growth of academic freedom in German universities centered around the developing concepts of *Lernfreiheit* and *Lehrfreiheit*. The former was concerned with the rights of the student to freedom in seeking his learning. He was free to travel about among universities, to choose courses or lectures wherever and in whatever order he wished, and to look after himself in his private life; responsibilty for learning was his. *Lehrfreiheit* was the freedom of the professor: freedom to explore his field, to evaluate evidence, to draw conclusions and to lecture on or publish his views. He also enjoyed a substantial freedom from institutional regulation, teaching as he chose. Generally, he was expected to advocate his personal convictions.[5]

In the United States, the early conflicts of educators with the community centered most importantly around neither the students nor the faculty but the presidents. The college president was a figure of great stature because the new colleges did not have senior, established faculties from which temporary rectors could be chosen. The president was likely to be the principal—perhaps the only—mature person involved in the operation of the college. Moreover, he was relatively permanent, while the faculty consisted largely of graduate students studying for the ministry, who would be teaching for only a few years. Boards of trustees consisted of clergy or of lay people. Because the junior age and inexperience of the faculty members made them inappropriate to guide the colleges, these boards—and even legislatures—often intervened directly in academic affairs.

A famous case of legislative interference is that of Harvard's first president, Henry Dunster, who refused to have his fourth child baptised. His refusal led the General Court of the province to recommend to the Overseers that they not keep as teachers or officers of the schools or colleges under their jurisdiction people who were 'unsound in the fayth." When Dunster resigned under this pressure, the General Court offered him a month in which to reconsider, but this gesture did not change his view.[6]

Another example is that of Thomas Cooper, one of the most distinguished men of American education at the time, who had been president of South Carolina College since 1820. His views were generally in accord with those of the community, except on the subject of religion. Not only was he a believer in materialism; he was also exceedingly articulate in his opposition to Calvinism and the Presbyterian clergy. In 1832, the Legislature finally sought to remove him, principally on the grounds of his religious views. Cooper constructed his defense on a state statute guaranteeing "freedom of religious belief and progession without discrimination or preference." His argument was extensive and laid out many patterns for academic freedom.

Cooper claimed for the educator the same rights of freedom of speech enjoyed by citizens in other occupations: "So, I may profess what I please in South Carolina, but not in the South Carolina College! Where is it laid down that the boundaries of South Carolina do not include the College?" He denied the right of the Legislature—and of the trustees as its agent—to explore the religious beliefs of candidates for collegiate offices. He pointed out that if views of one sect could determine the college policy at one time, those of another could set a different policy at another time. He expressed himself at length on the considerations to be expected of a teacher: that he treat the questions related to his subject fairly, impartially and fully, including difficult and unpopular aspects.[7] His sophistication was far advanced for his day.

A case of trustee consideration of religious views occurred at Columbia College in 1853. The board of trustees of Columbia College rejected the effort of some of its members to bring to the college Oliver Wolcott Gibbs, an outstanding chemist. Opposition was engendered by his Unitarian views, which were unpalatable to the Episcopalians who dominated the board. Gibbs became dean of the Lawrence Scientific School at Harvard and twenty years later was unanimously voted an LL.D. by the Columbia trustees.[8]

In the late eighteenth century, while student freedom of religious belief was expanding its base, orthodoxy was secured among the faculty largely by the process of selection. The views of potential faculty members were thoroughly explored, and appointments were granted only when their views were in accord with those of the governing powers. During this period, however, the faculty was increasing its control over the curriculum, both the subjects to be included in the program and the books to be studied.

With the introduction of scientific studies came the beginnings of a new attitude toward education: an interest in searching for new knowledge and a willingness to assert the validity of scientific evidence. In 1755, for example, John Winthrop, a professor at Harvard College, had mercilessly excoriated the Reverend Thomas Prince, an overseer of the college, in a lecture in the Harvard Chapel. Prince had called the erection of lightning rods around Boston blasphemous, basing his argument in part on the displeasure evidenced by God through a recent earthquake.[9]

The big breakthrough in the influence of scientific thinking on academic freedom of inquiry came with the publication in 1859 of Charles Darwin's *The Origin of Species*. Until about this time, professors had generally thought of themselves as conservers and transmitters of knowledge. Now they assumed a major responsibility for the discovery of knowledge.

A significant issue resulting from this development was joined in 1877, when Rudolph Virchow, a German pathologist, argued that one should teach the accepted beliefs of the day unless a contrary hypothesis had been indisputably proven true. He was answered by a biologist, Ernst Haeckel, who asserted that conflict of opinions is the only sound way to improve knowledge.[10] Haeckel's argument was characteristic of the German academic tradition of espousing one's personal view. In the United States, on the other hand, a professor is expected to present all views impartially, though he may indicate his own view if he does not attempt to force his students to accept it.

The history, even in recent years, of the abuse of academic freedom through dismissal under outside pressure is a sorry tale. Such abuses have occurred at both private and public institutions—and from presidents who have spoken out most vigorously for academic freedom. Let me cite two instances. In 1950, President Robert M.

Hutchins of the University of Chicago dismissed Mr. W. T. Couch, the able head of the University of Chicago Press, without hearings or charges, apparently for having published a book which the University of California had asked the University of Chicago not to publish. In the face of conflicting opinions about the legalities of the situation, President Hutchins refused to permit Mr. Couch even to obtain expert legal advice on the positions of the various parties at interest.[11]

In 1953, President Minard W. Stout of the University of Nevada dismissed Dr. Frank Richardson—associate professor of biology, head of department (on tenure) and president of the local chapter of the American Association of University Professors—for two offenses: (1) distributing to the faculty copies of an article critical of educationist training, in which Dr. Stout had received his degree, and deploring the decline of the disciplines in American colleges; and (2) criticizing the president's action in abolishing entrance requirements to the university without consulting the faculty. An assistant professor was also forced to resign when his salary was cut to a figure below that of his assistant.[12]

Many issues are not yet clear. Although freedom from the churches' dictates has been increasing substantially, it is not yet complete. Churches still seek to indoctrinate their tenets. In a pluralistic society such as ours, it is generally accepted that any church (or any other group) may justifiably organize a college for its own purposes. In church institutions, one may find areas of "revealed truth" and areas of "discovered truth." A few years ago, one college which had ceased to be church-controlled but which called itself a "Christian college" sought to determine with greater precision what this label meant. After exploring the problem, the faculty came to the view that if the institution was truly Christian, it could not be truly a college; and if it was truly a college, it could not be truly Christian. Other colleges which consider themselves Christian currently believe quite the contrary.

Granted that individual professors have the right to express their own views, however controversial, does an institution have the right to build a department in a controversial field (such as, in today's world, economics or political science) all of whose members hold the same major view? Departments of like-minded faculty are sometimes attacked today on grounds that they betray the responsibility for objectivity which is a correlate of academic freedom.

Are students to be entitled to academic freedom under social circumstances far different from those surrounding the *Lernfreiheit* of the German university? And what is the proper responsibility of a residential institution for its resident students?

With these and many other questions still unresolved, we might well ask: what is academic freedom today? Arthur Lovejoy, author of the article on academic freedom in the *Encyclopaedia of the Social Sciences,* defined it as "the freedom of the teacher or research worker in higher institutions of learning to investigate and discuss the problems of his science and to express his conclusions, whether through publication or in the instruction of his students, without interference from political or ecclesiastical authority, or from the administrative officials of the institution in which he is employed, unless his methods are found by qualified bodies of his own profession to be clearly incompetent or contrary to professional ethics."[13]

Perhaps the most authoritative statement for us today is the joint statement of principles of academic freedom endorsed in 1940 (a revision of a statement similarly endorsed in 1925) by the Association of American Colleges and the American Association of University Professors. It reads in part:

> The purpose of this statement is to promote public understanding and support of academic freedom and tenure and agreement upon procedures to assure them in colleges and universities. Institutions of higher education are conducted for the common good and not to further the interest of either the individual teacher* or the institution as a whole. The common good depends upon the free search for truth and its free exposition.
>
> Academic freedom is essential to these purposes and applies to both teaching and research. Freedom in research is fundamental to the advancement of truth. Academic freedom in its teaching aspect is fundamental for the protection of the rights of the teacher in teaching and of the student to freedom in learning. It carries with it duties correlative with rights.
>
> Tenure is a means to certain ends; specifically: (1) Freedom of teaching and research and of extramural activi-

---

* The word "teacher" as used in this document is understood to include the investigator who is attached to an academic institution without teaching duties.

ties, and (2) A sufficient degree of economic security to make the profession attractive to men and women of ability. Freedom and economic security, hence tenure, are indispensable to the success of an institution in fulfilling its obligations to its students and to society.

ACADEMIC FREEDOM

(a) The teacher is entitled to full freedom in research and in the publication of the results, subject to the adequate performance of his other academic duties; but research for pecuniary return should be based upon an understanding with the authorities of the institution.

(b) The teacher is entitled to freedom in the classroom in discussing his subject, but he should be careful not to introduce into his teaching controversial matter which has no relation to his subject. Limitations of academic freedom because of religious or other aims of the institution should be clearly stated in writing at the time of the appointment.

(c) The college or university teacher is a citizen, a member of a learned profession, and an officer of an educational institution. When he speaks or writes as a citizen, he should be free from institutional censorship or discipline, but his special position in the community imposes special obligations. As a man of learning and an educational officer, he should remember that the public may judge his profession and his institution by his utterances. Hence he should at all times be accurate, should exercise appropriate restraint, should show respect for the opinions of others, and should make every effort to indicate that he is not an institutional spokesman. . . .

Academic freedom has not come easily; it has been wrested by academicians from those outside or within institutions of higher learning who sought to control them. This freedom is founded on the common good, but that foundation is by no means fully and readily recognized by the lay public. The major recent gains have come from the activities of the American Association of University Professors, founded in 1915, whose investigations have led it to censure many institutions for violations, in its view, of the requirements of academic freedom. Motivated by a legitimate desire to help those of its constituents who may be suffering unwarranted abuses, it has not with equal fervor urged its members to live up to their responsibilities.

Beginning with the apparent intention of fulfilling professional responsibility, the AAUP early established two committees: Committee A on Academic Freedom and Tenure, and Committee B on Professional Ethics. Committee B, however, quickly became inactive and remained so for forty years, while Committee A was vigorously pursuing thousands of cases of violations of rights. If such a respected association of academic people can thus lose its professional balance, one can understand the hesitancy—and often the reluctance—of administrators, most of whom are former faculty members, to take for granted the objectivity of individual faculty members—especially those who, while ardently pushing a single point of view outside the classroom, claim that in class they present all views of their subjects objectively and impartially.

REFERENCES

1. Unpublished manuscript of Professor W. H. Cowley, Stanford University.
2. Richard Hofstadter and Walter P. Metzger, *The Development of Academic Freedom in the United States* (New York: Columbia University Press, 1955), pp. 8-9.
3. Arthur O. Lovejoy, "Academic Freedom," *Encyclopaedia of the Social Sciences,* (1930), Vol. I, p. 387.
4. Hofstadter and Metzger, *op. cit.,* pp. 240-241.
5. *Ibid.,* pp. 383-407.
6. *Ibid.,* pp. 86-91.
7. *Ibid.,* pp. 263-269.
8. *Ibid.,* pp. 269-273.
9. *Ibid.,* pp. 197-198.
10. *Ibid.,* p. 388.
11. Russell Kirk, *Academic Freedom* (Chicago: Henry Regnery Company, 1955), Chapter III.
12. *Ibid.,* pp. 59-72.
13. Lovejoy, *op. cit.,* p. 384.

COMMENTARY

Not long ago a professor of agriculture in a state with a sizeable dairy industry was asked to leave his teaching job because he claimed that oleomargarine was a satisfactory substitute for natural butter. Since then America's sophistication on these matters has developed rapidly, and, at least with respect to higher education, such an overt attack on academic freedom now seems unlikely to recur. Still, the issues and problems associated with the rights of academicians, on the one hand, and their responsibilities, on the other, are numerous, important and, therefore, worth examining.

The relationship between a man's employment security and his productivity varies from one occupation to another. No doubt a lumberjack fells more trees if he knows that low output will cost him his job than he does if he cannot be fired. However, society sees some occupations in a different light. For example, its collective feeling is that the social value of civil servants and judges would decrease if they could be fired, and so, in many instances, their appointments are for life. According to Professor Byse, we must take care to understand that such appointments are in no way designed as sinecures. Rather, their aim is to protect society. And so it is with academic tenure. Society claims that a teacher in an institution of higher learning is, in this regard, like a judge and a civil servant, rather than like a lumberjack. Thus it is viewed as socially advantageous if an economist who believes in free trade can espouse its virtues without fearing that the wrath of New England's textile industry might effect his dismissal.

Many well-informed people, Professors Byse and Harris included, contend that, on the whole, academic tenure is a good thing; but they also allow that, as an institution, it is not always properly managed. Professor Harris argued that administrators, who are often instrumental in hiring faculty, sometimes fail to understand the full financial implications of a tenure appointment. He estimated that when a top-flight institution gives such an appointment to a man in his early thirties, which is the average age these days, it is in effect earmarking approximately $1-million dollars in operating revenue over a period of roughly thirty-five years. Harris suspects that the more administrators learn to view the matter in these terms, the more care they will take in choosing their appointees.

Indeed, as the latter point suggests, the crucial concern of those charged with making tenure appointments should be to select the very best people available. Unfortunately, doing so is sometimes difficult. Many administrators assign equal weight in their mental scales to teaching and research abilities as important attributes of any faculty member, but whereas identifying an outstanding researcher is usually easy, identifying an excellent teacher often is not. Members of the seminar expressed a number of views about the process of evaluating teachers. Billy E. Goetz, professor of industrial history at the Massachusetts Institute of Technology, noted that although institutions often state what they consider to be the characteristics of good teaching, they make little effort to learn whether the faculty, in their daily classroom work, live up to those standards. One reason for this failing is that, in practice, the task would be difficult to accomplish since, according to Goetz, for reasons of decorum a university simply could not ask some of its faculty members to attend their colleagues' classes to grade their teaching. Byse took exception to this point and contended that although the situation might prove slightly embarrassing to one party or the other, there is nothing inherently wrong with having some professors grade the teaching of others. He also noted, however, that there are other ways of achieving the same end. For one thing, ordinary personal contact can reveal a great deal to an insightful examiner. People are rarely so Jekyll-and-Hyde-like that a boor in normal social intercourse becomes an inspiring teacher the moment he enters a classroom.

Another method which some members of the seminar thought useful for evaluating a teacher is to seek the opinions of his students. Byse suggested that if students were to be consulted, the experiment should be controlled. Specifically, a dean would ask student A to evaluate teachers B and C. Having already formed his own impression of B, the dean would be most inclined to let student A's impression of C influence him if A's evaluation of B is roughly equivalent to his own. This matter of students rating teachers has advanced beyond the stage of speculation. Recently the University of Washington received a grant to study the subject. The results showed that virtually all categories of students—graduates and undergraduates, those having high grades and those having low grades, and so on—tended to evaluate a given teacher in roughly the same way. However, there was a general conflict between the ways in which students, on the one hand, and faculty, on the other, appraised a given man's teaching.

A truly thorny question is how to evaluate the teacher who deliberately botches his presentation—perhaps by spouting such information as "x plus x equals x squared" or "Before drafting the Declaration of Independence, George Washington consulted James Buchanan"—in order to keep his students alert. There are numerous stories in circulation about teachers who, either deliberately or unconsciously, are so poor that their students must work with extra diligence and independently in order to master the syllabus. Not infrequently, such students ultimately gain a better knowledge of the material than do those whose teacher was routinely accurate and reliable. Naturally, irrespective of the results, unconscious botching cannot be condoned; but when it is done purposefully, that is another matter. In evaluating botching as a deliberate teaching device, we would do well to go along with Goetz' conclusion that many techniques of teaching are potentially satisfactory, but each can be handled both skillfully and clumsily. The Socratic method, for example, so popular in the law schools, is extremely effective—if the man who applies it as a Socrates. If not, it can produce a rather aimless, hour-long bull session, which has as its only apparent advantage, for student and teacher alike, the fact that neither need prepare for class. And so it is with the technique of deliberate botching: its success is not inherent in the method itself but depends upon the skill of the person who uses it.

In addition to the matter of selecting men who, at the time of their appointment, excel on some form of intellectual endeavor, academic tenure raises another problem and one which is exceedingly complex. Over the years, one's talents as teacher and scholar do not remain constant; often they deteriorate noticeably between the times of appointment and retirement. A person who was eminently qualified to be on the faculty when he was thirty-five may be a total misfit for such a position at the age of fifty-five or sixty. However, since tenure means a marriage between school and scholar until retirement do them part, administrators are not free to deal with this situation in what would be, from their point of view, the most satisfactory way: discharging the man. In short, once an institution gives someone a tenure appointment, for all practical purposes it is stuck with him until he reaches the compulsory retirement age. To remain employed, he need not be intellectually productive at all. He must only behave himself.

Professor Harris views this particular restriction on the institution as costly, and he suggested two possible paths for corrective policy. First, he would penalize delinquent professors by having their salaries grow slower than the general cost of living. Byse objected to making such manipulation of the financial carrot an overt policy of the institution, but he approved of using the technique informally. Harris' second idea was to reduce the compulsory retirement age and perhaps to make it flexible, according to reasonable criteria, rather than uniform for all professors. In dealing with this problem of deterioration,

Dr. Louis Joughin of the American Association of University Professors emphasized the importance of being able to convince a man who is past his prime to modify his activities around the institution and to undertake only limited teaching duties. As an extreme illustration related to these general matters, he mentioned a professor in hygiene who one day became completely obsessed with sex, seeing sexual motivation in every act of human life, and who thus lost his usefulness as a teacher. Fortunately the man had received a medical degree, and so he was transferred to the student health center, where he spent the rest of his years on tenure studying chest X-rays.

No one is complacent about the problem of holding on tenure someone who has become unqualified for the position, but in the opinion of Dr. Joughin, this danger is less serious than its alternative at the other extreme: what Joughin called the problem of the "fluid bottom." Many institutions, New York's municipal colleges included, give tenure with the fourth consecutive twelve-month appointment, irrespective of rank. But many academicians receive three such twelve-month contracts, then a fourth for nine months with the same total salary, and are then released to seek employment elsewhere and presumably to start climbing the academic ladder again from the bottom rung. They become the "fluid bottom." According to Joughin, this system permits scandalous exploitation of youth and is a pressing current issue relating to America's academic marketplace.

16. The Challenge of Growth for University Management

PAPER BY . . . *Vernon R. Alden*
President, Ohio University

The challenge of growth which confronts higher education today is almost overwhelming. The ever-increasing number of students enrolled, the constant need to expand the physical plant, the rising level of living costs and other costs—these problems plague the university administrator daily. He is under pressure simultaneously to raise the level of instruction and research, to accommodate more students and to reduce operating costs so that more funds can be channeled into faculty salaries, research activities, financial aid to students and other essential educational expenditures.

These pressures will continue to increase in the foreseeable future, and traditional patterns of organization and financial management are no longer sufficient to cope with them. There must be new solutions. I believe that three such developments now taking place will influence higher education substantially during the next ten or fifteen years. First, there will be new forms of regional organization and federation. Second, there will be new ways of supplementing traditional teaching methods. And third, there will be better accounting and control systems than we have seen in the past. I should like to discuss each of these directions of growth in turn.

Regional planning for higher education: Over the years, private colleges and even state universities have grown without much outside direction. Each institution has been free to develop its own undergraduate program, its graduate offerings and its physical resources with-

333

out much concern about wasteful duplication or conflict with other institutions. We are now moving very rapidly, however, toward planning by regional areas—and even on a state-wide or national basis. The University of California is probably the best-known example of state-wide master planning; but many states will encounter population growth comparable to California's in the next fifteen to twenty years, and it seems certain that other states will develop master plans of their own.

My university—Ohio University—is planning jointly with other state-assisted universities in Ohio for a substantial expansion of student population. The main Athens campus now has over 10,000 students, and another 5,000 are enrolled in seven branches scattered throughout southern Ohio. These are not junior colleges or community colleges; they are *branches*, offering fully accredited Ohio University courses. Students can qualify for an associate in arts degree at the completion of two years work, or they can continue toward a bachelor's degree on the Athens campus. The branch program is administered by a dean who maintains academic standards with the same vigor as the deans of the seven colleges and professional schools situated on the main campus. This branch program is being centrally administered from Athens through a director at each branch.

Looking ahead, I suspect that by 1970 we shall increase the size of the main Athens campus from 10,000 to around 18,000 students. Our long-term growth will take place in the seven branches. We will probably add another 7,000 students to our present branches in the next eight years, so that our total university population in 1970 is likely to be around 30,000. The other state-assisted universities in Ohio will also expand through their present branch programs and perhaps in new branch locations as well.

As we grow, we shall be concerned about maintaining our present standards. As a matter of fact, I hope that we can even improve the quality of our academic work. By controlling the size of the main Athens campus and the branches, we hope to be able to maintain close personal relationships between faculty and students, as well as the distinctive quality and personality of each campus unit.

The cost to the student at one of our branches is only $350 a year, in contrast to $1,500 a year for room, board, tuition and books on the Athens campus. The branches thus offer real economies to the student who could not otherwise afford to go to college. He can live at home, eat at home and even work part-time while he is taking fully accredited academic work.

Regional planning is also taking the form of federations among private colleges in the same geographical area. These associations permit the institutions to share faculty members, physical resources and, in some cases, central services.

The Associated Colleges of the Mid-West was one of the first of these experiments. The group comprises ten institutions: Carleton, Saint Olaf, Lawrence, Ripon, Beloit, Grinnell, Monmouth, Knox, Coe and Cornell. One of their most important achievements was to improve their individual medical-insurance coverages; they were able to reduce its cost as well. All this was accomplished through mutual inquiry with counsel. These colleges are sharing facilities, such as language laboratories, and are jointly exploring new techniques of teaching languages. They have also decided to undertake cooperative admissions recruiting.

Another interesting combination of institutions is the Associated Colleges in Claremont, California. This group includes Pomona, Scripps, Harvey Mudd, Claremont Men's College and Claremont Graduate School. These colleges have a common business office (with its obvious advantages), a library which is the central resource for all five colleges, a common heating plant and a joint health service. They share a large auditorium and a combined concert series. Upperclass students may take courses at any of the five colleges, and there is a combined faculty for the graduate school.

Pennsylvania's Harrisburg Center is a relatively new development. Lebanon Valley and Elizabethtown College offer joint courses and degrees, and they have associated themselves with three large universities in the state—Temple, Pennsylvania State and the University of Pennsylvania. They can therefore offer graduate work and are able to compete with other, larger institutions which offer opportunities for graduate study.

The University Center of Virginia, Inc., has tied together twenty-two different institutions ranging in size from Hampden-Sydney to the University of Virginia. These institutions have cooperative professorships and offer joint adult-education programs. They share portable scientific equipment, which moves from campus to campus by van; each college is thus spared the expense of investing in its own equipment. Because these colleges share research facilities, they can approach a foundation or a government agency with an attractive proposal: they can draw on the faculties and physical resources of all twenty-two colleges. They are in a much better position to attract research money than one small institution would be.

More such associations and federations are likely to develop in the next decade throughout the United States. Small institutions in some of the underdeveloped parts of the country have great difficulty attracting the support of corporations or foundations. Without such support, they will be handicapped in recruiting new faculty and first-rate students. Many of these colleges will die unless they merge—or relate in some way—with stronger institutions. In the Southeast, for example, Duke University can be a major force in helping small liberal-arts colleges scattered throughout North and South Carolina and Georgia. The resources of a large, well-endowed university such as Duke can enrich the educational offerings of all the private colleges in the area.

New economies of operation will develop from such associations. A small college cannot usually afford expensive electronic-computing equipment, but a group of ten or a dozen can. There would be economies for all, as well as improved record keeping. The next step will be central investment of endowment funds. Several colleges will pool their portfolios, as the schools at Harvard and other universities have done. Opportunities for diversification of funds, for investment in special situations and for economies which come from managing a large portfolio are attractive possibilities.

Small colleges within easy commuting distance can strengthen their educational offerings through cooperative planning. Advanced programs in engineering, physics and chemistry are expensive, but one college might agree to offer high-quality advanced work in engineering, another in chemistry and a third in physics. More and more students will take their freshman and sophomore liberal-arts work in one college and their advanced programs at another institution. The traditional undergraduate pattern will be substantially different in the world of 1975.

Ivy League colleges might well consider cooperative arrangements with other institutions as a potential solution to the pressure on admissions. Some of the smaller, less well-known colleges in New England could become satellites or branches of Harvard, Yale or Princeton. Faculty members could be loaned to these colleges, and centralized administrative resources could strengthen weak organizations. A plentiful supply of first-rate students who fail to gain admission to an Ivy League college in the freshman year could be assured to these colleges, whose attractiveness would be enhanced by the prestige of association with an Ivy League college. As pressure for admission to the better-known colleges continues to increase, the resources of these institutions must be used to strengthen alternative opportunities for excellent students.

New methods of teaching: An even more dramatic development in higher education is the new image of education in the mass. One commentator has said that education in the future may be simply a student sitting in his own home in front of a television set. This image may not be too far-fetched. Others are already weighing the possibilities of using Telstar to teach the uneducated masses in Asia, Africa and Latin America. As our own student population outraces the building of facilities, this may be the educational process for large numbers of people here as well.

The Chicago TV College already offers a complete two-year program on television. A student has a choice of about eight courses; he watches his course on his television set, and when the series is over, he goes to the TV College Center and takes his exams. As of 1961-62, nearly 3000 students were enrolled in these courses for credit; another 5,000 viewers watched them on a noncredit basis. Similarly, Continental Classroom provides televised courses in physics, chemistry, mathematics and American government, for which 160 colleges throughout the country offer full credit. It is quite possible that someday large numbers of professors at Harvard, Penn State, Berkeley, Chicago and Ohio will be signed up by major television networks. They may even have commercial sponsors!

A number of well-known professors are also making video tapes for use on both closed-circuit facilities and educational television networks. The tapes can be run and rerun indefinitely. If these facilities had been available some years ago, we could still be watching the great teachers of yesterday. As it is, we can disseminate for many years the very best lectures of today's finest teachers, until new giants replace them or new knowledge calls for new tapes.

Educational television can thus make the most distinguished professors in America available to colleges throughout the country. There would be no need for struggling, small colleges to recruit "name" professors. Students could watch the very best lectures and laboratory demonstrations on television, then participate in supplementary discussions and receive personal attention from their campus professors at the home colleges.

On a larger scale, some planners point out that numerous small movie theatres throughout the country are foundering because they can no longer attract sufficient customers. The proposal has been made that educational institutions or local communities buy or rent these small theatres and institute closed-circuit educational television programs. Whether the courses are offered for credit or not, the opportunity to provide continuing education to thousands of people in isolated communities staggers the imagination.

Technically, at least, this use of closed-circuit television is entirely practical. Several years ago, for example, doctors expressed a good deal of interest in a new technique for operating on a carcinoma of the liver. With the help of a pharmaceutical advertising firm, a closed-circuit television program was presented showing the actual operation taking place in a hospital in St. Louis. A Wednesday evening was selected for telecasting the program to doctors in rented theatres and ballrooms throughout the country. One half of all the doctors in America came, many through rain or snow, to see the live operation on television.

Television, then, can be a major force in adult education and in undergraduate instruction. It can help universities to meet the challenge of growth, if only we put our minds to the task. But resistance from well-meaning teachers and administrators is great, as it is with any new idea. Some advocates of educational television slow down the process of innovation by making overly dramatic claims. Some opponents insist that television will make the teacher obsolete. This charge is pure nonsense. The teaching profession will not be downgraded, nor will the teacher's job become less exciting or less stimulating.

We must distinguish between the teacher's job of *informing* his students and his responsibility in actually *teaching* them. Information can be transmitted by tape, by textbook material and by programed-learning machines. These media free the teacher to do the job of actually teaching, which is to respond to the needs of the student by asking him questions and by challenging him on the information he has learned. The teacher thus gives relevance and meaning to the material.

Thanks to these new methods of teaching, the dialogue between classroom teacher and student will be improved. The teacher will have more time to reach the students as individuals. He can actually spend his time challenging and stimulating individual students, rather than spending arduous hours delivering the necessary factual raw material. Teachers will not be replaced by machines. They will be elevated and liberated. They will be freed from the drudgery of parroting the text.

Improved accounting and control systems: These far-reaching developments in institutional organization and teaching methods will make mandatory a more precise method of fiscal control over university funds. Improvements in this area have long been desirable; and I have found among trustees, regents and legislative bodies a growing and healthy awareness of the problems of financing higher education and controlling costs. There is also an increasing sophistication about the related problems of class size, academic calendar and space utilization.

In Ohio, for example, as legislators debate the biennial appropriations for our state-assisted universities, they look carefully at these and other questions, including the proportion of educational costs that should be passed on to students and parents. This will be a continuing concern, and one of my major responsibilities as president of Ohio University is to examine carefully and continuously how we are spending tax-appropriated funds. Our biennial requests to the Legislature for capital and operating funds must be well-documented and based upon careful evaluation of our needs.

This is appropriate. We should be able to document clearly and to justify our expenditures of large amounts of money. If we are to continue to receive about $10-million every year from the State of Ohio, we must be able to show the legislators, the citizens of Ohio and the governor that we are putting our money to good use on essential educational activities.

Traditional university accounting has not been very helpful in the control of costs and in presenting an institution's needs for fund-raising purposes. At the Harvard University Business School, while I was its associate dean, we began to develop a *functional* budget and control system. Instead of breaking our budget down into familiar, line-item units (salaries, services, travel, capital equipment and so on), we lumped our expense items by operating units or educational programs and projects. We were dealing with fairly large amounts, the operating budget for 1960-1961, for instance, was about $7.5-million. About half of the income needed came from tuition charges, around 35 per cent from current gifts and the remaining 15 per cent from endowment income.

We first divided our budget into three major categories: (1) educational programs, (2) general educational activities and (3) general administrative services. In 1961-1962, we developed another unit: (4) general university services. This was done because we wanted to recognize—and we wanted faculty members and students to recognize—the many services we were receiving from Harvard's central administration, services purchased from the buildings and grounds, dining halls and personnel departments and from the treasurer's and comptroller's offices. For these services, we paid a fixed annual charge, which has been going up steadily, probably appropriately so. As a general contribution to the university we paid about $90,000.

Under "educational programs" we grouped our major programs, such as the two-year master's degree program, the doctoral program, the Advanced Management Program, the Program for Management Development and the Trade Union Program. Under each of these budget units, we included the salaries, travel expenses, research funds and secretarial services of the faculty members specifically assigned to that program. We also tried to allocate the charges of administrative people who worked full-time and part-time on a given program. This system enabled us to say precisely what any program was costing us each year, including all faculty and administrative services, operating costs for housing and feeding participants, promotional costs and miscellaneous expenses attributable to the program.

On the income side we listed, for each program, its tuition income, dining hall receipts, room rentals and all fees that were obtained from its participants. We were able to say at any time, therefore, whether the program was losing money or was making a net financial contribution to the other essential units at the school, such as the library or the division of research.

To take one specific example, we looked rather closely at the Trade Union Program of the Harvard Business School. The program had not been supported financially by the major American labor unions, nor had they sent many participants to it. It had consistently run a deficit, which could at last be stated precisely. We were thus able to ask: "Is the program significant enough for us to carry it at this loss? Should we take tuition income away from the master's degree program or the Advanced Management Program in order to continue to support this activity? Are there educational reasons that justify the continuing financial drain on other activities?"

We tried to make the same kind of cost analysis for other activities —research, case collection and distribution, our audio-visual department and special institutes. Naturally, our decisions were not based exclusively on income and expense data, but they did take into account financial information which few other institutions have at hand even today.

Some twenty or more individuals at the Harvard Business School, many of them full-time faculty members, are responsible for individual budget units. For each "cost center" there is one person responsible for the expenditure of funds. This person receives monthly statements comparing his budget estimates with his actual expenditures as reported by the comptroller's office, which is able to provide data corresponding to the units of the functional budget. Each responsible individual can thus tell from month to month precisely how much money he is spending in comparison with the allotted budget. Each month during the academic year, he receives evidence which permits him to curtail or accelerate expenditures in order to carry out the objectives of his program or activity. This system, taken as a whole, has been very helpful in guiding funds into the most important educational projects and preventing their being wasted on less fruitful activities.

In the preparation of our budget each year, we invited each individual responsible for a separate budget unit to submit a budget estimate. The form used for providing the data is divided into two major categories. Under Section A are included all items, such as salaries, services and capital equipment, for which he has no direct responsibility. Section B includes budget projections for such controllable items as supplies and printing, travel, postage, subscriptions and books, meetings and honoraria for speakers. In short, the responsible person from each department formulates his own operating budget. The dean's office then prepares the final budget, which is submitted to the president and the governing board of the university for approval.

Perhaps what is done at Harvard is not appropriate for other colleges and universities. Since we were able to break down our activities into functional units and discrete educational programs, we could clearly identify the faculty members and administrators who were concerned with each program. We could easily identify the income that came from each program as well as the costs attributable to each. The traditional four-year undergraduate college cannot so readily isolate units of income and expense.

Still, if we stretch our imaginations, every institution should be able to devise ways in which to group units by functions, by disciplines, by physical location and so on. It should be able to arrive at a functional budget which rather closely approximates that of a business-type operation—a budget which relates salaries, equipment and operating expenses to specific programs and provides an opportunity to compare expenditures with income derived from each program. In many institutions, under traditional methods of fiscal control, the responsible individuals simply do not know how expenses are related to specific offsetting income until the end of the year. Then it is too late to take appropriate action.

One of my colleagues said a few years ago, "Things are changing so quickly that I don't see how we can humanly manage to control the directions in education and other areas. There is no precedent, no previous human experience, to help us cope with the revolution of the space probe, the repercussions of Sputnik, the expanding physical plants and the swelling student enrollment. Perhaps by 1975 we may be able to wave away some of the missile vapor and take a long view back. We may be able to say, 'so this is how it all turned out.' "

My own view is that if we are capable of designing and executing such technological wonders as Telstar and the Saturn missile, we are certainly capable of planning the new directions in education and the accompanying new directions in administrative practices and policies. More and more, administrative officers in education will be asked to make changes. Let us be responsive and open-minded to innovation, but let us also approach change with critical analysis and tough-minded realism. We must understand what to conserve and what to give up. Daring must be combined with responsibility.

COMMENTARY

Academicians view the business world with ambivalence. On the one hand, they deplore what they consider its me-first-last-and-always attitude. On the other hand, they respect its principle of economizing. They recognize the desirability of getting what former U.S. Secretary of Defense Charles E. Wilson might have called the biggest educational bang for a buck. This latter attitude has only become respectable, especially around private institutions of higher learning, quite recently, but its effects have already been wide-ranging. For one thing, it has inspired a flurry of literature about potential educational economies; it has also raised the prestige of business-office personnel on American campuses.

A firm which manufactured soap would not support its counterpart of a university's classics department, and in the ramifications of this simple point lie the differences between the business unit and the educational institution as they are classically defined. We must not assume, however, that because institutions of higher learning are unconcerned with profits, they are also indifferent about costs. Only by knowing what projects cost can any educational administrator label them worthwhile or wasteful, for until he has data on costs, he cannot know what undertaking one project means in terms of foregone alternatives. The cost question is relatively simple when the institution is a liberal-arts college and most complex when it is a university whose product mix is extremely diverse. It is hard, for example, to know how much of a professor's salary to allocate to undergraduate instruction when, in addition to teaching undergraduates, he may direct a research laboratory, guide graduate students, publish books, advise Government officials, edit a scholarly journal and so on. Some skeptics feel that in situations like this, any attempt to allocate costs is strictly abitrary and thus meaningless. Increasingly, however, the alternative view is gaining popularity: sensible allocations of costs, albeit arbitrary ones, can be derived, and they are a better guide to decision-making than the purely intuitive, nonempirical approach.

One of the basic questions concerning the financial interrelations of segments of large universities is this: to what degree should a university's individual subdivisions be responsible for raising their own operating funds, or, conversely, to what degree should the relatively affluent sectors subsidize those whose income potential is more limited? At Harvard, for example, each dean must keep his own financial house liquid, but deans do not draw on the various sources of income in the same proportions. The law and business schools are well nurtured by tuition and private gifts, whereas the schools of public health and public administration rely rather heavily on Federal funds. Harvard's system has certain merits, but it seems destined greatly to strain some deans long before others grow their first gray hairs.

The alternative approach to this basic issue is for a university's profitable undertakings to subsidize its loss leaders. Inevitably, certain administrators will oppose this scheme. Indeed one current dean of a business school refused to accept his appointment until the university's president promised that he could keep the funds he raised. The dean's argument was that without such license he could not hope to hire a first-rate faculty and to compete with those business schools which were not financially obligated to the more indigent members of their university families. Furthermore, the general argument in favor of this second approach is that if divinity schools, for example, are guaranteed their support, they will not even attempt to raise those funds which, without too much effort, they probably could get. This last consideration led Mrs. Mary I. Bunting, president of Radcliffe College, to pose yet a more general question: what is the optimum number of pockets, collecting agencies, for a university to have in order to maximize its operating revenue independently of any ideas about distributing those funds? The answer is far from obvious, but the question, as Mrs. Bunting emphasized, is vitally important.

The combined phenomenon of capital gains and restricted gifts is the source of a knotty financial quandary for educational institutions with large endowments. Suppose that in 1870 a man bequeathed to a university $1-million, the income from which was to be used only to purchase Latin textbooks. Irrespective of interest and strictly as a result of capital gains, $1-million invested in a sensible portfolio in 1870 is worth a great deal more than that today; it is now worth perhaps as much as $5-million. The basic issue, which the university's present administrators must consider, is whether the income from $1-million or from the appreciated value of $5-million should be used today to purchase Latin textbooks. If the $1-million is deemed appropriate, there is, as Professor Harris pointed out, a very real sense in which the dead man is being cheated, his will violated. On the other hand, many modern administrators are reluctant to call $5-million the relevant principal because doing so restricts the outlets for too large a portion of the university's income. They want the freedom to spend their resources in ways that will serve what they believe are the best interests of modern education. They do not want their policies to be restricted by the well-intentioned but outdated notions of some nineteenth-century philanthropist. As concern with financing education has grown, this particular issue has become a source of much dispute. So far no administrator's judgment about the use or value of restricted funds has been contested in the courts, but no doubt such a decision will be challenged someday. When that happens, the result seems likely to be some interesting litigation, as well as the establishment of a formal legal precedent on the matter.

Long ago it was observed that Mohammed's traveling was only one of two possible ways of uniting man and mountain. More recently, department stores in search of customers learned the lesson, and the suburban shopping center was born. Now educational institutions seem to be catching on, and the result, as President Alden noted, is the emergence of branch colleges. Much has been said about this development, but one of its important aspects has not been well publicized: it can serve as a technique for blessing with public subsidies those private institutions which are currently faltering. In order to make this point clearly, it will be helpful to note three facts. First, public universities are the institutions which will most probably be enthusiastic about opening branches. Second, their branches are likely to be near—in fact those which either are contemplated or exist now are often near—small, indigent private institutions. Third, qualified manpower to staff the branches of public universities will be in short supply. In the light of these facts, the plan which one well-known public university has already instituted promises to become widespread. In order to acquire some of the staff for its branches, it hired on a part-time basis a number of faculty members from local private colleges. This arrangement is mutually beneficial to all the institutions involved. The public branch college gets teachers at a reasonable price, in contrast to the very high wage it might have to pay if it imported them. The private colleges benefit because many of their teachers earn money which these colleges cannot afford to pay them for doing work which they cannot provide. These private colleges are thus enabled to retain faculty members who might otherwise seek more lucrative jobs, especially in the near future, when the market will favor sellers rather than buyers of teaching talent. The effectiveness of this scheme, of course, depends upon the willingness of the large universities to let it function, and some do look upon it with at least mild skepticism. In general, however, those present felt that it has a significant future.

There are other techniques for economizing on scarce teaching personnel, and one of the most promising is television. One of Professor Harris' stories on this subject is of some interest. A producer in California approached a physicist and asked him how much he would charge to do a certain amount of teaching on television. The man replied $18,000. Soon, however, it was discovered that, before appearing, he had to be sanctioned by a local union. The union asked the physicist how many lectures he intended to give, and when he told them, they said that he could not perform for $18,000. He had to get $30,000. And he did. Amusing and interesting though this story may be, the complications which it suggests can probably be avoided when the distinction between educational and commercial networks is more clearly made.

Considerations of educational television on a grand scale have so far placed primary emphasis on the economies it may produce.

The aspect of the matter which has not received as much attention as it should—but which is perhaps instructional television's largest potential contribution—is its educational value. Television will facilitate bringing an increasing number of students into the classrooms of the truly great teachers. Naturally, it will also help to increase the degree of specialization among teachers and thus pave the way for expanding their productivity, which will, in turn, justify paying them higher salaries. But this function is perhaps best thought of as a by-product of its major potential result: improving the quality of American education.

This session's final topic was the need to inform consumers about the educational product and, more generally, to police educational standards. Most American products are heavily advertised, and consumers usually have especially detailed knowledge about those for which they intend to spend several thousand dollars. Services, however, are a different matter, and in general consumers know very little about the educational product they purchase. Those who are concerned about this state of affairs suggest that America should establish an agency, perhaps private, perhaps governmental, to evaluate institutions of higher learning, to inform potential students and their families about them and to enforce certain minimum educational standards. Hopefully, such an agency would improve and expand upon the rather disappointing work which the various accrediting boards are now doing. In essence, it would be to education what the Securities and Exhange Commission is to financial markets. The agency's basic purpose would be to enlighten the consumer and thus make the process whereby a youngster selects a college somewhat more rational than it now seems to be.